Animating the Victorians

Children's Literature Association Series

Animating
the
Victorians

Disney's Literary History

Patrick C. Fleming

UNIVERSITY PRESS OF MISSISSIPPI / JACKSON

The University Press of Mississippi is the scholarly publishing agency of the Mississippi Institutions of Higher Learning: Alcorn State University, Delta State University, Jackson State University, Mississippi State University, Mississippi University for Women, Mississippi Valley State University, University of Mississippi, and University of Southern Mississippi.

www.upress.state.ms.us

The University Press of Mississippi is a member of the Association of University Presses.

Copyright © 2025 by University Press of Mississippi
All rights reserved
Manufactured in the United States of America

∞

Library of Congress Control Number: 2024948361
Hardback ISBN 978-1-4968-5537-4
Paperback ISBN 978-1-4968-5538-1
Epub single ISBN 978-1-4968-5539-8
Epub institutional ISBN 978-1-4968-5540-4
PDF single ISBN 978-1-4968-5541-1
PDF institutional ISBN 978-1-4968-5542-8

British Library Cataloging-in-Publication Data available

Contents

Acknowledgments vii

Introduction: Disney and the Victorians xi
    Chapter Overview xv

Chapter One: Disney and the Victorian Tradition 3
    The Golden Age of Children's Literature. 5
    Copyright Law, the Victorian Business Ethos, and New Technologies 8
    Victorian Theater and Disney's Films 16
    Victorian Public Entertainments and Disney's Theme Parks 23
    Dickens, Disney, Oliver, and Company 31

Chapter Two: Alice from Gag to Franchise. 41
    Alice's Appeal 42
    The 1920s: Cartoon Gags and *Alice's Wonderland*. 47
    The Early 1930s: Mary Pickford and Disney's First *Alice* Feature 51
    The Late 1930s: Alice in the Archives. 56
    The 1940s: Aldous Huxley and Alice after the War 60
    After 1951: The Alice Franchise 65

Chapter Three: Animating Hans Christian Andersen. 73
    Competing Version of Walt Disney's Life 75
    Andersen among the Victorians 78
    From Provincial Origins to Global Fame 83
    Sexual Desire and Self-Deprivation 87
    Ugly Ducklings and Walt Disney's Andersen Adaptations. 94
    Hans Christian Andersen and the Disney Renaissance 100
    Andersen and the Politics of Twenty-First Century Interpretation. 106

Chapter Four: Princesses and Pirates 113

Disney's and the Victorians' Gender Ideologies 114
Fairy-Tale Princesses: Charlotte and Victoria 118
Feminist Princesses: Victoria's Daughters 126
The Victorian Princess Brand: Tennyson's *The Princess* 131
Pirate Masculinity: Historical and Theatrical 139
Disney's Victorian Pirates 144

Conclusion: Post-Corporate Art and Criticism 150

Appendix: Disney Studies and Victorian Studies 157

Why Disney? 158
Why the Victorians? 161
Why "Disney's Victorians"? 165

Notes 169

Works Cited 201

Index 229

Acknowledgments

This book is, at least in part, an attempt to reconcile the personal and professional. My wife Kate and I had season passes to Walt Disney World when we lived near Orlando (we both thoroughly enjoyed a behind-the-scenes tour), and our first son, Penn, was born as the idea for this book was taking shape. More than a few pages were written with him on my lap, and his love of books expanded my own reading. I made the final edits with our second son, Asa, on my lap. Listening to them, and to friends and family who also enjoy Disney, helped me realize the wider appeal of the literary and historical minutiae to which my academic training had attuned me.

All teachers, of course, make such appeals in the classroom. In the fall of 2014, I was scheduled to teach a seminar for English majors. I had chosen the title "Disney's Victorians," which I thought might appeal to students and allow me to teach some Victorian standards like *Oliver Twist*, *Alice in Wonderland*, and *Treasure Island*. That summer I participated in an NEH Summer Seminar in Santa Cruz, California, led by Sharon Weltman, on the topic of "Performing Dickens." Sharon had set aside a few days in the schedule for participants to visit any archives that might support our teaching or research. I had read about the Walt Disney Archives, located in Burbank, a few hours from Santa Cruz, and thought perhaps there would be something interesting there that I could share with students. I made contact with Steven Vagnini, who worked in the archives at the time. He pulled some materials for me, organized a studio pass, and invited me to come down. This book owes a major debt to Steven's willingness to meet with me and to respond to later inquiries about archival materials (Steven is a wealth of Disney knowledge and coauthor of *A Portrait of Walt Disney World: 50 Years of The Most Magical Place on Earth* and *Disney A to Z*). On the trip I stayed with my friend Michael Konik, whose Hollywood home isn't far from Burbank. Mike was the first "real" writer I knew personally, and I fondly recall reading his books of gambling stories as a teenager. Later on, Mike was kind enough to read some parts of this book and to give feedback from a perspective outside academia. Whether I found anything of interest during that visit, the following chapters must show.

That archival research made me realize a book like this was possible, and the NEH seminar also introduced me to adaptation studies, which provided a critical framework for the argument. My thinking was enriched both during and after the seminar by my fellow summer scholars, especially Carrie Sickman Han, Rob Jacklowsky, Taryn Hakala, Kirsten Andersen, and Becky Richardson. Carrie was kind enough to read my *Alice in Wonderland* chapter in a near-final version, and her feedback much improved that portion. I'm also grateful to Carolyn Williams, who was a guest lecturer at the seminar and whose work is quoted frequently in this book, and to John Jordan, who scheduled the NEH seminar as part of the Dickens Universe. I had the privilege to attend Dickens Universe again following year, when a few of us were invited back to present our work. I shared a portion of this book and met some wonderful scholars. I also want to thank the students in my "Disney's Victorians" seminar, which I taught twice, in 2014 and 2015.

The same summer that I attended the NEH seminar, I also participated in a Jessie Ball duPont seminar at the National Humanities Center, hosted by Laurie Langbauer on the theme of "Constructing Childhood." Laurie supported me in many ways, and it was also there that I met Jen Cadwallader, who has read several parts of this book over the last few years and whose feedback I value immensely. Jen and Laurie are fellow members of the Children's Literature Association, whose annual conference I look forward to each year. Conversations with ChLA members have greatly enriched my thinking about many of the topics with which this book engages. I presented the initial idea at ChLA in 2014, and other portions of it over the next few years. In 2019 I was awarded a Faculty Research Grant from ChLA, which helped me complete the manuscript.

I'm also grateful for the feedback I've received at other conferences. I presented portions of this book at conferences hosted by Interdisciplinary Nineteenth-Century Studies (INCS), Narrative, and the Dickens Society. I am especially thankful for the Victorians Institute, where I presented parts of each chapter over a period of several years and heard from fellow attendees whose scholarship provided insight into what other Victorianists were writing about. That broader context is crucial to this book's argument. I also had the privilege to serve on the executive board of the Victorians Institute, and I treasure the friendships I made at the annual meetings.

In 2016, I moved to Nashville, Tennessee, to work at Fisk University, where I wrote most of this book. I'm grateful to the students and colleagues who listened to me blather on about it, especially Holly Hamby and Katie Burnett.

In Nashville I also met Rachel Teukolsky, who was kind enough to invite me to the eighteenth- and nineteenth-century studies faculty reading group at Vanderbilt, which she hosted with Scott Jeungel. There I met Jay Clayton and Elizabeth Meadows at the Curb Center for the Humanities, and they kindly included me in two SEC colloquia and a winter edition of Dickens Universe. Rachel, Scott, Jay, and Elizabeth helped me find a community of fellow Victorianists in Nashville, without whom this book wouldn't have been the same. At a later stage, Erica Wright's feedback on the introduction and conclusion helped me to shape the core ideas. I left Fisk in 2020, and currently work for the National Endowment for the Humanities; this book represents my own views and not those of the NEH or the federal government.

A UNCF Mellon-Mays summer seminar, led by Cynthia Neal Spence in July 2019, convinced me that this book was achievable. I came into the seminar with about a third of a manuscript, and I thought that I would complete it a few years down the road. I came out with a complete proposal, which I sent to the University Press of Mississippi a few weeks later. I appreciate the support of everyone at the press, especially Katie Keene, who had first expressed interest in the manuscript after reading an excerpt published in the *Children's Literature Association Quarterly* (vol. 41, no. 2, Summer 2016). Chapter one includes material from that article, as well as content previously published in *Neo-Victorian Studies* vol. 9, no. 1 (December 2016), reprinted with permission. Throughout the book, I quote from materials held by the Walt Disney Archives. Margaret Adamic from Disney's legal department and Disney archivist Kevin Kern reviewed the manuscript. They made some excellent suggestions about citations, and requested that I alter the original title (which was "Disney's Victorians") and move the company's name to the subtitle rather than the main title. This book is not endorsed by the Walt Disney Company and contains no copyrighted materials.

Introduction

Disney and the Victorians

The Cambridge professor F. R. Leavis begins his book *The Great Tradition* (1948) by stating that "the great English novelists are Jane Austen, George Eliot, Henry James, and Joseph Conrad."[1] Leavis adds no qualifiers. Not "I take the great English novelists to be," or "some of the great English novelists include." Just "the great English novelists are." Such a bold pronouncement is necessary, says Leavis, because "far from all the names in the literary history really belong to the realm of significant creative achievement."[2] Leavis felt it his scholarly duty to pass judgment about which authors are worthy (or unworthy) of attention. He took seriously the job of passing on, as his title puts it, "the great tradition."

One of Leavis's contemporaries had a different view of such scholarly judgments. When he heard that viewers found symbolic meaning in *The Three Little Pigs* (1933), Walt Disney is said to have replied, "I make the pictures for entertainment, and then the professors tell us what they mean."[3] Disney, the self-educated Midwesterner who cultivated his persona as "Uncle Walt," thought that creative achievements should speak for themselves. He did once attempt to draw on a professor's expertise. In the 1930s, he invited an art scholar to speak to his animators, hoping that the visit might help them to improve their technique. As he later told the *New York Times*, he stopped the lectures because "none of us knew what [the professor] was talking about."[4]

Both Disney and Leavis perceived a divide between creatives and critics. While Leavis thought that a scholar's role was to guide an uncritical public toward the greatest creative achievements, Disney dismissed professors for conveying far-fetched interpretations in esoteric language. Such rhetorical posturing, though, belies the fact that critics and creatives are not antagonists but allies, each enriching the other. As the Victorian poet and critic Matthew

Arnold puts it, all worthwhile artistic creation "implies a great critical effort behind it."[5] No work of art is an island unto itself, and artists of all kinds recognize their place within a tradition. Walt Disney is no exception. Despite his dismissive remarks about "professors," materials in the Walt Disney Archives reveal the influence of academic scholarship on the studio's films. That influence expanded in the twentieth century, as college attendance became common. Today, most Disney creatives and executives have college degrees, and many, including former chairman and CEO Michael Eisner, were English majors. They bring with them the approaches they internalized during their own educations. Eisner presided over the company in the 1980s and 1990s, when cultural studies professors critiqued Disney's films for reinforcing a patriarchal hegemony. Four decades later, those professors' students have risen in the executive ranks, and Disney is accused of being *too* influenced by academic ideologies and catering to "woke" culture. This book aims to add some nuance to these extreme viewpoints by considering more closely the relationship between Disney's products and academic literary scholarship.

For all their intellectual differences, Disney and Leavis had two things in common. Besides having served in the ambulance corps during World War I, both men made it their business to keep abreast of current trends. Each had a finger on the pulse of the Anglophone world, and each recognized that mid-twentieth-century audiences were particularly drawn to the literature and culture of the Victorian period. Leavis felt motivated to defend the "great tradition" of Austen, Eliot, James, and Conrad against "the present vogue for the Victorian age."[6] Disney, for his part, contributed to that vogue. Not only were his feature films characterized by a "Victorian sensibility,"[7] but many of them were adaptations of Victorian stories. Of the feature films Disney released between *Snow White* (1937) and the opening of Disneyland in 1955, two thirds were based on Victorian texts.[8]

As a historical adjective, "Victorian" refers to the reign of Queen Victoria, from 1837 to 1901. The Victorian period is one of the six literary periods into which English literature is traditionally divided.[9] These divisions—a practice known as "periodization"—have practical consequences and are reinforced by institutional practices. Most university English departments require students to take courses spanning different periods. A 2016–17 report from the Association of Departments of English asserts that, despite critiques of periodization, "literary history continues to provide the most common curricular framework for the major."[10] This framework, including both chronological periodization and the separation of British literature from American literature, determines not only which courses are offered but also the expertise of the professors hired to teach them, and so the scholarly publications that those professors produce and the structure of the graduate programs in which they are trained. To study literature is to study literary history and to work within literary periods.[11]

The history of the Walt Disney Company is often divided into phases analogous to literary periods. The same basic structure is adopted by scholars in several fields,[12] by journalists and fans,[13] and even by D23, Disney's official fan club.[14] Walt Disney's oeuvre is separated into three parts: the early animated shorts; the feature films following *Snow White and the Seven Dwarfs* (1937); and the years after 1955, when he opened Disneyland and embraced the new medium of television. Following Walt's death in 1966, the company struggled, facing risks of bankruptcy and corporate takeover. In the 1980s, the so-called "Disney Renaissance" commenced under the leadership of Michael Eisner. Eisner stepped down in 2005, beginning a fifth period under the direction of Robert Iger, characterized by major acquisitions like *Star Wars* and Marvel and, more recently, the launch of the streaming service Disney+.[15] Each era provides a framework for understanding the works produced in those years, just as literary periods provide a framework for understanding historical texts. Disney historians use the conceptual tools of literary historians.

Leavis and Disney may have imagined a separation between the film industry and "the professors," but institutional realities tell a different story. The two are intertwined. Not only do college graduates become Disney Imagineers and executives, but the history of the Walt Disney Company runs parallel to the history of Victorian studies as an academic discipline. The journal *Victorian Studies*, which "in effect defined the field,"[16] was founded in 1957, two years after Disneyland and about a decade after Leavis recognized a "vogue" for the Victorians. As a new field bridging traditional disciplines like literature, history, and sociology, Victorian studies "sought to create something intellectually greater than the sum of the disciplines from which it grew."[17] The inaugural issue of *Victorian Studies* claimed both a distinct character for the Victorian period and a relevance to the twentieth century. "Although the division of history into periods is an artificial procedure," states the issue's preface, "certain times may have their own complex and individual characters; the Victorian period has such a character."[18] Walter Houghton's *The Victorian Frame of Mind*, published the same year, similarly identified a Victorian ethos that helps us "see our own situation a little more clearly."[19] From the very beginning, Victorianists—scholars of the Victorian period—looked to the era not merely for its own sake but to better understand the present.

Midcentury Victorianists shared a fairly limited set of theorists and conceptual frameworks, but over subsequent decades new theories and methods such as Marxism, feminist theory, and postcolonial studies drastically changed how literature is studied and taught.[20] Victorianists have often been at the vanguard of new critical trends,[21] and even the most cutting-edge scholars work within established literary periods. Scholars in digital humanities and environmental justice, for example, maintain the Victorian period as an organizing concept.[22] Despite an increasing diversity of theories, methods, and texts, Victorian studies persists as an academic discipline, still devoted to achieving Houghton's goal of using the Victorian period to see our own situation more clearly.[23]

Unlike F. R. Leavis, few professors today see their role as gatekeepers of a "great tradition." University curricula may keep some texts current while allowing others to be forgotten,[24] but our shared culture is increasingly determined not by teachers and scholars but by multimedia corporations like the Walt Disney Company. Scholars have recognized this shift, and Disney in particular has been the subject of foundational works of feminist and postmodern theory. Sandra M. Gilbert and Susan Gubar's reading of Disney's *Snow White* is one of the most memorable in *The Madwoman in the Attic*, and Disneyland features prominently in Jean Baudrillard's *Simulation and Simulacra*.[25] In the wake of cultural studies, Disney films appear frequently on course syllabi in a variety of departments.[26] The Walt Disney Company and its productions have been the subject of scholarship in several academic disciplines,[27] and an *International Journal of Disney Studies* will launch in 2025. Today, readers can find rich discourses of interdisciplinary scholarship both about the Victorian period and about Disney. This is the first book to link those two discourses together.

Victorian studies and the Walt Disney Company developed in tandem, and despite their shared histories, the connection between the two has yet to be fully explored. The following chapters work within an existing disciplinary structure—a literary period—and each one explores the relationship between the Walt Disney Company and the Victorians in a different way. I move back and forth between the two, considering both how works are produced (their creators' biographies and historical contexts) and how they are received (how they were interpreted by their first audiences and how those interpretations shifted over time). Throughout the book I draw on materials from the Walt Disney Archives, some of which have never, to my knowledge, been discussed in print.[28]

I hope this book provides some new ways of thinking about both Disney and the Victorians, and also about the future of literary studies in a world increasingly shaped by global media corporations. Readers who are interested in the theories and methods from which this book emerges may wish to begin with the appendix, which engages more directly with the scholarship from which my own argument emerges. In an academic monograph, that engagement usually comes here, in the introduction. I have made the choice to place it instead in an appendix, so that it may be consulted (or not) as you so choose. The same could be said for the chapter summaries that make up the rest of this introduction.

CHAPTER OVERVIEW

Chapter one argues that the Walt Disney Company owes its very existence to cultural, legal, and business systems that emerged during the Victorian period. By the end of the nineteenth century, family structures, decreasing printing costs, and universal public education had provided a context in which modern children's literature could emerge: the Victorian period is often called "golden age" of children's literature. The same period saw the emergence of technologies like photography and film and of an entertainment industry featuring both theatrical and non-theatrical productions. Disney would work with those technologies and within those industries. The career of Charles Dickens, in many ways an analogue to Walt Disney, spanned the middle half of the century, and the chapter ends with a case study, tracing the history of Dickens's *Oliver Twist* from its serial publication in the 1830s to Disney's *Oliver & Company* (1988) a century and a half later.

Chapters two and three explore Disney's decades-long relationships with a single Victorian text (*Alice's Adventures in Wonderland*, in chapter two) and a single Victorian author (Hans Christian Andersen, in chapter three). Walt Disney first began adapting the *Alice* books in the 1920s, before he left Kansas City for Hollywood. Thirty years of short films, research reports, press releases, and unfinished drafts preceded the 1951 animated musical, *Alice in Wonderland*. The initial release was underwhelming, but the film provided the foundation of a franchise whose merchandising, theme-park attractions, and sequels have made the *Alice* books inextricable from the Walt Disney Company. The history of the relationship between the two provides insights into both the internal workings of the Walt Disney Company and the reception history of Lewis Carroll's *Alice* books.

Chapter three focuses on Hans Christian Andersen, whose stories Disney has adapted more than the works of any other author. During his lifetime, Andersen presented his biography as a rags-to-riches tale, promoting the link between his life and his works by publishing three autobiographies and traveling throughout Europe, reading his works aloud and crossing paths with major Victorian writers. Today Andersen's biography is more often associated with his social anxieties and his non-normative sexuality, but his tales are always linked to his life experiences—and not only by scholars and biographers. Walt Disney, who also presented his life as a rags-to-riches tale, at one point planned to collaborate on a biopic about the fairy-tale author, whom he likely saw as a kindred spirit. All of the Disney company's Andersen adaptations, from cartoon shorts in the 1930s to *Frozen 2* in 2019, were shaped by understandings of the author's life. Differences among those adaptations reveal overlaps between scholarly biography and media production.

Chapter four links two Disney brands, princesses and pirates, to issues of gender and sexuality in the Victorian period. Actual nineteenth-century princesses, Tennyson's feminist epic *The Princess*, and the emergence of the pirate hero on the Victorian stage provide a background to Disney Princesses and Disney Pirates. This background reveals how Disney's brands, criticized for promoting outdated gender ideologies, shift along with changing cultural norms. Brands are as fluid as gender and sexuality, and uncovering their literary-historical origins can help us understand their impact on the present.

Finally, the conclusion draws an analogy between postcolonial Victorian studies and the metaphor of a Disney empire to imagine a "post-corporate" future. Both Victorian literature and Disney films are important parts of our cultural history. Studying that history means not excising works we find objectionable but providing a way to discern the values that cultural products promote and a context in which to discuss them. This is a never-ending process, since our culture is constantly shifting. By linking an academic discipline to a global multimedia corporation, this book provides a history of both, and a method for applying literary history to corporate productions.

Animating the Victorians

Chapter One

Disney and the Victorian Tradition

T. S. Eliot's "Tradition and the Individual Talent" (1919)—which has been called "the most influential English-language literary essay of the twentieth century"[1]—argues that any individual work of art must be considered as part of a tradition, a constellation of other works that came before and after it. Creating or interpreting a work of art, says Eliot, requires "a perception, not only of the pastness of the past, but of its presence."[2] The Walt Disney Company takes Eliot's statement a step further, recognizing the presence of the past not only in its creative products but also in its corporate practices. Disney's acceptance of Eliot's credo is encapsulated in the orientation course for Disney employees, or "cast members." The course is called "Traditions."[3]

Diane Disney Miller, Walt Disney's daughter, once remarked that "mom and dad both loved the Victorian period."[4] Though the immediate reference is to her parents' home décor, it might be expanded to include not only the numerous Victorian texts that Disney adapted (many of which I discuss in this book) but also to Victorian culture more broadly. Many of the traditions that inform the Walt Disney Company's output, structure, and ethos have their roots in Victorian literature and culture.

Walt Disney traveled through Europe after the London premiere of *Alice in Wonderland* (1951), visiting several sites that had opened during the Victorian period, such as Denmark's Tivoli Gardens, which opened in 1843, and Neuschwanstein, the Bavarian castle built in the 1880s and opened to the public after King Ludwig's death in 1886. Upon his return, Walt "plunged back into Disneylandia and his park."[5] Neuschwanstein would be the basis for the theme park's centerpiece, Sleeping Beauty's Castle, and Tivoli Gardens has distinct themed areas, which may have given Disney the idea to divide his own park into Adventureland, Frontierland, Tomorrowland, and Fantasyland. The latter, Disney told audiences in the first episode of the *Disneyland* television series, was inspired by Wonderland and Never Land, from two quintessentially Victorian texts.

In London, Disney couldn't have missed the Festival of Britain, which was being celebrated on the South Bank during his visit. The festival marked the centennial of the Great Exhibition of 1851, the high-water mark of Victorian culture. The Great Exhibition, held inside a glass building known as the Crystal Palace, inspired the World's Fairs that were common over the next century. Walt Disney's father worked as a carpenter at the 1893 Chicago World's Columbian Exposition, and the 1964 World's Fair was an important event for Disney: he produced four exhibits, all of which were later incorporated into his theme parks.[6] In 2023, Disney celebrated its centenary with "Disney 100: The Exhibition," which toured the United States and Europe. Its title quietly evokes London's Great Exhibition, as does the Crystal Palace restaurant in Florida's Magic Kingdom.

Disney's films were frequently based on Victorian texts and its theme parks had important Victorian precursors. But "tradition," in the sense that Eliot means it, is more than simply a set of works. Eliot builds on the Victorian critic Matthew Arnold, who wrote that for artists to produce their best work, "two powers must concur, the power of the man [sic] and the power of the moment."[7] The same might be said for a corporation. The Walt Disney Company took shape in the mid-twentieth century, with the concurrence of the right cultural institutions (a widely shared children's literature and a vast entertainment industry), legal protections (cross-media and international copyright), and technologies (moving pictures and sound recording). Those institutions, protections, and technologies all emerged during Victoria's reign. In the 1830s, writers like Charles Dickens had no control over stage adaptations of their novels, nor did they profit from the pirated editions sold in the United States, unauthorized spin-offs of their works, or the merchandising of their characters and stories. The invention of photography in the 1840s and of motion pictures at the end of that century further threatened authors' control over their works. But revisions to copyright law began to protect adaptations across media, and the 1886 Berne Convention formulated the first international copyright law. By 1901, when Victoria died and Walt Disney was born, the stage was set for a global media corporation built on adaptation franchises.

THE GOLDEN AGE OF CHILDREN'S LITERATURE

In the twenty-first century, one can't think of "Snow White," "Cinderella," or "Beauty and the Beast" without thinking of Disney's versions. Lamenting this hegemony, Jack Zipes, a folklorist and expert in the history of fairy tales, titled his most famous essay "Breaking the Disney Spell."[8] But fairy tales had begun to homogenize long before Disney. Originally an oral genre, fairy tales shifted to print culture in the eighteenth century and became popular in England after Edgar Taylor translated Jacob and Wilhelm Grimm's *German Popular Stories* (1823). The tales the Grimms collected had existed in various forms across multiple countries. Over the course of the nineteenth century, those tales, and their corresponding tropes, solidified into the versions we recognize today. Victorian illustrated narratives and stage performances distilled the Cinderella story into the elements that Disney would feature in its 1950 film; it was the Victorians who established the stepsisters' ugliness and who made Cinderella's most prominent feature her beauty rather than her personality.[9] Similarly, the tropes of the princess's trance, the palace that sleeps alongside her, and the heroic prince who awakens her with a kiss are Victorian revisions to the "Sleeping Beauty" story.[10] "Beauty and the Beast" was one the most popular Victorian fairy tales, circulating in fairy-tale collections, picture books, and theatrical genres like the fairy extravaganza and the pantomime.[11] Disney's fairy-tale films may have cast a spell on the fairy tale in the mid-twentieth century, but the tales on which those films were based were not timelessly authentic. They were Victorian. And the same cultural factors that consolidated the fairy-tale tradition—the emergence of child consumers, legal protections for artists, and new media—also laid the groundwork for the Walt Disney Company.

Walt Disney expected whole families, not just children, to enjoy his films. "Dad never thinks of children as his primary audience," remarked Diane Disney Miller. She quoted her father as saying, "When we make our movies, we try to please ourselves instead of some composite, imaginary child."[12] Such a qualification would not have been necessary in the early nineteenth century, as the "composite, imaginary child" had not yet come into being. A separate literature for children is a relatively new phenomenon. Only in the mid-eighteenth century did publishers begin marketing works explicitly for children; John Newbery's *A Little Pretty Pocket-Book* (1744) is commonly cited as the first children's book. Early children's texts balanced entertainment with instruction, addressing a child who presumably needed only knowledge and practice to become a full-fledged adult.[13]

In the early nineteenth century, poets like William Wordsworth instead envisioned childhood as an innocent, imaginative state, helping change the general cultural image of the child. Teachers, psychologists, and social reformers also began to identify childhood as a separate stage from adulthood. In school, children interacted mostly with peers of their own age, and the Victorians established juvenile detention centers instead of prisons and separated children from their parents in the workhouses for the poor.[14] By the turn of the century, it had become possible to envision the "composite, imaginary child" to which Disney refers.

As childhood began to be considered a separate state from adulthood, the boundaries between children's and adults' reading were constantly shifting. Most reading took place in the home, and even literature not explicitly aimed at children was influenced by Victorian family structures.[15] Victorian readers found the widest selection of reading material at subscription-based libraries. The most famous library, Mudie's, opened in 1842 and became synonymous with the era's moral strictures. Mudie's helped ensure that mid-nineteenth-century fiction was appropriate for reading aloud in a family setting. Novels that wouldn't be approved for purchase at Mudie's likely wouldn't be published, and savvy writers adjusted their works accordingly.[16] Mudie's proprietors didn't openly adumbrate the forbidden content, but publishers and novelists were keenly aware of the implied moral guidelines.[17]

Many of the informal restrictions associated with Mudie's were later codified by the Motion Picture Production Code of 1930. Known as the Hays Code, this document governed film content from 1930 through the late 1960s. As Nora Gilbert has argued, the Hays Code's explicit constraints drew on the implicit moral guidelines from the Victorian period, and filmmakers' language about the code echoes the self-imposed restrictions of nineteenth-century writers.[18] All of the films that Walt Disney produced during his lifetime would have been governed by the Hays Code, and those films established the brand for which the company is still known.

The Walt Disney Company struggled after Walt's death in 1966, and its challenges are usually attributed to the death of its founder. But the Hays Code was suspended the same year, and Disney was not alone in its declining profits. Blockbusters like *The Graduate* (1967), *The Godfather* (1972), *The Exorcist* (1973), and *Jaws* (1975) featured violence, sexuality, and sacrilegious content that would have been prohibited a decade earlier. These taboo-breaking films alienated some viewers, shrinking the market and threatening the major studios.[19] The market recovered as studios began targeting niche audiences, and this new structure left a space for Disney to profitably distribute the same films they had been producing for decades.[20] Disney produced family friendly content not because of externally imposed restrictions but because a more subtle, self-imposed, censorship based on an understanding of the marketplace. In this sense, Disney had more in common with Victorian writers than with some of his Hollywood contemporaries.

The setting that Mudie's imagined for its customers, reading aloud in the family, was a long-established activity. Expanding educational opportunities, however, meant that by the end of the Victorian period most children could read by themselves. It was a major change. Children had few educational opportunities prior to Victoria's reign. Boarding schools like Eton and Harrow had long histories, and the Enlightenment brought about a range of Dissenting Academies, which not only offered a new curriculum, including the sciences, but also educated girls as well as boys. Nonetheless, these institutions served a very small proportion of English children. Things began to change in the early 1830s, as the broadly progressive movement characterized as Reform led to public funding for elementary education.[21] The 1870 Education Act started a push towards universal mandatory education, and after 1880 basic schooling was both state-funded and mandatory. The last generation of Victorian children would nearly all have known how to read.

Increasing literacy rates and changing perceptions of childhood corresponded with, and indeed helped bring about, the first Golden Age of children's literature.[22] By the end of the century, children had a literature of their own. In *Juvenile Literature As It Is* (1888), Edward Salmon wrote, "it is only within the last quarter of a century that [children's] literature has deservedly assumed a high place in the public regard."[23] Salmon describes both the quantity and the quality of newly available children's literature, including English writers like Lewis Carroll and Robert Louis Stevenson as well as Americans like Louisa May Alcott and Europeans like Hans Christian Andersen and Jules Verne. Much of the new children's literature came in juvenile periodicals like the *Boy's Own Paper*, which published Verne's stories, and *Young Folks*, where Stevenson's *Treasure Island* was first serialized. These respectable publications competed with myriad "penny dreadfuls" like *Boys of England*, which flooded the market in the last quarter of the nineteenth century, providing young readers with cheap (and mostly forgettable) fiction. By the end of the century, children's literature was a wide open market, and authors and publishers rushed to fill it.

COPYRIGHT LAW, THE VICTORIAN BUSINESS ETHOS, AND NEW TECHNOLOGIES

Children's literature was by no means the only genre to expand rapidly during the late nineteenth century, and its expansion was not merely the result of education and literacy. Legal protections, corporate structures, and print technologies played an equally important role in the explosion not just of children's literature but of all kinds of media.

The Walt Disney Company has a reputation for being especially litigious in defense of its copyrights. Under Michael Eisner the company's synergistic strategy relied on deploying its trademarked characters across different media, and in protecting those characters the company went so far as to sue a daycare center that had painted Disney characters on the walls and even the Academy Awards for an unlicensed use of Snow White in a performance during the 1989 Oscars.[24] Disney remained synonymous with copyright enforcement even after Eisner's tenure. In 2015, amidst debates about the Trans-Pacific Partnership, Mickey Mouse became synonymous with American media exports, protection of which was a key component of the international trade agreement.[25]

In the twenty-first century, however, with the rise of social media and widespread online piracy, Disney has revised its hardline policies. The synergistic strategy that required dogged defense of copyright in the 1990s now benefits from more relaxed enforcement, as unlicensed parodies, compilations, and clips on sites like YouTube expand films' reach and drive visitors to in-person experiences like theme parks and stage shows.[26] But a foundational legend about Walt Disney helps perpetuate the company's reputation for defending its intellectual property. In the first extended biography of Walt Disney, Diane Disney Miller told the *Saturday Evening Post* how Charles Mintz had wrested away control of Disney's first popular animated character, Oswald the Lucky Rabbit, and also poached several of his top animators.[27] Disney learned that he had lost the rights to Oswald when he visited New York in early 1928. According to legend, a frustrated Disney came up with a new character on the train ride back to California. He called the character Mortimer Mouse. His wife, Lillian, suggested a different name, and by May Disney and his few remaining animators had finished *Plane Crazy*, the first Mickey Mouse cartoon. *Steamboat Willie* debuted in November. Years later, a Disney executive explained that the event shaped Walt's business ethos, and that he always "negotiates like he's afraid someone might take another Oswald the Rabbit away from him."[28] The anecdote, in the legend of Disney's biography, provides not only an origin story for Disney's most famous character but also an object lesson in copyright protection.

Not everyone takes kindly to Disney's copyright practices. Pointing out the irony that so many Disney films are based on works in the public domain, Jonathan Lethem calls the company "the most pernicious source hypocrites of all time."[29] As early as the 1960s, Frances Clark Sayers was arguing that Disney "shows scant respect for the integrity of the original creations of authors."[30] Richard Schickel worried that Disney's merchandizing "had a natural tendency to blanket the original" and he quotes a joke about Disney being the author of *Alice in Wonderland*, *Encyclopedia Britannica*, and the works of William Shakespeare.[31] The joke is clever, but it belies an ineluctable fact about cultural production. New works always incorporate precursors. Shakespeare famously borrowed freely from his predecessors, and to the Victorians he was the quintessential example of an individual genius transforming others' stories into new creative works. In Dickens's *Nicholas Nickleby* (1838), the hero grants that Shakespeare "brought within the magic circle of his genius, traditions peculiarly adapted for his purpose, and turned familiar things into constellations which should enlighten the world for ages."[32] *Romeo and Juliet* and *Hamlet* are no less original for using borrowed stories.

The fact that some texts are more closely associated with Disney than with their original authors is one of the main assumptions underlying this book. Opinions vary about that association, as they do about the company's staunch defense of its own trademarks. But the legal possibility is the result of Victorian developments. *Nicholas Nickleby* was the first novel Dickens published after *Oliver Twist*. As would be the case for all of Dickens's novels, unauthorized productions appeared on stage while the novel was still being serialized. The stories were pirated before they were even finished. Nicholas Nickleby, who voices Dickens's frustrations, contrasts Shakespeare, who adapted the "plots from old tales and legends in general circulation," with a "literary gentleman" who adapts novels for the stage without their authors' permission. Nicholas accuses the playwright of stealing "the uncompleted books of living authors . . . which have doubtless cost him many thoughtful days and sleepless nights,"[33] and then goes on to chastise him for dragging "within the magic circle of your dulness, subjects not at all adapted to the purposes of the stage."[34] Such criticism echoes what Lethem, Sayers, and Schickel say about Disney.

Nicholas Nickleby rebukes the plagiarist on personal, moral, and aesthetic grounds, but the practice he denounces was not illegal. In legal terms, copyright is a business arrangement granting the exclusive right to make and sell a particular work, and the arrangement holds because it is "respected by colleagues in the industry and guaranteed by the state."[35] Today we take it for granted, but copyright was barely a century old when Dickens was born. Only in 1710 did the Act of Queen Anne establish an author's rights to their work, and well into the Victorian period it was common practice for most writers to sell those rights to a printer or publisher.[36] However much we think about intellectual property as belonging to a single creative genius, in legal terms it is a business arrangement, and most often it is the domain of a company rather than an individual.

In the 1830s, Dickens's novels were protected by copyright but his characters and stories were not. Others could freely adapt them into other forms, writing new stories about them or transferring them to other media.[37] Stage performances were an especially a grey area of nineteenth-century copyright law. Because performance involved a collective effort, a playwright was considered just one among many creators. The 1814 Copyright Act restricted printed copies of a play but didn't limit performances.[38] The 1833 Dramatic Literary Property Act finally extended protection to playwrights, but only for works written expressly for the stage; novelists still had no legal recourse if their stories were adapted into theatrical productions.[39] Dickens advocated for changes to copyright law, and with his Christmas stories he tried to find loopholes by releasing his own stage production simultaneously with the text. But he would not live to see a legal solution to the problem of other writers adapting his novels for the stage, even before he had written the ending.

The case of Gilbert and Sullivan's *H.M.S. Pinafore* (1878) and *The Pirates of Penzance* (1880) demonstrates the continued absurdity of performance copyright a decade after Dickens's death. *Pinafore* was wildly popular but plagued by copycats from the start. A dispute among investors led to a theater riot, and the investors took the original costumes and props and launched their own production. So even in London, Gilbert and Sullivan's *Pinafore* competed with another production of the same play at a different theater. Things were worse in America, where eight productions of *Pinafore* ran simultaneously in New York City, and over a hundred nationwide.[40] Gilbert and Sullivan received no compensation for any of these performances, and they were determined to better secure the rights to their next work. But they faced a paradox. They could secure English copyright only after a first performance. Stage productions typically premiered a "copyright performance," which could be simply a reading of the play for a small public audience, often acquaintances of the playwright who would accomplish the legal fiction by paying for tickets.[41] But such a performance secured only the English copyright. The American rights to a play required the first premiere to be in America, effectively meaning that a work couldn't be copyrighted in both nations at once.[42] To subvert this absurdity, Gilbert and Sullivan arranged a fully staged English premiere of *Pirates of Penzance*, and then set sail for America to premiere the show in New York. The two premieres occurred on the same day, in different nations, ensuring copyright in both.[43]

As this anecdote suggests, the expanding American market raised the need for international copyright agreements. Americans could legally pirate British books for most of the nineteenth century. A 1790 ruling had denied US copyright protection to foreign authors, and the US and Britain did not come to an international copyright agreement until 1891.[44] Mark Twain's *The Adventures of Tom Sawyer* (1876), a cornerstone of American literature, was published in London before it was published in America, so that Twain could secure the English copyright. Charles Dickens fumed about American piracies of his works, giving regular speeches on the subject during his first trip to America in 1842. The speeches had a significant impact. A few decades later, an *Atlantic* writer, remembering the visit, remarked that "Dickens's opinion of the country rose or fell, according to the chances of its passing an international copyright bill."[45] Cheap reprints of British books made American readers intimately familiar with British culture. Harriet Beecher Stowe, whose *Uncle Tom's Cabin* (1852) was the century's best-selling novel in both America and England, called the English canon "a glorious inheritance."[46] And as public education expanded at the end of nineteenth century, the Victorians featured prominently in American textbooks whose publishers were free from legal restrictions.[47]

Dickens's complaints about American piracies and the steps that Gilbert and Sullivan took to even *try* to protect their intellectual property reveal the tenuous state of international copyright law during the Victorian period. Dickens didn't live to see it, but modern international copyright would take shape by the turn of the twentieth century. In the wake of these laws, newly published British literature actually became less available in America (and American books less available in Britain).[48] For this reason, twentieth-century American audiences further associated British books with the Victorians, who were the most recent authors in the public domain and whose works were frequently included in textbooks and anthologies. This association no doubt contributed to the midcentury "vogue" for Victorian literature and culture, to which I refer in the introduction.

The copyright laws that emerged at the end of the Victorian period ensured that Walt Disney could both adapt classic texts and claim copyright of his own productions. Copyright made Disney's business possible. And the Walt Disney Company is, first and foremost, a business. In an oft-quoted memo, Michael Eisner claimed that a media company's only obligation is to make money. "We have no obligation to make art," Eisner stated. "We have no obligation to make history. We have no obligation to make a statement." The line, which appears in numerous memes, sounds like a capitalist manifesto and captures one view of Disney as a corporation. Eisner's next sentence, however, is less frequently quoted. "But to make money," Eisner continued, "it is often important to make history, to make art, to make some significant statement."[49] Art and entertainment are a business, a fact that was as true in the Victorian period as it is today.

During the Victorian period, commerce became, in the words of Samuel Taylor Coleridge, the "paramount principle of action in the nation at large."[50] Soon after Victoria's coronation, Thomas Carlyle prophesied that the culture's obsession with money would soon give way to a new society, helmed by industrial leaders rather than military or political heroes.[51] Today they might be called "innovators" or "disruptors," but Carlyle, situating the new entrepreneur within the heroic tradition, called them "captains of industry." The phrase became "the most widely echoed Victorian reconfiguration of masculinity."[52] Practical businessmen appear frequently in Victorian fiction. In George Eliot's *Middlemarch* (1870), for example, Caleb Garth expresses his disappointment that his son has "taken to books instead of that sacred calling 'business.'"[53]

Samuel Smiles's *Self Help* (1859) further popularized the commercial spirit. Smiles presented brief biographies of exemplary captains of industry such as James Watt, the inventor of the steam engine, and Josiah Wedgwood, the eighteenth-century potter whose china and porcelain company is still in business today. Although he includes artists and writers among his exemplars of industrious men, Smiles is clear that money measures success. He goes so far as to suggest that Shakespeare took more pride in the practical management of the theater company than in his writing.[54] Critics called *Self Help* "a eulogy of selfishness,"[55] but such accusations did little to detract from the book's popularity. *Self Help* was an immediate bestseller.

Self Help not only celebrates practicality but also derides culture and education. Smiles writes, "we find in daily life so many instances of men who are well-informed in intellect, but utterly deformed in character; filled with the learning of the schools, yet possessing little practical wisdom."[56] Such a statement exemplifies the anti-intellectualism that went hand in hand with the Victorian business ethos. Even the sciences, when not directly applied, were deemed impractical. Speaking at the inauguration of a scientific college in 1880, Thomas Henry Huxley identified two groups who opposed introducing the physical sciences into university curricula.[57] He spends most of the speech responding to classical scholars who saw teaching science as inimical to education's primary goal of propagating tradition. Matthew Arnold wrote a famous rejoinder,[58] and Huxley's essay is most often remembered in the context of their exchange. In the mid-twentieth century, the dispute was resurrected in a debate between C. P. Snow and F. R. Leavis, for which Snow first coined the phrase "two cultures" to refer to the split between humanists and scientists.

But before addressing the classicists, Huxley first acknowledges objections from "the men of business who pride themselves on being the representatives of practicality."[59] Huxley speaks of these men of business in the past tense, assuming that most businessmen have since come to recognize the "demonstrative evidence of the practical value of science."[60] And rightly so. For all his dismissals of formal education, many of Smiles's exemplars built their fortunes on technical innovations. By the end of the century, the Victorian business ethos had come to include science and technology. Walt Disney shared that ethos. The Carousel of Progress, which debuted at the 1964 World's Fair and was later installed at Disneyland and the Magic Kingdom at Walt Disney World, showcases new technologies by portraying family life in different decades.[61] It starts in the twentieth century but nevertheless reveals Disney's interest in the history of technology.

Steamboat Willie, arguably the most important cartoon in Disney's early history, was a technological triumph in itself. It so successfully linked the visual gags with the soundtrack that it was immediately recognizable as something new.[62] Its content also references a technology that had transformed the globe in the previous century: the steam engine. The first sounds heard in *Steamboat Willie* are those of smokestacks and steam whistles, both of which had become a part of life during the Victorian period. In 1842, Dickens expressed his astonishment at the "Britannia steam-packet" that transported him to America.[63] A decade later he described the fictional Coketown, in *Hard Times* (1854), as "a town of machinery . . . where the piston of the steam-engine worked monotonously up and down, like the head of an elephant in a state of melancholy madness."[64] Even William Wordsworth, best remembered for poetry celebrating the natural world and the pleasures of country life, welcomed the new technologies. In "Tintern Abbey" (1798), his best-known poem, Wordsworth laments "the din / Of towns and cities" and affirms that "Nature never did betray / the heart that loved her."[65] Such a poet might be expected to denounce the incursions of railways and steamships. But an 1833 sonnet, "Steamboats, Viaducts, and Railways," asserts that "Nature doth embrace / Her lawful offspring in Man's art."[66] At the start of the Victorian period, it was already clear that the world would be changed by new technologies.

Steam technology transformed all aspects of Victorian life. Steam powered not just the ships that brought Dickens across the Atlantic but also the railways that transformed the English landscape. In 1902, H. G. Wells claimed that the steam-powered train was the defining symbol of the nineteenth century.[67] The first line connecting two major cities, the Liverpool and Manchester Railway, opened in 1830, and by the end of the century railways were ubiquitous both in England and in its colonies. Building on the already-established systems of stagecoach travel, the railways fundamentally altered England's sense of community.[68] Transportation networks facilitated by railways and steamships drastically reduced postal costs and led to unprecedented communications both locally and globally.[69] The tedium of a long journey could be alleviated by railway editions of novels, cheaply produced thanks to steam-powered technologies in printing and paper-making.[70] Railways altered time itself. Railway Time was introduced at stations in 1840, and the construction of Big Ben in 1859 (assisted by steam-powered machinery) created a monument to standardized time.[71] In *Mrs. Dalloway* (1925), Virginia Woolf describes the sound of Big Ben as "leaden circles dissolving in air," providing an acoustic symbol of Londoners' shared experience.[72]

Like the burgeoning business ethos, new technologies raised questions about their moral and environmental impact. By the end of the nineteenth century, London was the largest city that had ever existed, and industrial modernity had changed the very atmosphere: the word "smog" was coined in 1905, describing for the first time a human-caused climate feature.[73] Dickens's *Dombey and Son* (1846) chronicles the destruction and displacement of a London neighborhood, Stagg's Gardens, by the introduction of the railroad. "The first shock of a great earthquake had, just at that period, rent the whole [of Staggs's Gardens] to its centre," writes Dickens. "In short, the yet unfinished and unopened Railroad was in progress."[74] The novel returns to the same scene, years later. "There was no such place as Staggs's Gardens. It had vanished from the earth . . . The carcasses of houses, and beginnings of new thoroughfares, had started off upon the line at steam's own speed, and shot away into the country in a monster train."[75] *Steamboat Willie* celebrates a technology that changed the world but nonetheless had always been viewed with ambivalence.

Advances in transportation technologies were matched by new media technologies. By midcentury, photography, first invented in the 1820s, had displaced painting as the favored mode for realist representation. While painting is necessarily connected to an individual artist, photography claimed to represent its subject without bias. Unlike the human eye, susceptible to changing moods and attention spans, the camera "seemed relatively neutral and impervious to such influences, as only a machine could be."[76] This new form initially seemed a marker of modernity. In *Great Expectations* (1861), the retrospective narrator remarks that he'd never seen his parents because "their days were long before the days of photographs."[77] But cheaply available photographs, and new methods for printing them, quickly made pictorial items like mass-printed photographs a part of daily life.[78] In the 1880s, photography was common enough to be a children's pastime, and both *Boy's Own Paper* and *Girl's Own Paper* encouraged readers to learn photographic skills, form clubs, and enter competitions.[79] Just a quarter-century after *Great Expectations*, the search for Mr. Hyde (in Robert Louis Stevenson's *The Strange Case of Dr. Jekyll and Mr. Hyde* [1885]) is rendered difficult both because witnesses can't accurately describe him and because he had never been photographed.[80] These two facts sit casually side by side, as if, by 1885, being photographed was as normal as being seen.

The quotations from Dickens and Stevenson imply that photography accurately represents the world, but not all Victorians shared that view. Victorian art photographers combined and altered images, creating "photographic fictions." Rather than faithfully replicating real-life scenes, Victorian photography was "pressed into the service of fictional creation."[81] Film and sound recording would later be similarly associated with realist representation, but like photography, these technologies were equally interesting for their ability to defy the laws of the physical world. If *The Jazz Singer* (1928) offered an experience analogous to seeing Al Jolson perform live, *Steamboat Willie* presented an unrealistic spectacle, as objects and animals are transformed into musical instruments. Those transformations, and Mickey's impossible bodily contortions, have roots in Victorian photographic fictions.

A plethora of optical toys like the thaumatrope (1825), the phenakistoscope (1832), and the zoetrope (1843) educated the Victorians in different visual effects, not only shaping the contours of modern children's media but also laying the groundwork for moving pictures.[82] In February 1896, Robert W. Paul exhibited the first film in London, at the Finsbury Technical College. A month later he rebranded the apparatus and moved the display to the Alhambra Music Hall in Leicester Square. The relocation marks a shift in how film was perceived.[83] What had first been a technical wonder, akin to optical toys and exhibited at a technical college, now became a public entertainment, displayed in a music hall. Sound recording, also a Victorian innovation, followed a similar trajectory. Thomas Edison traveled to England to record the voices of famous personages; thanks to Edison, we can listen to Victorian poets Alfred Tennyson and Robert Browning. But phonograph recordings quickly became entertainment fare. In 1888, Horatio Nelson Powers composed "The Phonograph's Salutation," a poem told from the perspective of the phonograph and purposely composed to showcase the technology.[84] Edison's electric company also helped spread entertainment culture in the early twentieth century. Electric companies and trolley companies built amusement parks at the ends of their lines, as a way to entice customers to ride the trolleys on weekends. Disneyland was originally envisioned in direct contrast to those parks.

By the turn of the twentieth century, a family culture, international and cross-media copyright laws, a business ethos, and new media technologies were firmly in place. All had emerged in the decades following the 1830s. And as these disparate elements developed, a public entertainment industry was emerging to unite them. Victorian theatricals, elaborate spectacles with musical accompaniment, readied the public for Disney's animated musicals in the twentieth century, while public displays like wax museums, panoramas, and the Great Exhibition laid a conceptual foundation for Disney's theme parks.[85]

VICTORIAN THEATER AND DISNEY'S FILMS

By the time he died, Walt Disney presided over a company whose diverse revenue streams included film and television, music and publishing, theme parks, and merchandising. He seems to have been especially attuned to what would later be called "synergy," as each part of the company enhanced the whole. The soundtrack for *Snow White and the Seven Dwarfs*, for example, was the first instance of a now-ubiquitous musical genre: original songs from motion pictures.[86] The *Disneyland* television specials not only provided the studio an early foray into television but also promoted both the theme parks and the films, not to mention merchandise like the Davy Crockett coonskin cap.[87] This synergy intensified under the leadership of Michael Eisner, who oversaw the opening of international theme parks and the purchasing of ABC and ESPN, and then Bob Iger, who spearheaded the purchase of the Marvel and *Star Wars* franchises, the acquisition of 21st Century Fox, and the launch of Disney+.[88] Twenty-first-century media companies rely on successful franchises, and no company holds more valuable ones than Disney, whose "accumulation of ideational and material capital" makes it a case study in "cultural capitalism."[89]

The proliferation of adaptations in new media technologies—from film and television to theme parks and smartphones—continues a long-established trend. Victorian texts also moved fluidly across media, a word that postdates the period but has nevertheless been called the era's "defining aesthetic."[90] Charles Dickens offers a case study. The text of Dickens's novels was enhanced by pictures (all of his novels were illustrated), and later in his life he gave public readings, allowing audiences to hear his novels through his own voice. These "official" multimedia texts competed with unlicensed spin-offs, including not just stage productions but also prose imitations, unauthorized illustrations, and all manner of consumer products. From the beginning of Dickens's career, each novel was not just a book but "a phenomena, a mania."[91] The same was true for countless other nineteenth-century novels. "The Victorians," writes Linda Hutcheon, "had a habit of adapting just about everything—and in just about every possible direction."[92] Public entertainments took advantage of new technologies, and by the start of the twentieth century, they had solidified into the entertainment industry that the Walt Disney Company would come to dominate.

The theater was the most important Victorian precursor to Disney's amusement empire, both for its popularity among audiences and for its influence on film history. Partly because stage performances are so ephemeral, the influence of theatrical productions on early film is often downplayed or outright ignored. The director Sergei Eisenstein famously claimed that early cinema aesthetics borrowed from nineteenth-century novels,[93] but well into the twentieth century those novels had nearly always been adapted into highly successful stage shows before they were made into films. The stage productions were at least as influential as the written texts.[94] A. A. Milne's script, *Toad of Toad Hall* (1929), to cite an example relevant to this book, brought new audiences to Kenneth Grahame's *The Wind in the Willows* (1908). Milne's play, rather than Grahame's novel, likely inspired Disney's *The Adventure of Ichabod and Mr. Toad* (1949) and Mr. Toad's Wild Ride, which was among the attractions when Disneyland opened in 1955.

Victorian theater, even more than Victorian literature, shaped the film industry in the first half of the twentieth century. And not just live-action films. The influence of the theater on Disney's early films is confirmed by reports from the late 1930s, preserved in the Walt Disney Archives. Al Perkins, writing an internal report about *Alice in Wonderland*, devotes several pages to Eva Le Gallienne's production at the Civic Repertory Theater in New York.[95] Perkins clearly admired Le Gallienne's play, but his report also notes how a Disney version might fill gaps left by the production and by recent films. Referring to the scene when Alice gets stuck in the White Rabbit's house, Perkins writes, "our treatment of this scene would be brand new stuff to everyone, for it was not even attempted in Paramount's or Eva Le Gallienne's version, and Tenniel only did two episodes."[96] Perkins grounds his ideas in Carroll's text, but he also considers how a Disney cartoon might fit into previous adaptations, including film, theater, and illustration.

Le Gallienne and co-writer Florida Friebus chose *Alice in Wonderland* because they already had *Peter Pan* in their repertoire and they wanted another play that would attract both kids and adults.[97] Their version of *Peter Pan* was also influential, and Disney storywriter Dorothy Blank discusses it in her research report about J. M. Barrie's story, along with many other stage productions. Blank focuses on the performers, and especially on Maude Adams, who had played Peter in the first American production in 1905 and reprised it multiple times. Adams, whom a 1907 biographer called the "most popular of all the women stars on the American stage today," was best known for her roles in Barrie's plays.[98] Blank notes that in London *Peter Pan* is staged every Christmas, and so "the flesh and blood embodying him appear to have been disregarded."[99] But to American audiences, "Peter Pan was Maude Adams and Maude Adams, Peter Pan."[100] Other actresses, like Marilyn Miller, who played Peter at the Knickerbocker in 1924, and Betty Bronson, who starred in the Paramount film the same year, were compared (unfavorably) to Adams. Blank also refers to a production at the Wilshire Ebell, a theater in Los Angeles, and implies that she and Walt (to whom these memos are addressed) had seen it.[101]

Blank argues that an animated version of *Peter Pan* has distinct advantages over a stage play or a live-action film. Nana, the Darling family's Newfoundland nursemaid, is "undoubtedly one of the very best characters in the story. . . . Critics have often expressed regret that Nana did not play a more important part." Since an animated dog is much easier to handle than a live one, Nana is "ideal for our purposes."[102] Blank loved the character so much that, in early versions of the story, Nana accompanies the children to Never Never Land. She also thought the casting of Peter could contrast with the stage productions. On stage, Peter is usually played by an adult woman. This wasn't critically popular, and audiences wished for "a more robust portrayal." So Blank suggests that "in our character of Peter Pan we remove forever any doubts about sex, and make our hero <u>all boy</u>."[103] In Disney's *Peter Pan*, Peter is voiced by Bobby Driscoll, who also starred in Disney's *Treasure Island* (1950) and in one of the studio's most controversial films, *Song of the South* (1946).

Though it earned a special award for actor James Baskett and won the 1947 Academy Award for Best Original Song ("Zip-A-Dee-Doo-Dah"), *Song of the South* remains an outlier in Disney's catalog. Its characters and the song were repurposed for the Splash Mountain ride in the early 1990s, but Disney has otherwise attempted to forget it. It was the only film never released on home video, and it was not made available on Disney's new streaming service, Disney+.[104] In 2020, Disney announced that even Splash Mountain would be rethemed, to be based instead on *The Princess and the Frog* (2009).[105] The new attraction, based on Disney's first Black princess, will displace a film that has long been considered racially insensitive. *Song of the South* is based on Joel

Chandler Harris's *Uncle Remus* stories, which Disney claimed to have loved as a child. A few scholars have praised the film's racial politics, noting that Baskett's special Academy Award made him the first Black male honored by the Academy and that the film also featured Hattie McDaniel, who in 1939 had become the first Black entertainer to win an Oscar for her performance in *Gone with the Wind*.[106] But *Song of the South* is more often condemned for its overly sentimental depiction of the "Old South" and implications of "happy slaves," elements that led the NAACP to boycott the film.[107]

Harris's Uncle Remus stories were published in Victorian period. This contemporaneity, coupled with the fact that Harris, a white writer, appropriated Black folktales, brings to mind a particular nineteenth-century stage practice that became central to film history, including Disney's early animation: blackface minstrelsy. Blackface was a prominent feature of nineteenth-century theater in both Britain and America, and its images and styles remained legible in popular culture well into the twentieth century.[108] Mickey Mouse's white gloves, wide eyes, and trickster behavior place him in the minstrel tradition.[109] *Steamboat Willie* features "Turkey in the Straw," which had become famous as a minstrel tune. The musical connection underscores the image of *Steamboat Willie* as an adaptation of minstrel music, and perhaps also of *The Jazz Singer* (1927), the first feature-length sound film. *The Jazz Singer* had been released the year before *Steamboat Willie*, and starred Al Jolson in blackface. Audiences for the first sound cartoon would have made the connection.

Mickey Mouse was far from the only animated character who borrowed the tropes of blackface, and it has been argued that the whole animation industry owes its origins to minstrelsy.[110] One Disney cartoon, however, engages directly both with blackface and with nineteenth-century theater more generally. "Mickey's Mellerdrammer" (1933) begins with Mickey putting on blackface and starring in a stage production of Harriet Beecher Stowe's *Uncle Tom's Cabin*.[111] Stowe's book was the bestselling novel of the nineteenth century, not only in America but also in Britain and its colonies (where, with no international copyright protection, it sold a million and a half copies).[112] Like other popular novels, *Uncle Tom's Cabin* was immediately adapted for the stage. The Howard family, headed by the American actor-manager George C. Howard, starred in the most famous stage production. Four-and-a-half-year-old Cordelia Howard was cast as Eva, the tragic white child who was a favorite among readers; her father thought Cordelia perfect for the role after seeing her in a family production of Dickens's *Oliver Twist*.[113] Cordelia's mother played another of Stowe's most famous characters: Topsy, an enslaved Black child. Caroline Howard (who is white) became famous

Audiences enjoyed reproductions of famous battles and productions on horseback at Astley's Amphitheatre. Drawing by Thomas Rowlandson and Augustus Pugin (1808–1811).

for the role, performing it over 5,000 times before her retirement in 1886.[114] While Eva epitomized the innocent, angelic white child, Topsy was the prototype for what Robin Bernstein calls the "insensate pickaninny," a Black child depicted as "resistant if not immune to pain."[115] Topsy's image was printed on a remarkable array of products, from soaps and crackers to sheet music and ashtrays. "The repetitious ubiquity of the insensate pickaninny," writes Bernstein, "de-sensitized white readers and other consumers of African American pain."[116] Read in this context, the formulaic violence of the cartoon gags in "Mickey's Mellerdrammer" takes on a very different register.

Blackface minstrelsy is only one element of nineteenth-century theater parodied in "Mickey's Mellerdrammer." The title plays on the word "melodrama," evoking what was far and away the period's most popular theatrical genre. Melodrama owed its origins to the Licensing Act of 1737, which limited spoken drama to just two London theaters, Drury Lane and Covent Garden. Shows at other venues were deemed "illegitimate," and were legally required to distinguish themselves from spoken drama. By the end of the eighteenth century, an entire culture of illegitimate theatricals had emerged, with standard conventions for distinguishing those performances from the legitimate productions at Drury Lane and Covent Garden.[117] Most performances included music, and many featured animal acts, puppetry, or dance. The censorship led to extravagant creative feats. At Sadler's Wells and Astley's Amphitheater, for example, audiences could experience recreated battles, including land engagements featuring cavalry and naval battles in water tanks.[118] Serious performances of Shakespeare's plays (some of them staged on horseback, a genre called "hippodrama") existed alongside parodies of the Bard that set the soliloquies to popular music, changed the blank verse to rhyming couplets, and added topical references, often "digs at the famous actor playing Shakespeare straight next door."[119] These various "illegitimate" performances fell under the general heading of melodrama.

Victorian melodramas were multimedia performances, and music would typically underscore the dramatic action, or dramatic speeches might alternate with songs. Melodramas also featured moments of "static pictorial composition," known as tableaux.[120] Actors would group together to form a scene, maintaining a static pose. For Victorian audiences, a tableau was not just a respite between scenes; it was "the master-convention of melodrama's visual semiotics," occurring at climactic moments (often the ends of scenes) and inviting audiences both to recall important earlier moments and to postulate what would happen next.[121] A particular subset of tableaux, known as "realizations," imitated famous works of art. Realizations relied on audiences' familiarity with particular images, a familiarity that became increasingly likely as Victorian advances in printing made images cheaply reproducible.[122] Stage adaptations of novels were often structured around realizations of the illustrations that appeared alongside the text.[123]

Melodramas also took advantage of new technologies for astounding stage effects. A water tank featured as the central spectacle in Benjamin Webster's 1853 performance of *The Thirst of Gold* at the Adelphi Theater. The tank held machinery to raise two "icebergs" through the tank, and a tableau featured the ice breaking apart, stranding the captain's orphaned child on the last piece of ice.[124] As they were invented, technologies like photography and railroads also made their way into melodramatic plots, often as narrative devices. The plot of one of the period's most popular melodramas, Dion Boucicault's *The Octoroon* (1859), turns on a photograph. Carolyn Williams has argued that these elements of the melodrama—the musical soundtrack running alongside the drama, static scenes coming together into a narrative whole, and the integration of new technologies—paved the way for early cinematic forms.[125]

Because the music and stage effects were at least as important as the plot and dialogue, theatricals owed their success less to individual playwrights than to theater managers (many of them women).[126] Stage productions were commercial ventures as much as artistic. Gilbert and Sullivan's first collaboration, *Thespis* (1871), puns on the word "company," linking its theatrical meaning to its business one. The "thematic coherence" of the work derives from the dual meaning of "company management," and Williams calls it a fitting start to the "well-functioning machine" that characterized the duo's subsequent collaborations.[127] Gilbert and Sullivan's theatrical company, each member working in a disciplined system to create a final product billed under someone else's name, might be seen as a precursor to Disney's studio. Despite periodic challenges from animators and a midcentury artists' strike, a unique style emerged in Disney's early films. That style, which continues in a recognizable form into the twenty-first century, is associated with the company, rather than any individual animator, voice actor, or singer.

By the early 1940s, Walt Disney had positioned himself not as an individual artist (the creator of Mickey Mouse, which had earned him his first Academy Award) but as a corporate franchise.[128] In a popular anecdote, when a child heard that Walt Disney didn't draw or write his films, he asked what he *did* do. Disney responded by comparing himself to a honeybee, flying between different aspects of the production as a bee flies between flowers.[129] Just as audiences today associate the films with Disney, rather than with a particular writer or animator, Victorian audiences were more likely to be fans of a particular theater, or of a particular actor or actress, than an individual playwright.[130] Both theater and film are fundamentally collaborative. This aspect, as well as the broad public appeal, the narrative and formal structure, and of course the actual performances that Disney's writers researched or viewed, links Disney's animated musicals to nineteenth-century theater.[131]

Children were active participants in Victorian theatrical culture, both as performers and as audience members.[132] Lewis Carroll's diaries record frequent theatrical trips accompanied by child friends.[133] Fairy tale and pantomimes were popular among child audiences early in the century, and a separate theater aimed specifically at children would emerge in the last quarter-century. As I discuss in the next chapter, Carroll worked with Henry Clarke Saville on a stage version of the *Alice* books. Frances Hodgson Burnett, who like Charles Dickens objected to unauthorized productions of her works on stage, adapted *Little Lord Fauntleroy* (1886) into a theatrical performance in 1888. Unlike Dickens, she successfully defended her rights to the story, in a landmark case of international copyright law.[134] Though it premiered shortly after Victoria's death, J. M. Barrie's *Peter Pan* (1904) would become the era's most famous play. Carroll, Barrie, and Burnett were forerunners in establishing children's theater as its own genre.[135]

Theater is among the oldest literary genres, but a separate theater for children was a relative latecomer—so late, in fact, that it was nearly contemporaneous with children's film. The Lumière Brothers' *L'Arroseu arrosé* (*The Sprinkler Sprinkled*, 1895) features a child playing tricks on an adult, and some US theaters were offering separate screenings for children as early as 1896.[136] Barrie and Burnett lived long enough to see their works adapted into film. Burnett attended the 1921 premiere of *Little Lord Fauntleroy*, with Mary Pickford in the starring role.[137] Barrie lived until 1937, though there is no evidence that he saw Betty Bronson as Peter Pan in Herbert Brenon's 1924 film.

The link between theater and film is a natural one, and as I stated at the start of this section, theater exerted a far greater influence on early film than did the novel. But as I demonstrate in the next section, moving pictures emerged within an entertainment industry that far exceeded stage productions.

VICTORIAN PUBLIC ENTERTAINMENTS AND DISNEY'S THEME PARKS

Charles Dickens's *Hard Times* (1854) famously opens with Thomas Gradgrind instructing a schoolmaster to "teach these boys and girls nothing but facts. Facts alone are wanted in life."[138] Dickens juxtaposes Gradgrind's school with Sleary's circus, to which Gradgrind's children sneak away. As a counterpoint to Gradgrind's dictum, the lisping circus-master Mr. Sleary provides his own maxim: "People mutht be amuthed."[139] Sleary's circus was part of a newly emerging amusement industry. As workers' rights movements gradually restricted the burden that industrialists placed on their workforce, workers could decide how to spend their newly acquired leisure time. Sleary's circus, and the theaters discussed in the previous section, competed with "gin palaces" and grand music halls, with seaside resorts attracting crowds via rail and steamship, and with "palatial winter gardens" and exhibition grounds offering "mechanized amusement rides."[140] Many of London's public museums and art galleries also opened during the Victorian period, becoming competitors in an industry that has always balanced instruction with amusement.[141]

Frances Burney's epistolary novel *Evelina; or, the History of a Young Lady's Entrance into the World* (1778) offers a tour of the city's entertainment scene as it existed in the late eighteenth century. Evelina attends the opera and the theater, but also visits displays like Cox's museum, where she is impressed by a mechanical pineapple, and pleasure gardens like Vauxhall and Marylebone.[142] Those pleasure gardens were perhaps eighteenth-century London's closest analogue to a theme park. They combined fireworks shows with art exhibitions and other performances, and attracted a remarkably socially diverse crowd. William Thackeray's *Vanity Fair* (1847), which is set at the beginning of the century, describes "all the delights of the Gardens" as the characters visit Vauxhall:

> the hundred thousand extra lamps, which were always lighted; the fiddlers in cocked hats, who played ravishing melodies under the gilded cockle-shell in the midst of the gardens; the singers, both of comic and sentimental ballads, who charmed the ears there; the country dances, formed by bouncing cockneys and cockneyesses, and executed amidst jumping, thumping and laughter; the signal which announced that Madame Saqui was about to mount skyward on a slack-rope ascending to the stars; the hermit that always sat in the illuminated hermitage; the dark walks, so favourable to the interviews of young lovers; the pots of stout handed about by the people in the shabby old liveries.[143]

Everyone enjoyed the lights, music, dancing, and acrobatic performances, but those "dark walks" and "pots of stout," combined with the mixing of social classes, gave Vauxhall a reputation for rowdy crowds. That reputation, and the increased ticket prices established in the hope to control those crowds, diminished Vauxhall's reputation. In the 1840s, Thackeray's readers would have felt a sense of nostalgia at his description, and the Georgian pleasure gardens like Vauxhall were nearly all closed.[144] The form persisted, though, with new pleasure gardens in London and other major cities like Birmingham and Manchester. They entertained thousands of attendees each night, their managers spending thousands of pounds a season on new entertainments in an attempt to keep pace with the rapidly developing mass entertainment industry.[145]

The pleasure gardens' most direct competition came from the music hall, which has been called "Britain's first indigenous and fully capitalized mass culture form."[146] Early music halls were "flourishing in towns and cities across the nation by 1850," and reached new heights with the 1854 opening of Charles Morton's Canterbury Hall in Lambeth.[147] Morton had opened a fairly modest public house a few years earlier, with a small concert room. The adjoining space was sufficiently successful that Morton expanded it to a capacity of between 1,500 and 2,000. Contemporary journalists noted its size and grandeur, and the theatrical space quickly overtook the public house. Unlike nearby theaters, the Canterbury was attached to a pub, and Morton catered to a mixed-gender audience, which distinguished his music hall from gentleman's clubs that offered similar entertainments. The Canterbury's sheer size helped establish its reputation for "ostentatious respectability," and Morton employed a corps of professional performers, including trained opera singers, who helped ensure that the entertainments maintained a veneer of respectability, attracting audiences from different social classes.[148] Despite fears of "moral panic" expressed by mid-Victorian critics like Henry Mayhew, music halls proliferated over the subsequent decades, reaching their "commercial zenith" in the late Victorian period and remaining popular through the first World War.[149] Music hall songs, typically bawdy comic songs with a chorus that invited audience participation, became a popular genre. Star performers became recognized as "the true curators of their culture," and music halls remained synecdochic for working-class Englishness throughout the twentieth century, legible in theatrical productions like Lionel Bart's *Oliver!* and British pop bands like the Beatles.[150]

But music was by no means the only entertainment enjoyed by Victorian audiences. Pleasure gardens and smaller, more specialized sites offered crowds the chance to experience entertainments that had been impossible a century earlier. By midcentury, the mechanical pineapple that so impressed Evelina would have paled in comparison to magic lantern and dissolving-view shows and elaborate waxworks. Waxworks had begun as religious relics, and a wax body features in the plot of Ann Radcliffe's *The Mysteries of Udolpho* (1794). Over the course of the nineteenth century, however, Madame Tussaud, whose name remains synonymous with the form, adapted the form as an entertainment. Tussaud displayed her waxworks in London around the turn of the century before embarking on a three-decade tour through England and Ireland.[151] In the 1830s, she returned to London, setting up shop with her sons, who kept up the attraction after her death in 1850.[152] It was still going strong at the turn of the century, and the first sentence of E. Nesbit's *The Railway Children* (1906) lists Tussaud's as a favorite children's destination along with the magicians Maskelyne and Cook's, the pantomime, and the zoological gardens.[153] In 1884, Tussaud's grandsons relocated to Marylebone Road, where the waxworks remains open today. Its franchises have expanded across the globe.[154]

When Alice first meets Tweedledum and Tweedledee in *Through the Looking-Glass* (1871) they are standing "so still that she quite forgot they were alive." She is roused by Tweedledum, who tells her that if she thinks they're waxworks, "you ought to pay, you know. Wax-works weren't made to be looked at for nothing."[155] The joke relies on the reader's familiarity with waxworks, both as an object and as a product within a fee-charging industry. Disney could still rely on that familiarity in the mid-twentieth century, and *Alice in Wonderland* (1951) maintains the joke. Shortly after that film's release, Disney was planning his own waxwork exhibit at Disneyland: a walk-through attraction featuring pirates. But at the 1964 Worlds Fair, Disney debuted his first Audio-Animatronics human, Abraham Lincoln. Audio-Animatronics figures—programmable, realistic robotic puppets—proved superior to waxworks, and the pirate waxworks evolved into the Pirates of the Caribbean boat ride.[156]

Disney's Audio-Animatronics displays were a technical wonder, but like other media products, they drew on a long tradition. George Cruikshank, the illustrator who provided the pictures for Dickens's *Oliver Twist*, later produced *I Dreamt I Slept at Madame Tussaud's* (1847), imagining Tussaud's figures coming to life and interacting with each other. The notion was not as unrealistic as one might think. Clockwork automata, like the mechanical pineapple that Evelina sees at Cox's Museum, had been popular attractions in the eighteenth century. The Mechanical Turk, a chess-playing machine, debuted in 1770 and remained popular well into the nineteenth century. It was eventually revealed to be an elaborate hoax, and not a true automaton, but it was only the most famous among many human figures that moved via clockwork. Mrs. Salmon, whose waxworks had been popular before Madame Tussaud's, displayed waxworks that moved via springs and clockwork.[157] These displays were precursors to Disney's Audio-Animatronics figures.

In 1802, before her eponymous shop became a global phenomenon, or even a permanent London attraction, Madame Tussaud had first exhibited her waxworks at the Lyceum,[158] a venue that provides an index to changing trends in Victorian entertainments. Built by the Society of Artists in 1772, the Lyceum displayed a variety of exhibitions in the late eighteenth century, including "astronomical demonstrations, air balloons, waxworks, 'philosophical fireworks,' boxing matches, circuses, programs of humorous recitations, and concerts."[159] The original building burned down in 1830, and after being renovated it staged more traditionally theatrical performances. In the late 1840s, it was managed by some of the era's most famous theatrical couples, including the Robert and Mary Anne Keeley (from 1844 to 1847) and Charles Mathews and Lucia Elizabeth Vestris (from 1847 to 1855).[160] The offices of Dickens's magazine *Household Words* opened across the street, and Dickens commented on the crowds who came to see the fairy extravaganzas.[161] Hans Christian Andersen saw two performances at the Lyceum when he stayed with Dickens in 1857,[162] and before he partnered with Arthur Sullivan, W. S. Gilbert began his career in 1863 with a "curtain-raiser" at the Lyceum.[163]

In the last quarter of the century, the Lyceum came to be associated with the actor-manager Henry Irving and his wife Ellen Terry, who became famous for their Shakespeare performances. Irving's 1874 *Hamlet* was "one of

DISNEY AND THE VICTORIAN TRADITION

the most influential and talked about theatrical roles in the latter part of the nineteenth century,"[164] and his performance was parodied in W. S. Gilbert's *Rosencrantz and Guildenstern.*[165] Bram Stoker worked for Irving, and his time at the Lyceum familiarized him with the theatrical traditions that permeate *Dracula* (1897). The venue remained popular in the twentieth century. *Alice in Ganderland*, the "first feminist adaptation" of the *Alice* books, played there in 1911.[166] More recently, since 1999 the Lyceum has hosted Disney's *The Lion King*, a play that might be said to continue the theater's legacy. It is partly an adaptation of *Hamlet*, in tune with Irving's legacy, and combines two distinct trends of twentieth-century pop culture: the animated musical and the Broadway play.

The Lyceum hosted various entertainments, both theatrical and otherwise. Other entertainments required the construction of entirely new structures. Panoramas were elaborate and detailed landscapes painted on the inside of cylindrical buildings several stories tall. Visitors climbed stairs or rode newly invented elevators to view representations of distant geographies or famous battles, and by the 1840s panoramas were often supplemented with lectures and live performances.[167] Panoramas let Victorian audiences travel the globe, becoming a visual metaphor for distant places both real and imaginary. In George Eliot's *Middlemarch*, Lydgate imagines his potential move to London as seeing his future in "a magic panorama."[168]

In its heyday, the panorama must have been an exciting experience, and after it declined at midcentury, its legacy lived on in other visual entertainments like the diorama, a flat picture given the illusion of depth and movement by lighting and sound.[169] Other entertainments were even more elaborate. To access Thomas Hornor's Colosseum, audiences entered through a 100-foot circular room, the Saloon, and then up an "ascending car" into the first of four galleries. They were "overwhelmed by a flood of sensory information" as they moved through exhibits as varied as the roof of St. Paul's Cathedral, an African glen, and a Glaciarium (an indoor skating rink).[170] The Colosseum was an immersive experience. Like a theme park, it promised not just a representation of reality but an escape from it.

At times the whole of Victorian London must have had the feel of a theme park. Thomas and Jane Carlyle complained that fireworks kept them awake at night.[171] Accustomed to London, Dickens was struck by the quietness of the New York streets when he visited in the 1840s. "Are there no itinerant bands; no wind or stringed instruments?" he wondered, expressing surprise at the absence of "Dancing-dogs, Jugglers, Conjurors, Orchestrinas, or even Barrel-organs."[172] Such entertainments were common throughout the city, but London's popular entertainment industry was centered in the neighborhood

Prince Albert initially planned the Great Exhibition to be in Leicester Square, the heart of London's entertainment industry. It was moved to Hyde Park instead, but was nevertheless a sensation, captured in images like David Roberts's *The Inauguration of the Great Exhibition: 1 May 1851* (exhibited in 1852).

around Leicester Square, which had been the location of the first panorama and which, by 1850, was "virtually synonymous with miscellaneous exhibitions and entertainments."[173] It retains its reputation, and Disney's *Alice in Wonderland* premiered at the Leicester Square Theater.

Leicester Square was Prince Albert's initial choice for an entertainment event that would ultimately eclipse all others: the Great Exhibition of the Industry of All Nations. Ultimately located in the more spacious Hyde Park, the Great Exhibition was a sensation, drawing crowds from Europe and America and seeming to "monopolize public and private discourse."[174] Wilkie Collins captures the mass of tourists descending on the city in *The Woman in White* (1859), describing how Mrs. Rubelle and her husband "had taken a house in the neighbourhood of Leicester Square, to be fitted up as a boarding-house for foreigners, who were expected to visit England in large numbers to see the Exhibition of 1851."[175] By linking technological innovation with public entertainment, the Great Exhibition epitomizes the entertainment scene of Victorian London. Walt Disney was certainly aware of it, and not just because the Great Exhibition inaugurated the tradition of the World's Fairs in which he so actively participated. Disney was in London for the 1951 premiere of *Alice in Wonderland*, where he would have witnessed the centennial of the Great Exhibition, celebrated by the Festival of Britain on the South Bank. The centerpiece of the Great Exhibition was the Crystal Palace, a massive glass structure in Hyde Park. A restaurant called the Crystal

Palace in Walt Disney World's Magic Kingdom offers a further connection to the Great Exhibition, as does another restaurant, Victoria and Albert's, in the adjacent Grand Floridian Hotel.

The Great Exhibition caused an "unprecedented tourism boom" in London, and crowds spilled over into other London sites.[176] The Crystal Palace was expanded and remodeled, and then relocated to its own extensive landscaped grounds in Syndenham, South London. While the Great Exhibition had been partly a national and educational project, designed to showcase industrial progress around the world, and especially Britain and its colonies, "the new Crystal Palace in Sydenham was fundamentally a commercial venture," owned by a joint-stock company chaired by railroad entrepreneur Samuel Laing, whose transportation connections helped ensure crowds could travel to the new site (much like funding from trolley and streetcar companies led to a twentieth-century boom in amusement parks).[177] The Crystal Palace never entirely abandoned its predecessor's educational mission, continuing to offer public lectures on art, geography and science as well as adult education classes.[178] But in order to remain permanently open, the site had to attract thousands of visitors over a sustained period. Its managers and investors recognized that this would require novel and exciting entertainments suited to the structure.

The Crystal Palace at Sydenham included a winter garden, with parrots and tropical plants maintained by miles of iron pipes. The rest of the palace included self-contained "courts," showcasing the architecture of different historical periods and providing visitors an experience "halfway between walking through a museum and a series of historically themed theatrical sets."[179] The grounds around the palace featured landscaped gardens of the type normally associated with country estates (and so inaccessible to most of the English public) and a set of fountains designed to rival Versailles.[180] To keep crowds coming, the palace adopted strategies associated with the pleasure gardens. Musical performances, from weekly operatic concerts to a triennial Handel Festival, were the most profitable attraction, and the site featured staple pleasure garden entertainments like balloon ascents and firework displays.[181]

The Syndenham Crystal Palace remained open for fifty years, finally closing in 1909. During that period, it had faced competition from other sites inspired by the Great Exhibition. Over the next half-century, they took their place among the theaters, music halls, pleasure gardens, and various attractions at Leicester square and elsewhere in London. In 1899, the Greater British Exhibition at Earl's Court included the instructive and colonialist exhibits reminiscent of its predecessor a half-century earlier, but also a Great Wheel (the first Ferris wheel having premiered in Chicago a few years earlier) and the Great Canadian Water Chute, a flume ride in a flat-bottom boat.[182] These rides further link the legacy of the Great Exhibition to Disney's theme parks.

The Great Exhibition fundamentally changed the London entertainment scene. Charles Kean, manager of a "previously rather unimportant" theater, developed programming to capture the crowds drawn by the Exhibition.[183] Kean's productions aimed for an immersive authenticity that imitated what visitors would see at the Exhibition and at the growing numbers of London museums. Kean created a place for theater in what has been called the "emerging West End 'Theme Park.'"[184] It was in this context, with multimedia theatrical performances existing alongside other visual entertainments, that the first films were exhibited. Well into the twentieth century, film was rarely viewed in isolation, and was not primarily considered a narrative medium. Even as late as the 1950s, a film might "cap a program that included cartoons, shorts, newsreels, a support feature or even live acts."[185] Just as the panoramas had depicted scenes of interest, whether natural sites or scenes of historical events, early films (most of which were no more than a minute) depicted "street scenes, processions, public events, dancers, variety turns and such like."[186] The earliest audiences appreciated the technology as much as the content. Rather than the story-driven plays of legitimate theater, those audiences would have associated moving pictures with the visual spectacle of the panorama, the tableaux and other stage effects of melodrama, and the myriad exhibits at the Great Exhibition and the World's Fairs.[187]

Motion pictures began being exhibited publicly in London in 1894, and by the end of the century, ninety London businesses specialized in their production, distribution, or exhibition.[188] Sales figures grew steadily in the mid-1890s, with peaks each year in September when most films premiered, coinciding with "the new autumn season for the music halls and variety theatres," as film exhibitors adopted the expectations of the industries with which they competed.[189] In 1844, Victoria had been the first English monarch to be photographed, and she was also the first to be captured in a motion picture. Her diary for Saturday, October 3, 1896, records the family being "photographed by Downey by the new cinematograph process, which makes moving pictures by winding off a reel of films."[190] She died just a few years later, and there was a "phenomenal demand" for footage of the funeral in February 1901. The footage prompted an off-season spike in demand, helping prove that films could draw crowds even outside the normal entertainment season.[191]

Victoria's death had a notable impact on the emergence of the film industry, which began to take shape during her lifetime. Walt Disney, born the year Victoria died, would come to dominate that industry. Other groundwork for the Walt Disney Company, such as the emergence of children's culture, legal and technological advances, and a burgeoning industry of popular entertainment, had also been laid during Victoria's reign. To see how those disparate factors coalesce, the last section of this chapter turns to Charles Dickens, a Victorian media celebrity whose life and career were not so different from Disney's, and whose first novel the company adapted at a crucial point in its history.

DICKENS, DISNEY, OLIVER, AND COMPANY

As visitors approach the Disneyland ticket counter, their view of the park's centerpiece, Sleeping Beauty's Castle, is obstructed by the train station. To enter, guests pass through tunnels running below the train and flanked on either side by coming attractions posters, which advertise the park's rides and shows. The train station functions as a curtain, the posters as previews. Even at the opening of the park each morning, the smell of popcorn wafts through these tunnels, not because guests necessarily want popcorn for breakfast but because the smell adds to the movie-theater ambience.[192] Characters are staged throughout the park, and even non-costumed Disney employees are "cast members" trained to think in terms of "on stage" and "off stage." Storywriters and animators were closely involved in constructing Disneyland and since its opening in 1955 the architectural, metaphoric, and even olfactory experience has been framed as a performance.[193]

Disneyland is the benchmark for themed entertainments, even those whose themes are a far cry from Disney's. Following the announcement of a Charles Dickens theme park in the dockyards of Chatham, Kent, a writer for the *Evening Standard* quipped, "Forget Disneyland, try Dickens World."[194] Comparisons to Disney remained commonplace even as Dickens World didn't quite live up to expectations. *The Guardian* called it "Disney gone to the dark side."[195] *Christian Science Monitor* compared it to "Disney World dipped in rust-colored paint and starved of the Florida sunlight."[196] But while journalists saw Disney as synonymous with entertainment quality, defenders of the British tradition feared that Dickens World would be a "Disneyfication" of Dickens and the era in which he lived.[197]

Reactions to Dickens World reenact the disagreement between F. R. Leavis and Walt Disney that I presented in the introduction: the divide between elite critics and popular entertainment. Dickens World, in its attempt to appeal to both groups, came to stand for more than a single author. Unlike Shakespeare, whose stories have proved temporally and culturally fluid, Dickens is closely associated with the time and place in which he lived: most adaptations of his novels are set in Victorian England.[198] Dickens is a brand unto himself, "his name authorizing any and all iterations of Victorian figures, experiences, and products."[199] The value of his name was already apparent in the 1840s, when London guidebooks featured titles like *A Ramble in Dickens-land.*[200] Nearly two centuries later, he is still synonymous with the Victorian period. Dickens's world is the Victorians' world.

But the content of the Dickens brand is hard to pin down. Dickens was a passionate social reformer, quick to point out social injustices like the hypocrisy of the Poor Laws (in *Oliver Twist*) and the harsh conditions of factory workers (in *Hard Times*). Those injustices are often called "Dickensian," an adjective frequently applied to "perceived ideas of Victorian England" as a whole.[201] But scholars' concerns that this "real Dickens" might be lost in Disneyfication obscure the fact that Dickens was not primarily a social reformer. He was, like Walt Disney, a "self-created celebrity and mass media entrepreneur."[202] His mass appeal caused some critics to disparage him. In 1865, five years before Dickens's death, a young Henry James wrote, "Mr. Dickens is a great observer and a great humourist, but he is nothing of a philosopher."[203] George Orwell recalled "having Dickens ladled down my throat by schoolmasters" and thought that "no grown-up person can read Dickens without feeling his limitations."[204] Leavis agreed, quipping that "the adult mind doesn't as a rule find in Dickens a challenge to an unusual and sustained seriousness."[205] James, Orwell, and Leavis dismissed Dickens as a popular entertainer, better suited to childhood amusements than to serious adult reading.

In fact, for much of the twentieth century, Disney was considered a more serious artist than Dickens. Disney garnered multiple awards in the early 1930s, and before World War II reviews and essays typically portrayed him as "an artistic genius and a modernist pioneer."[206] In 1943, he was named a trustee of the Museum of Modern Art in New York, and he recruited the executive director of the Los Angeles County Museum of Art to help him find artists interested in collaboration.[207] The company had become financially viable only after the release of *Snow White* (1937), and even then the associated merchandising accounted for most of the profits.[208] Other studios balked at how much money Disney spent in pursuit of his artistic goals and even stockholders complained that he was "an artistic success and a commercial failure."[209]

Since the 1940s, Dickens's and Disney's reputations have reversed. In 2013, Dickens World shifted its business model, abandoning the initial theme-park idea and instead offering guided tours with a more educational focus. It closed permanently in 2016.[210] The same year, the Walt Disney Company opened its sixth theme-park resort, in Shanghai. Dickens looms large both in the classroom and in serious scholarship about the Victorian era, but doesn't have the popular appeal to sustain a theme park. By contrast, Disney products are taken less seriously in classrooms and scholarship, but it would be utter folly to call the Walt Disney Company a commercial failure.

Given the influence the Disney brand holds today, it is perhaps difficult to imagine how uncertain was the company's future after Walt Disney's death in 1966, and especially after the 1971 death of his brother Roy. In the early 1980s, the Walt Disney Company faced bankruptcy or absorption into another company. Many top animators left the studio, citing reduced investment in the quality of the films.[211] When Michael Eisner took over as CEO in 1984, he sought to revitalize the animation department, which he saw as the company's core business. He and chairman Jeffrey Katzenberg held "gong show" meetings, at which animators would pitch story ideas. At one such meeting, in 1985, Ron Clements, a Disney animator who was at work on a film about a Sherlock Holmesian mouse, suggested "The Little Mermaid"—it got the gong, as it was considered too similar to the just-released *Splash* (1984). Clements then offered "*Treasure Island* in space." It was also rejected. Finally, Pete Young pitched an idea, and his was the one the executives chose. The next Disney animated feature would be "Oliver Twist with dogs."[212]

When Charles Dickens began serializing *Oliver Twist; or, the Parish Boy's Progress* in *Bentley's Miscellany* in 1837, he was just beginning his career. The novel responds to a recent parliamentary act (the Poor Laws) and a fad genre (the Newgate novels, which glorified the lives of criminals). It climaxes with the violent, sexually charged murder of a prostitute, followed by the murderer's madness and then his gruesome death. The murder was so central to the novel that Dickens selected that scene to read aloud when he began performing his novels for audiences. Such a story would seem an odd choice for a family friendly company like Disney. But in the century and a half between its serialization in *Bentley's* and Disney's decision to make the film, *Oliver Twist* moved from the pages of the magazine to the stage, to the screen, and back to the stage again. By the 1980s, a Disney animated musical "*Oliver Twist* with dogs" was far more likely than the novel's plot indicates. What's more, drafts of *Oliver & Company* (1988)—the fruition of Young's idea—reveal that Disney writers engaged with that textual history and the adaptations across media. These drafts, and other materials from the Walt Disney Archives, show Disney's connection not only to Charles Dickens but also to period he has come to represent.

As was common for Victorian fiction, all of Dickens's novels were illustrated. In fact, his first major work, *The Pickwick Papers* (1836), had initially been envisioned as a vehicle for the illustrator Robert Seymour, who was more marketable than the then-unknown Dickens. Dickens was hired merely to provide textual anecdotes to accompany Seymour's pictures. His prose, however, quickly built his fan base. Seymour's suicide after the first few installments ensured that *The Pickwick Papers* would be remembered more for its words than its illustrations. The work also initiated Dickens's practice of publishing his works in weekly or monthly parts, keeping readers in suspense while they waited for the next part of the story.[213]

Oliver Twist contained pictures by the famed illustrator George Cruikshank, but it was first and foremost a Dickens novel. And it had a political purpose. From the very first paragraph, Dickens takes aim at the Poor Law Amendment Act of 1834. Oliver is born in one of the workhouses the Act had established, and within days the London *Times* excerpted a scene from the novel to show the Act's inhumanity. *Oliver Twist* helped shape public discourse about the law.[214] But as Dickens's first readers noticed, Oliver's story is soon overshadowed by Nancy's. Nancy is murdered by her lover, Bill Sikes, while trying to protect Oliver. An 1839 reviewer remarked, "we all sympathise with Nancy's melancholy fate: her death is drawn with a force which quite appalls."[215] For nineteenth-century audiences, the politics of poverty were not the primary focus of *Oliver Twist*. The novel's climax was Nancy's murder.

Nancy's centrality to the narrative was enhanced by Dickens's reading tours, which he began in the late 1850s. The tours gave both English and American audiences a chance to hear in person a voice they had been reading for decades (much as, a century later, Walt Disney's television appearances let audiences connect "the likable, avuncular man to the theme park and media products that carried the Disney name").[216] Evidenced by the underlining and marginalia in his reading texts and by the testimonies of those who heard him, Dickens was an active performer. Among his most notorious readings was "Sikes and Nancy," a selection from *Oliver Twist* that focused on the death scene that had "appalled" early reviewers. His friends "adamantly opposed" this addition to his repertoire because they were "fearful of the extraordinary physical and physiological demands it made upon" him.[217] His manager George Dolby believed that these performances, especially "Sikes and Nancy," hastened the author's death from a stroke.[218] Dickens's histrionic reading of the scene, together with the subsequent rumors of its connection to his death, further elevated the importance of Nancy's murder to the popular imagination of *Oliver Twist*. It is this "Sikes and Nancy" element with which *Oliver & Company* seems most incongruous. And that element was even more central to the stage and film adaptations than to the novel.

Oliver Twist borrows many conventions from the stage, and even cites the influence. "It is the custom on the stage," begins chapter seventeen, "in all good murderous melodramas, to present the tragic and the comic scenes, in as regular alternation, as the layers of red and white in a side of streaky bacon."[219] Dickens's use of stage conventions in his fiction, combined with his popularity, made his novels fine candidates for dramatic (and later, cinematic) adaptations. In the absence of copyright law protecting reproductions in different media, those stage adaptations were produced without his permission or control. And because his novels were serialized, they were typically performed onstage before they were even finished—much to his chagrin. Dickens's friend and biographer John Forster recalls accompanying the novelist to an unauthorized production of *Oliver Twist* at the Royal Surrey Theatre in 1838, while the novel was still being published. "In the middle of the first scene," writes Forster, Dickens "laid himself down in a corner of the box and never rose from it" until the play was over.[220]

Naturally, and despite the author's objections, these performances shaped the public's reception of his novel. The script for the performance that Dickens attended at the Surrey was written by George Almar. It is "a full blown 'murderous melodrama,' of the sort that Dickens discusses" in the "streaky bacon" passage.[221] Nancy's murder is the play's "undeniable climax" and Almar presents the story as a revenge tragedy built around that scene.[222] Though it was staged before the novel was finished, Almar's was not the first *Oliver Twist* theatrical. C. Z. Barnett presented a stage version in May 1838, when only thirty of the novel's eventual fifty-three chapters had been published. Nancy's murder closes chapter forty-seven, which had not yet appeared, so Barnett could not structure his story around that scene. But he still enhances Nancy's role. The "dramatis personae" lists her as "Sikes's wife" and she helps bring about the story's denouement.[223]

These theatrical adaptations promoted the elements of *Oliver Twist* that Dickens would later highlight in his public readings, and his "Sikes and Nancy" performance was probably motivated by the prominence that Nancy had earned onstage. Together they ensured that Nancy's murder was the focal point of the narrative. Film and television adaptations continued that focus. The first Dickens film was the American Mutoscope Co.'s *The Death of Nancy Sykes* [*sic*] (1897), and for the first half of the twentieth century *Oliver Twist* was the most adapted Dickens text, beating out even the now-ubiquitous *A Christmas Carol.*[224] In the process, certain excisions occurred. The Poor Laws had been crucial both to the novel's first readers and to early stage adaptations. Barnett's version features the orphans in the workhouse singing, "The Poor Law Bill! / The poor man's shame! / It bringeth him ill, / And it bringeth him pain!"[225] But in her survey of screen versions, Juliet John finds only one allusion to the bill, even though most versions keep the Victorian setting.[226]

The Death of Nancy Sykes continues the legacy of the dramatic adaptations and Dickens's own readings, but later silent films changed the story's tone, emphasizing the community and marketability of the text. Frank Lloyd's 1922 version, for example, built on the popularity of Jackie Coogan, who had recently won acclaim for his performance in Charlie Chaplin's *The Kid.*[227] But after World War II, those early adaptations were overshadowed by two British productions, David Lean's film *Oliver Twist* (1948) and Lionel Bart's musical *Oliver!* (1960). Lean's film reclaimed *Oliver Twist*'s "Englishness" and shifted the public's sense of the novel "from the cheery and sentimental tone of the early American films toward the stark austerity of postwar England."[228] Lean's stated goal was to be as faithful as possible to Dickens's original text, and he based his costuming and casting choices (including a prosthetic nose for Alec Guinness, who played Fagin) on Cruikshank's illustrations. That fidelity came with a price. Viewers accused Lean of anti-Semitism, and the film caused riots in Berlin and was initially banned in the United States.[229]

It was in this context that Lionel Bart produced the stage musical *Oliver!*, which had a record-breaking theatrical run in London's West End. Lean's screenplay had already reduced the long novel into a manageable script, providing a narrative structure for Bart's libretto: most of the scenes in *Oliver!* correspond with scenes in Lean's *Oliver Twist.*[230] And perhaps in response to the criticism of Lean's film, Bart's musical reduces Fagin's villainy. Fagin sings one of the musical's biggest numbers ("Reviewing the Situation") and is the focus of the play's ending. As a result, *Oliver!* concentrates the villainy in a single character, Bill Sykes.[231] One effect of that concentration is to focus the narrative on its most violent scene, the murder of Nancy. Nancy's role is even larger in the musical than in the book, as the subplot of the "strange and seemingly fruitless romance" between her and Bill competes for attention with Oliver's and Fagin's stories.[232]

Oliver! was (and remains) a staple of school and community theaters. Since it calls for a cadre of child performers, budding actresses and actors often encounter it at a young age. Even during the musical's first run on the West End, the producers received letters from schoolchildren "in hopes of getting permission to perform songs from the show in recitals."[233] That association helped make Dickens's story an appropriate source for a Disney film. When Disney announced *Oliver & Company* in the 1980s, they promoted the link to Dickens. The *New York Times* mentioned Eisner and Katzenberg's desire "to make a contemporary live-action musical version of Charles Dickens's 'Oliver Twist' set in New York City."[234] The featurette "The Making of *Oliver & Company*" similarly envisions it as a contemporary Dickens story. But in terms of production, the stage musical *Oliver!* was a more important precursor than the novel *Oliver Twist*. Sharon Weltman posits that the title *Oliver & Company* may be a tacit acknowledgment of the play's importance, since several musical numbers in *Oliver!* are designated as being performed by "Oliver and Company."[235]

Oliver & Company's link to Broadway is further solidified by the voice cast and the production team. In addition to headliners Bette Midler and Billy Joel, the *New York Times* review highlights Sheryl Lee Ralph's "1,200 Broadway performances in 'Dreamgirls'" and "Roscoe Lee Browne, a veteran of Joseph Papp's New York Shakespeare Festival."[236] Even more importantly, *Oliver & Company* marked Howard Ashman's Disney debut. Ashman had recently written the hit musical *Little Shop of Horrors* (1982) with Alan Menken, who would soon join him at Disney. With *Oliver & Company* and subsequent films, Disney approached its animated musicals as if they were Broadway shows. This approach especially characterized the films of the Disney Renaissance: *The Little Mermaid* (1989), *Beauty and the Beast* (1991), *Aladdin* (1992), and *The Lion King* (1994).[237] *Oliver & Company* isn't typically considered part of the Disney Renaissance, but it shares some key characteristics with those films.

Yet even with the popularity of *Oliver!* among family audiences, Disney's "*Oliver Twist* with dogs" presented a challenge. A century and a half of *Oliver Twist* adaptations, from the earliest stage productions to Dickens's readings, and from early films through the hit musical, had placed Nancy at the center of the plot. The "Oliver Twist Musical" (as internal memos referred to the work when still in progress)[238] would need to account for her character—and her murder. Draft scripts in the Walt Disney Archives show how writers approached the problem. From the beginning, the drafts follow Bart's lead, and further change the power dynamic between Sykes (spelled with a "y" in Disney's script) and Fagin. For all Sikes's violent tendencies, it is Fagin, in Dickens's novel, who controls the action. Sikes fears him. *Oliver!* had made Fagin less villainous, and the earliest character description in the Disney Archives follows that same trajectory, describing Fagin as "a bum with a heart of gold."[239] The intention seems to have been to concentrate the villainy in Sykes.

Other changes are also evident in the early drafts. Initial story concepts involved a plot to steal a panda from the Central Park Zoo, and a zoo break-in was the story's climax as late as August 1986.[240] Perhaps most notably, the pathos of Oliver's abandonment is relegated to the opening credits. The image most audiences associate with *Oliver Twist* is the young Oliver, cupped hands outstretched, asking, "Please sir, I'd like some more." Disney completely omits the workhouse setting that makes that plea necessary. Instead, the film opens with a box of abandoned kittens, of whom Oliver is the only one not adopted. Disney seems never to have considered an analogue to the workhouse setting. The earliest extant draft begins with an overview of New York City and then Jenny receiving Oliver as a birthday present.[241] Oliver later pleads with Dodger to share some stolen sausages, but in the absence of anything like a workhouse setting, the plea lacks the same significance.

These drafts make it clear that Disney never planned to stick closely to Dickens's novel or even to Bart's libretto. The Brownlow and Maylie households are condensed into the child Jenny and her butler Winston, and Disney adds an antagonist, Jenny's pet poodle Georgette, whose primary role seems to be as a vehicle for Bette Midler.[242] Yet Nancy's character, and even her murder, still feature prominently in the early scripts. The earliest memo is dated September 24, 1985, though reference to storyboards already in progress indicates prior drafts. A cover sheet lists the goals of the revision: "1. Give Oliver an attitude; 2. Show a more defined relationship between Dodger and Oliver; 3. To develop a warm relationship between Oliver and the Tina character."[243] Tina Turner was slated to sing the opening song and perhaps lent her name to the character. But as the relationship with Oliver indicates, Tina is clearly based on Nancy. In Dickens's novel, Nancy plays the role of Oliver's protector. The script assigns that role to Tina. She is the only female in the group of dogs whom Oliver befriends. When Sykes and his Dobermans arrive, "Tina, using her female charm, sweet-talks the Doberman and distracts him, saving Oliver from certain death."[244] The ending is even more revealing:

> Tina agrees to show Oliver the way through secret alleys, since she is the one who got him involved in the first place. . . . In one of the alleys, they are overtaken by the Dobermans . . . she stalls the Dobermans. As Tina and the Dobermans approach each other growling, we cut to Dodger and the others.[245]

After the plot resolves, Oliver "runs into an alley, he comes to a sudden stop. Horrified, his eyes fall on Tina, bloodied and dying. . . . Oliver, with tears in his eyes, rests his head on Tina's paw as she dies."[246] Oliver's presence makes the scene all the more poignant, as does the location in the narrative. The draft puts her death after the resolution of the main storyline (and so not spurring a "revenge plot," as in earlier versions) but before the final scene, which is still "a happy moment for all."[247] Just two days later, the writers already seem unsure about this scene. The next script reads, "could have a death scene here, OR Tina survives."[248]

The connection between Tina and Nancy is made more explicit a month later. The typed copy in the archives is annotated in blue pen, and each appearance of "Tina" has been crossed out and replaced with "Nancy." The alley scene remains: "In a back alley the Dobermans overtake ~~Tina~~ Nancy." And after the plot resolves, "Oliver and the gang race off to look for the missing ~~Tina~~ Nancy. They find her bloodied and helpless."[249] But now she survives, and in the final scene we see "Fagin and the gang, including the bandaged ~~Tina~~ Nancy."[250] In this version, the alley scene is also sexually charged, as the plot had earlier implied a relationship between Nancy and one of Sykes's Dobermans. When the Dobermans first appear, the script notes, "Both dogs are cruel, but one a bit less so. We find out that he's ~~Tina's~~ Nancy's ex."[251] By August, the character's name had been changed again, to Rita, as it would remain in the final version. But her sexuality is still featured. Rita turns on the television "with a sexy bash of the hip," and when the Doberman Roscoe first sees her, "The two eye each other. There's a history there."[252] Playing up these aspects links Rita to Dickens's Nancy and adds a sexual undertone to the alley scene.

That scene is cut from the film's final version. Katzenberg called Rita "the conscience of the gang,"[253] and she is the first to feel guilty about the gang's kidnapping Oliver from Jenny. (Unlike the kidnapping in the novel, this is portrayed as a good faith act, returning Oliver to his friends.) But Rita's conscience is far less legible in the final version than in the early drafts. She is a minor character, no more developed than the other caricatured dogs in the gang.

Removing Nancy as a major character makes space to enhance the Artful Dodger, who plays only a minor role in Dickens's novel. After introducing Oliver to Fagin, Dickens's Dodger fades into the background until his capture and trial, which mostly provide comic relief. But *Oliver!* had already elevated the Dodger's character. "Consider Yourself," which he sings to welcome Oliver into the gang, is one of the play's most famous songs, and its performance marked a turning point on the show's opening night.[254] Voiced by Billy Joel, Disney's Dodger plays an even larger role. The archives show how that role developed. The earliest memo states the goal of defining the relationship between Oliver and Dodger, and later it was suggested that "as a means of strengthening our story structure, OLIVER could be told through Dodger's rather than Oliver's point of view. . . . This would deepen our understanding of the entire cast . . . and clearly focus the story's attention on its centerpiece: Dodger and Oliver."[255] Already Dodger has replaced Nancy as Oliver's most important relationship and the presumed centerpiece of the story.

Oliver & Company is one of Disney's less memorable films. Unlike Disney's other franchises (like *Alice in Wonderland*, which I discuss in the next chapter, or the princess franchises I discuss in chapter four), *Oliver &*

Company did not lead to sequels, spin-off television series, or theme-park attractions. But the film is nevertheless important to the studio's history, as it introduced Ashman to animation and marked an early success for Eisner and Katzenberg, who would go on to break records with the next few films. Drafts of *Oliver & Company* in the Walt Disney Archives also reveal insight into the Disney's creative process, showing how Disney's writers engage closely with what Paul Davis would call the "culture text" of *Oliver Twist*: not just the text itself but the history of its reception and adaptations.[256] *Oliver & Company* is by no means an outlier in this regard. The studio has always been attuned not only to market forces (like the midcentury vogue for Victorian texts) but also to histories, both its own internal history and the histories of the texts it adapts. As this chapter has demonstrated, not only have Victorian adaptations been cornerstones of the company's success, but its very existence depends on legal and cultural concepts that emerged in the Victorian period. The remaining chapters further examine Disney's entanglement with the Victorians, considering a Victorian text, a Victorian author, and Victorian ideologies of gender and sexuality.

Chapter Two

Alice from Gag to Franchise

In 1946, the Walt Disney Company published a two-page ad in *American Weekly*, announcing a feature film based on Lewis Carroll's *Alice in Wonderland*. The ad quotes Walt Disney as saying, "No story in English literature has intrigued me more. . . . It fascinated me the first time I read it."[1] In the late 1940s, Alice appeared in board games and jigsaw puzzles from Parker Brothers, in comics like *Superman* and *Raggedy Ann*, and even on the cover of *Life* magazine. The *American Weekly* ad might seem like just another example of postwar Anglophilia. But Disney's fascination with Carroll's book predates the "Alice mania." In fact, by the 1940s he had been making cartoons based on Lewis Carroll's story for two decades.

Walt Disney produced *Alice's Wonderland* (1923) while living in Kansas City, long before he founded his eponymous company. The short film doesn't use Carroll's characters or episodes, but conceptualizes the cartoon medium through the lens of the Victorian nonsense novel: a live-action Alice steps into a cartoon world. Disney brought the film with him when he moved to Los Angeles, and a series of fifty-six Alice comedies marks the real beginning of his career. He never stopped thinking about Alice, even as he moved on to other cartoons. A 1931 *New Yorker* profile noted that, "since the success of Mickey Mouse, Disney is continually receiving requests to make the original Alice in his own medium."[2] He made several attempts to oblige those requests, and research reports, early drafts, and press releases provide evidence of several "phantom adaptations," films that were begun but never completed.[3]

Disney's *Alice in Wonderland* was finally released in 1951, but it was not particularly successful. Walt Disney thought it too "intellectual."[4] The film was by no means the company's last *Alice* adaptation, however. Scenes from the film were incorporated into the television special *Disneyland*, and when the park opened in 1955 it featured two attractions based on the movie. In the second half of the twentieth century, Disney produced Alice merchandise of all kinds, as well as rereleases and adaptations of the 1951 film.

The history of Disney's *Alice* adaptations not only provides insights into Disney's internal workings and external marketing but also shows how interpretations of *Alice in Wonderland* changed over the course of the twentieth century. More generally, it provides a case study in literary adaptation, revealing the "stakeholders, institutions, commercial arrangements and legal frameworks which govern the flow of content across media."[5] Today, Disney's *Alice* is not merely a film but a franchise.

ALICE'S APPEAL

The *Alice* books have a famous origin story. Charles Lutwidge Dodgson, a professor of mathematics at Christ Church College, Oxford, first told the story to Lorina, Alice, and Edith Liddell (the daughters of the Dean of Christ Church) during a trip down the River Thames in the summer of 1862. Alice asked Dodgson to write the story down, and he produced a manuscript with his own illustrations, titling it *Alice's Adventures Underground*. Encouraged by friends, he revised the story and published *Alice's Adventures in Wonderland* in 1865, using the pseudonym Lewis Carroll. The book includes a poem alluding to the story's genesis. It begins, "All in the golden afternoon, / Full leisurely we glide" and puns on the girls' last name (Liddell): "both our oars, with little skill, / By little arms are plied." The poem alludes to the river trip and to the "cruel Three" who ask for a story and demand, "There will be nonsense in it!" It concludes, "Thus grew the tale of Wonderland."[6] With this prefatory poem, the story's private origins became part of its public reputation. Disney's *American Weekly* advertisement mentions the origin story, and even states Dodgson's name, rather than just the more famous pseudonym. (Disney does not mention the scandalous accusations about Carroll's sexuality that were just beginning to come to light.)[7]

Neither *Alice's Adventures in Wonderland* nor its slightly darker sequel, *Through the Looking-Glass and What Alice Found There* (1871), has been out of print since their first publication. Since the 1880s, the books have remained current through stage and film adaptations.[8] Carroll clearly recognized the value of his stories, both as works of art and as marketable commodities. He paid close attention to the design of the physical books. The manuscript included his own illustrations, but he chose John Tenniel, already well-known for his illustrations in *Punch*, for the published version. When Tenniel thought the paper used for the first print run was too thin and obscured the illustrations, Carroll bore the costs of reprinting (the poor quality copies were sent to America).[9]

Carroll proved to be "a skillful entrepreneur who carefully cultivated and controlled his Alice industry."[10] After the release of *Wonderland*, he published frequently under the name Lewis Carroll, presumably so readers began to associate it with nonsense verse, and he worked closely with Macmillan, his publisher, "to identify potential periodicals that might review the text."[11] Like Disney, Carroll recognized the link between his artistic product and the economic results. Modern critics celebrate the books' resistance to didacticism, but as the books expanded into other markets Carroll "substantially changed the supposed moral-free nature of *Wonderland* and *Looking-Glass*," producing versions of the stories like the *Nursery Alice* (1890), which teaches letters and numbers. These versions make Alice "a far more didactic and marketable heroine," showing Carroll's knowledge of the children's literature market and his willingness to meet purchasers' desires.[12] And when those desires extended to merchandise like date books, stamp cases, tablecloths, biscuits tins, and ivory-carved parasol handles, Carroll took an active role in creating them.[13]

Carroll also recognized the value of adapting the *Alice* books into other media. He mentioned a potential stage version of *Wonderland* in a letter to his brother within two years of its initial publication, and over the next few years corresponded with playwrights and theater managers.[14] In 1876, he explored the idea of working with W. L. Beare to produce magic lantern slides based on Alice.[15] Finally, in 1886 two theaters approached Carroll about staging the stories, and he began collaborating with Henry Savile Clarke to produce an operetta.[16] They worked closely together for several months, and Carroll's letters evidence the interest he took in the details of the production. The result was advertised as "A Musical Dream Play, in Two Acts, for Children and Others," and opened on December 23, 1886, in the Prince of Wales's Theatre in Coventry Street.[17] Each act condensed one of the books, the first act treating *Wonderland* and the second, *Looking-Glass*. Clarke's play was wildly successful, becoming a staple of London's Christmas season. It was produced nearly every year from 1898 through 1927.[18]

Clarke's collaboration with Carroll is not the only theatrical version of *Alice in Wonderland*. More than forty were staged by 1920, and more than

Lewis Carroll collaborated with Saville Clarke for a stage adaptation of the *Alice* books. *Alice in Wonderland: A Dream Play for Children* premiered in 1886.

100 by 1951, the year of Disney's cartoon.[19] Eva Le Gallienne's 1932 New York production was especially influential, and a 1947 revival of Le Gallienne's play made the April cover of *Life* magazine. Film studios also recognized the appeal. Alice appeared in silent films as early as 1903, and in 1933 Paramount produced a feature-length Alice musical starring W. C. Fields, Cary Grant, Edna May Oliver, and Gary Cooper.[20] These adaptations shaped public perceptions of the *Alice* books and provided a backdrop for the Disney versions I discuss later in this chapter.

The plurality of adaptations also raised questions about the intellectual property rights to the story, characters, and images. In the *American Weekly* ad, Disney claims to have acquired the film rights to *Alice in Wonderland* "as soon as I possibly could after I started making animated cartoons."[21] The statement fits the marketing plan, which is grounded in Walt's long-term fascination with Alice, but it rather oversimplifies the text's copyright status. In Carroll's lifetime, copyright protected a work for forty-two years, or for seven years after the author's death, whichever is longer. Carroll died in 1898, and so the text of *Alice's Adventures in Wonderland*, published in 1865, came out of copyright in 1907. New editions of *Wonderland* began to appear immediately, usually with new illustrations to appeal to younger audiences.[22] But copyright law changed in 1911, when *Through the Looking-Glass* (1871) was still in copyright and John Tenniel was still alive, extending the copyright to his illustrations. The new law extended copyright protection to the life of the author plus fifty years. Tenniel died in 1914, and under the new law his illustrations remained in copyright until 1964.

A text's copyright status can have a profound effect on its reception.[23] The importance of Tenniel's illustrations, and their different copyright status, helps explain Disney's insistence on acquiring the rights to a book that, at least in textual form, was already in the public domain. Despite the myriad modern illustrations, Tenniel's images remained the most recognizable (at least until Disney's 1951 intervention). Filmmakers as well as illustrators attempted to remain faithful to Tenniel. Paramount took such pains to reproduce Tenniel's illustrations that the all-star cast is unrecognizable. Plaster masks hid the faces and muffled the voices of Gary Cooper (the White Knight), Edna May Oliver (the Red Queen), and Cary Grant (the Mock Turtle).[24]

Thomas Leitch has suggested that a focus on Tenniel's illustrations has led most film adaptations to treat the *Alice* books as "a series of set pieces or episodes."[25] But the episodic structure is inherent in Carroll's text. Each *Alice* book has a simple frame narrative: Alice visits Wonderland and looks for a garden, or steps through the Looking-Glass and maneuvers across a chessboard. The story concludes when she wakes up from a dream. Within this frame, individual episodes are built around a single idea. The Mad Tea Party, probably the book's best-known episode, juxtaposes two proverbs ("mad as a hatter" and "mad as a march hare") with the expected orderliness of a tea party. For a Victorian girl, a tea party must have been the epitome of a rule-based event, and the episode parodies the no-doubt bewildering experience of a child learning the rules of "civil" behavior. The characters crowd together in one corner of a large table, leaving most of the seats empty. Yet they cry "no room, no room" as Alice tries to sit down. They trade accusations of incivility. The idea of "teatime" sets up another series of jokes. The March Hare gloomily ponders why even "the *best* butter" didn't fix the Hatter's watch, and the Hatter refers to "murdering the time" in his rendition of "twinkle, twinkle, little bat."[26]

The Mock Turtle's sequence has a similar structure. His story about going to school in the sea gives way to an extended series of school-related puns. The tortoise "taught us" lessons in "Reeling and writhing," "the different branches of Arithmetic—Ambition, Distraction, Uglification, and Derision," "Mystery, ancient and modern, with Seaography," "Drawling, Stretching, and Fainting in Coils," and "Laughing and Grief," and all of these lessons "lessen from day to day."[27] As with the tea party, a single concept unifies the jokes, most of which break established rules: rules of behavior, rules of language, and even the rules of the physical world (like Alice's growing and shrinking). Neither the tea party nor the Mock Turtle's story have much to do with the chapters that precede or follow them. The *Alice* books are held together not by a continuous narrative but by a formal technique, the breaking of familiar rules. In the language of early film comedy, this technique is called "business" or "gags."[28]

The *Alice* books were especially well-suited for the cartoon shorts that were popular in the late 1920s. Cartoons privileged gags over the story, so much so that when Disney began production on *Snow White*, others in Hollywood called it "Disney's folly" because nobody thought an audience would sit through a feature-length cartoon.[29] Like Carroll, animators began with a concept (like a tea party or an undersea school) and came up with related gags.[30] Thematic relationships between the gags, rather than an extended narrative, unified each cartoon. At the start of his career, Disney recognized a similar structure in the *Alice* books. He kept returning to Carroll's texts as he began to include more complex narratives in his cartoons, and the studio's gag department gradually evolved into the story department. The balance between gags and story remained at the center of Disney's decades-long process in producing *Alice in Wonderland*.

THE 1920s: CARTOON GAGS AND *ALICE'S WONDERLAND*

Walt Disney claimed to have been a fan of the *Alice* books since childhood.[31] At some point, he must have realized that the story's governing metaphor, a child's navigation of a world with strange, unfamiliar rules, could be applied directly to cartoons. Viewers could accompany a child through a cartoon universe, just as readers accompany Alice through Wonderland. Perhaps Disney came to this realization on his own, but it's equally possible that he got the idea from Edwin G. Lutz's *Animated Cartoons: How They Are Made, Their Origins and Development* (1920), which he checked out from the Kansas City Library around 1921.[32] The final chapter of Lutz's book, "Animated Educational Films and the Future," discusses "educational subjects," a category in which Lutz includes "any theme, or story for children, even if a slight touch of the humorous or diverting is to be found in it."[33] As "a good example of the type of fanciful tale on the order of which animated cartoons could be made for children," Lutz offers *Alice in Wonderland*, noting that "Tenniel's interpretations of the characters seem to have been created especially for translation to the animated screen."[34]

Tenniel's illustrations were still under copyright, and it would be another decade before Disney would acquire them. But Lutz's remark must have sparked his imagination. In early 1923, he watched an advertisement starring the four-year-old Virginia Davis, and felt he had found the child who would guide viewers into the cartoon world. They signed a contract on April 13 and began work on a film initially titled *Alice in Cartoonland*.[35] The final version, under the altered title *Alice's Wonderland*, would launch Disney's career.

Early cartoons balanced three elements: the visual quality of the drawings and the animation; the characters and story; and the use of "gags," or "business." The latter was the most important. "We try to create as many gags as possible in a sequence and then give the situation a quick twist," Disney explained to a *New York Times* reporter in 1934. "Portrayal of human sensations by inanimate objects such as steam shovels and rocking-chairs," he added, "never fails to provoke laughter."[36] Other common gags included the distortion of a character's body (stretching their neck to see over a wall, for example), body parts used in unexpected ways (like a cat using its tail as a sword or a spring), or inanimate objects coming to life and interacting with characters.

Disney developed his gag style while still in Kansas City. His earliest cartoons include a series of modernized fairy tales in which, as Timothy S. Susanin explains, Disney developed a repertoire of gags. *Little Red Riding Hood* (1922), for example, features a "frequently used Disney gag" in which, when a cat is injured, "nine spirits—the cat's nine lives—ascend upwards from the cat." *The Four Musicians of Bremen* (1922) "also contains several gags Walt would reuse in future productions, including the cat's removal of his tail to bat away incoming cannonballs" and a "swordfish's removal of his 'sword' to use as a saw."[37] Disney also learned from other animators. The most prolific producer of cartoons was Paul Terry, who produced weekly cartoons based on Aesop's fables. By mastering shortcuts like cycling and repeating actions, Terry "established the cartoon production on an industrial basis."[38] Disney cited him as an early influence and *Alice's Wonderland*—with its "great variety of animals, all moving in cycles and repeats"—evokes Terry's films.[39]

Max and Dave Fleischer's Out of the Inkwell series also influenced Disney's early cartoons. The series features a cartoon clown named Koko who emerges from an inkwell and interacts with a live cartoonist. Dave Fleischer, who had worked as an usher in the Palace Theater in New York, cited vaudeville's influence on Out of the Inkwell, which envisions the animator as a performer.[40] The Fleischers' series built on a tradition of cartoons that made the animation process part of the content, self-consciously emphasizing the labor that goes into producing them.[41] John Randolph Bray's *The Artist's Dream* (1913), for example, alternates a live-action artist with animated scenes in which his drawings come to life.[42] The first film Disney screened (part of a series of short cartoons satirizing local current events, which he called "Laugh-O-grams") began with a live-action scene of Walt preparing to draw.[43] In the fall of 1921, Walt and his friend Fred Harman left their advertising jobs to start their own animation studio, and their first cartoon, *The Little Artist*, also featured an easel coming to life.[44]

The first sequence of *Alice's Wonderland* belongs to this tradition. Alice visits an animation studio and meets with Walt and the other animators. As the animators watch and laugh, cartoon animals come to life on the easels. A cartoon mouse jousts with a live-action cat, and two cats box while the animators cheer them on. Like Out of the Inkwell, this sequence features animators as performers. It lasts about two and a half minutes, before Alice bids goodbye to the animators.[45] But in the next scene, Alice's mother puts her to bed, and a title card introduces a dream sequence: "that night when the sandman came. . . ."[46] Here Disney's film distinguishes itself from its predecessors, inverting the concept so that rather than a cartoon character interacting with a live actor, Virginia Davis enters a cartoon world.

The film's title and the dream concept make it clear that Disney had Carroll's text in mind. For both Disney and Carroll, the dream world allows standard rules to be broken. Alice acts as a surrogate for the reader or viewer, her surprise mimicking our own. To make the film, Disney would shout out what would be happening in the animation so that Davis could react.[47] The absence of sound made this interaction invisible in the final cartoon. So while cartoons like Out of the Inkwell foregrounded the production process, Disney elided it. The Fleischers emphasize the realism of the animation, bringing animated characters into the artists' world. By contrast, Disney emphasizes the *difference* between the real world of the animators' studio and the dream world to which Alice travels. Davis's Alice, just like Carroll's, navigates a fantastic universe with strange rules.

Alice's Wonderland set the tone for Disney's early career, establishing a "comic vocabulary" that he would continue to deploy for the next decade.[48] "Disney gags are intrinsically no better than other studios," write J. B. Kaufman and Russell Merritt, "but they were frequently organized with greater skill, with particular concern for detail, and as Disney matures, a concern for building comic routines, for making gags pay off."[49] *Alice's Wonderland* shows that skill developing. The dream sequence begins with standard train gags. A train stops at a canyon, looks down in fear, then leaps over it. Alice steps off the train to meet circus animals holding signs saying "Welcome Alice" and "Cartoonland," as well as a welcoming committee of four dogs in top hats. She is carried by an elephant as the animals take her on parade, and dances to music by a band of cats. While this happens, a lion in a cage seems to go mad: he eats the bars of the cage and escapes, followed by other lions. In a scene reminiscent of the first scene on the animator's easel, the lions chase Alice into a tree. She fights them offscreen, smoke emerging from the tree to represent the violence. The gag repeats twice more (the second time with a rabbit's hole rather than a tree), before the lions chase Alice to the edge of a cliff, recalling the first train gag. The repetition of gags provides some structural balance, and the film ends when Alice leaps from the cliff.[50] In Carroll's story, Alice falls for so long that "she had plenty of time to look about her, and to wonder what was going to happen next."[51] The end of *Alice's Wonderland*, an extended shot of Alice falling, directly references this scene from the book.

Disney completed the film in April 1923, and in May he pitched it to Margaret Winkler, who had begun her career at Warner Bros. and gone on to become "the first female distributor and producer of animated cartoons."[52] Winkler distributed the two most popular animated series of the early 1920s, Pat Sullivan's Felix the Cat and the Fleischers' Out of the Inkwell. Disney explained his concept and offered to send her *Alice's Wonderland*. Winkler replied immediately and asked to see it. Disney's Laugh-O-gram company went bankrupt by July, leaving him unable to finish the film. But he wrote to Winkler again in August, informing her that he had started a new studio in Los Angeles and planned to continue the idea with higher-quality acting and production.[53]

The timing was fortunate. Disney's letter arrived as Winkler's contracts for Out of the Inkwell and Felix the Cat were about to expire, and she offered to buy a twelve-film series of Alice comedies.[54] The rights to *Alice's Wonderland* had been sold to Pictorial Films shortly before Laugh-O-gram went bankrupt, but Disney set to work on a new film following the same concept. With a contract to produce a series, Disney abandoned the Wonderland concept in favor of themed settings like the ocean (*Alice's Day at Sea*), a haunted house (*Alice's Spooky Adventure*), and the wild west (*Alice's Wild West Show*). The films maintained the structure of *Alice's Wonderland*. Animated scenes, replete with gags, were framed by live-action sequences at the beginning and end of the film.[55] The initial twelve-film series was successful enough to justify two more, and Disney eventually produced fifty-six Alice comedies.

A July 1924 *Los Angeles Times* review, "Actors Mix With Cartoons," highlights the novelty of Disney's concept.[56] But as that novelty wore off, the Alice comedies began to distinguish themselves through gags. Rudy Ising recalled story meetings from the mid-1920s, at which the animators would come up with an idea (such as Alice playing a fireman) and then brainstorm gags around that theme.[57] After Winkler complained that *Alice's Day at Sea* was "not all that it was expected to be," Disney promised to "inject as many funny gags and comical situations into future productions as possible."[58] By the sixth film in his contract (*Alice the Peacemaker* in August 1924), "the live action became a true framing device, and the animation the clear center of interest."[59] By the tenth film (*Alice the Piper*, in December 1924), Disney had dispensed with the frame, focusing only on the live Alice interacting with the animation.

In 1924, while the Alice comedies were being produced, Winkler married Charles Mintz. Mintz took over the distribution business after the marriage, and began to make changes. He refused to renew Virginia Davis's contact after the first twelve-film series because, as Davis remembered it, he had become "more sold on the cartoon gags rather than the human animation."[60] But from Disney's perspective "the tyranny of the gag sharply restricted narrative development and characterization," and he was often at odds with Mintz.[61] Mintz thought *Alice Hunting in Africa* totally unusable, and when Disney sent him *Alice the Jail Bird* (1925) ahead of schedule, Mintz refused to pay. They nevertheless reached an agreement for another twenty-six Alice films, and when Mintz signed a contract with Universal Pictures for a cartoon series starring a rabbit named Oswald, he hired Disney to create it.[62]

Oswald the Lucky Rabbit was Disney's first big break. The Alice cartoons had been distributed on a states-rights deal, the Winkler firm contracting with local representatives. But Universal was a major studio that could distribute Disney's cartoons nationally.[63] The final Alice cartoon was released in August 1927. A month earlier, Oswald had premiered in *Trolley Trouble*. Universal complained that it was "merely a succession of unrelated gags" without "even a thread of a story." Initially, Walt pushed back. He thought the short cartoon format didn't give enough time to develop a story, and that an attempt at narrative would distract from the gags.[64] But he changed his mind as the series continued. With the later Oswald cartoons, Disney began using "rough sketches, six to a page, that established the general appearance of each scene."[65] These sketches forecast the storyboarding process that the studio would soon develop, ensuring a storytelling style that would help separate Disney's cartoons from his competitors.'

Lewis Carroll's *Alice in Wonderland* had been doubly inspirational for Disney. It not only provided an underlying metaphor for his first cartoon series but also, in its episodic structure, helped him conceptualize the gag as an organizational alternative to narrative. Over the next half-decade, as Disney learned to blend gags with character and story, Carroll remained on his mind. After becoming the undisputed leader in the genre of animation, Disney would return to the *Alice* books.

THE EARLY 1930s: MARY PICKFORD AND DISNEY'S FIRST *ALICE* FEATURE

In 1928, while Walt was creating the first Mickey Mouse cartoons, the *Alice* books were making headlines across the Atlantic. Alice Hargreaves (born Alice Liddell, and the child to whom Carroll first told the story of Wonderland in 1862) put her personal copy of *Alice's Adventures Underground* up for auction. Much to the chagrin of the British public, the British Museum's bid of £12,500 was surpassed by the American A. S. W. Rosenbach, who paid £15,400 (the equivalent of almost $2 million today).[66] The manuscript was therefore in America on the centennial of Carroll's birth, in May 1932. Columbia University invited Hargreaves to New York, awarding her an honorary degree. Her visit caused "Alice fever," and again brought Carroll's text into the spotlight.[67] Eva Le Gallienne's theatrical version premiered on Broadway the year of Hargreaves's visit, and Paramount's film was released the following year. (Hargreaves reportedly saw Paramount's film before her death in 1934.)[68]

Walt Disney was aware of these events. Hargreaves reportedly saw three Mickey Mouse cartoons during her trip,[69] and Disney mentions the sale of the manuscript in the *American Weekly* advertisement.[70] By the early 1930s, Disney was known nationwide as the creator of Mickey Mouse, but the Alice comedies were still in the public memory. According to a 1931 *New Yorker* profile, Disney regularly received requests to adapt *Alice in Wonderland*.[71] Less than a year after Hargreaves's visit, he announced a return not only to Alice but also to the combination of live-action and animation: Mary Pickford would star in *Alice in Wonderland*, appearing alongside animated characters.[72] The film never progressed beyond screen tests, making it the first of Disney's "phantom" *Alice* adaptations. But its concept and publicity reveal how copyright law, distribution rights, and Hollywood's star system combine with limits of material production, raising a question Disney spent nearly two decades asking: are Carroll's books, which had been ideal for cartoon shorts, suitable for a feature film?

The years between the last Alice comedy and the proposed Pickford film had seen major changes both in the Disney studio and in the genre of the cartoon. Oswald the Lucky Rabbit both brought Disney national attention and changed his approach to cartoons. Disney used only a very general sketch of a story for cartoons like *Little Red Riding Hood*, produced in Kansas City. The title did most of the narrative work. When he came to Hollywood he generally abandoned the pretense of complex narratives, and instead his cartoons "set up simple conflicts between small, vulnerable characters and oversized menaces."[73] The barest narrative sufficed as a vehicle for the gags. In the early 1930s, though, Disney began to pay more attention to character and story. Evening gag meetings had been routine since the mid-1920s. In 1931, Disney began bringing typed story outlines to these meetings, and by January 1932, he was telling his animators that "all scenes will depend on the characters acting as natural as possible without any exaggerated tricks."[74] Narrative and characterization were beginning to overtake the gags as the most important feature of the cartoons. By the end of 1931, some of Disney's staff "functioned only as writers and were thus truly specialized, in a way that no one on the Disney staff had been before."[75]

A *New York Times* essay from the early 1930s describes the Disney studio's process. The story team would search "a library of fairy tales and folk music" and provide rough synopses of potential projects to the editorial team, who must "return it at the end of two weeks with action and gags suggested."[76] Drawings originated in the story department. As the stories became more involved, animators started pinning the drawings to a bulletin board in chronological order, rather than spreading them out on a table. This "storyboarding" process became one of the studio's most important contributions to the industry.[77]

In December 1932—the same year Alice Hargreaves visited the US—Disney circulated a three-page outline of "The Three Little Pigs," along with a copy of the story from Andrew Lang's *Green Fairy Book*.[78] Disney's notes to the outline made clear it would not be "a straight story," and the animators should "gag it in every way we can and make it as funny as possible." But he also insisted the pigs wear clothes, use props, and be "more like human characters."[79] Disney sensed the future of the cartoon medium. He knew the gags and "business" that had sustained cartoon shorts for nearly two decades wouldn't suffice. He wanted characters that could hold an audience's attention long enough for a feature film.

At the same time, Disney was being inundated with recommendations for feature film projects. Douglas Fairbanks invited him to collaborate on *Gulliver's Travels*, and the cartoonist James Thurber suggested Homer's epics.[80] An obstacle to these productions was that Disney animators could not yet convincingly draw human figures.[81] Mary Pickford finally approached Walt with a project that must have appealed to him. Pickford, along with Fairbanks (to whom she was married), the famed director D. W. Griffith, and Charlie Chaplin, had founded the production company United Artists in 1919. Disney signed a distribution deal with United Artists in 1932, and when Pickford returned from Europe in March 1933, she told the *New York Times* that she and Disney were working on an *Alice in Wonderland* feature. "I would be the only living character in the picture," she reported. "The others would be his creations."[82]

Pickford likely knew of Disney's fondness for Alice: the announcement in the *Times* about his signing with United Artists had referred to the Alice comedies as the "'Alice in Wonderland' series with a real little girl."[83] She was excited about the project, offering to "guarantee an advance equal to seven of his cartoons and underwrite the production costs."[84] Between this financial incentive and Pickford's star power, the project was perfect for Disney. A mix of live-action and animation would both recall his first animated series and obviate the need for animated human characters. Art director Ken Anderson remembered Disney being "impatient with the restrictions of the cartoon."[85] Animated sequences were a way to break into feature films without having to overcome all those restrictions at once.[86] An *Alice in Wonderland* feature starring Mary Pickford seemed an ideal vehicle for those sequences.

In 1934, however, Disney told the *New York Times* that he wasn't ready for a feature film.[87] That may have been true, but copyright was another hurdle. When they first began the project two years earlier, Roy Disney had determined the rights for *Alice in Wonderland* to be in the public domain.[88] But Disney and Pickford were not the only ones with their eyes on an *Alice* feature. Columbia and Paramount Pictures were in competition to purchase the film rights from the English actor Edgar Norton, who claimed ownership of the screen rights to both Carroll's text and Tenniel's illustrations.[89] The

The Mickey Mouse short *Thru the Mirror* (1936) reimagines John Tenniel's illustrations for *Through the Looking-Glass* (1876).

"'Alice in Wonderland' situation," as a 1933 *Times* article puts it, was cleared up by Paramount Pictures' announcement of a deal with Norton.

The Pickford collaboration, which had seemed so promising, would remain a "phantom adaptation." Some of the gags envisioned for the it might have been used in a Mickey Mouse short that premiered in 1936, two years after Disney announced he had given up on the Pickford film. *Thru the Mirror* opens with Mickey having fallen asleep reading *Alice through the Looking-Glass*, which remains on his bed. He dreams about climbing through the mirror. After eating a nut, Mickey grows and shrinks, as Alice does when

The Mickey Mouse short *Thru the Mirror* (1936) reimagines John Tenniel's illustrations for *Through the Looking-Glass* (1876).

she eats the mushroom in *Wonderland*.[90] Besides this gag, the concept and Mickey's book are the only direct references to Carroll. Mickey dances with the queen of hearts and leads a deck of cards in a marching line, but the gags are based around shuffling and cutting cards and the king of hearts getting jealous. The short doesn't seem to allude to any particular card gags from *Wonderland*, and the chess pieces from *Looking-Glass* do not appear. As with the Alice comedies, *Thru the Mirror* uses Carroll's idea only for an opening scene. Any other ideas the studio had for the *Alice* feature were temporarily set aside. As it happened, though, they weren't set aside for long.

THE LATE 1930s: ALICE IN THE ARCHIVES

A live Mary Pickford interacting with the animals and caricatures that populate Wonderland would have solved a practical problem: Disney's animators hadn't yet mastered the movement or emotional range needed for human characters. With the help of drawing classes and live models, however, their skills were vastly improving. In 1933, the studio released five *Silly Symphonies* with human characters.[91] (One has a Victorian connection: *The Pied Piper* had been popularized by Robert Browning's 1842 poem and adapted for children by late-Victorian illustrators like Kate Greenaway). Those improvements, combined with the success of *Three Little Pigs*, made a feature-length cartoon a plausible idea. *Snow White and the Seven Dwarfs* premiered in December 1937, becoming the highest-grossing sound film of all time (it was surpassed by *Gone with the Wind* in 1939).[92]

In April 1938, just months after *Snow White*'s premiere, Roy Disney purchased the rights to Tenniel's illustrations as part of "an acquisition spree of properties for future features."[93] A month later, Al Perkins—who would write the screenplay for *The Reluctant Dragon* (1941), based on Kenneth Grahame's 1898 story—submitted his first report about *Alice in Wonderland*. It is dated May 27, 1938, one week after the *New York Times* announced Disney's purchasing of the rights from Carroll's publisher, Macmillan.[94] Perkins begins with a scene-by-scene analysis of both *Alice* books, highlighting content appropriate for a Disney film.[95] Over the next few months, he read reviews of film and stage adaptations, taking special note of Paramount's 1933 film, Eva le Gallienne's 1932–33 production at the Civic Repertory Theater, and Clarke's 1886 operetta. He produced a second report in September. Around the same time, Dorothy Blank was producing a similar report about *Peter Pan*. The studio may have planned these two titles as the next feature films. In the opening sequence of *Pinocchio* (1940), Jiminy Cricket sits atop the book *Pinocchio*, and *Peter Pan* and *Alice in Wonderland* are visible in the background.[96]

That Disney staff would review not only primary texts but also competing adaptations is unsurprising. Scholars' inattention to intermediary stage version is one of the biggest differences between the theory and the practice of film adaptation.[97] What *is* surprising, though, is that both Blank and Perkins also consulted biographical and scholarly sources. In her report on *Peter Pan*, Blank summarizes Patrick Braybrooke's *J. M. Barrie: A Study in Fairies and Mortals* (1924) and H. M. Walbrook's *J. M. Barrie and the Theatre* (1922), and reproduces a chapter from F. J. Harvey Darton's *J. M. Barrie* (1929).[98] Another of Darton's books, *Children's Books in England: Five Centuries of Social Life* (1932), was a landmark in children's literature studies. Darton established categories and approaches to children's literature that continue to inform scholarship today, and his book is regularly cited. His appearance in Blank's report (which I discuss further in chapter four) marks a notable overlap between Disney's creative process and academic scholarship.

Perkins also consulted scholarly works for his *Alice* report. He quotes from critical biographies of Lewis Carroll by Belle Moses, Harry Morgan Ayers, Walter de la Mare, and Stuart Dodgson Collingwood. He dismisses de la Mare's 1932 study as too "high-brow," and he finds in Ayers's *Carroll's Alice* (1936) "nothing of any use to us in interpreting 'Alice in Wonderland' for the screen."[99] But Belle Moses brought to Perkins's attention Clarke's operetta, which convinced him that the story could be usefully set to music. The biographies also gave Perkins an idea for the opening shot. He proposes

> a shadowy boat with shadowy forms drifting down river . . . either a narrator's voice (man) starting to tell the story, or a woman off scene singing . . . scene could fade out into the first scene of Alice's adventures, and, at the end of the picture, we could fade back into the same river scene with the boat drifting out of sight and the narrator or singer finishing the story.[100]

This suggested opening alludes to Carroll's famous 1862 trip down the Thames. The idea continues to pop up in discussions of the film over the next decade. A full paragraph of the 1946 *American Weekly* advertisement is devoted to describing the river trip, perhaps priming audiences for its inclusion in the film.[101] At this stage, Disney was considering not only the text and adaptations of the *Alice* books but also the story of their production.

Perkins's report offers some evidence for how adaptation practitioners address concepts that scholars have theorized. Early work in adaptation studies was concerned with providing alternatives to a "fidelity discourse," seen as overly focused on whether an adaptation is faithful to its source.[102] At times, Perkins does seem concerned with staying close to Carroll's text. And adaptation scholar Linda Hutcheon distinguishes between "knowing and unknowing" audiences, those who are very familiar with a source text and those who are not.[103] Perkins makes a similar distinction and is explicit about the need to appeal simultaneously to these distinct groups. He writes, "we should try to keep as much of the original dialogue as is still effective" because "the book has been so widely quoted and is so universally read and loved."[104] His desire to keep the original dialogue came from his recognition that the "knowing audience," the fans of the books, were a large and vocal minority.

But fidelity is by no means a priority for Perkins. He dismisses Paramount's film because it tried too hard merely to reproduce Carroll's books.[105] The report becomes increasingly insistent on the making significant changes to Carroll's text. "The more I get into the 'Alice in Wonderland' story," he writes, "the more I am convinced we are going to have to change it radically all the way through to make a successful picture that will hold the audience's attention," even though this choice "might offend those who think the book is a classic that must not be tampered with."[106] He also makes suggestions based on what he took to be Carroll's desires. He notes, for example, that the White Rabbit doesn't wear eyeglasses in Tenniel's illustration, but Carroll thought he should have. Perkins recommends, "we ought to fuss him up in every possible way."[107] In the 1951 cartoon, the White Rabbit dons a pince-nez, a high-collared shirt, and a bowtie.

Rather than trying to faithfully reproduce Carroll's text, whether its printed form or its ideal in the author's mind, Perkins's research into the original text, supplemented by his study of intervening adaptations, helped him to imagine what a Disney adaptation might look like. He thought the *Alice* books have too many "characters and incidents" and that neither book "contains the fundamental theme or story that we should have."[108] "To make 'Alice' believable on the screen," he suggested, the studio should "forget the structure of the book."[109] Instead, he recommended getting the "spirit" of the Alice books, as Eva Le Gallienne did in her stage production. Originally performed in 1932, Le Gallienne's play was an important intervening adaptation. The play was revived in 1947 and is mentioned in Disney's *American Weekly* advertisement.[110]

Partly because the animators felt an affinity with the illustrator, and partly because Roy Disney had just acquired the rights to the drawings, Tenniel also features prominently in Perkins's report. Among the options for the opening sequence, Perkins imagines a shot of Tenniel "in his studio, holding Carroll's manuscript in one hand, as with the other he finishes an illustration which we could truck down on and animate as our story begins."[111] The suggestion reveals the complex relationship between Disney's film and the original books. Carroll's text literally features in the scene, but is mediated by the figure of Tenniel, who stands in for Disney's animators. When Perkins notes that this scene is a variation on the opening shot of *Snow White*, which features a book in the opening sequence, he grounds his ideas in Disney's own oeuvre. Featuring the illustrator/animator in the film also harkens back to "Alice's Wonderland" and the Fleischer's Out of the Inkwell cartoons that had inspired it.

In his second report, from September 1938, Perkins provides a chapter-by-chapter analysis, reproducing most of Carroll's text and underlining scenes, characters, and dialogue that would best fit the studio's style. In Carroll's novel, Alice often talks to herself, which Perkins feels "might be awkward on screen." He suggests "giving Alice some kind of companion on this journey," such as Dinah (her cat) or even a teddy bear.[112] And although he finds the caucus race chapter "pretty weak" overall, he thought the birds "swell characters for our medium" because they would give animators "a wide-open chance to inject a lot of our own comedy without interfering with the book."[113]

By "our own comedy," Perkins means gags. He is especially attuned to the unique contribution a Disney adaptation could make. Chapter four, when Alice gets stuck in the White Rabbit's house, "would be brand new stuff," he writes, "for it was not even attempted in Paramount's or Eva Le Gallienne's version."[114] He quotes the paragraph about the animals deciding who will go down the chimney, which "suggests a hell of a funny scene where all these little animals could come with their elaborate props and lay siege to the house. . . . There is opportunity here for all sorts of gags if we want them—rope gags, sliding ladder gags, roof pole gags."[115] Only someone with Perkins's expertise could see this opportunity in Carroll's texts.

Perkins is equally aware of what he *doesn't* think will work. The Mock Turtle's school-related puns, he thought, "would lay a terrific egg with a modern movie audience."[116] And he is careful about characterization. He recognizes that Carroll's Caterpillar is "one of the most <u>famous</u> characters in the book," yet worries that the scene is "all dialogue, no action." Giving physical gags to the Caterpillar might be "contrary to the spirit of the book," so Perkins instead suggests giving him "as much <u>business</u> as we can while he talks."[117] "Business" is another word for gags, and this vision would be realized in the 1951 cartoon, where the caterpillar's smoke forms visual puns based on his dialogue.

In his initial report, from May, Perkins had called the tea party "one of the best scenes in the book."[118] In September, he remained impressed. Here again we see Perkins drawing on other genres. Although the "dialogue as Carroll wrote it would not be funny to audiences today," he sees the Hatter, the March Hare, and the Dormouse as "a trio of screwballs that could act like the Marx Bros., the Ritz Bros., or any other group of haywire comedians. Because of the teapot and food props at the table I would see them acting like a trio called Willie, West, and McGinty, who used to be in vaudeville."[119]

Drawing on his knowledge of the cartoon medium and of contemporary comedians, Perkins makes a convincing case that *Alice in Wonderland* had the stuff of a good Disney feature. But he also notes a significant obstacle. "It is pretty much agreed among the story men of the studio," he writes, "that 'Alice' <u>must</u> be changed around so that it contains an authentic story that will hold an audience's interest."[120] Disney's story men were not the first to come to this conclusion. Early silent film adaptations had struggled "because the *Alice* books are not action driven," relying instead on dialogue and wordplay.[121] The same elements that made *Alice in Wonderland* an ideal choice for a cartoon short posed a problem for a feature film.

Perkins's report would shape the studio's approach to the *Alice* books for the next decade. The influence of this report is evident in the 1946 *American Weekly* advertisement, the 1951 cartoon, and Walt Disney's essay about his film, "How I Cartooned Alice." The latter lists "three fundamental problems" in making an Alice film: Carroll's interest in fantasy over narrative, the abundance of characters, and the length of the stories.[122] Perkins had identified all three problems, but it took over a decade to solve them. That decade brought an animators' strike, a world war, and a script by a famous British novelist.

THE 1940s: ALDOUS HUXLEY AND ALICE AFTER THE WAR

At a story meeting in January 1939, just four months after Perkins's report, Walt Disney dismissed concerns about "English audiences and Carroll fans," instructing the animators to update the jokes and dialogue for American audiences.[123] The statement shows Disney's frustrations with the project, and his directive contravenes both earlier and subsequent efforts. In June, the British artist David Hall produced about 400 paintings, drawings, and sketches from Perkins's report, and in November, Stuart Buchanan (who voiced characters in *Snow White* and *Pinocchio*) recommended they bring in an Alice "fiend" to help with plotting.[124] The production team met again in April 1941, but that would be the last meeting for several years. In May, Disney's animators went on strike. Pearl Harbor was attacked in December. The strike, followed by the draft and then Disney's wartime propaganda films, put Disney's feature films on hold. When Disney returned to *Alice in Wonderland* in the late 1940s, he doubled down on the text's Englishness. The next draft would frame Alice's journey down the rabbit hole with a story about her creator enmeshed in the politics of university life, childrearing, and the Victorian theater. It was written by a renowned British writer with a keen interest in Lewis Carroll and strong family ties to the Victorian period.

Aldous Huxley is most famous for his 1932 dystopia *Brave New World*, a mainstay of high-school reading lists. But he comes from a family of eminent Victorians. His grandfather was the Victorian scientist Thomas Henry Huxley, known as "Darwin's bulldog" for his fierce defenses of evolution. He was also related to the educationalist Thomas Arnold (one of the four personages named in Lytton Strachey's *Eminent Victorians*) and his son, the poet and essayist Matthew Arnold. In 1937, having already established himself as a famous novelist, Aldous Huxley left England and settled in Los Angeles. One of his friends, the screenwriter Anita Loos, recommended him to write the dialogue for MGM's adaptation of *Pride and Prejudice* (1940). He felt guilty accepting a large payment "while my friends and family are starving and being bombed in England," but Loos reminded him that he could send the money back home.[125] He accepted the gig. He later worked on several other projects, including MGM's *Jane Eyre* (1944). Disney must have learned of Huxley's experience adapting nineteenth-century British novels for the screen. He was considering Margaret O'Brien, a child actress under contract with MGM, for the role of Alice,[126] so perhaps Huxley's MGM connection was also part of the appeal.

In October 1945, Huxley wrote to Loos to say that he had committed "to sign up with Disney for the script of an Alice in Wonderland."[127] A company memo indicates he signed a contract by that month, and was to deliver his synopsis by Thanksgiving.[128] Huxley was tasked with creating a live-action frame, providing a transition into Wonderland and some narrative structure. His letter to Loos, however, indicates that he had much bigger ideas. Huxley describes his vision:

> a cartoon version of Tenniel's drawings and Carroll's story, embedded in a flesh-and-blood episode of the life of the Rev. Charles Dodgson. I think something rather nice might be made out of this—the unutterably odd, repressed and ridiculous Oxford lecturer on logic and mathematics, seeking refuge in the company of little girls and in his own phantasy. There is plenty of comic material in Dodgson's life and I think it will be legitimate to invent some such absurd climax as a visit of Queen Victoria to Oxford and her insistence on having the author of Alice presented to her, in preference to all the big wigs— the scene dissolving, in Carroll's fancy, to the end of Alice: "They're nothing but a pack of cards"—and the Queen and her retinue become ridiculous cartoon figures and are scattered to the four winds.[129]

Huxley's letter makes clear his commitment to the Victorian context of *Alice's Adventures in Wonderland*. While Perkins had floated the idea of a frame narrative involving Carroll, Huxley took it to much deeper waters.

The synopsis that Huxley delivered in November lives up to the promise of his letter. In the opening scene the vice-chancellor of Oxford learns that Queen Victoria, who loved *Alice's Adventures in Wonderland*, wants him to

Charles Dodgson's photograph of the actress Ellen Terry. Reprinted in Collingwood, *Life and Letters of Lewis Carroll* (1898). Courtesy of the *Victorian Web*.

discover the identity of Lewis Carroll, rumored to be the pseudonym for an Oxford don.[130] This plotline has some historical basis. Carroll sent a presentation copy of *Alice's Adventures in Wonderland* to Princess Beatrice, Queen Victoria's youngest daughter. It was rumored that Victoria so enjoyed the story that she wrote to the publisher, Macmillan, requesting the author's next book. The punchline is that his next book was *An Elementary Treatise on Determinants, with Their Application to Simultaneous Linear Equations and Algebraical Geometry* (1867). The anecdote was sufficiently popular that thirty years later Carroll felt compelled to disavow it in one of his last books, *Symbolic Logic* (1898).[131] Belle Moses mentions the "funny tale" about delivering the mathematical treatise to Queen Victoria in his 1910 biography of Carroll.[132] In Perkins's report about the *Alice* books, the suggestion to frame the cartoon with Carroll's life comes in the middle of a paragraph about Moses's book, so Perkins may have noted the rumor.[133] But only Huxley would draw inspiration for a Disney film from a bit of Victorian gossip.

Huxley's frame story takes place sometime after the publication of *Alice's Adventures in Wonderland*. The opening scene continues with Dodgson reading a playbill and expressing his interest in the actress Ellen Terry, whom he had known as a child.[134] Dodgson really did know Terry, as Huxley was certainly aware. According to Collingwood's *Life and Letters of Lewis Carroll*—another of the works consulted in Perkins's report—Dodgson saw the nine-year-old Terry perform in *A Winter's Tale* in 1856.[135] He took her picture in 1864, and by the 1880s they were, according to Collingwood, "excellent friends."[136] In Huxley's script, Dodgson visits Terry in her dressing room. Terry discovers that Dodgson is Lewis Carroll, and the two discuss Alice's future visit to the theater.[137] Terry is dressed to play Ophelia, another subtle reference to Victorian entertainment history. Terry was known as a Shakespearean actress, and Ophelia was the first role she played at the Lyceum, alongside the actor-manager Henry Irving. As I discuss in chapter one, the Lyceum not only features prominently in Victorian theater history but is also where Disney's *The Lion King* has played since 1999.

Dodgson was a prolific amateur photographer, and Terry was far from his only subject. His photography is an important element in Huxley's plot, as Alice's guardian has hired Dodgson to take a picture of Alice to send to her parents, who are away in India.[138] Langham (the Oxford vice-chancellor and the frame story's antagonist) disapproves of photography, of the theater, and of associating an Oxford professor with a children's book. Among the plot's first conflicts is the "imperious" Langham's opposition to Dodgson's application for a librarianship.[139] In a scene intended to intensify Dodgson's desire to be a librarian (and thus escape his teaching responsibilities), two undergraduates laugh at Dodgson's stutter. According to Huxley's parenthetical comment, the students are based on characters from *Tom Brown at Oxford* (1859) and so are "authentically of the period."[140] The aside reveals Huxley's commitment to a Victorian period aesthetic, and also the differences between his synopsis and Perkins's earlier report.

Huxley prioritizes pathos rather than humor in this scene, declining to seize the opportunity for gags.

The second antagonist in Huxley's synopsis is Mrs. Beale, the governess who makes Alice recite "one of Dr. Watts's edifying rhymes for children."[141] It's a nice joke, since in Wonderland Alice recites a parody of Isaac Watts's "How doth the little busy bee," rendering it "How doth the little crocodile."[142] Dodgson is Alice's logic tutor, and he angers Mrs. Beale by encouraging her interest in the theater. Mrs. Beale punishes Alice by locking her in a garden house, from which Alice escapes. She goes to London, arriving at the theater and meeting Terry. To pass the time, Terry repeats to Alice some of the scenes from *Alice's Adventures in Wonderland*, which the synopsis glosses as "dissolve into animation." Dodgson arrives at the theater and joins in the storytelling until, at the climactic "off with their heads" moment, Mrs. Beale bursts in to demand Alice return home. Beale is furious at Dodgson, but he is saved by a *regina ex machina*, as Queen Victoria arrives hoping to meet the author of the *Alice* books. The plot resolves and Dodgson is awarded the librarianship.[143]

Huxley shared his synopsis with Disney and his writing team. The subsequent story meeting focused primarily on relationships among the characters, especially Miss Beale, who as the central villain would provide the film's narrative tension. Disney insisted that the story foreground a lesson about nonsense, in contrast with Miss Beale's insistence on practicality.[144] Huxley also expressed his desire to maintain some historical accuracy. He recommended they keep Victoria in the background, partly to keep her a remote comic figure but also because "she was an old woman without any sense of humor at all."[145] Though the initial meeting seems to have gone well, the animator Dick Huemer recalled Walt talking so much that Huxley felt he couldn't get a word in, and the collaboration lasted only five meetings.[146] But the *Alice* books' relationship to the Victorian period, and the idea that they promote nonsense over seriousness, remained central to Disney's conception of the film. The *American Weekly* ad not only mentions Dodgson and retells the story of the river trip but also refers to the *Alice* books challenging a "serious Victorian tradition."[147]

Huxley probably used some of the same sources as Perkins, but his frame story takes Dodgson's biography much further. It was a plausible approach, since his synopsis provides some narrative conflict and the humor could fit Disney's style. Ultimately, Disney decided not to devote so much screen time to the Victorian setting. The only remnant of the frame story that survives in Disney's cartoon is the opening image, which shows Oxford in the background and a rowboat that may be an homage to the story's first telling.[148]

After the disappointing reception of *Song of the South* (1946), Disney was also beginning to realize the difficulty and expense of producing films that alternate between animation and live-action. As I discuss in the next chapter, he had been considering this combination not only for *Alice in Wonderland* but also for a feature film about Hans Christian Andersen. That project also stalled in the mid-1940s. But with the Huxley script Disney seems to have committed the studio to a feature-length *Alice in Wonderland*. The *American Weekly* advertisement appeared in August 1946, less than a year after the Huxley meetings. The studio would continue to work on the project.

AFTER 1951: THE ALICE FRANCHISE

By the late 1940s, Disney and his staff had abandoned Huxley's script and were beginning to get frustrated with *Alice in Wonderland*. They had publicly announced the film and had too much money invested in the project to abandon it. But they had been working on it for so long, without solving some of the problems with the narrative, that the animators had lost their enthusiasm.[149] Disney's *Alice in Wonderland* was finally released in 1951. It lost about $1 million and was lampooned both by film critics and by "Lewis Carroll loyalists who felt that Disney had maligned the book."[150] Diane Disney Miller quotes her father as saying, "Alice is a literary classic with an intellectual appeal, but no emotional appeal."[151] *Alice in Wonderland* was a prime example of the Disney studio's Anglophilia, which may have distanced the company from its own artistic history and "the socio-cultural context in which it was produced."[152] The film still draws critics' ire. Writing about the sesquicentennial of Carroll's book for the *New Yorker*, Adam Gopnik refers to Disney's film as "dreadfully sweetened and stupid."[153]

The problem with *Alice* had always been the narrative. The concept was well-suited for short, gag-heavy films like the Alice comedies and the Mickey Mouse cartoon *Thru the Mirror*, but by the postwar years the Disney studio was focused on feature films. In 1938, Perkins worried, "if we do not get real suspense into this picture at some point, it will not hold an audience, no matter how full of cute and funny stuff it may be."[154] The final film never achieved that suspense and arguably failed to hold an audience. But Perkins was working under a different business model. In the media culture that emerged in the late twentieth century, the value of a feature film lies not only in its ability to hold an audience's attention but also in its ability to support a franchise. Modern audiences need not sit through Disney's film to be aware of it. Today they might hear its soundtrack, or play a video game, or watch a clip on YouTube, or purchase an Alice-themed product, or ride an attraction at one of Disney's parks. The "cute and funny stuff" of the individual episodes matters far more than the unifying narrative. The episodic nature of Disney's *Alice in Wonderland* (a problem Disney spent decades trying to solve) turned out to be its greatest benefit. Disney's film "marked a turning point in the history of *Alice*, as it moved from a textual artifact to a sound-and-motion one in the public imagination."[155] Adaptations and retellings of the *Alice* books continue to proliferate across media,[156] but none is as recognizable nor as omnipresent as Disney's. *Alice in Wonderland* may not be a great film, but it provided the basis for a very successful franchise.

Walt Disney attempted something of a defense of *Alice in Wonderland* the year of its release. He wrote in *Films in Review*, "The animation of *Alice in Wonderland* presented the most formidable problems we have ever faced in translating a literary classic into a cartoon medium."[157] He goes on to explain how his story department approached a text with so many characters and so little story by condensing dialogue, combining characters, and moving "the dry history lesson from its original context in the Caucus race, to the opening scene of our picture," a move that gives "coherence to all that follows, since it puts the reason for Alice's descent into the rabbit hole where it is most effective dramatically, i.e., at the beginning."[158] Disney implies that Alice descends to Wonderland to escape from the oppressive, adult-centric Victorian nursery. That is a plausible interpretation of Carroll's books, which are often read as celebrating childhood imagination in contrast to nursery-room ideologies. But such a reading depends on knowing those ideologies in the first place. Alice is a socialized child, and "Carroll's target audience clearly consists of similarly socialized children. The humor of the opening scenes, in which Alice misremembers what she has been taught, depends on child readers knowing the right answers."[159] And even if Disney saw *Alice in Wonderland* as a defense of the imagination against Victorian prudery, some critics find the Disney film "much more stereotypically Victorian than its nineteenth-century British source."[160] The film's ending forestalls Alice's sense of adventure, which the book had celebrated. Carroll's Alice takes control of the episodic narrative with a performative exclamation, "You're only a pack of cards!" The realization wakes her up, and so gives her control over the dream.[161] But in Disney's cartoon that line is uttered while Alice flees in terror from a dream that has gotten out of control. By imposing an ending on the feature film, Disney wrests that control away from her.[162]

What Disney's *Alice in Wonderland* lacks in narrative coherence, it makes up for in gags and animation. Disney's animators demonstrate mastery of their medium. All film versions of Carroll's text faced the same challenge

Disney did. The books' humor often depends on Carroll's wordplay, his breaking of the rules of language. Perkins thought that Paramount's 1932 film had failed "to distinguish between the language of literature and the language of the screen."[163] Other filmmakers struggled with this same distinction, as did Disney for several decades. But ultimately, as Kamila Elliott writes, Disney's *Alice in Wonderland* "offers a fluid path between verbal and visual modes and posits each as the content of the other."[164] The smoke rings the Caterpillar blows, for example, initially form vowel letters as Alice approaches. As they begin conversing, the letters form visual puns like the "R" in "who are you?" and the "C" in "I do not see." These visual puns then transform from letters to images, as the smoke forms a knot in his response, "I do not know."[165] And at the tea party "Disney's half-cup of tea, sliced in half yet miraculously holding tea . . . violates both linguistic conventions and physical laws."[166] While it may not have come together into a great story, this is precisely the kind of "business" at which Disney excelled.

Many twenty-first century readers (perhaps even *most* readers) come to Carroll's books with at least some awareness of the Disney film. These "knowing" readers, to use Linda Hutcheon's distinction, know Disney, not Carroll. They might be surprised that *Wonderland* and *Looking-Glass* are two different books, or that the speaking doorknob is original to Disney's film, and doesn't appear in either book. Moreover, the distinction between knowing and unknowing audiences is a continuum rather than a binary. This is especially true as adaptations expand beyond a single film into a franchise characterized by "vast quantities of interlinked media products and merchandise."[167] In the twenty-first century, media franchises are the norm rather than the exception. Original productions carry a risk, while sequels and franchises are more predictably profitable.[168]

Disney was a pioneer in franchising. Mickey Mouse was among the first characters to be widely licensed. Just a few years after Mickey premiered in *Steamboat Willie*, a *New Yorker* article reported that he inspired 40 percent of novelties offered at a Leipzig trade show, appearing on velvet dolls, wooden figures, mechanical drummers, metal sparklers, coloring books, writing paper, radiator caps, and comics in twenty-seven languages.[169] Disney received royalties from this merchandise and continued to innovate. The soundtrack to *Snow White and the Seven Dwarfs* was the first commercially available record of songs from a movie.[170] Today, the Walt Disney Company owns television stations, publishing houses, and theme parks, allowing it to take full advantage of both homegrown franchises like Disney Princesses and *Pirates of the Caribbean* and more recent acquisitions like Marvel and *Star Wars*. According to a 2018 article, the Walt Disney Company owns eleven franchises each earning over $1 billion dollars a year.[171] Though there are exceptions (like *Pirates of the Caribbean*), the franchises typically begin with a movie and build on that success with other products. Those products in turn promote the movie, and the cycle is continually reinforced. Disney's *Alice in Wonderland* was adapted into television specials, theme-park rides, stage productions, a live-action film, and every imaginable product from tea sets to T-shirts. As the Alice franchise grew, scenes and characters from Disney's film became more familiar than Carroll's text or Tenniel's illustrations. And with each adaptation the absence of a unifying narrative mattered less and less.

One of Disney's first adaptations of its own version of *Alice in Wonderland* came before the film was even released. In 1950, Disney made his first foray into television with *One Hour in Wonderland*, essentially an advertisement for the upcoming film. Disney was among the earliest film producers to adopt the new television medium. A few years after the theatrical release, scenes from *Alice in Wonderland* were again adapted for television as part of *Walt Disney's Disneyland*, which aired from 1954 to 1958. Televising *Alice in Wonderland* so soon after its release has been cited as evidence that the film "bombed," as Ward Kimball put it.[172] In hindsight, though, the decision was a savvy one. The *Disneyland* series, like *One Hour in Wonderland*, functioned as both entertainment and advertisement. Disney produced the series to promote his theme park, which opened in 1955.[173] The television special helped introduce an entirely new concept, which over the next half-century would distinguish Disney from its competitors and create entirely new revenue streams.

As the *Los Angeles Times* recognized, Disneyland differed from its pre-decessors and competitors: the newspaper coined the term "theme park" to describe it.[174] Amusement parks and "trolley parks" (built at the end of street-car lines to encourage weekend usage) had emerged in the late nineteenth century and flourished in the first half of the twentieth century. These parks offered rides and games but had no unifying theme. By the 1950s, they developed a reputation for being somewhat unseemly. From the start, Disneyland was envisioned as a complete immersive experience, one that visitors could enjoy "without ever setting foot on a ride."[175] The *Disneyland* TV series conveyed Disney's vision. The first episode, "The Disneyland Story," emphasizes the narrative strategy deployed throughout the park. The episode moves from the Burbank studio, with behind-the-scenes clips about creating several of Disney's films, to explain the division of the park into separate themed lands: Frontierland, Adventureland, Tomorrowland, and Fantasyland.[176] The second episode condenses *Alice in Wonderland*, as guests' entrance to Disneyland parallels Alice's descent into Wonderland.[177] The episode prioritizes the characters and musical set-pieces, merely gesturing to a coherent frame narrative. Within just a few years of its release, *Alice in Wonderland* was once again being separated into its component parts.

Alice in Wonderland was linked to Disneyland in more than just its promotion. One of the original rides was the Mad Tea Party, in which riders sit in giant spinning teacups. The ride is "inspired by the Mad Hatter's party sequence," and the promotional material invites riders to celebrate their "un-birthday."[178] The ride reproduces a scene from Disney's film, along with one of its more famous songs, and has become one of Disney's most popular attractions. A few years after opening, Disneyland premiered a second Alice-themed ride, giving it the same title as the film. Alice in Wonderland is a "dark ride," a variation on a common theme-park attraction.[179] The typical dark ride, in which "the customer rides in darkness through a labyrinth, encountering various surprises," is usually "a random sequence of shocks and scares," rather than a narrative.[180] Disneyland, however, includes several dark rides based on its films, many of them among the park's original attractions. These rides are envisioned as narratives, either "recapitulating the film" (as in Peter Pan's Flight) or adapting material into new stories (as in Snow White's Scary Adventure or Mr. Toad's Wild Ride).[181]

The Alice in Wonderland dark ride takes advantage of its form. Unlike filmgoers, riders do not necessarily expect a narrative, and the ride omits the frame of Alice and her sister, which Walt Disney had claimed gave coherence to the film.[182] Instead, riders climb into caterpillar-shaped vehicles and follow the White Rabbit, putting them in the same position as the heroine. The ride also makes a key narrative change. The film's final scene is the Red Queen's terrifying injunction "off with their heads," an ending that disempowers Alice, as she awakens in fear rather than (as in Carroll's book) with the realization that she is dreaming.[183] In the ride, this scene occurs in the middle rather than at the end. The ride concludes with the Mad Hatter's "unbirthday," which is probably the film's most famous scene. This ending both provides a more lighthearted conclusion and connects the dark ride to the nearby teacups.

The Alice in Wonderland franchise has remained central to Disney's theme parks as they expanded beyond California. The Alice in Wonderland dark ride is unique to Disneyland, but a version of the Tea Party features at all Disney's theme parks, including those in Florida, Paris, Tokyo, Shanghai, and Beijing. Disneyland Paris, which is perhaps "the park with the most Alice content," also includes Alice's Curious Labyrinth, a hedge maze "punctuated with models of minor and some major characters from the film."[184] Like the tea cups, the maze takes its theme from *Alice in Wonderland*, but omits the narrative.

Alice in Wonderland merchandise is available near all these attractions, and at Disney stores beyond the theme parks. Disney also licenses the characters to other companies. The merchandising opportunities for the film are seemingly endless: there are Alice-themed costumes and tea sets, Alice-themed bouquets of roses from Rosehire, a checkbook from the Bradford Exchange, and a Swarovski crystal figurine. One can also purchase several doorknobs, themed after the talking doorknob, the only character original to the film and not drawn from the books.[185] In the 1970s, Disney licensed a youth musical version of *Alice in Wonderland*, intended for use in schools.[186]

Among the most intriguing components of Disney's *Alice* franchise, however, is the live-action film *Alice in Wonderland* (2010), directed by Tim Burton. Unlike the live-action remakes of its other cartoon musicals—like *Cinderella* (2015), *The Jungle Book* (2016), and *Beauty and the Beast* (2017)—and despite its title, *Alice in Wonderland* is a sequel to the 1951 cartoon, rather than a retelling. And it expands the Victorian frame that had been considered in the 1940s. Alice (played by Mia Wasikowska) has reached adulthood but is still suffering under the repressive Victorian norms that, in Disney's own interpretation, had motived Alice's descent into the rabbit hole in the first place.[187] After a flashback to a scene from Alice's childhood, when she tells her father about her recurring dream about Wonderland, Alice and her sisters travel through London en route to a party where a lord is about to propose to Alice. The frame story is rife with Victorian allusions: Alice's father is named Charles Kingsleigh, a nod to Carroll's contemporary, the Cambridge professor and author of *The Water Babies* (1862); a reference to swimming in "Havisham's pond" alludes to *Great Expectations*; and Alice is enjoined to marry by being told she doesn't want to end up like her aunt Imogene, whose name recalls Edwin Arlington Robinson's 1902 poem "Aunt Imogen." Alice again follows the White Rabbit down the rabbit hole into Wonderland, and when she returns she rejects the marriage proposal, stands up to her sister, and collaborates with Lord Ascot to pursue her father's imperial trade expansions.

Kamilla Elliot argues that the 2010 film is an adaptation of the books, rather than a sequel, since it "adapts many scenes and most characters from the Alice books" and "quotes many of its lines verbatim."[188] Combining Carroll's two books into one story, Burton's film "builds on Carroll's 'portmanteau' words . . . not only at the level of diction . . . but also at the levels of character and plot," shutting the Red Queen and the Queen of Hearts together into Helena Bonham Carter's character, for example.[189] Given that these statements all hold true of the 1951 Disney film, however, Burton's film seems less an adaptation of Carroll's book than of Disney's franchise. The opening scene presents a nine-year-old Alice telling her father about her dream, falling down the rabbit hole and encountering a blue caterpillar.[190] The chromatic specificity references the Disney film: Tenniel's illustrations were in black-and-white, Carroll doesn't mention a color, and early twentieth-century picture-books depicted the caterpillar in various colors. In Wonderland, Alice encounters the same mix of characters from the two books, including Tweedledee and Tweedledum and the Jabberwocky (characters from Carroll's *Through the Looking-Glass*, not *Wonderland*). And even the moralizing structure, with Alice escaping a repressive Victorian culture, is consistent with how Walt Disney explained the first film.

The tone of the 2010 film (and its 2016 sequel, *Alice through the Looking-Glass*) contrasts with the cartoon. The aesthetic follows the darker interpretation of Alice popular in the twenty-first century,[191] and is consistent with Tim Burton's other films. Prior to the film's release, many viewers perceived "aesthetic affinity between Carroll and Burton" and had high hopes for the adaptation.[192] The casting of Johnny Depp and Helena Bonham Carter, the latter Burton's long-time partner and the former a frequent star in Burton's films (as well as Disney's *Pirates of the Caribbean* franchise), reinforces *Alice in Wonderland* as a Tim Burton film. The movie also has a stronger narrative drive than either Carroll's text or the 1951 film. The Jabberocky gives Wonderland a primary antagonist, and the film has a clear moral, asserting Alice's control over her identity in the face of societal expectations, both in and out of Wonderland.

Yet these differences merely serve to highlight the franchising effect. To use Hutcheon's terms, the film is "repetition with variation," and the pleasure comes from the "piquancy of surprise" at how it differs from its precursor.[193] By establishing its own film as the primary precursor, Disney reasserts ownership of the Alice franchise. And because Disney's Alice no longer depends on a unified narrative, characters and episodes can be readily transported to unlikely contexts. A Las Vegas fashion show with scantily clad models promoting Alice-themed jewelry, for example, might seem foreign both to the *Alice* books and to Disney's corporate identity. But because they reassert Alice as a Disney product, such tie-ins strengthen rather than diminish the franchise.[194]

The Disney studio has been adapting Lewis Carroll's *Alice in Wonderland* for nearly a century. The book's narrative style initially made them appropriate for short, gag-laden cartoons. The popularity of the *Alice* books, bolstered by Alice Hargreaves's visit, made them attractive as a feature film, and Mary Pickford was a promising partner. Competition with other studios, the material challenge of drawing believable human characters, and a contentious copyright situation put the film on hold until a postwar Anglophilia made it plausible again. Disney never really solved the problem of finding a narrative for *Alice in Wonderland*. But by spending decades with the text, the studio adapted the scenes and characters to its own medium. Those elements, and the music, were sufficient to displace nearly all competing adaptations.

Part of Wonderland's appeal is its separation from reality. This separation makes it all the more surprising that throughout Disney's decades-long relationship with the *Alice* books—from the initial concept (a vehicle for gags) through several phantom adaptations, an animated musical, and ultimately a franchise—the studio has prioritized their Victorian origins. During the same period, *Alice in Wonderland* was regularly appearing on college syllabi, as Victorian studies developed into a discipline. Disney's adaptations no doubt shaped students' conceptions of the story. And as the next chapter will demonstrate, Disney also responded to changing interpretations of text and authors it chose to adapt.

Chapter Three

Animating Hans Christian Andersen

Hans Christian Andersen's tales like "The Ugly Duckling" and "The Emperor's New Clothes" are as proverbial as the classic fairy tales on which Disney based films including *Snow White* (1937), *Cinderella* (1950), *Sleeping Beauty* (1959) and *Beauty and the Beast* (1991). But those centuries-old stories emerged from an oral tradition that spans multiple cultures. In contrast, Andersen's tales were the work of a single individual, and during his lifetime they were inextricable from their author's own life story. Andersen not only performed his stories at royal courts and aristocratic households throughout Europe, but also wrote several autobiographies, one of which he titled *The Fairy Tale of My Life*. In person and in print, Andersen presented himself as an ugly duckling, initially unappreciated until he found the right community. This version of Andersen's life persisted into the twentieth century. Especially in America, critics highlighted how Andersen used his innate talents to rise from poverty to worldwide fame.

Walt Disney likely saw a kindred spirit in Andersen. He adapted more stories by Andersen than by any other author. Both grew up in provincial towns but leveraged their artistic talents to become world-famous. Disney made two cartoon versions of "The Ugly Duckling" (1931 and 1939), and in the 1940s, he began collaborating with Samuel Goldwyn on a film about Andersen's life. Disney was to produce animated scenes based on the fairy tales while Goldwyn would be responsible for the live-action frame scenes from Andersen's life. The Samuel Goldwyn Company eventually produced the Danny Kaye musical *Hans Christian Andersen* (1952) without Disney, but the animation studio preserved the concept art. Work begun for the biopic became the basis for several films, from short cartoons in the *Silly Symphonies* series and *Fantasia 2000* (1999) to features like *The Little Mermaid* (1989). Disney had a version of Andersen's "The Snow Queen" in production for most of the twentieth century, and that work finally culminated in *Frozen* (2013). Andersen's biography remained a key touchstone for all these films.

By 2013, however, the critical understanding of Andersen's biography had changed substantially. The Romantic notion of innate artistic genius fell out of favor in the late twentieth century, as scholars began to focus instead on the cultural and historical circumstances that make literary production possible. From this perspective, Andersen's tales convey the "dynamic tension" between his sympathy with the poor and his dependence on the dominant classes, both royal and mercantile.[1] Scholars who link Andersen's success to his navigation of Denmark's rigid social structures emphasize the role of his patron and surrogate father Jonas Collin, to whose family he remained close throughout his life.[2] Other biographers argue that the most important person in Andersen's life was not Jonas Collin but his son Edvard, with whom Andersen formed a romantic attachment. Andersen's romantic desires have puzzled biographers since the beginning of the twentieth century, and recent works by Jens Andersen, Alison Prince, and Jackie Wullschlager see his fairy tales as reflections of a "bizarre or downright abnormal" sexuality.[3]

These different biographical emphases—Andersen's rags-to-riches narrative, his obsession with social class, and his sexuality—shaped Disney's adaptations at different points in the company's history. As I'll demonstrate in this chapter, Disney's adaptations show an awareness not only of Andersen's life but also of the shifting interpretations of that life. Viewing Disney's adaptations alongside different biographies of Andersen reveals how adaptations become intertwined with the author on whose works they are based and change along with perspectives on the author's life.

Before turning to Andersen, however, I will consider a somewhat simpler question, which sets up the stakes of this discussion: who determines how to interpret an artist's life and why might that interpretation matter? I'll consider that question by taking Walt Disney as a case study.

COMPETING VERSIONS OF WALT DISNEY'S LIFE

"Celebrate the Magic," a nightly show that for many years preceded the fireworks at Disney's Magic Kingdom theme park in Florida, featured a black-and-white Walt Disney reciting a mantra that is simultaneously modest and boastful: "I only hope that we don't lose sight of one thing—that it was all started by a mouse."[4] The brief clip, interspersed with scenes from Disney's films projected onto Cinderella's Castle, moves seamlessly from the singular "I" to the collective "we," a plural pronoun that both recognizes film as a collaborative enterprise (the "we" standing for everyone involved in producing the films) and welcomes the audience into a knowing inner circle. In the second clause, the pronoun "it" remains tantalizingly vague. Lacking an antecedent, the pronoun suggests a sense of wonder and happiness that, reinforced by the word "hope" in the preceding clause, encapsulates the Disney brand.

The clip of Disney uttering this phrase, which appears frequently in documentaries, commercials, and other representations of Walt Disney, is just one example of how Walt's image stands in for the corporate brand. The image of "Uncle Walt," cultivated on the *Disneyland* television program, embodies the family values for which the company still stands. The Walt Disney Family Museum, which opened in 2009, lends the brand archival support, and the company still portrays itself as continuing Walt's legacy. Michael Eisner, head of the studio during the "Disney renaissance," thought of himself as "like Walt, a storyteller at heart."[5] When animators and directors turned against Eisner in the early 2000s they deployed the same rhetoric, stating in a letter to shareholders that "Mr. Eisner's rejection of Walt Disney's heritage has been a colossal failure."[6] In 2016, *Life* magazine marked the fiftieth anniversary of Walt's death with a special issue that begins with Walt's childhood in Marceline, Kansas, and ends with the Walt Disney Company's global expansion, epitomized by the opening of Shanghai Disney.[7] While men like Ray Kroc, Steve Jobs, Mark Zuckerberg, and Elon Musk remain closely associated with the companies they started, no company leans as heavily as Disney on its founder's life story.

But biography is a tricky concept, and by placing Walt's life at the center of its corporate brand, the Walt Disney Company competes with journalists and scholars who might frame that life differently. Perhaps the earliest biography of Walt Disney is Gilbert Seldes's 1931 profile in the *New Yorker*, published just three years after *Steamboat Willie* introduced audiences to Mickey Mouse.[8] Seldes refers to Disney as a "mediocre draughtsman" whose talent is not for drawing pictures but for inventing stories. He recounts how Walt worked diligently to bring his stories to life, refusing to be satisfied until his vision is achieved. He covers Walt's life before Hollywood, including his studies at the Art Institute in Chicago, his stint as an ambulance driver in World War I, and his time as a commercial artist in Kansas City. He acknowledges Walt's older brother Roy as "the businessman of the firm," and refers to the siblings' frugality, as they reinvest profits into the company, share meals in a cafeteria, and live in middle-class houses on the same plot of land.

Disney was thirty when the *New Yorker* profile was published, and so, Seldes writes, "too young to have had a history, too young to have developed oddities and idiosyncrasies."[9] Yet the portrayal differs very little from biography that the company promotes today.[10] A century later, Seldes sounds almost prescient. He points out that while Disney lives frugally and pours the money back into the company, "experts think that he is only at the beginning of his great success."[11] Those experts were right, of course. In 1931, Disney was producing twenty-six cartoons a year: thirteen Mickey Mouse cartoons and thirteen *Silly Symphonies*. A few years later, he would enter the feature film business with *Snow White*, and in the 1950s, he opened Disneyland and adapted to the new medium of television.

Walt Disney also recognized new avenues for profit. The first Mickey Mouse Club launched in January 1930 at the Fox Dome Theater in Ocean Park, California. Local businesses provided Mickey-themed ice cream or piggy banks, merchandise that not only helped see many small businesses through the Great Depression but also made Mickey a household name.[12] By 1932, the clubs boasted over a million members, roughly the size of the Boy Scouts and Girl Scouts, and Disney hired Herman Kamen to lead a merchandising department.[13] From the 1930s through today, licensing profits form a large portion of Disney's revenue, and those profits bolster the films, television shows, and theme-park attractions. By the time the company celebrated its centennial in 2023, it stood among the most powerful media corporations in the world.

The public imagination draws little distinction between Walt Disney and The Walt Disney Company. Books about Disney's corporate practices are a genre unto themselves, and most are grounded in the company's history and in Walt Disney's biography.[14] But versions of Walt's life have also proliferated well beyond a single magazine profile. Pete Martin's 1956 series in the *Saturday Evening Post*, which was based on interviews with Walt's daughter Diane, was the first extended biography of Walt Disney, and may have been arranged to preempt a more critical biography.[15] Martin lauds Disney's inventiveness and risk-taking, from his first experiments in Kansas City to his belief that *Snow White* would succeed, even while others in Hollywood called it "Disney's Folly." He also includes humanizing anecdotes about Disney crying at his daughter's wedding and preferring macaroni and hot dogs to expensive steaks.

But just as charming anecdotes about Walt's life bolster the company's family image, critiques of the man could be turned into critiques of the company. Less than two years after Walt's death, Richard Schickel's *The Disney Version* (1968) envisioned the Walt Disney Company as a machine "designed to shatter the two most valuable things about childhood."[16] Schickel criticizes Disney's labor practices and his refusal to grant credit to his collaborators, seeing both as precursors to the animators' strike in the 1940s. Rather than the family man from small-town America who just happened to create a popular character, Schickel portrays Disney as a capitalist whose goal had always been to become "a wildly successful entrepreneur of art."[17] According to Schickel, "Walt Disney's greatest creation was Walt Disney."[18]

Some later biographers reinforced the avuncular image of the *Saturday Evening Post*, while others extended Schickel's critiques of Disney's paternalist and capitalist ideology. Critical and unauthorized biographies like Marc Eliot's *Hollywood's Dark Prince* (1993) compete with "company-approved 'sanitized' biographical material" like Bob Thomas's panegyric *Walt Disney: An American Original* (1976), which was rereleased in 1994, the year after Eliot's book.[19] Most biographies fall somewhere between these two poles. Neal Gabler, whose 2007 biography is probably the most extensively researched of the bunch, called Walt "as much a commodity as a man."[20] One's perspective on that "commodity" affects how one interprets both the Walt Disney Company itself and the films and other entertainment products it produces.

My aim in this chapter is not to promote or to challenge any particular interpretation of Walt Disney's life. Instead, I wish to show how different interpretations of an author's life can lead to different interpretations—and, more to the point, different adaptations—of their works. I argued in chapter one that Charles Dickens is a Victorian analogue to Disney, and I might have written this chapter about Dickens rather than Hans Christian Andersen. Dickens is the quintessential Victorian, and I could certainly trace a trajectory through biographies of Dickens that mirrors the above paragraphs about Disney's.[21] But as the next section will show, Hans Christian Andersen was also omnipresent in the Victorian world. And because Disney adapted so many of Andersen's stories at so many different points in its corporate history, the relationship better demonstrates the relationship between literary biography and the Walt Disney Company.

ANDERSEN AMONG THE VICTORIANS

Andersen was born in 1805, an auspicious moment for the literary fairy tale, which had only recently transitioned from oral culture to the print tradition. Adaptations by French writers like Charles Perrault and Madame d'Aulnoy were popular throughout eighteenth-century Europe. The first of the Brothers Grimm's tales were published in 1812, and they were quickly translated from German into other European languages. (Edgar Taylor produced the first English translation in 1823; it was illustrated by George Cruikshank, who would later do the pictures for *Oliver Twist*.) Perrault, D'Aulnoy, and the Grimms, however, did not claim the fairy tales as their own creations. D'Aulnoy drew on stories that circulated in French salons, and the title of Perrault's *Histoires ou contes du temps passé, avec des moralités* (*Tales from the Past, with morals*) conveys the nature of his collection. The Grimms were linguists who hoped to unify Germany by establishing a national language. For them, the fairy tale's most important feature was its folk heritage, divorced from any single individual creator.

In contrast, Andersen's fairy tales are original works, often reflecting his own experiences. His contemporaries knew him as not only a fairy tale author but also a novelist, a playwright, and a travel writer. His extensive travels brought him into contact with contemporary luminaries, including the Grimms, whom he met in the 1840s.[22] He was also an inveterate performer, entertaining audiences with renditions of his stories. These performances underscored a key aspect of his writing. In Andersen's works, regardless of genre, "everything is personal, for his ambition was always literary creativity."[23] His fairy tales are consistent with his larger oeuvre, distinguishing him from his predecessors in the fairy tale genre.

Andersen moved in a pan-European artistic circle that overlapped with many eminent Victorians, both on the continent and in England. The first of his works to be translated into English were novels. Mary Howitt (author of the well-known poem "The Spider and the Fly," parodied in *Alice in Wonderland*) translated *The Improvisatore*, *Only a Fiddler!*, and *O. T.* in 1845, which were published by Richard Bentley. Andersen's *Eventyr* (*Tales*) did not appear in English until the next year. They were immediately popular, and circulated in cheap periodicals before Bentley published a collection in 1846.[24] By the time Andersen visited England in 1847, most of the major literary journals had already favorably reviewed his work. The invitation to England was extended by William Jerdan, editor of the *Literary Gazette*, and "no reader of *The Literary Gazette* in the years 1845–47 could fail to know Andersen's name."[25] He quickly became a mainstay of English literature and children's culture. In 1887, Edward Salmon wrote that a work by either Andersen, Aesop, or the Grimms "is almost certain to be selected by the parent among the first books placed in the hands of children."[26]

Among Andersen's early admirers was Charles Dickens. Dickens lived in London, but in July 1847 had rented out his house and was spending the summer in Kent. When he learned of Andersen's visit (perhaps from Bentley, owner of *Bentley's Miscellany*, where *Oliver Twist* was first serialized and which Dickens also edited) he traveled to London with the express purpose of meeting Andersen. The two had dinner, and Dickens was the last person Andersen saw before he departed.[27] They continued to correspond over the next few years, and Dickens encouraged Andersen to return to England and to stay at his house.[28] Andersen took him up on the offer and stayed with the Dickens family when he returned to England in 1857. Dickens's biographers depict the visit as something of a farce. Andersen intended to stay a week, but the trip extended to more than a month. The patient but exasperated family put up with their Danish visitor's eccentricities. Dickens's daughter Kate thought him a "bony bore who stayed on and on."[29] After the visit, Dickens supposedly pinned a note above a mirror that read, "Hans Andersen slept in this room for five weeks—which seemed to the family AGES!"[30]

Shortly after the visit, Dickens wrote to a friend that Andersen "speaks no language but his own Danish, and is suspected of not even knowing that."[31] Andersen's poor English was certainly a source of frustration for the Dickens family, but this negative view may also have been influenced by Mary Howitt, who was an acquaintance of Dickens's.[32] The year before traveling to England, Andersen had been dismayed to learn that Howitt's translations of his works had been pirated in America, where they him no royalties.[33] His friend Joseph Hambro, a Danish banker in London, called Howitt a "translation factory" and thought she had offered Andersen an outrageously small sum for the translation rights to Andersen's works.[34] For her part, Howitt was territorial about her translations, which faced competition from other translators as Andersen's popularity grew. She and Andersen had an awkward meeting during Andersen's first London trip in 1847. Hambro and Richard Bentley eventually took over the negotiations on Andersen's behalf, and dropped Howitt as the translator—much to her chagrin. She later wrote a vengeful memoir, calling Andersen childish and egotistical.[35]

Andersen seemed to have been aware that his English skills caused friction in the Dickens family. He dwells on the subject in both his letters and his diary. A diary entry records, "little Kate sarcastic, and the aunt is certainly weary of me."[36] Andersen refers to Dickens's daughter and his sister-in-law Georgina, who lived with the family. But he didn't see that weariness extending to Dickens himself. Ten days after his arrival, and about to depart, Andersen wrote in his diary, "Dickens begged me most charmingly not to go before I had seen the performance they were giving for Jerrold's widow."[37] The invitation to stay was just the sort of kindness that appealed to Andersen, who was always seeking approval from those around him.

Andersen's diary entry refers to an amateur performance of *The Frozen Deep*, intended as a benefit for the family of the playwright Douglas Jerrold, who had died in June. The play was written by Dickens's friend Wilkie Collins and had first been performed at Dickens's home earlier that year. Dickens played the starring role and contributed significantly to the script. The July performance was attended by Queen Victoria and her husband Prince Albert, as well as the King Leopold of Belgium and Prince Frederick of Prussia (who would marry Victoria's eldest daughter the following year). Andersen enjoyed the proximity to royalty and was moved by Dickens's performance. He also attended an after-party at the office of *Household Words*, the magazine Dickens had founded in 1850. But he closes his diary entry with a parenthetical, "Not at all in good humour really the whole evening."[38] Andersen sensed tension in the Dickens household, especially from Georgina Hogarth, whose weariness he had noted in his diary.

Andersen couldn't have known that the Dickens household's veneer of domestic happiness would be shattered within a year. Dickens would soon recruit a professional cast for *The Frozen Deep*, including the young actress Ellen Ternan. His affair with her would lead to the end of his marriage. Catherine Dickens moved out of her husband's house; Georgina stayed, with all but one of the children. Details of the affair were not public knowledge during Dickens's lifetime, but the separation was sufficiently scandalous that Dickens published a plea for privacy in *Household Words* in June 1858, less than a year after Andersen's departure. To modern audiences the events are well-known, and the affair is the subject of a feature film (*The Invisible Woman* (2013), starring Ralph Fiennes). But in 1857 Andersen was unaware that his extended presence in the household probably heightened tensions that already existed.

Dickens was not the only famous Victorian writer on whom Andersen left an impression. In Rome, he visited the American sculptor William Wetmore Story, at whose house his fondness for children, and their fondness for him, impressed a young Henry James. James's biography of Story includes an anecdote about Andersen keeping all the old tin soldiers and broken toys that children would give to him.[39] At Story's home, Andersen also met Robert and Elizabeth Barrett Browning. Robert "sat in a circle of children and read two of his poems to them."[40] The Brownings' son Pen reportedly called Andersen an ugly duckling.[41]

According to Andersen's diaries, Elizabeth Barrett Browning "graciously expressed her pleasure at my visit," but Andersen thought she "looked very sickly."[42] It was an astute observation; Barrett Browning died a month later. One of her last poems, "The North and the South," imagines a conversation between the two regions of Europe. Such contrasts were a common nineteenth-century trope, with the natural beauty and fecundity of the southern climate often set against the moral and physical strength supposedly bred in the north. Byron's *Don Juan* contrasts the "happy nations of the moral north" with the "sultry" Spanish climate.[43] Thomas Carlyle addresses English readers as "sons of the icy north,"[44] and John Ruskin refers to a "northern energy" in his architectural history, *Stones of Venice*.[45] In Barrett Browning's poem, the north asks for a climate that bears olives and grapes, while the south requests, "a poet's tongue of baptismal flame, / To call the tree or the flower by its name!" The poem's last stanza reads:

> The North sent therefore a man of men
>> As a grace to the South;
> And thus to Rome came Andersen.[46]

Andersen read the poem three years later, while staying with the son of the novelist Edward Bulwer-Lytton, and he found it "very flattering."[47]

Even English writers who didn't meet Andersen were familiar with his works and expected their readers to recognize even passing references. In the famous preface to *Middlemarch*, George Eliot retells the parable of Saint Theresa, founder of a religious order. For Eliot the story introduces the possibility of the many mute, inglorious Theresas, "foundresses of nothing" who "found for themselves no epic life."[48] To emphasize her point, Eliot offers a brief analogy. "Here and there a cygnet is reared uneasily among the ducklings in the brown pond," Eliot writes, "and never finds the living stream in fellowship with its own oary-footed kind."[49] The reference is to "The Ugly Duckling," as Eliot imagines those unlucky swans who grow up with ducklings but never learn their true potential. From that one sentence, Eliot expects her readers to recognize the story, extrapolate its moral, and then connect its obverse to the rest of the preface. Such an allusion implies a readership that is fluent in Andersen's tales.

Two years before Eliot's novel was published, the novelist and critic Charlotte Yonge wrote that Andersen's tales "have already acquired a sort of force, like a proverb, by their wonderful terseness of irony and truth."[50] Yonge's temporal adverb—that these tales are *already* proverbial—makes clear how famous Andersen's tales had become, in just a few decades, among

Augustus Vilhelm Saabye's statue of Hans Christian Andersen in Rosenborg Castle Gardens. Andersen objected to Saabye's initial idea because he felt it pigeon-holed him as a children's writer.

Victorian readers. His works were performed on stage, often in pantomimes. In the summer of 1888, Charles Dodgson (Lewis Carroll) saw Isa Bowman perform in Savile Clarke's tableaux based on Andersen's fairy tales, and the performance "suggested to Dodgson the possibility of Isa as Alice."[51] Bowman would go on to star in the production, and so Andersen also has a direct connection to the stage adaptation of *Alice's Adventures in Wonderland*.

Unlike Oscar Wilde, whose fairy tales were popular among adults, "Andersen remained a children's author, absorbed into the cult of Victorian childhood."[52] English readers typically neglect his works for adults, and even the more mature and nuanced tales, in favor of the fairy tales that fit best into the burgeoning children's literature market. Scholars have posited several justifications for Andersen's English reputation, including the paucity of English genres of short fiction and the poor quality of the early translations.[53] Taken from German editions rather than the original Danish, these translations "ironed out his idiosyncrasies and made his writing more sentimental and moralistic."[54] Andersen was still living in 1869, when Yonge counted him among the best modern writers for children. As examples, Yonge lists "True Princess," "Emperor of China's Clothes," and "Lark."[55] These tales are better known as "The Princess and the Pea," "The Emperor's New Clothes," and "The Nightingale," and Yonge's rendition of the titles hints at the dismal translations available to Victorian readers.

Andersen titled his first three fairy-tale collections *Eventyr, fertile for Børn* (*Tales, Told for Children*), and in the early 1830s expressed to his friends that he envisioned a child audience.[56] But he dropped the subtitle "for children" from the 1843 collection, which includes "The Ugly Duckling" and "The Nightingale."[57] A quarter-century later, he balked when the American publisher Horace E. Scudder proposed to publish his tales in the *Riverside Magazine for Young People* because he didn't think a children's magazine was an appropriate venue.[58] And in 1875, just two months before he died, he recorded in his diary a complaint about plans for a statue by Augustus Vilhelm Saabye, which portrayed Andersen surrounded by children. He told Saabye, "my tales were just as much for older people as for children."[59] (The finished statue, which now stands in Rosenborg Castle Gardens in Copenhagen, depicts Andersen without the children.) So while the earliest tales envisioned a child audience, over the next three decades Andersen (and his Danish and German readers) came to see his works in a different light.

To English readers, however, Andersen remains primarily a sentimental author for children. In that genre he has been remarkably successful. Andersen contributed to English children's literature "that vein of fantasy and imaginative invention that is often regarded as peculiarly English" and he influenced writers like J. M. Barrie, Rudyard Kipling, Kenneth Grahame, Lewis Carroll, and A. A. Milne.[60] That those authors were the basis for some of Disney's most successful films further underscores the company's connection not only to Andersen's tales but also to his legacy and his life story.[61]

FROM PROVINCIAL ORIGINS TO GLOBAL FAME

Hans Christian Andersen was born in Odense, Denmark. In the early nineteenth century, Odense was provincial enough to maintain a connection to the folk culture that would inform Andersen's works, but large enough that it also presented him with "the intriguing possibilities of bourgeois culture which shaped his ambition."[62] Like Disney and Dickens, Andersen had a lifelong interest in the theater. As a child he would act out Shakespeare's plays with puppets, in a toy theater his father built for him, and by his early teenage years he was regularly reciting and singing at homes throughout Odense.[63] At fourteen he left for Copenhagen, determined to work at the Royal Theater. When his unsuccessful attempts at dancing, singing, and writing left him impoverished, he began dropping in for unannounced visits to artists and theatrical patrons. This unorthodox strategy eventually paid off. Crown Princess Caroline heard about the odd, talented boy, and called him to recite at Frederiksberg Castle.[64] He performed small theatrical roles and eventually earned the patronage of Jonas Collin, director of the Royal Theater. The wealthy, well-connected philanthropist would remain a lifelong friend to Andersen, paying for his education and supporting him throughout his career.

Andersen's childhood experiences presage much of his later life. He maintained a high opinion of his own talent and an equally high desire for others to recognize that talent. In 1837, the year he published his third collection of tales, he wrote that fame "is the only thing I live for."[65] Andersen envisioned himself not as a provincial writer but as a European artist. He feared that his success was hampered by his being from a small nation whose national language was not widely spoken. Travel helped him to "shake off his Danish provincialism," and he reveled in the company of famous artists and aristocrats throughout Europe.[66] For all his internationalism, however, he did little writing while abroad, and always returned to Copenhagen.

In addition to invigorating and inspiring Andersen, who was at his most productive when returning from a trip abroad, travel helped him secure a European reputation. On his first trip to Germany in 1831, he was already methodically cultivating his fame. He met with the German writer Ludwig Tieck, who had read Andersen's first novel *Walking Tour*, and in his autobiography later claimed this as evidence of his growing reputation on the continent. What he doesn't mention is that he himself had, a year and a half earlier, sent Tieck a copy of the novel. He would later repeat this strategy with other European artists of note. Andersen often claimed they had come across his works on their own, but before the 1840s that was rarely true—he sent his works in advance of his visits.[67]

Andersen took pride in his acceptance among elite circles. "People say the aristocracy in England excludes all artists from their circle," he wrote in his diary, recalling what his friend Carl Alexander, the hereditary Duke of Weimar, had told him. "I can't say that—I found the friendliest people, the heartiest reception. They say that Dickens and Disraeli are excluded from these circles; they acknowledged me, they accepted me."[68] Among the many royals he visited was the Bavarian King Maximilian, whose son was so enamored with "The Steadfast Tin Soldier" that when he found his own toy soldiers broken, he became distressed at what Andersen would think.[69] This child grew up to be Ludwig II, who built the fairy-tale castle that inspired Disneyland's centerpiece, Sleeping Beauty's Castle.

Andersen further cultivated his European reputation with a series of autobiographies. He wrote his first autobiography in 1832, though it remained unpublished until it was rediscovered nearly a century later. His first published autobiography accompanied an 1847 German edition of his collected works, and he revised it slightly into a standalone work, *The Fairy Tale of My Life*, in 1855. He added additional chapters for Horace Scudder's American edition of the complete works in 1871.[70] His autobiography was widely reviewed in America, receiving "more reviews than any other single work he wrote."[71] The reviews typically highlighted "the moral fabric of the life portrayed in the book," in the tradition of biographies as moral exemplars.[72] Reviewers highlighted "the 'romance' of Andersen's ascent from poverty to acclaim," a bootstrap narrative that had "particular resonance in mid- and later nineteenth century America."[73] These reviews bolstered the vision of Andersen that he himself tried to promote. Walt Disney saw his own life in similar terms, and the connection likely motivated him to consider a biographical feature about Andersen.

Andersen basked in his fame and delighted in finding his own books on sale in foreign countries. His diary entry for his first day in England records that in Trafalgar Square he saw "a window with my own picture in it from *Howitt's Journal*; bought a copy later."[74] In small doses one might find such anecdotes charming, especially mixed with the mundanity that often characterizes his diary entries (his entry about visiting the princess of Prussia, for example, also includes an episode about a misplaced umbrella).[75] But some of Andersen's friends and countrymen thought his fame-seeking a "sickly flaw" in his character.[76]

Andersen successfully cultivated powerful friends both at home and abroad, and these friends formed a network that facilitated his travels. Whether he was dining with friends in Copenhagen or visiting kings and dukes in Europe, Andersen's hosts expected that he would draw a crowd and "provide a good deal of the entertainment at the dinner table and in the evening hours."[77] The entertainments included festive bouquets and table decorations (Andersen was famous for his paper cutouts), but surely the biggest draw was his reading his stories aloud. Danish friends like the Collin family and Captain Alexander Wilde, Germans like the composer

Felix Mendelssohn-Bartholdy, and English visitors like Edmund Gosse all agree that Andersen's seductive reading style drew listeners into his fairy-tale worlds.[78]

Like Charles Dickens's public readings (discussed in my first chapter), Andersen's performances bolstered his reputation. By the 1870s, he had received several invitations to visit the United States. His friend Henriette Wulff encouraged him to visit, pointing out that he could join Jenny Lind (the famed singer known as the "Swedish nightingale," whom Andersen had earlier befriended) on her tour with P. T. Barnum.[79] Years later, the poet Henry Wadsworth Longfellow also invited Andersen to do a reading tour. Longfellow promised to arrange everything in advance if Andersen could read just three tales in English. Andersen could rehearse to overcome the language barrier, and Longfellow assured him, as Andersen records in his diary, "a whole fortune. I could earn money over there the way Dickens did."[80] Both the money and the comparison to Dickens must have appealed to Andersen, but he turned down the chance. Henriette Wulff had drowned en route to New York, and his fear of crossing the Atlantic was a major factor in declining Longfellow's invitation.

Yet his fame in America continued to grow. In 1874, he received a letter with an American dollar bill and a newspaper article exhorting children to repay him the debt they owed for his tales. He later heard that the American ambassador had brought more money from American children. Andersen, by that time both pensioned by the Danish monarchy and earning a substantial income from collections of his works, was outraged that American children thought him indigent.[81] At a dinner party with the American ambassador he proposed a toast, which he recorded in his diary:

> Once England was our distant neighbor, but time has made everything looser, and now America is closer to us than England once was. People from the North visited and knew about America before Columbus knew about it . . . it has become precious to me because of the love flowing out to me from the hearts of its young people. The children of America have broken open their piggy banks to share what they have with the old Danish writer they believe to be living in need. It has been a whole page in the fairy tale of my life.[82]

By the end of his life, American readers had shown a fondness for Andersen's tales, a fondness bolstered by his biography (as it was presented to them). Andersen, in turn, felt a fondness for the readers across the Atlantic, who helped ensure the fame he had craved his whole life.

In the preface to his third collection of fairy tales—which included "The Little Mermaid" and "The Emperor's New Clothes"—Andersen addressed his critics. "In a small country, the writer is always a poor man," he wrote.[83] In light of such statements, one might assume that Andersen's courting of fame was financially motivated. Dickens and Andersen discussed royalties for their works during Andersen's first visit in 1847, and Dickens had been shocked to learn how little Andersen was making.[84] Dickens had recently returned from America, where he had been outspoken about the need for international copyright protection. Though no record of the conversation exists, it seems plausible that the two men spoke about copyright. Andersen had always worried about his earning capabilities as a writer from a small country, and as his reputation grew he secured contracts with both German and English publishers to ensure a wider distribution of his work. Indeed, the purpose of Andersen's visit to England was to work out a deal with Richard Bentley, securing copyright by publishing some of his works in English before they appeared in Danish or German. Bentley published several of Andersen's tales as *A Christmas Greeting to My English Friends* at the end of 1847, not only taking advantage of the Christmas book-buying season but also dedicating the work to Dickens, who since the 1842 publication of *A Christmas Carol* had been associated with the holiday.[85]

Andersen proved himself a savvy marketer of his works, leveraging his fame and his social connections to publish his writing. He was certainly conscious of his works as products for the market. Yet financial reward seems to have been less a motivator than personal fame. For Andersen, both writing and traveling served a psychological need. It may even have fulfilled an erotic need for a man whose sexuality was outside the norm for his society.

SEXUAL DESIRE AND SELF-DEPRIVATION

The Danish language did not have a word for "homosexuality" during Andersen's lifetime, but as early as 1826 Andersen recognized that his own desires did not fit the norms of those around him.[86] In letters to Jonas Collin and B. S. Ingemann, he labeled himself "womanish," "feminine," and "childish."[87] He later recorded in his diary the words of Karl Gutzkow, a German author with whom he had stayed in 1856. "He was so tactless as to ask whether I had ever been in love," Andersen writes, because "one couldn't tell from my books, where love came in like a fairy; I was myself a sort of half-man!"[88] As these remarks show, Andersen seems to have felt his sexual desires at odds with his masculinity. He conflates gender and sexuality not because he questioned his gender identity but because he lacked a language to better describe his sexual desires.

Scholars look for insight into Andersen's sexuality by considering how his fairy tales portray gender and desire. Jack Zipes identifies a consistent pattern in how Andersen depict boys and girls. Stories about boys tend to be "about the rise from rags to riches and fame," following an Aladdin motif.[89] One might see such tales as particularly biographical, since Andersen portrayed his own life story in a similar manner. But he may have identified even more closely with his girl protagonists, who don't fare as well in his tales. The heroine of "The Little Match Girl," for example, freezes to death while seeing visions of happiness. Stories like "The Red Shoes," "The Girl Who Trod on a Loaf," and "The Little Mermaid" similarly delight in the trials that girl protagonists undergo—trials that lead, at best, to an ambivalent ending rather than a happy one. As many scholars have argued, these tales convey Andersen's struggle to understand his own desires in a culture that did not tolerate deviation from accepted norms.

Andersen never married and claimed to remain a virgin his whole life. But as the editors of his diaries put it, he "lacked neither impulse, desire, nor opportunity for sexual relations."[90] "My blood is churning," Andersen recorded in Naples in 1834. "Huge sensuality and struggle with myself. If it really is a sin to satisfy this powerful urge, then let me fight it. I am still innocent, but my blood is burning."[91] He did occasionally "satisfy this powerful urge," and diary entries like this one often end with a cross, the symbol he used to record his masturbation. Andersen's biographers agree that the "sublimation of sexual urges" (prevalent throughout the diaries) was important to Andersen's "artistic professionalism."[92] But they disagree in how they interpret those urges.

Alison Prince's *Hans Christian Andersen: The Fan Dancer* (1998) is the least circumspect of the biographies. Prince argues that Andersen perpetuated a "complex and deliberate cover-up" of his sexuality, which later biographers continued.[93] She goes so far as to suggest that the literary critic Georg Brandes, in his 1886 *Creative Spirits of the Nineteenth Century*, avoided voicing his conviction about Andersen's sexuality only because he "had no wish to destroy a famous writer by involving him in a huge public scandal, nor to get involved himself in a libel action which would reverberate throughout the literate world."[94] Prince, of course, has the advantage of knowing about Oscar Wilde's 1895 trial for "gross indecency," which is perhaps the most famous instance of a writer persecuted for his homosexuality. She also reads a lot into Brandes's comments about Andersen's "maidenly" expressions and his mind being "devoid of sexual distinctions."[95] That Brandes saw something effeminate in Andersen's writing doesn't seem sufficient evidence that he necessarily thought Andersen a homosexual, let alone that the thought of libel entered his mind.

Jackie Wullschlager also places Andersen's sexuality at the center of her biography. For Wullschlager, Andersen's personal writings "leave no doubt that he was attracted to both sexes."[96] Earlier biographers, she writes, had based their denial of his homosexual encounters on the argument that the Collin family would have known about them, and if they had, "would not have allowed him to take their young sons and grandsons on foreign holidays."[97] She dismisses the assumption, pointing out that members of the family had discussed it openly with him. She also argues that his struggle to express his same-sex desires before "homosexual" became an available term was evident to astute contemporary readers. His fellow Dane Søren Kierkegaard recognized Andersen's ambivalent sexuality in a critical review of Andersen's 1837 novel *Only a Fiddler*. Kierkegaard thought "the lax and weak aspects of Andersen's writing were due to the author's sexual confusion."[98] And in the early twentieth century the lawyer Albert Hansen speculated about Andersen's sexuality. His study formed the basis for Hjalmar Helweg's psychiatric study of Andersen.[99]

Such arguments are far from universally accepted. A review of Wullschlager's book in *The Guardian* concludes that she "nails Andersen rather too definitely to the mast of homosexuality."[100] The Hans Christian Andersen Centre at the University of Southern Denmark insists that homosexual relationships "would have been entirely contrary to his moral and religious ideas."[101] There may be strong disincentives to discussing Andersen's sexuality. Andersen is to Odense, as Michael Booth puts it, as Elvis to Memphis or the Beatles to Liverpool: he is "their greatest international export, by an infinite margin."[102] Booth later implies that the Danes' Viking heritage rests on a masculine ideology that makes it hard to accept a fluid sexuality like Andersen's.[103] Booth is not a biographer but a travel writer following the itinerary in Andersen's *A Poet's Bazaar*. That he feels compelled to discuss Andersen's sexuality testifies to its prominence in discussions of his life and works.

The lack of a nuanced vocabulary through which Andersen might have expressed his sexuality is exacerbated by late nineteenth-century medical and legal discourse that defined homosexuality as an illness and a crime. Andersen's first biographers, especially Edvard Collin, were keenly aware of this fact, and may have destroyed evidence of his erotic relationships with men. When he died in 1875, Andersen left his estate to Collin. He also requested that Edvard and his wife, Henriette, be buried in the same triple plot as Andersen (this request was granted when Edvard and Henriette died, in 1886 and 1894).[104] As executor of Andersen's estate, Edvard was responsible for making decisions about the decades of correspondence that Andersen had saved. Not only did he heavily edit the letters on which he based his own book, but he also returned other letters to their senders, thus breaking up a record of the author's emotional life. Jens Andersen posits that some of Andersen's correspondents—most notably the dancer Harald Scharff—burned the letters to keep their youthful private lives from public scrutiny.[105]

The history is further complicated by the fact that Edvard Collin was not only Andersen's friend and biographer but also an object of his infatuation. Andersen had become enamored with his patron's son early in his life, and while several young men "now and then glittered more dazzlingly for Andersen, then receded into the background," his affection for Edvard persisted.[106] Like some other European languages, Danish has two second-person pronouns, *de* and *du*, the latter of which connotes a more personal relationship. In the early 1830s, Andersen asked Edvard to use the more personal pronoun, a request that Edvard flatly refused—and continued to refuse throughout their lifelong friendship.[107] In 1840, as Andersen left Denmark for his second European tour, he recorded in his diary, "Edvard Collin was the last one out there. I said goodbye; he pressed a kiss onto my mouth! Oh, it was as if my heart would burst!"[108] Collin likely would have objected to such a statement, but not necessarily because of the kiss. Male friendship in the early nineteenth century did not preclude such physical displays of affection. For someone like Edvard Collin, what would seem aberrant in Andersen's desire for a close relationship was his outpouring of emotion and pleas for affection—in this example, the feeling that his heart would burst.

One of Andersen's most autobiographical tales, "The Shadow," revolves around a character's refusal to use the more personal second-person pronoun and is almost certainly based on Edvard's denial of intimacy. Jack Zipes sees "The Shadow" as a turning point in Andersen's art. The tale shows him at the height of his powers, confidently exploiting all types of sources rather than relying only on folklore, and no longer considering his tales as predominantly for children.[109] Yet Zipes calls Andersen's sexual preferences a "side issue," referring to Andersen as "an emotional cripple who failed to satisfy his desires and needs in intimate relationships of any kind" and who often expressed "a certain fear of sexual and erotic arousal."[110] I disagree with Zipes on this point. It is clear from Andersen's obsession with building his European reputation and seeking the attention of the aristocratic and intellectual elite that he cared a lot about what others thought of him. Anxiety that he would be disavowed or condemned seems a more plausible reason for his "fear of sexual and erotic arousal" than his being (to quote Zipes's unfortunate phrase) an "emotional cripple."

Hans Christian Andersen in 1860 (Portrait by Franz Hanfstaengl).

Edvard Collin was not the only young man with whom Andersen had an intimate relationship. Wullschlager chronicles Andersen's relationships in the 1830s with Christian Voight, Edward Müller, and Henrik Stampe. He wrote love letters to Müller, a twenty-three-year-old theology student, and openly expressed his feelings to his friends. He was overjoyed to receive a response from Müller, but before he sent his reply his friend Mimi Thyberg (whose sister was engaged to Edvard Collin) admitted Müller's letter to be a forgery, a rather unkind joke.[111] The anecdote shows that Andersen was unafraid to share with his close friends his desires for intimacy with young men. But these relationships were unlikely to have been sexual ones. Close male friendships were a standard precursor to marriage, providing nineteenth-century men a kind of emotional preparation for married life.[112] Voight, Müller, and Stampe seem to fit that standard.

A later relationship provides better evidence of Andersen's attraction to another man. Andersen met the young ballet dancer Harald Scharff in Paris in 1857, and their relationship almost certainly developed into a love affair.[113] Andersen saw Scharff again in Munich in 1860, and they continued their relationship in Copenhagen, where Scharff was a dancer for the Royal Theater. In January 1864, Andersen recorded in his diary that he found Scharff "charming."[114] Scharff makes regular appearances in the diary over the course of the year: "I was at a party at Scharff's"; "Scharff has been visiting me regularly and often"; "A visit from Scharff, who showed up alone with a walking stick"; "Paid a visit to the Collins and after that to Scharff."[115] Andersen's infatuation was open and public enough to draw disapproval from the Collin family. Scharff moved in a circle of other young, unmarried men at the Royal Theater. Jonas Collin referred to the group of actors and dancers as a "swarm of confidantes," condescendingly expressing his disapproval of Andersen's relationship with them.[116] Theodor Collin, Andersen's doctor, "informed Andersen that he was advertising his feelings for Scharff much too openly," and people were beginning to notice.[117]

Though Andersen tried to maintain the intimacy (as his diaries indicate), Scharff grew distant within the year. The correspondence between the two was destroyed (or, with the same result, returned to Scharff) by Edvard Collin, as he prepared Andersen's biography in the homophobic climate of the 1870s.[118] Collin consulted his cousin Emil Hornemann, who had been one of Andersen's physicians for forty years, for a medical evaluation of Andersen's sexuality.[119] That Collin felt the need to do so, and that Hornemann, as a physician, would comment on Andersen's sexuality, gives us some insight into the medicalization of sexuality in the last quarter of the nineteenth century. If evidence of a sexual relationship with Scharff—or any other man—existed, it would likely have been destroyed in this period.

Andersen also developed close relationships with women. He typically addressed them as "sister," a term whose familial and spiritual resonance doubly excluded these women from the possibility of sexual attraction.[120] Often the women with whom he was infatuated were sisters of the young men who were also the subject of his affections. He met the Voights in the summer of 1830, and Wullschlager suggests that his infatuation with both of them "was the first hint at a pattern in Andersen's love affairs that was to establish itself forcefully over the years—that to fall in love with a woman, he needed two emotional objects, one male and one female."[121] Relationships with women like Riborg Voight (already engaged when she met Andersen) and Louise Collin (whose romance with Andersen the Collin family was unlikely to encourage) gave Andersen the opportunity to play the lover while remaining chaste—and also, perhaps, to establish a relationship with the men to whom his affections may really have been meant.

One exception to this pattern is Jenny Lind. Known as the "Swedish Nightingale," Lind was one of the most famous singers in Europe, and a tour sponsored by P. T. Barnum made her equally famous in America (the tour is a subplot of Disney's 2017 biopic about Barnum, *The Greatest Showman*). Andersen's story "The Nightingale," which takes as its theme the relationship between art and royal society, is based in part on Lind. Scholars and biographers debate whether Andersen's attraction to Jenny Lind was sexual or spiritual. While early scholars considered Lind his great unrequited love, Wullschlager notes that even if he *did* feel a sexual attraction to Lind, he was also courting Henrik Stampe around the same time.[122] Moreover, Andersen's "utterly disembodied" descriptions of Lind "never approached the type of sensuality that was often at play in Andersen's texts when younger representatives of his own gender—whether in tight-fitting uniforms, leotards, or bare-chested—were within sight."[123] Certainly "The Nightingale" lacks the eroticism of some of his other tales.

The sensual descriptions of men in leotards or uniforms notwithstanding, Andersen maintained a detached, aesthetic relationship to physical expressions of desire. His travels on the continent, especially to France and Italy, had tested his chastity for decades. But only in the 1860s did he come close to surrender. He visited a Parisian brothel on August 30, 1866, and recorded the experience in his diary.[124] Andersen had thought Paris a lustful city since his first visit in 1833, so it makes sense that it was in Paris that he chose to "investigate" the brothels, which he visited four times between 1866 and 1868 (including while visiting the Paris Exhibition). At least according to the diary entries, the visits never moved beyond conversation: Andersen returned to his hotel room to enter a cross in his diary, indicating masturbation.[125] Hornemann, a close friend of Andersen's as well as a physician, referred to Andersen's sexuality as "ascetic."[126] His self-denial in his brothel visits and the platonic nature of his relationships with both men and women seem to support that conclusion.

Biographers differ in their precise conclusions about Andersen's sexuality: whether he was a homosexual, as Prince and Wullschlager suggest; or whether his denial of same-sex relationships was part of his self-conception as an artist, as Jens Andersen sees it; or whether his sexual preferences are a side issue, as Zipes believes. Andersen's coded record of his masturbation in his diaries might support an argument for "autoeroticism," an alternative Eve Sedgwick posits to challenge the hetero/homosexual binary.[127] Sedgwick offers this alternative precisely to demonstrate the limitations of our modern

94   CHAPTER THREE

definitions of sexuality, and ultimately, I see no need to confine Andersen to any particular category. It suffices to say that erotic longing was an important element of his works, and that that longing did not fit the approved standards of his time.

By the end the twentieth century, the rags-to-riches framework through which Andersen had presented his own life story had been surpassed by consideration of his sexuality. As the next sections will demonstrate, the shift is mirrored in the Walt Disney Company's adaptations of Andersen's tales, which engaged in different ways with Andersen's biography over a span of eighty years.

UGLY DUCKLINGS AND WALT DISNEY'S ANDERSEN ADAPTATIONS

Andersen first had the idea for "the story of a duck" in July 1842, over a year before it was published. The collection in which it appeared (and which also included "The Nightingale," based on his friend Jenny Lind) was the first of Andersen's books to receive unanimously positive reviews, both from Danish readers and from audiences throughout Europe. "The Ugly Duckling" quickly became his most popular tale, and its popularity was bolstered by Andersen's travels. He read "The Ugly Duckling" aloud so often that it became his "calling card" among "the top echelons and royal courts all over Europe."[128]

To many readers, "The Ugly Duckling" conveys the idea that innate attributes will eventually be recognized. Hearing the tale in his own voice, Andersen's friends and hosts would certainly have connected "The Ugly Duckling" to his biography. Even those who didn't meet him personally could have seen the connection, since short portraits of Andersen regularly accompanied his works. These biographical sketches depicted Andersen's childhood poverty and his youthful trials in Copenhagen as preludes to his inevitable recognition as a brilliant artist. By 1847, the distinction between his life and work had almost entirely vanished.[129] In that year Andersen published the first of his autobiographies, *Das Märchen meines Lebens ohne Dichtung* (promptly published in English as *The True Story of My Life*), which served as a prelude to a thirty-volume German edition of his collected works and emphasized his life as rags-to-riches story.

Walt Disney shared this interpretation of "The Ugly Duckling" (and of Andersen's life). He produced two versions of the tale in the *Silly Symphonies* series. Neither makes any mention of Andersen, but Disney was certainly thinking about the Danish author; he would soon begin work on the planned biopic. In the 1931 black-and-white short, a duckling (not a swan) is born among chickens, and even the mother turns her back on it.[130] Like the other shorts, the film builds its momentum with a series of gags, as the mother hen teaches her chicks to drink water and the duckling chases after worms and meets other animals on the farm. After a tornado destroys the farm (and results in more gags), the chicks find themselves trapped in the river, and the duck rescues them just before they tumble over a waterfall, earning the affection of the mother hen. This version (besides, oddly, setting an actual duck among chickens) promotes active heroism rather than physical beauty, but maintains the core lesson of unrecognized abilities.

The Ugly Duckling (1939), for which Disney won an Academy Award for Best Short Subject, begins with a father duck fretting while the mother sits on the eggs.[131] Four ducklings hatch first, and the hatching of the "ugly duckling" spurs an argument between the father and mother ducks. An accusation of infidelity is implied, though there is no dialogue in the film, only quacking. As in the 1931 cartoon, the mother duck tries to rid herself of the unwanted offspring, whose honk jars against the ducklings' quacks in a persistent auditory gag. The audio takes advantage of the sound quality that had been a hallmark of Disney's shorts since "Steamboat Willie." The ugly duckling looks at his reflection in a stream and is shocked at his own ugliness. Abandoned, he wanders alone, encountering blue jays who chase him away when they hear his discordant honk and a plastic duck that ignores him, until he finally meets a family of swans who honk just like he does. The film gives one final view of the original duck family, until the swan holds his head high and swims off into the sunset with his family. So, while the 1931 cartoon had rewarded a specific action, the later version is more consistent with Andersen's tale (and his autobiographies); it promotes the ideology that innate gifts will inevitably be recognized and rewarded. The difference likely results from Disney's growing familiarity with Andersen's biography.

Andersen wrote his autobiography while traveling in southern Europe. He sent each part back to Edvard Collin, who served as his editor and who toned down Andersen's "sniveling" and "vanity," character traits Collin found especially annoying.[132] Collin's reaction hints at another reading of "The Ugly Duckling," an interpretation that undermines the parable associated with the tale. Zipes reads "The Ugly Duckling" as "an apology for Andersen's elitist thinking," and argues that the tale conveys "a secret disdain for the masses and his longing to be accepted by court society."[133] This reading is supported both by the context of the story's genesis and by the tale itself. Andersen began "The Ugly Duckling" during a summer visit to the country estates of various aristocratic Danish friends. He must certainly have had in mind his own relationship to the upper classes, on whom he depended for patronage.[134] In Andersen's tale, the narrative perspective begins not with the ugly duckling but with his mother, who tries her best to be optimistic. In response to the other ducks, who suggest the ugly duckling is perhaps a turkey, she responds, "See how nicely he uses his legs, and how straight he holds himself. He's my very own son after all, and quite good-looking if you look at him properly."[135] This defense, of course, accepts the premise that looks are important, and the mother duck also teaches her children obeisance to the "noble" ducks. She tells them, "Don't turn your toes in. A well-bred duckling turns his toes way out." The other ducks are cruel to the ugly duckling, who is "sad because he was so desperately ugly, and because he was the laughing stock of the whole barnyard."[136] The duckling is sad not only because the other birds make fun of him but also because he internalizes their judgment about his appearance.

The ugly duckling's acceptance of his own ugliness is reaffirmed after he runs away. Observing the swans, he thinks that he "had never seen birds so beautiful." His reaction is consistent with his earlier attitude: he loves the birds because they're beautiful. When the swans return, the duckling tells himself, "I shall fly near these royal birds, and they will peck me to bits because I, who am so very ugly, dare to go near them. But I don't care. Better be killed by them than to be nipped by the ducks." He approaches them and bows deferentially, and it's only in this submission that he sees his image in the water. The story ends, "Being born in a duck yard does not matter, if only you are hatched from a swan's egg."[137] That last sentence is typically given as the moral of the tale, but in the context of the story it is far more conservative than it is usually interpreted. Instead of recognizing personal traits, the final sentence reinforces the importance of parentage and heredity.

"The Ugly Duckling" can also been read as a parable of Andersen's sexuality. The duckling initially accepts the dominant discourse of those around him. When expelled by his family he has difficulty overcoming the feelings of aberrance that he has internalized. But once he finds a community that accepts him, he gains "a fuller understanding of his own good fortune, and of beauty when he met with it."[138] It's a story about recognizing one's self worth, regardless of what others think. Andersen felt ostracized by his own difference and was unable to reconcile his desires with the normative expectations of those around him. "The Ugly Duckling" could be seen as a hopeful fantasy of how he might thrive under different societal expectations.

The contrasts among these varying interpretations underscore the complexity of Andersen's tale and the different ways his biography can be interpreted. This third interpretation differs from Andersen's autobiography and from Disney's cartoons because it leaves open the alternative that George

Eliot imagines in *Middemarch*. It was always possible that the duckling would *not* find acceptance among his "own oary-footed kind."[139] This interpretation also takes a different view of Andersen's personality. He is not, as Zipes would have it, an obsequious writer groveling for acceptance from aristocrats. Instead, he is a tragic figure inhibited by social expectations. This tragedy, that unlike the ugly duckling Andersen never found a community in which he could express his true desires, is evident in another of Andersen's tales, written nearly two decades after "The Ugly Duckling" but using the same metaphor: a society of ducks.

"In the Duckyard" begins when a songbird is chased into an enclosure inhabited by ducks and chickens. The ducks initially take care of him, fixing his broken wing and showing him off to other birds that visit. But they eventually grow annoyed with his singing, and after remarking, "I'll have to teach you good manners," the duck who had been taking care of him "bit off the Songbird's head, and he lay there dead."[140] The other birds gather around and initially pity the songbird, but the story ends with a coldhearted remark: "Let us now think about getting something in our stomachs. . . . If one of our playthings is broken, why, we have plenty more of them!" Andersen had earlier envisioned the artist as a songbird in "The Nightingale," published in the same collection with "The Ugly Duckling." That tale was inspired by the "Swedish Nightingale" Jenny Lind, but its theme of underappreciated artists equally applies to Andersen. "In the Duckyard" unites the two earlier tales. The brutal ending reveals that even in the 1860s, when Andersen had been near-universally revered for almost two decades, he still felt the sting of being an outsider, the "plaything" of the upper classes. The sexual and class anxieties evident in his early tales persisted throughout his life. He never found his community of swans.

Andersen wrote in Danish, of course, and my English quotations in this book rely on a translation by Jean Hersholt. The Danish-born Hersholt edited a collection of Andersen's letters and published several articles about him. His translation, *The Complete Andersen* (1949), remains the standard version.[141] Walt Disney owned a copy of Hersholt's *Hans Christian Andersen: Fairy Tales* (1942).[142] But during his lifetime, Hersholt was known not as a scholar but as an actor. He had a successful career starring in silent films and in the long-running radio series *Dr. Christian*, whose eponymous character is named for Hans Christian Andersen. Hersholt portrayed Shirley Temple's grandfather in *Heidi* (1937), released the same year as *Snow White*, and from 1945–49 he was president of the Academy of Motion Picture Arts and Sciences. The Academy continues to honor him annually with the Jean Hersholt Humanitarian Award.[143] Besides owning a copy of his Andersen

98 CHAPTER THREE

translation, Disney knew Hersholt personally. In 1948, during Hersholt's tenure as president of the Academy, Disney urged him to consider an Academy Award for James Baskett, who had played Uncle Remus in Disney's *Song of the South*. Hersholt also granted Disney access to his extensive collection of Anderseniana.[144]

It's hard to gauge the extent of Hersholt's influence on Disney's adaptations, if any. But by 1940 Disney was planning a feature film based on Andersen's works. In 1939 (the year *The Ugly Duckling* won an Oscar), he registered two titles with the copyright office: "The Story of Hans Christian Andersen" and "Tales of Hans Christian Andersen." Samuel Goldwyn, who had already registered "The Life of Hans Christian Andersen," asked Disney to withdraw the former title, which implied a biographical film rather than just the tales. In March 1940, Disney suggested they collaborate. A "flurry of correspondence" resulted in three scripts, but they were deemed inappropriate; two of them purportedly included several scenes set in a Copenhagen bordello.[145] Al Perkins (who wrote the research report for *Alice in Wonderland* I discuss in chapter 2) and Dick Creedon came up with another idea, and, on September 17, 1943, the *Hollywood Reporter* announced the collaboration.[146] The planned film would mix live-action and animation, a combination Disney was also considering for other projects, including *Alice in Wonderland* (as I discuss in the previous chapter). Goldwyn would produce the live-action biographical scenes, which would frame Disney's animated versions of tales.[147]

Disney had plenty of prior work to draw on, since his studio had worked on several Andersen adaptations the previous decade. "The Ugly Duckling" was not the only Andersen story that Disney had attempted as part of the *Silly Symphonies* series. In 1936, Ted Sears and Merrill de Maris were developing a cartoon short based on "The Emperor's New Clothes," but couldn't find a strong enough ending.[148] A second crew picked up the story in 1938, this time as a Mickey Mouse cartoon. Mickey, Donald, and Goofy star as the poor tailors who provide the emperor with "invisible" thread when they can't pay their tax bill. The storywriters still couldn't make it work, though. They felt the tale lacked sufficiently sympathetic characters and they were reticent to feature Mickey, Donald, and Goofy as dishonest tailors.[149] Disney writers also attempted a version of "The Nightingale," first in the late 1930s, then again in 1960, when T. Hee and Bob Kurtz made a stop-motion paper sculpture film, and again in the 1980s as a Mickey Mouse sketch for a sequel to *Fantasia*.[150] The Danish illustrator Kay Nielson, who drew the storyboards for the *Bald Mountain* sequence of *Fantasia* (1940), also produced pastel sketches for "The Little Mermaid," though at the time "Andersen's parable of Christian sacrifice also seemed too bleak to film."[151]

Nielsen's sketches were eventually used as a basis for the 1989 film, which credits him as a 'visual developer.'"[152]

In the spring of 1947 a list of potential Disney features included both *Treasure Island* and the Hans Christian Andersen feature. But the profits from *Song of the South* did not justify the labor and expense that had gone into the film, and the studio became convinced that the combination of live-action and animation was not worth it.[153] Disney may also have shied away from a biography of Andersen because the bleak endings of his stories contrast with the studio's reputation for optimism[154] or because crediting another author would threaten the "auteur" persona he had developed.[155]

Whatever the reason, Goldwyn completed the biopic without Disney. The resulting film, *Hans Christian Andersen* (1952), remains the best-known portrayal of Andersen's life. Danny Kaye portrays Andersen as a fanciful cobbler (Andersen's father's profession) who is at odds with the community because he's always telling stories to children. The film features versions of "The Emperor's New Clothes," "Thumbelina," and "The Ugly Duckling," the latter of which is told to a child whose father, a newspaperman, prints it. Exiled from his small town, Andersen travels to Copenhagen. In a plot that perhaps combines his love interests Jenny Lind and Harald Scharff, he falls in love with a ballerina and writes "The Little Mermaid" for her, which she turns into a ballet.[156] Kaye's performance in the film led many viewers to conflate the actor's life with "the film's biographically simplified Andersen," as Kaye became "indelibly associated with children."[157] In 1954 (the year he starred in *White Christmas*, which beat out Disney's *20,000 League's Under the Sea* for the year's highest-grossing feature), Kaye was appointed the first Goodwill Ambassador for the United Nations International Children's Emergency Fund (UNICEF). A quarter-century later, he hosted two TV specials for Disney, one celebrating the twenty-fifth anniversary of Disneyland in 1980, the other, the 1982 opening of EPCOT. One can only speculate about what Kaye's relationship with Disney might have been during the intervening period, had the Disney-Goldwyn collaboration come to fruition.

Hans Christian Andersen culminates with a balletic performance of "The Little Mermaid." There is a long tradition of adapting Andersen's tales as ballets, and Goldwyn's choice to feature ballet may have been partly inspired by the success of Michael Powell and Emeric Pressburger's film *The Red Shoes* (1948), an Andersen adaptation that, a few years earlier, had won two Academy Awards and had been nominated for Best Picture. But Andersen also had close associations with the art form. As a child he had hoped to be a dancer and auditioned for Copenhagen ballerina Anna Margrethe Schall, and the nature of his relationship with the ballet dancer Harald Scharff has been the subject of much biographical speculation.[158]

The choice to conclude with "The Little Mermaid," rather than "The Ugly Duckling," also presents a different view of Andersen's life. The Danish-born choreographer Kim Brandstrup made a similar choice in her own version of Andersen's life, *The Anatomy of a Storyteller*, which she created to celebrate the bicentennial of Andersen's birth. Brandstrup noted that people would often whistle Kaye's "The Ugly Duckling" when she told them about the project. She hoped that her work would introduce audiences to a grown-up version of Anderson, balancing out the "chirpy, sentimental Hollywood biopic."[159] Brandstrup's ballet, with its emphasis on Andersen's sexuality and outsider status, reveals how profoundly perspectives on the fairy-tale author's biography had shifted between the 1950s and the early 2000s.

Brandstrup believed that "The Little Mermaid," with its theme of illicit romantic desire, best captured the understanding of Andersen's life that she wanted to convey.[160] The centrality of this tale, rather than "The Ugly Duckling," had been building over the previous two decades, due in no small part to a Disney animated musical. Disney's *The Little Mermaid* (1989) marked a new era both for the Walt Disney Company and for approaches to Andersen's biography.

HANS CHRISTIAN ANDERSEN AND THE DISNEY RENAISSANCE

Although is hard to fathom, given the company's current global success, in the 1980s the Walt Disney Company was facing threats of bankruptcy and hostile takeover. Michael Eisner, who began his tenure as CEO of the Walt Disney Company in 1984, is often credited with turning the company around. The early years of Eisner's tenure are often referred to as the "Disney Renaissance." Under Eisner's leadership, Disney purchased ABC Studios and ESPN, and began expanding the company into the global media empire it remains today. But in many ways the Disney company of the 1990s represented a return to its roots in the 1930s. Walt Disney had expressed a fondness for the Victorian period, and Eisner, consciously continuing Walt's legacy, felt a similar connection. The first three animated films produced under Eisner's leadership all adapted Victorian texts: *The Great Mouse Detective* (1986, based on a children's series about a mouse living under Sherlock Holmes's floorboards); *Oliver & Company* (1988, based on Charles Dickens's *Oliver Twist*); and *The Little Mermaid* (1989, based on Hans Christian Andersen's tale). In 1991, *Newsweek* praised Disney for keeping to its traditions even as studios like MGM and Warner Bros. were becoming "impersonal corporate giants."[161] The return to the Victorian period in general, and to Andersen in particular, helped Disney remain synonymous with family entertainment in general and animation in particular.

The Little Mermaid is not the only Eisner-era Disney film to draw on Andersen's tales. In *Lilo & Stitch* (2002), the alien Stitch chooses "The Ugly Duckling" from a shelf. Lilo tells him the duck is "sad because he's all alone and nobody wants him," until on the next page his family finds him and the duckling is happy "because he knows where he belongs."[162] *Fantasia 2000* also includes an Andersen story, "The Steadfast Tin Soldier." The tale follows a similar theme to "The Ugly Duckling," and even features wax swans (animals that, in Andersen's oeuvre, often represent the aristocracy) swimming around "a marvelous castle of cardboard."[163] Of twenty-five tin soldiers, all look alike except one, who has only one leg. "But just you see," writes Andersen, "he'll be the remarkable one." The soldier falls in love with a paper lady in the castle, who has her leg raised like a ballerina (and so appears to have only one leg). The toy soldier is knocked out a window, then undergoes a series of mishaps. He is eventually eaten by a fish that ends up in the kitchen of his original home. He is returned to the other toys, only to be thrown into the fireplace. The ballerina is blown into the fireplace as well, and the two burn up together. As he burns, the soldier wonders whether the heat he feels is from the flames or from his love.

"The Steadfast Tin Soldier" was the first of Andersen's purely original fairy tales, with no folk-tale precursor.[164] In the soldier's loyalty, the longing for someone of a higher class, and the ambivalent ending, the story prefigures themes that appear frequently in Andersen's tales. These themes, and the envy of the ballerina, link "The Steadfast Tin Soldier" to Andersen's life. It is one of his best-known stories, and the subject of a 1981 ballet by George Balanchine. Disney may have been spurred towards its own version, however, by the success of another film about living toys. *Toy Story* (1995), which received three Oscar nominations, was based on the Pixar short *Tin Toy* (1988), which had won the Oscar for Best Animated Short Film.

Toy Story 2 (1999) appeared shortly before *Fantasia 2000*, and audiences would likely have made the connection between that series and the toys coming to life in *Fantasia 2000*. Set to Dmitri Shostakovich's *Piano Concerto No. 2*, "The Steadfast Tin Soldier" cuts the number of soldiers from twenty-five to five and enhances the Jack-in-the-Box's villainy. In Andersen's tale, the "black bogey" threatens the tin soldier, and is mentioned, though not directly blamed, whenever something bad happens. When the soldier is knocked out the window it is unclear "whether the bogey did it, or there was a gust of wind," and when at the end a boy throws the soldier into the fire the "black bogey in the snuffbox must have put him up to it."[165] In *Fantasia 2000*, the jack-in-the-box's actions are more direct. He leers at the ballerina in the opening segment, grabs the tin soldier just as he is about to grasp the ballerina's hand, and, after a short fight, knocks the tin soldier out the window and traps the ballerina under a glass. As in Andersen's tale, the soldier returns after being swallowed by a fish, and this time it is the jack-in-the-box who is tossed into a fire at the end. Disney thus replaces Andersen's sad irony with poetic justice, consequently removing the biographical element of Andersen's tale.

Under Eisner's leadership, the studio planned to release another *Fantasia* movie, which was also to include a Hans Christian Andersen tale, "The Little Match Girl." The pathos of that story is unavoidable, and biographers link it to Andersen's own experiences with poverty and rejection.[166] The first paragraph introduces the "poor little girl, bareheaded and barefoot," who is "shivering with cold and hunger" while trying, unsuccessfully, to sell matches during a snowstorm.[167] For fear of being beaten, she doesn't dare go home without earning the money from the matches. She burns the matches, and with each one sees an image of warmth: first a stove, then a table with a "shining dinner service," then a Christmas tree, and finally her grandmother's face. She burns the remaining bundle of matches in an attempt to keep view of her grandmother, and "both of them flew in brightness and joy above the earth, very, very high, and up there was neither cold, nor hunger, nor fear." The girl's body is found the next day, and the story ends with the remark that none of the passersby "imagined what beautiful things she had seen, and how happily she had gone with her old grandmother into the bright New Year." That last image provides a touch of optimism, which may have inspired Disney's animators.

Though the *Fantasia* film was eventually scrapped, the segment featuring "The Little Match Girl" was completed and released separately as a short in 2006, accompanied by Alexander Borodin's *String Quartet No. 2*. The short keeps the two first fantasies and combines the others into a single scene, a sleigh ride bringing the girl to her grandmother's where she sees a Christmas tree. The film begins in primarily gray tones, brightening into color when the girl lights the matches. It ends with the girl's grandmother finding her hunched over in the street, and only the visuals (the grandmother, initially in gray, brightens into color when she picks the girl up) imply that this is also a vision.[168] The short film maintains the pathos of Andersen's tale instead of adding a happy ending. Even more than the other Andersen adaptations, it maintains a fidelity to Andersen's text that may result from a commitment to reflecting his life story.

Fantasia 2000 and *Lilo & Stitch* came late in Eisner's tenure, by which time animators and directors had begun to turn against him. Their letter in support of Roy E. Disney (who had challenged Eisner's policies) claims, "Mr. Eisner's rejection of Walt Disney's heritage has been a colossal failure. . . . A unique American art form, the Disney cartoon feature, hangs precariously in the balance."[169] A decade earlier, however, Eisner had helped reignite that unique American art form with an Andersen adaptation closely linked to the fairy-tale author's biography.

Ron Clements (who was at the time working on another Victorian adaptation, released in 1986 as *The Great Mouse Detective*) first pitched an animated musical based on "The Little Mermaid" at a story meeting in 1985. The idea was initially rejected because it seemed too similar to *Splash* (1984), the romantic comedy about a mermaid and a human released the year before by Disney's subsidiary, Touchstone Pictures. But Eisner liked the idea, and he and Jeffrey Katzenberg encouraged Clements to pursue it.[170] Howard Ashman, who had worked on *Oliver & Company*, brought along his collaborator Alan Menken, with whom he had written the hit 1982 musical *Little Shop of Horrors*. The two began a partnership that would characterize the start of the Disney Renaissance.

The Little Mermaid was well-received. Critic Roger Ebert wrote that the film restored "the magic of animation," and praised Disney for presenting a "fully realized female character who thinks and acts independently, even rebelliously, instead of hanging around passively."[171] Academic readers, however, found the film more troubling. Like *Fantasia 2000*'s "Steadfast Tin Soldier," *The Little Mermaid* locates evil in a single character, Ursula the Sea Witch, excising the Christian worldview and the moral ambiguity of Andersen's version. Waller Hastings connects these changes to the "conservative American ideology of the 1980s" and to President George H. W. Bush's "transformation of the Gulf War from a geopolitical conflict into a crusade against the person of Saddam Hussein."[172] And despite Ariel's rebelliousness and independence (the traits Ebert highlights), feminist critics could not ignore the fact that she literally gives up her voice in pursuit of a man. *The Little Mermaid* provides the titular endpoint for *From Mouse to Mermaid*, a collection of essays critical of Disney. (I discuss those arguments in the next chapter, considering *The Little Mermaid* in the context of "Princess Culture.")

In light of Andersen's biography, however, critiques of the film's conservative politics or its marriage plot are less notable than interpretations of the musical as a parable for sexuality. Andersen's "The Little Mermaid" has been called "an existential and poetic reflection and clarification of his love for Edvard [Collin]."[173] This biographical connection provides one reason for interpreting Disney's adaptation as reflecting contemporary politics of sexuality, as well as geopolitics and gender ideologies. The production of *The Little Mermaid* at the Disney studio in the 1980s reinforces the connection. As Sean Griffin has pointed out, many films that Disney and its subsidiary labels released during the period—such as *Down and Out in Beverly Hills* (1986), *Three Men and a Baby* (1987), *Big Business* (1988), *Dead Poets Society* (1989), *Newsies* (1992), *Swing Kids* (1993), and *Tombstone* (1993)—directly or indirectly raised questions of sexual identity.[174] These films were influenced not only by Disney's financial struggles in the previous years (the struggles that Eisner was hired to alleviate) but also by changing attitudes toward sexual identities. "When Disney moved to find new markets," Griffin writes, "it was probably inevitable that the studio would reach out to the untapped 'gay community' for their dollars."[175] Taking the studio's output as a whole, including animated and live-action films as well as television shows like *Ellen* (1994–98), Griffin sees "Disney's increased manifest representation of homosexuality" as a "momentous event for both the company and lesbian/ gay culture."[176]

The films of the Eisner era particularly embraced the aesthetics of camp, the "signpost of contemporary popular culture and of pre-Stonewall queer-ness."[177] Perhaps the strongest link between Disney and camp is the frequent featuring of Bette Midler, who became almost synonymous with Disney during in the 1980s and who "began her career by singing in gay male bath-houses in New York City, an experience that helped her to fashion a camp star persona as 'the Divine Miss M.'"[178] Midler starred predominantly in live-action films, but her connection to Disney helps explain the otherwise odd character of Georgette in *Oliver & Company*. And Midler is far from the only link between Disney and camp. Ursula, the villainous half-octopus in *The Little Mermaid*, was based on the cult transvestite star Divine, and the song "Under the Sea" was conceived a parody of Busby Berkeley, who has been called "the patron saint of movie camp."[179]

Animated features are collaborations surpassing the contributions of par-ticular individuals, but scholars have noted that several of the most important contributors to *The Little Mermaid* were openly gay. The animator Andreas Deja, for example, "has announced in various interviews that his sexual ori-entation has had its effect on the characters he draws."[180] Deja is known for working on male villains like *Aladdin*'s Jafar and *The Lion King*'s Scar, and hypermuscular men like King Triton in *The Little Mermaid* and the epony-mous hero of *Hercules* (1997). Gaston, from *Beauty and the Beast*, brings the two types together.[181] These characters "spectacularize the male body in a way rarely seen in Disney animation prior to *The Little Mermaid*."[182]

ANIMATING HANS CHRISTIAN ANDERSEN

But the artist whose sexuality is most often connected to *The Little Mermaid* is the lyricist Howard Ashman. Ashman was diagnosed with HIV in 1988 and died of AIDS in 1991, shortly after the first screening of *Beauty and the Beast*. That film, which is dedicated to Ashman, would earn him and Menken two Academy Awards; it was also nominated for Best Picture and won the Golden Globe for best musical or comedy. In the wake of the film's success, a high-water mark in the Disney Renaissance, CBS News anchor Dan Rather published his interpretation of the film in the *Los Angeles Times*. The Beast, Rather wrote, "reminded me of somebody else, somebody I've seen over and over as I've covered the news in the last decade: a Person With AIDS."[183] A viewer might feel the Beast's loneliness and frustration more acutely, Rather argued, if they connected the magic spell he is under to AIDS, "with the same arbitrary and harshly abbreviated limitations on time." He connects this interpretation with Ashman's death and draws on Susan Sontag's *Illness as Metaphor* to suggest that *Beauty and the Beast* is the first AIDS film to achieve such widespread success. The next year, Tom Hanks won Best Actor for his role as an attorney with AIDS in *Philadelphia*.

Sean Griffin extends Rather's argument, seeing the musical number "Kill the Beast" as a parallel to the violent panic of some political and religious responses to the spread of AIDS.[184] Though Disney had a tradition of "gay-tinged" villains, Ashman's musical numbers allow "mainstream audiences and reviewers to positively revel in the campiness of their villainy."[185] Songs Ashman wrote for Disney's heroines also reveal a shift away from "wish songs" like *Snow White*'s "Some Day My Prince Will Come" or *Cinderella*'s "A Dream Is a Wish Your Heart Makes," which had expressed a desire to find happiness in everyday (heteronormative) life. By contrast, Ashman's heroines "specifically want to forsake the 'normal' world and find happiness somewhere else."[186] Both *Beauty and the Beast* and *The Little Mermaid* depict "a gay dilemma of trying to choose between different worlds—one explicitly associated with family and marriage, the other configured along the lines of fantasy, escape, and forbidden romance."[187] While these films acknowledge "the fears and misdirected anger that both sides feel," they ultimately "bear a stamp of reconciliation and acceptance." *The Little Mermaid* ends with King Triton creating a rainbow, a symbol of gay pride that, in the film, builds a metaphorical bridge between the two worlds.[188] The ending of the Disney adaptation, in this interpretation, finally achieves the acceptance that Hans Christian Andersen sought his entire life.

On its surface, *The Little Mermaid*, the story of girl literally giving up her voice for a man, supports the notion that Disney's films uphold a regressive hegemony. The film delivers the heteronormative ending it had promised from the beginning. The argument I've just made, that the 1989 animated musical connects to Andersen's sexuality, requires reading allegorically and metaphorically, recognizing the undertones of camp aesthetics, the auteurship of openly gay artists like Deja and Ashman, and veiled references like the rainbow at the end and Ursula being based on Divine. But audiences have been more than willing to read between the lines, whether they come to bury Disney's films or to praise them. In the 1990s, Disney films were condemned for upholding patriarchal and imperialist values.[189] Now, in the 2020s, condemnation comes from the other side of the political spectrum, as conservatives accuse Disney of bending to a progressive agenda not just when it comes to gender and sexuality but also issues of racial representation. The politics of interpreting both Disney's output and its corporate practices are now characterized by the tension between these viewpoints. And as this chapter's final section will demonstrate, a Hans Christian Andersen adaptation is again at the center of the discussion.

ANDERSEN AND THE POLITICS OF TWENTY-FIRST CENTURY INTERPRETATION

The Little Mermaid was released at "a moment of unprecedented cultural richness, cohesion, and assertiveness for many lesbian and gay adults."[190] A few months later, a group of 3,000 gays and lesbians from central Florida coordinated to wear red shirts to Walt Disney World, inaugurating a tradition, Gay Days at Disney, which by 2010 was drawing 150,000 visitors a year and had become "one of the largest gay-pride events in the world."[191] Gay Days is not an official Disney event, but the company generally evinces "a progressive attitude toward LGBT people," not only in the content of its films but also in its corporate practices.[192] In 2016, the company threatened to stop filming in Georgia in protest of an anti-LGBTQ+ bill.[193] And, in 2022, then-CEO Bob Chapek announced the company's opposition to a Florida bill restricting teachers from discussing LGBTQ topics.[194]

Not everyone has been pleased by Disney's progressive attitude. In the 1990s, Gay Days at Disney sparked a backlash from religious and conservative groups, with some calling the company "sex perverts and anti-family feminists."[195] The Southern Baptist Convention boycotted Disney for almost a decade.[196] The response to Chapek's announcement became even more heated, and likely contributed to Chapek's removal as CEO (his predecessor, Bob Iger, returned to fill the role). Florida governor Ron DeSantis revoked the special tax district granted to Walt Disney World, and in May

2023, Disney filed a lawsuit alleging DeSantis had violated the company's constitutional rights.

Headlines about Disney's feud with the state of Florida coincided with a controversy about its live-action remake of *The Little Mermaid* (2023). The film continues the tradition begun with *Alice in Wonderland* (2010), as Disney adapts its own animated musicals with live performers. Halle Bailey stars in the title role, and outlandish claims circulated online that Disney was being unfaithful to the original tale by casting a Black actress. Several media outlets picked up the story, often pointing out both that mermaids are fictional characters without race and that Disney's 1989 cartoon was not in fact the "original tale." Writing for *Vox*, Aja Romano called Andresen's version "a sublimated allegory for a closeted queer man."[197] A *Forbes* article quotes a Twitter user calling Andersen's mermaid "a queer man's self-insertion character, longing to be able to be in a relationship with another man."[198] That publications like *Vox* and *Forbes* not only mention Andersen but make confident assertions about his sexuality demonstrates how mainstream this biographical viewpoint had become.

But it was not *The Little Mermaid* that brought Andersen's sexuality into public discourse. A decade before Bailey was cast as Ariel, Disney's *Frozen* (2013) offered an alternative to the heteronormative marriage plot typically associated with Princess franchise. (I discuss Disney Princesses in chapter 4.) Released to audiences both attuned to subtext and accustomed to broadcasting interpretations on social media, *Frozen*, which is based on Andersen's "The Snow Queen," was frequently linked to Andersen's life, and especially his sexuality. It was also a blockbuster, becoming the fifth-highest grossing film of all time (and the highest-grossing animated movie by a wide margin) and winning two Academy Awards, for Best Animated Feature and for Best Original Song.[199] That success brought attention to Andersen, whose biography was of particular interest to a culture wrestling with questions of gender and sexuality identity.

"The Snow Queen," one of Andersen's longest fairy tales, is divided into seven parts. The first story tells of a "terribly bad hobgoblin" who creates "a mirror which had this peculiar power: everything good and beautiful that was reflected in it seemed to dwindle to almost nothing at all, while everything that was worthless and ugly became most conspicuous and even uglier than ever."[200] The mirror shatters into tiny fragments that lodged into people's eyes and "made them see only the bad side of things," and into people's hearts, turning them to ice. The second story is set "in the big city" and tells of two children, Kay and Gerda, who "were not brother and sister, but they loved each other just as much as if they had been." The eponymous

Snow Queen is first mentioned when Kay's grandmother refers to the falling snow as "white bees swarming," and he asks if these bees also have a queen. When she tells him about the Snow Queen he says, "let her come! . . . I would put her on the hot stove and melt her." She later frightens him when she appears in the window, but nothing happens until summer returns and he gets a shard of the goblin's mirror in his eye. Kay's behavior turns wicked, and that winter he disappears with a mysterious white sleigh that appears in the town square and takes him to the Snow Queen.

The remaining stories tell of Gerda's journey to rescue Kay. A witch hides the roses in her flower garden so that they won't remind Gerda of Kay. Two crows bring Gerda to meet a prince and a princess in a castle, and then she is kidnapped by robbers and befriends a reindeer who knows of the Snow Queen's summer palace. She learns of the sliver in Kay's heart, and the reindeer asks a Finn woman for a magical gift. "No power that I could give could be as great as that which she already has," the woman tells him. "Strength lies in her heart, because she is such a sweet, innocent child." Gerda rescues Kay and they return to the city, where it is summertime.[201]

The grandmother's first mention of the Snow Queen grounds the fairy tale in the oral tradition from which Andersen drew much of his inspiration, and several tropes link this tale to other Andersen works. As in many of Andersen's tales, the role of art and artists recurs throughout. The opening story comments on art's ability to mirror the world. References to picture books insist that reality is preferable to representation and the flowers in the witch's garden recite their own fairy tales. The talking flowers in the witch's garden are reminiscent of Andersen's tale, "Little Ida's Flowers." Birds feature prominently in Andersen's tales, and "The Snow Queen" includes swallows who insist on Kay's being alive, crows who bring her to the castle, and pigeons who tell her they have seen Kay. Andersen's father had been a cobbler, and shoes are often a powerful metaphor in his stories, most notably "The Red Shoes." In "The Snow Queen," Gerda's "dearest possession" is her pair of red shoes.[202]

But the tale's visual imagery is perhaps even more captivating than its thematic richness. The Snow Queen appears "dressed in the finest white gauze which looked as if it had been made from millions of star-shaped flakes. She was beautiful and she was graceful, but she was ice—shining, glittering ice." Her palace has walls of "driven snow," and the "windows and doors were the knife-edged wind. There were more than a hundred halls, shaped as the snow had drifted, and the largest of these extended for many a mile. All were lighted by the flare of the Northern Lights." Disney's animators recognized the "obvious cinematic possibilities" of these visual descriptions.[203] The *Frozen* production visited an ice hotel in Quebec and the Norwegian fjords, hoping to gain a better sense of how to bring Andersen's images to life.[204] The studio also developed a new technology to render the snow as animation.[205]

The real challenge Disney faced, however, was creating a narrative to justify those visuals. The studio began working on "The Snow Queen" at least as early as the 1940s, when a concept painting was produced for the Goldwyn collaboration. Over the next seventy-five years, Disney Imagineers attempted adaptations of "The Snow Queen" in various mediums, including a theme-park ride designed by Marc Davis in the early 1970s and a stage show written by Alan Menken for Disney's Tokyo theme park in 2006.[206] Several writers, including Harvey Fierstein (who won a Tony Award for *Mulan*) and Glen Keane (who worked as an animator on *Tangled*), also pitched the story as an animated feature film.[207] The basic idea behind *Frozen* was evident a decade before the film's release, in storyboards Mary Jane Ruggels presented for a "Snow Queen feature." Ruggels suggested bringing Andersen's tale into the Disney Princess franchise. In Andersen's tale, the crow tells Gerda about a princess who "made up her mind to marry as soon as she could find the sort of husband who could give a good answer when anyone spoke to him."[208] Ruggels suggested making this princess the Snow Queen herself, and giving the suitors the challenge to melt her heart. In Ruggels words, the character would be a "terrible bitch. . . . When her suitors try to melt her heart, the Snow Queen freezes them."[209] Remnants of Ruggels's idea are evident in *Frozen*, especially in the character of Prince Hans, the suitor who aims to take over Arendelle.

Once Disney decided to not to make the Snow Queen the villain, however, they were left with little narrative tension. The solution, says producer Peter Del Vecho, was to make the two protagonists sisters, humanizing the Snow Queen by depicting her childhood relationship.[210] Gerda, renamed Anna, is the princess who is pursued by the suitor, Hans. Kay's character is divided between Elsa, whom Anna tries to rescue, and Kristoff, Anna's love interest. The resulting story differs substantially from Andersen's "The Snow Queen." "There is snow and there is ice and there is a Queen," says Del Vecho, "but other than that, we depart from it quite a bit."[211] Fidelity to an original tale was not a priority. In fact, the link to Andersen himself may have been just as important as the narrative of "The Snow Queen."

Andersen's biography factored into the production of *Frozen*. To start with, Disney writers incorporated a second Andersen tale, "The Snow Man." Written late in his life, this tale begins with a snowman complaining that it is "so bitterly cold that my whole body crackles."[212] He has a staring contest with the sun, refusing to blink at its glare while wishing he could move and slide like the boys who made him. When he voices his wish, a dog tells him,

"The sun will teach you how to run. I saw your predecessor last winter, and before that *his* predecessor. Away! Away! And away they all go!" A young couple approaches the snowman, marveling at the beauty of the trees and bushes in winter, which "looked like a forest of white coral, while every twig seemed smothered with glittering white flowers." They remark that summer "can't show us a lovelier sight," and include the snowman in their praise. The snowman asks the dog about them, and he tells about the master's family and household, and how he used to live in the house and warm himself by the stove, "which is the finest thing in the world at this time of year." The snowman peers through the window at the stove and a "very strange feeling swept over" him. He doesn't understand it, "but all people who aren't snow men know that feeling." The dog warns him that he'll melt, but he remains enamored of the stove. As the weather gets colder, "it was just the sort of weather a Snow Man should most thoroughly enjoy. But he didn't enjoy it; indeed, how could he enjoy anything when he was so stove-sick?" As the Snow Man begins to melt, it becomes evident that he was built around a wooden pole, a stove rake, to which the dog attributes the snowman's feelings. The tale ends abruptly as little girls in the house sing a song welcoming spring. The last sentence is: "Nobody thought any more about the Snow Man."[213]

Those familiar with *Frozen* will connect this synopsis to the snowman Olaf, a comic sidekick who sings the song "In Summer," which centers on his desire to be warm.[214] Later in the film, Olaf lights a fire and is enamored by a stove as he rescues Anna. The core of that joke is plausibly drawn from Andersen's tale, and Disney writers must have recognized the humor of a snowman in love with a stove. Read biographically, however, "The Snow Man" treats themes that appear often in Andersen tales: unsanctioned love and the neglect of beauty. The Snow Man desires to be a part of a community from which he is excluded, and his desires are seen as inappropriate, even dangerous. Yet his feelings are nevertheless natural, and "all people who aren't snow men know that feeling."[215] The image of the stove-rake at the core of his body underscores this naturalness, while the tale's final line comments on how quickly beautiful objects are forgotten. Andersen had visited Harald Scharff in Munich about a month before writing "The Snow Man," and Wullschlager interprets the tale as a "veiled, self-mocking autobiography" expressing "Andersen's view of love as a burning, unreciprocated pain."[216] While *Frozen* ignores the tale's tragedy in favor of its comic elements, the choice to incorporate a second Andersen tale underscores the relationship with his biography.

Frozen's Olaf belongs to a Disney tradition of comic sidekicks who accompany the princess protagonists, but in this case, the character also plays an important thematic role. Viewers are primed by the first half of the film, and its link to the Disney Princess genre, to anticipate a marriage plot. Early in the film, Anna meets Hans, and the two sing a duet, "Love Is an Open Door." After Elsa accidentally freezes Anna'a heart, Kristoff brings her to the magical trolls, "love experts" who explain that "only an act of true love can thaw a frozen heart." They suggest a solution that forms the climax of Disney films from *Snow White* to *Sleeping Beauty* to *The Little Mermaid*: true love's kiss. But when Anna returns to Prince Hans, he turns out to be a villain. Olaf helps rescue her and asks, "What happened to your kiss?" "It wasn't true love," Anna explains, and says she doesn't know what love is. Olaf tells her it is "putting someone else's needs before yours." Anna looks up to see Kristoff, who has put her needs before his own, and in a different film that realization would be the romantic climax. But the primary narrative conflict—Anna's frozen heart and Elsa's inability to control her ice powers—has yet to be resolved. In the next scene, as Hans attacks Elsa, Anna steps in front of his sword, choosing to save her sister rather than run to Kristoff. The "act of true love" that defines the film, then, rejects heteronormative marriage in favor of sorority.

This final scene has its origins in "The Snow Queen." Andersen himself was immersed in the fairy-tale tradition and well aware of the "true love's kiss" motif. When the Snow Queen kisses Kay, however, it is more like the kiss of death: "That kiss was colder than ice. He felt it right down to his heart, half of which was already an icy lump. He felt as if he were dying, but only for a moment. Then he felt quite comfortable, and no longer noticed the cold."[217] When she kisses him again he forgets Gerda, his grandmother, and everyone else he knew, and she warns him that she won't kiss him again, "or else I should kiss you to death." When Kay appears again in the last story, he "was blue, yes, almost black, with the cold. But he did not feel it, because the Snow Queen had kissed away his icy tremblings, and his heart itself had almost turned to ice." The act that finally saves Kay is not a kiss but tears. Upon seeing him, "Gerda shed hot tears, and when they fell upon him they went straight to his heart. They melted the lump of ice and burned away the splinter of glass in it." Kay "cried so freely that the little piece of glass in his eye was washed right out." In *Frozen*, Elsa's tears similarly unfreeze Anna after she sacrifices herself.

Reviewers called *Frozen* "refreshingly" and "satisfyingly" feminist, and praised it for "rescuing" the genre of the princess film, since "the love between the two sisters takes precedence over any man."[218] Many also recognized a gay subtext to the film. Some conservative critics condemned the film for "normalizing" homosexuality, but the more common reaction was to embrace a queer interpretation.[219] *Frozen* was referred to as "perhaps the queerest animated film ever produced by Disney,"[220] seen as "a parable for homosexuality" that is "rife with subtext,"[221] and even called "a crash course in queer studies" that preaches acceptance and questioning gender."[222] The scenes of Elsa locked in her bedroom were compared to the "misery of the closet" and the song "Let It Go" (which won an Oscar) was interpreted as a coming out anthem.[223] These fan responses were sufficiently widespread that some hoped the sequel, *Frozen 2* (2019), would make manifest what is latent in the original: the hashtag #GiveElsaAGirlfriend trended briefly in advance of the film's release.[224] The sequel maintains the subtext of the first film, and does not provide a love interest for Elsa.[225] Ultimately, Elsa's remaining "unattached and focused instead on coming to know and accept herself" may be even more revolutionary than making her openly queer.[226] By rejecting the assumption that "an act of true love" necessitates a heterosexual kiss, *Frozen* opens itself to these other possibilities.

Biographers see "The Snow Queen" as one of Andersen's least biographical tales. It has been interpreted as fundamentally a tale about "woman's redemption of man,"[227] or about the idea that "a child's faith was a magic wand that could appear at any time because it was waved by the force of the emotions and not reason."[228] By combining it with "The Snow Man," however, Disney's *Frozen* brings "The Snow Queen" in line with Andersen's life. In that sense, the film culminates Disney's seventy-five-year relationships with Hans Christian Andersen. The 1940s-era biopic never came to fruition, but it made the studio aware of Andersen's biography, and its influence is felt in later Andersen adaptations.

In 1843, Hans Christian Andersen was among the guests invited to the opening of Copenhagen's new amusement park, Tivoli Gardens.[229] Walt Disney visited Copenhagen during his European tour in the early 1950s, and Tivoli Gardens helped shape his ideas for Disneyland. Perhaps, as he strolled through Tivoli Gardens, he thought about Denmark's famous fairy-tale writer, who like him had grown from humble, provincial origins to become a global celebrity. Neither could have foreseen the global success of an animated musical version of "The Snow Queen," nor could they have predicted how central Andersen's queerness would be to that success. Andersen's tales have always been read as autobiographical, and Disney's decades-long relationship to Andersen reveals how, despite an individual's (or a company's) best efforts to control how a life story is received, each generation brings its own values to earlier texts.

Chapter Four

Princesses and Pirates

My college swim coach used to bring her daughter with her to our practices. She was about eight, and often wore the same dress, a version of Belle's from Disney's *Beauty and the Beast*. I didn't know it at time, but this was not just a single young girl's eccentricity. She was at the vanguard of a nationwide trend. And while my coach seemed patient with her daughter's costume (worn over several swim seasons), other mothers were becoming fed up with the "princess culture" the outfit represented.

The Disney Princess franchise was fairly new when I was in college in the early 2000s. Disney's consumer products division had struggled the previous decade, as their strategy of marketing products based on individual films was beginning to falter.[1] When Andy Mooney, newly hired as the chairman of Disney's Consumer Products Division, attended a production of *Disney on Ice*, he noticed that many of the girls were dressed up as the princess characters, but they were wearing homemade costumes. He grasped the opportunity and combined the Disney heroines into the "Disney Princesses" franchise.[2] The brand exploded. By 2019, Disney Princesses ranked seventh on *Business Insider*'s list of the most profitable media franchises, behind Mickey Mouse and *Star Wars* but ahead of both Harry Potter and Marvel.[3]

Not everyone was thrilled with the princess marketing, and some at Disney objected to bringing together princesses from different storyworlds. But the franchise's success quickly overcame those objections.[4] A more serious condemnation was encapsulated in Peggy Orenstein's 2011 bestseller, *Cinderella Ate My Daughter*. For Orenstein, Disney Princesses are a metonym for twenty-first century girlhood or, as her subtitle puts it, "the new girlie-girl culture."[5]

Orenstein worries about the effect of "playing princess" on girls' self-esteem, and how it might reinforce certain ideas about girlhood: that girls should be focused primarily on their appearance; that they should care very much about how others perceive them; and, most importantly for their passage into heteronormative womanhood, that they should be searching for their prince. Though writing for a non-academic audience, Orenstein echoes the arguments feminist scholars had been making since the early 1990s.[6]

Among the ways that Disney has leveraged its Princess brand is the Bibbidi Bobbidi Boutique, a theme-park attraction providing children the opportunity to get a "princess makeover."[7] It is among the most popular attractions at Disneyland in Anaheim and at the Magic Kingdom in Florida. Young girls dressed as Disney princesses are a common sight throughout Disney's parks, and the makeover was featured on a 2013 episode of *The Big Bang Theory*.[8] Although nothing prevents boys from getting a princess makeover, they're not the target audience. Instead, Disney offers masculine alternatives. In Fantasyland, the segment of the park containing the Bibbidi Bobbidi Boutique, children can dress up as a "knight" (perhaps chosen over "prince" so as to seem less like a second-tier supplement to the princess). But the more popular costume is located across the park in Adventureland, near the water ride that inspired another of Disney's billion-dollar franchises. The masculine alternative to the Disney Princess is the pirate.

These two tropes—the princess and the pirate—encapsulate a gender binary evident in Disney's marketing. But Disney did not invent those tropes, any more than it invented the concept of a gender binary itself. Drawing a historical connection between Disney's marketing campaigns and Victorian images of princess and pirates, both real and imaginary, helps us see that neither trope is inherently regressive. A famous Victorian poem depicts a princess as a feminist icon, and even the Disney Princess franchise has evolved: films like *Brave* (2012), *Frozen* (2013), and *Moana* (2016) do not feature a prince at all. Gender, like other cultural constructs, is constantly being renegotiated, and media portrayals, whether in Victorian poems or Disney cartoons, are never as simple as they seem.

DISNEY'S AND THE VICTORIANS' GENDER IDEOLOGIES

The Disney Princess brand contributed to the notion that Disney's depictions of gender were especially retrograde, or even "Victorian." Applied to gender politics, the adjective "Victorian" conveys a general sense of strict and outdated morality. Victorian families didn't really cover their piano legs out of modesty, but they did impose rather rigid gender expectations. "The man's power is active, progressive, defensive," wrote John Ruskin in 1864, while "the woman's power is for rule, not for battle, and her intellect is not for invention or creation, but for sweet ordering, arrangement and decision."[9] Ruskin espouses the idea of "separate spheres," which assigned different societal roles to men, responsible for the public work of industry and empire, and women, responsible for maintaining domestic life.

The ideology pervades Victorian culture. The period's dominant genres were the domestic novel and the domestic melodrama, both of which followed the ubiquitous "marriage plot." Victorian texts typically limited women to three archetypes, which live on in modern culture, including (though of course not limited to) Disney's films. The exemplary Victorian woman was most memorably captured in Coventry Patmore's 1854 poem, "The Angel in the House." Patmore's title became associated with the unreachable feminine ideal. As Virginia Woolf put it a generation later, Victorian women were expected to be "immensely charming," self-sacrificing, and "utterly unselfish."[10] The "angel in the house" ethos persists in Snow White cleaning up the Dwarfs' house while singing "Someday My Prince Will Come," or in Ariel giving up her voice to be with Prince Eric.

Disney's young, marriageable princesses are often contrasted with two other female archetypes: wicked, middle-aged villains and elderly, benevolent fairy godmothers.[11] These types also had Victorian roots. Opposite the "angel in the house" stood the "fallen woman," a term that came to encompass not only prostitutes but also unwed mothers and unmarried women living with men. Fallen women came to represent cultural anxieties about women's loss of control, their inability to live up to the ideal expected of them, and the possibility that any woman might "fall."[12] Such anxieties manifest in Disney tropes like the poisoned apple offered to Snow White, or the contract Ursula cajoles Ariel into signing.

Even Victorian women who did not "fall" faced dire prospects. The proportion of single women of marriageable age increased in England as their potential husbands traveled abroad in service of the expanding British Empire. The doctrine of separate spheres had created a taboo preventing middle-class women from working outside the home, and these "redundant" or "surplus" women were caught in a double bind, unable either to work or to marry. Like fallen women, surplus women were excluded from the dominant domestic ideology.[13] As they aged, they were categorized as old maids or spinsters. They could hope, at best, to play the role of fairy godmother to a younger friend or relative, but more likely were treated as comic figures, like Flora, Fauna, and Merryweather in Disney's *Sleeping Beauty* (1959).

The Victorian cultural imagination, like Disney's princess culture, left few desirable options beyond the charming, self-sacrificing domestic angel. But if Disney's princess ideology has Victorian roots, so too does the feminist movement that has resisted and revised that ideology. The doctrine of separate spheres limited the options available to women, but also elevated the status of the domestic angel, providing a framework for early feminist reformers.[14] Josephine Butler, for example, argued vociferously for women's educational and work opportunities by stressing the importance of the home and even of women's centrality to it. "Home is the nursery of all virtue," wrote Butler in 1869, "the fountain-head of all true affection, and the main source of the strength of our nation."[15] Not allowing women to be educated and to work, Butler argued, threatened the values instilled in the home, and so threatened the nation itself. Granting women's demands was the only way to "tend to the restoration of the true home ideals."[16] Reformers like Butler used the rhetoric of domestic ideology to extend rights for married women, to expand access to education, and eventually to claim the right to vote.

While political reformers leveraged the powers of the "female sphere," poets and novelists parodied the underlying premise. A rich literary tradition, including novelists like Charlotte Bronte and George Eliot and poets like Christina Rossetti and Elizabeth Barrett Browning, satirized the notion of separate spheres. For example, the heroine of Barrett Browning's *Aurora Leigh*, written roughly the same year as Patmore's "The Angel in the House," is educated by her aunt. "I read a score of books on womanhood," recalls Aurora, "books that boldly assert / Their right of comprehending husband's talk / When not too deep."[17] The enjambment in the last line, which mockingly adds "when not too deep," undercuts the assertion that conduct manuals "boldly" allow a wife to "comprehend" her husband's talk. Aurora later refuses a proposal from Romney Leigh, the idealistic social reformer. "You want a helpmate, not a mistress," she tells him, "A wife to help your ends—in her no end."[18] Barrett Browning's heroine both cuts to the core of the doctrine of separate spheres and asserts her own vocation, that of a poet.

The Walt Disney Company is well aware of critiques of its Princess brand, and their films respond to it.[19] *Wreck It Ralph 2: Ralph Breaks the Internet* (2018) includes a scene inside the Disney Princess website. The scene's climactic gag is based on the one thing all the princesses have in common: their problems are solved when they met a big strong man.[20] Recent Princess films have also undercut the brand's supposed gender ideologies. In *Frozen*, Princess Anna is cursed by her sister, then told that the curse can be lifted only with "true love's kiss." An audience raised on *Snow White*, *Sleeping Beauty*, *The Little Mermaid*, and *Beauty and the Beast* can be counted on to recognize the trope, but the love Anna needs is neither that of her supposed beau Prince Hans (who turns out to be evil), nor the lovable buffoon Kristof, but her sister Elsa. *Frozen* has been so successful that Anna and Elsa are brands unto themselves, distinct from the Princess brand. And the two most recent additions to the Princess canon, Merida (from *Brave*) and Moana, appear in feature films with no male love interest at all. Researchers initially posited that engaging with Disney Princesses may lead to more stereotypically female play, but follow-up studies suggest that it could also lead to more egalitarian views of gender.[21] Some critics even see the brand itself as supporting "girl power."[22] Disney promotes that interpretation through its "Dream Big, Princess" campaign.[23] While the Disney Princess formula has historically implied a marriage plot featuring a heroine validated only by her choice of a husband, the brand is flexible enough to pivot to more progressive views as audiences' expectations change.

Disney's masculine alternative to the princess, the pirate, is even more fluid. In Disney lore, one becomes a princess by birth or by marrying a prince. At least on its surface, the term "princess" implies something immutable: once a princess, always a princess. "Pirate" is a purely situational identity. Any individual can claim to be a pirate, and the term can also be imposed or revoked by a group, either to justify punishment (the British navy might brand someone a pirate to arrest them) or to claim kinship (a pirate crew might welcome a new member). To claim the pirate as a masculine alternative to the princess is to accept the understanding of gender most famously framed by Judith Butler: "What is called gender identity is a performative accomplishment compelled by social sanction and taboo."[24] Gender, in other words, is not an essential characteristic but a behavior, a repetition of particular, stylized acts. Sometimes being a pirate means capturing ships and searching for treasure, behaviors associated with masculine norms. But just as often it means wearing an eye-patch or an earring, or having a pet parrot, or simply calling oneself a pirate.

The pirate becomes an even more intriguing trope when connected to sexual identity rather than gender identity. Since piracy is a crime, the state has the power to brand someone a pirate and to punish them. Pirates are defined as rebels by external forces seeking to exclude, punish, or demonize them. But they also claim the title as a badge of honor and work within their own system of rules. The "pirate code" lays bare the hypocrisy of the discourse that brands pirates outlaws in the first place. Pirates depend on invisibility to avoid prosecution but they also depend on performance to establish their identity and claim their place among a crew. This binary of secrecy and disclosure is akin to Eve Kosofsky Sedgwick's conception of the "closet." For Sedgwick, the closet provides an "overarching consistency to gay culture and identity," as members of the gay community must "come out the closet" (or not) with every new relationship.[25] The pirate occupies a similar space, choosing when (and when not) to self-identify as a pirate. As the masculine corollary to the feminine princess, then, the pirate challenges both the binary and the heteronormativity that Disney's gendered brands supposedly reinforce.

The princess's femininity changes through satire and revision and the pirate's masculinity is inescapably fluid. Such ambiguity would be problematic for an organization committed to conservative gender politics, but it's actually quite beneficial to a corporate brand. Andy Mooney has admitted that part of the genius of the Disney Princess brand is its ability to expand and contract as markets dictate.[26] The Disney Princess, and its concomitant gender ideology, are as fluid as gender and sexuality itself. This fluidity stymies critics' efforts to frame Disney as an anti-feminist, anti-democratic, "sinister corporate oppressor" (efforts that, in any case, never diminished the company's success).[27] Gender and sexuality are complex topics, with different meanings at different historical moments. And perhaps no tropes encapsulate these shifting ideas, both in the Victorian period and today, so well as the princess and the pirate.

FAIRY-TALE PRINCESSES: CHARLOTTE AND VICTORIA

Most European royal families were ousted during the revolutions of the nineteenth and early twentieth centuries. The English monarchy survived, but that survival was by no means assured. In fact, at the turn of the nineteenth century the English monarchy was at a low point. George III had been on the throne for forty years. American schoolchildren know him as the villain of the American revolution, the king who taxed without representation and from whom the revolutionaries declared their independence. He reigned until 1820, nearly a half-century after the American Revolution. During those years, England watched closely as democracy spread across Europe and revolutions toppled other European monarchies.

George III and his children were regrettable royal models for those revolutionary years. The king was declared mad in 1810 (English schoolchildren know him as "Mad King George"), and his eldest son ruled as prince regent until the king's death in 1820. The regent and his twelve adult siblings were notoriously spendthrift and immoral, a drain on the country's resources during a period of famine and expensive wars. William Hone mocked the regent as "the dandy of sixty" who "when Britain's in tears, sails about at his pleasure."[28] Two of George III's other sons were involved in public scandals: the Duke of York was accused of taking bribes for military commissions, and the Duke of Cumberland was rumored to have murdered his valet to cover up a homosexual affair. Percy Shelley's sonnet "England in 1819" laments "an old, mad, blind, despised, and dying King; / Princes, the dregs of their dull race, who flow / Through public scorn."[29]

But if the English public scorned the king and the princes, they saw hope in a young princess who would one day lead the nation through the already-tumultuous century. The perseverance of the English monarchy might be attributed Princess Charlotte and to her cousin, who would become Queen Victoria. Charlotte and Victoria were, of course, real people, with the same nuances and complexities as anyone else. But they were also public figures. The public encountered them daily, if not in person than through gossip, newspaper commentary, advertised commodities, and images.[30] Public depictions of Victoria and Charlotte—not to be confused with the royals' actual lived experiences—confined them to feminine archetypes: the young marriageable princess, the middle-aged wicked witch, and the matronly fairy godmother. As young women, Charlotte and Victoria were celebrated for their future potential, and especially the hope that they would marry and have children who would renew the ailing monarchy. They fit the archetype of the Disney Princess. Charlotte died young, leaving her image fixed. But Victoria would be portrayed differently as she aged, passing through the second and third archetypes. In middle age, Victoria was chastised for putting her own interests ahead of the nation, but by the end of her life she was depicted as the British Empire's fairy godmother. The shifting public perceptions of Charlotte and Victoria show how the same archetypes applied to Disney's princesses function in a different context. The rest of the chapter shows how those same archetypes can be upended by other cultural forces.

Born in 1796, Princess Charlotte was the only child of George III's eldest son. She was third in line for the throne (after her grandfather and her father), and as the king's only legitimate grandchild, she was the sole hope for the royal line. The public idolized her. Even as a child, Charlotte drew cheering crowds when she walked through the park, and the public constantly surveyed and discussed her "deportment, health, learning, accomplishments, dress, and appearance."[31] To the English public, Charlotte was a fairy-tale princess. Fairy tales had been flourishing on the continent since the eighteenth century, but it was only during Charlotte's lifetime that the English reading public developed a taste for the genre.[32] Cinderella, Snow White, and Sleeping Beauty provided an imaginary backdrop for Charlotte's public image, even as it became common knowledge that Charlotte herself led a sheltered and imprisoned life. Her paranoid father feared that she was plotting against him, and the family treated her as a minor royal and a "marriage pawn."[33] Byron, the era's best-selling poet, captured both the princess's distress and the public's hope for her reign: "Thy tears are virtue's tears," he wrote, "Auspicious to these suffering isles: / And be each drop in future years, / Repaid thee by thy people's smiles."[34] Byron's verse holds the promise that Charlotte's suffering, and the nation's, would end when she became queen. The public cheered when they learned she was to marry Prince Leopold of Saxe-Coburg in 1816. Even Charlotte, who was accustomed to large crowds at public events, was struck by the number of people who lined the streets for the royal wedding.[35] A year later, she and Leopold became patrons of the Royal Coburg Theatre, the first royals to officially patronize a theater in nearly 200 years.[36] As the public increasingly resented the mad king, the wasteful prince regent, and his immoral and spendthrift siblings, they saw in Charlotte and Leopold a more hopeful future.

When the couple announced Charlotte's pregnancy, the country prepared itself for the first legitimate royal birth since Charlotte's. But the event turned doubly tragic: the child was stillborn, and Charlotte died within a day. The whole country mourned their deaths. Theaters, courts, and the Royal Exchange were closed. Public buildings were draped in black. Shops that had been preparing souvenirs to celebrate the royal birth pivoted to "memorial cards, plates, cups, pitchers, and entire tea services," as well as rings and bracelets, often with an image of Charlotte ascending to heaven.[37] A planned celebration had become a period of mourning. Waxworks proprietors had prepared models of Charlotte, and they continued their planned tours, redressed in black. George Cruikshank, the famed illustrator and satirist who would later produce the illustrations for Dickens's *Oliver Twist*, recorded the event in a drawing titled *England's Only Hope Departing*. Charlotte and her child had been the future of the English monarchy. Two days of tragedy made that future uncertain.

After Charlotte's death, George III had thirteen living children and an estimated fifty-six grandchildren, but not a single legitimate heir. His sons immediately began considering legitimate marriages. Several married in the next few years. One of Charlotte's favorite uncles, the Duke of Kent, married Leopold's sister Victoire in 1818, and they had a daughter the next year, affectionately known as "Drina." Her birth was not accorded the same fanfare that her cousin Charlotte's had been. Among her own generation Drina was first in line to the throne, but she was preceded by her grandfather, three uncles (the prince regent, the Duke of York, and the Duke of

Clarence), and her father. Any of her cousins, or a brother, would precede her in the line of succession.

The Duke of York had been married for nearly three decades without children, and seemed unlikely to father a legitimate heir. The Duke of Clarence had lived with the actress Dorothea Jordan for twenty years. They had many children, but since they weren't married, all were illegitimate. He abandoned his mistress in 1811, and he secured a legitimate marriage after Charlotte's death. The couple had a child a few months before Drina's birth. The infant survived only a few hours, but there was every reason to believe there would be another, who would precede Drina to the throne. Drina's own parents also seemed likely to conceive again, and a male child would succeed the throne ahead of her. Charlotte had been the nation's hope, the princess who would someday be queen. Drina was just another princess.

Things gradually changed. Drina's father and King George III died before her first birthday, leaving only her three uncles between her and the throne. The Duke of York died in 1827, and King George IV in 1830. Her other uncle, the Duke of Clarence, had four more children, but three were stillborn and the fourth lived only a few months. When he became King William IV in 1830, he still had no legitimate children. Drina was next in line for the throne, followed by the Duke of Cumberland, the same Duke thought to have murdered his valet and "probably the most unpopular man in England."[38] Once again, the nation pinned its hopes on a young princess. When King William IV died in June 1837, an elaborate coronation ceremony signaled the start of a new era. The eighteen-year old princess was crowned Queen Victoria.

Innovations in printing and image-making, along with rising literacy rates and new railways bringing readings materials at increasing speeds, made Victoria the first "media monarch."[39] Over the next six decades, the press would portray her through a series of archetypes that "might well serve as the stock characters for a typical fairy tale"[40]—or, for that matter, a Disney movie. In the early years of her reign, Victoria fulfilled the ideal into which she and Charlotte had been cast. She lived, until the early 1860s, the "happily ever after" implied by the customary fairy-tale ending. Her diaries record the substantial time she spent sitting for portraits, which circulated as engravings and made her face familiar even before she became queen.[41] The earliest portraits portray Victoria as a princess and future queen. An 1833 portrait by George Hayter depicts the sixteen-year-old surrounded by a globe and books representing her education and her readiness for her future role. But in the corner her spaniel Dash playfully holds one of her gloves, leaving her hand bare and reminding the viewer of her youth.[42] Victoria's youthful femininity promised not just an intelligent, educated queen who would lead the nation

Early portrayals of Victoria, like George Hayter's *Queen Victoria and Dash* (1833), emphasized her youth but also her future role as queen.

through the nineteenth century but also one whose children could prevent the monarchial crisis her own birth had only just barely averted.

Earlier generations of readers would have been accustomed to commentary about the monarchy, whether it took the form of praise or opprobrium. But the new daily newspapers, made possible by the reduction of the stamp tax and increasingly cheaper paper, now had column inches to fill, and they provided detailed descriptions of royal activities.[43] Victoria was scrutinized as no monarch had been before. Such idealization continued after her marriage to her cousin Albert in 1840 and the births of their nine children. The portraits from this period showcase "the domestic, bourgeois values of stability, comfort, and security," an ideal household which her subjects could emulate.[44] In her private life, Victoria fulfilled the role of wife and mother, delivering on the promise implied by her earlier representation. And in public she and Albert "set the model for the serious duties and pleasurable diversions that we have come to expect from a constitutional monarchy."[45] Their self-conscious presentation as an ideal couple made possible the image that Disney would later market so successfully. Victoria proved the myth that Charlotte's death had shattered: a princess could go on to live happily ever after in domestic bliss.

But Victoria's domestic bliss was cut short when Albert died from typhoid fever in 1861. The queen wore black for the remainder of her life, earning her the moniker the Widow of Windsor. Her mourning has become legendary. Public statues and dedications—among them Royal Albert Hall and the Victoria & Albert Museum—were supplemented by more private remembrances. The room in which Albert died was memorialized and servants were instructed to lay out Albert's clothes and shaving water for the remaining four decades of Victoria's life.[46] Whereas Victoria's public and private lives had been united in a carefully orchestrated public image, after Albert's death she secluded herself. Privately she continued "the routine business of her station," but her withdrawal from ceremonial events contrasted starkly with the displays the nation had come to expect.[47]

The public complained of Victoria's absence from public affairs. An anonymous notice was posted on Buckingham Palace, indicating it was to be sold "in consequence of the late occupant's declining business."[48] Among the business she declined was the annual opening of Parliament, a symbolically important constitutional requirement that Victoria refused for three years.[49] On the third anniversary of Albert's death, the *Times* reprimanded the queen. "The living have their claims as well as the dead," the newspaper chided, asking that she "return to the personal exercise of her exalted functions."[50] Victoria refused, citing the toll that public appearances took on her

By the 1880s, Queen Victoria was portrayed as the nation's matriarch, as in this 1882 photograph of by Alexander Bassano.

health. The excuse came across as selfish, especially considering the public funds granted to her and her children. The annuities necessary for her nine children called to mind her spendthrift uncles, who had drawn the public's ire a generation earlier and whom Percy Shelley had called the "dregs of their dull race." Democratic revolutions continued on the continent, and

English anti-royalists "prophesied that Queen Victoria would at any rate be the last monarch of England."[51] Had Victoria died in the early 1870s "there can be little doubt that the voice of the world would have pronounced her a failure."[52] The fairy-tale princess whose domestic bliss had been so widely celebrated was now cast as the evil queen, spending the public's money while living in selfish seclusion.

The seclusion eventually came to an end. In 1870, Princess Louise became engaged to the Duke of Argyll, who was technically a commoner. Victoria approved of the marriage, and her prioritization of her daughter's happiness helped salvage her reputation. News of her own illness drew public sympathy, which increased when the Prince of Wales fell ill with typhoid, the same disease that had led to Albert's death. A failed assassination attempt further strengthened her public support. By midcentury, she was renewing her public appearances, and in 1876 Parliament bestowed upon her the title Empress of India. Her daughter Princess Alice died in 1878, and her son Prince Leopold in 1884. The English public was sympathetic to "the widowed mother weeping for her children."[53] With this renewed public support, Victoria entered a final stage of her life, this time fulfilling a third archetype, the nation's fairy godmother. Images of Victoria after 1880 portray her as calm and in control, presiding over an empire on which the sun never set. Images like Heinrich von Angeli's portrait, *Her Majesty the Queen wearing the Small Imperial Crown* (1885) and Alexander Bassano's 1887 photograph emphasize "the presence of a monarch rather than a mother."[54]

The events that perhaps best capture Victoria's reputation after her emergence from her widowed seclusion are the two Jubilee celebrations. Victoria herself largely funded the 1887 Golden Jubilee, which celebrated her fiftieth year on the throne. The event so successfully promoted England's unity and prowess that a Diamond Jubilee, in 1897, was funded by Parliament.[55] The celebrations were accompanied by "an extraordinary array of advertised commodities" that not only underscored the monarchy's public function but also established domestic imagery that would dominate advertising well into the twentieth century.[56] It is this image of Victoria that is best remembered today.

Of course, Victoria's life was more complicated than such a sketch allows. Her many biographers reveal her humanity and her struggles to maintain her composure as both an individual and a symbol. Nevertheless, her public life fits neatly into a three-part master narrative: an early life and romance with Albert; a widowed seclusion; and the symbolic longevity of her final decades. This tripartite feminine stereotype is how the public viewed Victoria. Both the hopeful young princess and the matriarch behind which the whole nation rallied fit the image of a self-sacrificing, charming feminine ideal, the "angel in the house." When she made the conscious choice to prioritize her own emotional needs, she was vilified for it. And as an elderly woman she gained a kind of benevolent magic aura. Collapsed into this narrative, Victoria's life might be seen, like the women who feature in Disney films, to encapsulate the restrictions placed on women in popular media.

FEMINIST PRINCESSES: VICTORIA'S DAUGHTERS

If Victoria's public image neatly fits the limited, stereotypical roles associated with princess culture, her daughters challenged those stereotypes and contributed to feminist causes that sought to break through those limitations. In the years after Albert's death, as Victoria faded from public view and began to draw the public's ire, her children took over many of the official duties that had initially endeared the couple to the British populace. By the late 1860s, Britain was accustomed to Victoria's absence and people "actively looked forward to seeing the princes and princesses instead."[57] Bertie, Victoria's eldest son and second-eldest child, was first in line for the throne. He eventually became quite popular, in the nearly six decades he lived before his mother died and he became King Edward VII. But he had a reputation as a playboy and his less-than-discreet affairs earned him the nickname "Edward the Caresser." He hardly fit the image the royal family hoped to convey. He also, from his childhood, seemed to display "a deep-seated repugnance to every form of mental exertion," a particular contrast to his elder sister, who was "an extremely intelligent child."[58] As early as the 1840s, it was clear that the intellectual powers of Victoria and Albert manifested themselves in their daughters rather than their sons—that is, in the princesses, not the princes.

By the mid-1860s, Victoria's three oldest daughters had all married European princes. Vicky, the eldest, married Frederick, son of the German Emperor Wilhelm II; Alice, the next eldest, another German prince, Louis of Hesse; and the middle daughter, Helena, Prince Christian of Schleswig-Holstein. These strategic marriages showcase one aspect of a princess's role, and Victoria's descendants held positions of power across Europe through the tumultuous first half of the twentieth century. Her two youngest daughters, Louise and Beatrice, would live until 1939 and 1944, respectively (both could potentially have seen a Disney film). Beatrice is remembered as an image of filial devotion, staying close to her mother in the decades after Albert's death. It was Beatrice who copied out Victoria's diaries, editing out anything controversial and destroying the originals. Lewis Carroll also sent Princess Beatrice the second presentation copy of *Alice in Wonderland* (he gave the first to Alice Liddell).

Vicky, Alice, and Helena married strategically to further Britain's European reach, and Beatrice stayed close to her mother. But in the 1870s, it was Victoria's second-youngest daughter, Louise, who captured the imagination of the British public. With Victoria withdrawn from public life, Louise was the "poster girl" for the royal family. Newspapers "loved to comment on the clothes she wore and her artistic sense of style" and celebrated that, unlike her siblings, Louise "refused to marry a foreigner."[59] Lucinda Hawksley recounts an 1878 visit to Liverpool from "the favorite of the queen's daughters . . . her smiling, pretty face replacing the dour expression of the black-clad queen."[60] To Victoria's chagrin, Louise's popularity surpassed her mother's. Yet despite her popularity among her contemporaries, less is known about Louise than about her siblings. Hawksley recounts difficulties getting access to materials about Louise, which had been relocated to the royal archives. "There has been some very careful sanitizing of Princess Louise's reputation," Hawksley writes, "and a whitewashing of her life, her achievements and her personality."[61] The royal archives, like the Walt Disney Archives, exist not merely as a historical record but as a private collection, ineluctably tied to a grand narrative that the collections' custodians can be loath to challenge. Louise was independent-minded, and where she seems most to challenge the official royal narrative is in her desire to have a political impact. In the constitutional monarchy that Queen Victoria helped initiate, the royal family is not meant to meddle in political affairs. Louise challenged that edict.

Besides being "the prettiest, the wittiest, and the best-dressed" of Victoria's daughters,[62] Louise had artistic talent. She studied with the sculptor Mary Thornycroft, who recommended her to the National Art Training School (which later became the Royal College of Art). She produced several sculptures, some of which were exhibited by the Royal Academy of Art.[63] Her artistic endeavors brought her into contact with the Pre-Raphaelite Brotherhood, a set of idealists who came to prominence around the time of Louise's birth. The PRB, as they mysteriously signed their earliest works, felt stifled by the art world's restrictive definitions of "beauty." They represented a radical movement when they first exhibited their works. The art critic John Ruskin wrote that "Pre-Raphaelitism has but one principle, that of absolute, uncompromising truth in all that it does."[64] But the PRB's works were controversial, especially those depicting sacred scenes. Charles Dickens was disgusted by John Everett Millais's *Christ in the House of his Parents*, which the National Academy of Art exhibited in 1850. He thought Millais's Mary "horrible in her ugliness," and found the whole painting "mean, odious, repulsive, and revolting."[65] Over such objections, the PRB helped expand the "proper" subjects of art. Their influence extended beyond the art world to Victorian culture more broadly. They were part of a larger cultural revolution that was beginning to chip away at Victorian authority.

When Louise was seriously pursuing her own art, she came to know the PRB socially as well as professionally.[66] Whether or not they directly affected her beliefs, their prominence underscores why the princess's artistic pursuits were not politically neutral. She moved in circles that made the royal establishment uncomfortable. As a child, Louise had accompanied her mother on visits to orphanages, hospitals, and asylums, where she was expected to passively observe. Those visits kindled a desire to use her royal reputation to improve the world. As an adult, inspired by the artistic circles in which she moved, she became more determined.[67] She was especially drawn to women's emancipation, a cause she shared with her sisters—but not with her mother.

Given her prominence as a female ruler of a quarter of the earth's population, Victoria no doubt inspired thousands of women. As feminist movements emerged in the 1850s and 1860s, she was among the individuals held up as an exemplar, showing what women could accomplish.[68] But privately she upheld the notion of separate spheres. "God created men and women different," she wrote in an 1870 letter, "let them remain each in their own position."[69] On this subject, her daughters vehemently disagreed. The two eldest, Vicky and Alice, were both living in Prussia, each married to a German prince. As married women living outside England, they were free to choose their own political causes to support. Alice sponsored two organizations, the Princess Alice Society for Women's Training and Industry, which promoted women's education, and the Princess Alice Women's Guild, which supported the training of nurses. Both were substantial organizations by the 1870s, and her innovations are still remembered in Darmstadt.[70] Vicky had similar views. As the Crown Princess of Prussia, she led a society for the employment of women in Berlin, a role she mentioned in a December 1868 letter to Josephine Butler.[71]

Butler was a prominent proponent of women's emancipation. A year after Vicky's letter, she published *Woman's Work and Woman's Culture*, a series of essays about women's causes ranging from marriage to education and suffrage. She was just beginning the role for which she is best remembered: the leader in the campaign to abolish the Contagious Diseases Acts. Passed between 1864 and 1869, these controversial laws gave police the power to forcibly "test" any woman suspected of having a venereal disease, and to detain her if she was deemed contagious. Ostensibly intended to protect naval and military men, the laws were an egregious invasion of women's bodies, and thousands were subjected to embarrassing and invasive "inspections." Women of different social classes organized in opposition to the laws.

A London historical marker refers to Josephine Butler as a "Champion of Women's Rights."

The first women's suffrage societies were founded at this time, and the Ladies' National Association shortly thereafter.[72] It was this group that led the campaign to repeal the Contagious Diseases Acts. Their active participation in the political movement "astonished and perplexed the press and public officials," who were unused to hearing women speak openly and publicly about issues related to sex and the body.[73] Their efforts were successful, and the acts were repealed in 1886. Looking back on the campaign a decade later, Butler called it "one of the most vital movements of Christian times."[74]

The successful campaign to repeal the Contagious Diseases Acts laid a foundation for the next half-century of feminist victories, including the suffrage movement in the first quarter of the twentieth century. Butler emerged as a "moral and charismatic leader" who exerted a "magnetic sway over popular audiences."[75] She was the public face of the campaign when she corresponded with Princess Vicky, whose letter describes her own work in Berlin and encourages Butler to correspond with her sister. Butler sent a letter to Louise, and received a prompt response. Louise's reply goes further than her sister's, expressing a desire "to do everything I can to promote all efforts" related to "the happiness and general well-being of women."[76] This desire was genuine, and the twenty-one-year-old princess hoped to assert her independence and use her popularity to support Butler's cause. She requested Butler's book, *Woman's Work and Woman's Culture* (1869), and Butler sent her a signed copy.[77]

But as an unmarried princess still in England, Louise's actions reflected on Victoria and the royal family more than Vicky's. The repeal of the Contagious Diseases Acts was an especially controversial subject. Pressured by her family, Louise was prevented from offering Butler any active support, and even returned the copy of her book. Royals could not take sides on political questions.[78] Louise nevertheless continued her correspondence with Butler, though she stressed the importance that Queen Victoria not know about it. In March 1869, she wrote to Butler about a journal, the *International Women's Review*, which Butler was in the process of planning. Louise expressed concern that the word "women" in the title would dissuade male buyers.[79] In this she echoed something Butler herself had written in the introduction to *Woman's Work and Woman's Culture*. Butler rejects the idea that the causes discussed in the collection were only women's causes. "We are human first; women secondarily," she writes. "We care for the evils affecting women most of all because they react upon the whole of society."[80]

Louise was not yet married when she corresponded with Butler, and she had always maintained she would not marry a foreign prince (as her sisters had done). In 1870, a new law may have nudged her towards matrimony. For centuries English common law held that a married couple was a single entity, and under the doctrine of coverture a woman's property became her husband's after marriage. Married women could not own property. The first major success of the burgeoning women's rights movement was the passage of the Married Women's Property Act of 1870, which gave married women the legal rights to money and property they earned or inherited. Louise had been unsuccessful in her attempts to assert her independence, first as a sculptor and later, following the example of Florence Nightingale, as a nurse. She perhaps began to realize that if she wanted to continue to support women's causes she would have more success as a married woman rather than a "spinster princess."[81] In 1870, she became engaged to the Marquess of Lorne, a relationship that (publicly at least) was touted as a love match rather than a political alliance.[82] The public welcomed the marriage, glad to have a princess married to an Englishman, and Victoria supported it as well.[83] The marriage corresponded with Victoria's reentry into public life. It had been nearly a decade since Albert's death, and the public was increasingly wearied of Victoria's seclusion. In 1871, the queen asked Parliament to grant a £70,000 dowry to Louise, plus an annuity of another £6,000. To appease the public, she opened Parliament that year.[84] The brief period of Victoria's unpopularity, when her daughters had become the most visible of the royals, was coming to a close. Louise traveled to Canada when her husband became governor general in 1878. She remained popular but was no longer the monarchial "poster child" she had been before her marriage, during Victoria's seclusion.

Victoria lived another quarter-century, entering a new stage as the imperial matriarch. Had she not lived so long, or had her daughters been more able to persuade her of their own feelings, perhaps Louise and her sisters would be remembered as the princesses who secured women's suffrage. As it happened, the political issue that divided Victoria from her daughters faded temporarily into the background. The 1886 repeal of the Contagious Diseases Acts was the last major legislative success for three decades, until the 1917 Representation of the People Act finally granted the right to vote to women over thirty.

THE VICTORIAN PRINCESS BRAND: TENNYSON'S *THE PRINCESS*

The princess trope links the gender dynamics of the Victorian era to our own. But the royal family is only part of the story, and fictional princesses abound in Victorian literature, including in original fairy tales by writers like George Macdonald (whose works include "The Light Princess" [1864] and *The Princess and the Goblin* [1872]) and novelists like Frances Hodgson Burnett (whose *A Little Princess* developed from a short story published in 1887). Perhaps the most important princess in Victorian literature, the one who might be the best candidate for a Victorian-era "princess brand," is Tennyson's Princess Ida, the eponymous heroine of *The Princess* (1847). Tennyson's poem engages directly with the politics of women's education, and has been read both as a defense of female empowerment and as a regressive satire that perpetuates the marriage plot. Such opposite readings may point to an even more radical conclusion, one that I suggest aligns with Disney's brand: the rejection of the gender binary itself.

Queen Victoria refers to Tennyson's poem in the same 1870 letter in which she calls women's suffrage a "mad, wicked folly," writing that "Tennyson has some beautiful lines on the difference of men and women."[85] She doesn't specify which lines she means, but the poem expresses the idea of "separate spheres" as directly as Ruskin's *Sesames and Lilies*, which I quoted in the introduction to this chapter. Here are the lines Victoria may have had in mind:

Man for the field and woman for the hearth:
Man for the sword and for the needle she:
Man with the head and woman with the heart:
Man to command and woman to obey;
All else confusion.[86]

These lines express the ideology of separate spheres at its most extreme. Men are active workers, while women are obedient, emotional, and homebound. The sentiment, however, is not Tennyson's. The speaker is a violent, misogynist king, at odds with the other characters in the poem. *The Princess* is about the founding of a university for women and in the context of the poem, the king's "tirades" are "a grotesque parody of male chauvinism."[87]

The Princess was published in 1847, but Tennyson had the idea for a poem about a women's college nearly a decade earlier. Debates about women's rights "filled the pages of periodicals in the 1820s and 1830s," while Tennyson was beginning his poetic career.[88] Victoria's ascension in 1837 had renewed discussions of female education, both Victoria's own (and the extent to which it prepared her for the throne) and the education of her future children.[89] Tennyson began *The Princess* the year Victoria was engaged to Albert, and he was still working on it a year later when she gave birth to Vicky, the first of the era's princesses.[90] He would surely have been thinking about the English royal family as he began writing *The Princess*, and must also have been aware of a political treatise with a very similar title, Machiavelli's *The Prince*. *The Princess* is a politically loaded poem.

Tennyson set the poem aside for several years to work on other projects, but he returned to it in 1845, perhaps after reading, or at least hearing about, Margaret Fuller's *Woman in the Nineteenth Century*, published that year.[91] Certainly he would have been aware of headlines about women's education. In 1848, F. D. Maurice helped found Queen's College, a school for girls that drew ire for teaching "masculine" subject matter like mathematics. Two decades earlier, Maurice had founded the Apostles Club at Cambridge. Tennyson was a member, and it was through the Apostles that he met Arthur Henry Hallam. Hallam died of a stroke at age twenty-two and is the inspiration for Tennyson's *In Memoriam A. H. H.*, the work that secured his status as poet laureate and provides the famous line, "'Tis better to have loved and lost / Than never to have loved at all."[92] *In Memoriam* consists of 131 lyrics dealing with his grief at Hallam's death. Tennyson wrote the first lyric shortly after Hallam's death in 1833, and was still working on the poem when he published *The Princess*. He was thinking about the Apostles, and no doubt aware of the founder's support for women's education.

A year after Maurice founded Queen's College, Elisabeth Jesser Reid founded a competing school for girls, the "Ladies College" in Bedford Square. Queen's College and Bedford College were pioneer institutions in women's education.[93] They emerged from the same public debates from which Tennyson drew his ideas for *The Princess*. An early reviewer thought the poem makes the case for women's education "with a force and an eloquence which the world has scarcely witnessed before."[94] The topic remained a focal point for Victorian feminists. Elizabeth C. Wolstenholme, who had recruited Josephine Butler to the campaign to repeal the Contagious Diseases Acts, contributed an essay on educating girls to *Woman's Work and Woman's Culture*. Writing in 1869, Wolstenholme thought that higher education for women "cannot as yet be said to have any existence."[95] But change was coming. University College began enrolling women in 1878, Cambridge, in 1881, and Oxford, in 1884.[96]

Tennyson's epic about higher education for women achieved the height of its popularity during the very years when English universities were opening their doors to women. Its success during those years was aided by two adaptations (an 1859 illustrated Christmas gift book and Gilbert and Sullivan's 1884 burlesque *Princess Ida*), and by the prominence of Tennyson himself, who lived until 1892. Only Charles Dickens rivals Tennyson in his close association with the Victorian period. Victoria herself was "much soothed" by reading *In Memoriam* after Albert's death in 1861,[97] and Tennyson has been called the first "media poet," complementing Victoria as the first "media monarch."[98] Edward Moxon's 1857 illustrated edition of Tennyson's *Poems* included woodcuts by the Pre-Raphaelites at the height of their fame and helped launch a "golden age" of book illustration.[99] *The Princess*, a wildly popular poem by the era's most prominent poet, helped shape Victorian ideas not just about women's education but about gender roles more generally. And it did so through the figure of a princess.

The Princess begins with a frame narrative. The narrator, a male university student, visits the estate of his friend Walter Vivian, along with five of their schoolmates. He is shown a chronicle of the Vivian family, a "hoard of tales that dealt with knights / Half-legend, half-historic," one of which is about "a lady, one that arm'd / Her own fair head, and sallying thro' the gate, / Had beat her foes with slaughter from the walls."[100] Walter asks, "lives there such a woman now?" and a response from his sister Lilia sets up the tale that will follow: "There are thousands now / Such women," Lilia tells him, "but convention beats them down: / It is but bringing up; no more than that."[101] Lilia asserts that gender differences are the result of education rather than biology. She then imagines a solution: "I wish / That I were some great princess, I would build / Far off from men a college like a man's, / And I would teach them all that men are taught."[102] Shortly thereafter the college friends describe a favorite pastime. One would begin a story, and each friend would then continue it, creating a seven-part tale. Lilia suggests they try the game now, and her brother proposes a protagonist: "Take Lilia, then, for heroine . . . make her some great princess."[103] And so the seven friends base their collaborative story—what the poem's subtitle calls a "medley"—on Lilia's assertion of women's intellectual abilities and her idea for a women's university.

The seven-part story can be quickly summarized.[104] The first-person narrator is a prince who, as a child, had been betrothed to Ida, a princess from a neighboring kingdom. When the time comes for the marriage he receives word that Ida refuses to marry him and instead plans to "live alone / Among her women."[105] Although he has never met her, the prince has seen her picture and believes himself to be in love with her. He and two friends travel to her kingdom, where her father informs them that several years ago two women had captured his daughter's attention and "fed her theories . . . maintaining that with equal husbandry / The woman were an equal to the man."[106] They convinced Ida that, as Lilia had asserted in the frame, gender inequality results only from education. The three women departed, "All wild to found a University / For maidens."[107] They haven't seen a man since, and men are forbidden to enter the university on penalty of death. Ida's justification for the university echoes Lilia's language from the frame story: "Here might they learn whatever men were taught."[108] The curriculum, which highlights famous historical and mythological women, includes astronomy, government, and geography.

The prince and his two accomplices dress up as women and enter the school. The disguised prince tries to convince Ida to honor the marriage contract, but she maintains her plan: "When we set our hand / To this great work," she tells him, "we purposed with ourself / Never to wed."[109] When some of her students later express doubts, she warns that they could be "dismiss'd in shame to live / No wiser than their mothers, household stuff, / Live chattels."[110] For Ida, domesticity is a prison. And as the prince (still incognito) fails to convince Ida to commit to marriage, he begins to see the virtue in her arguments. "Were we ourselves but half as good, as kind, / As truthful," he later tells his father, "much that Ida claims as right / Had ne'er been mooted, but as frankly theirs / As dues of Nature."[111] The prince becomes convinced of Ida's point, which is the same as Lilia's point in the frame narrative: equal access to education will lead to equality between the genders.

The men's ruse is revealed when Ida falls into a river and the prince rescues her. He and his friends escape the university and meet his father, who utters the remarks I quoted earlier, the ones that Queen Victoria likely refers to in her diary: "Man to command and woman to obey / All else confusion."[112] This gender essentialism accompanies a more literal violence. The king has arrived with a conquering army intent on taking the university by force. The prince protests, and they compromise with a tournament. The prince is wounded, as are many others, and Ida agrees to take the wounded into the university to care for them. Fairy-tale tropes take hold. Awakening to see Ida at his side, the injured Prince tells her, "I shall die tonight. / Stoop down and seem to kiss me ere I die."[113] She does, and "all / Her falser self split from her like a robe, / And left her woman."[114] Marjorie Stone sees the ending as a reversal of the "Sleeping Beauty" story:[115] Ida falls for the prince and the story ends with their renewed betrothal, this time both willing adults. But the prince remains convinced that "the woman's cause is man's."[116] The ultimate goal of Ida's university was never to separate the genders, but instead to unite them. Ida had earlier prophesied, "Everywhere two heads in council, two beside the hearth, / Two in the tangled business of the world."[117] In this rejection of separate spheres, men and women work together both in and out of the home. Ida and the prince fulfill that prophecy. The princess gets her prince, but she also achieves her political goal.

The end of *The Princess* returns to the frame narrative. The narrator remarks, "Ourselves are full / Of social wrong; and maybe wildest dreams / Are but the needful preludes of the truth."[118] Ida's university may be a wild dream, but this line implies Tennyson's support for the idea. Readers learn the same lesson as the prince, that "the woman's cause is man's," and Tennyson challenges Victorian gender ideologies to promote what some scholars see as "an ideal of androgyny."[119] Tennyson's revisions to the poem's second edition, in 1850, strengthen its "feminist sympathies" and have been interpreted as a rejoinder to readers who missed that argument in the first edition.[120]

Just as modern perceptions of *Alice in Wonderland* and Hans Christian Andersen's tales are shaped by Disney's adaptations, so adaptations of *The Princess* influenced the reception of Tennyson's poem. One could imagine an adaptation that celebrates Ida's university and highlights the prince's speeches that most support equality. Perhaps it might give more voice to the female characters or alter the ending so as to free the story from the confines of a marriage plot. But that is not the direction taken by the two most influential adaptations. In 1859, Edward Moxon (whose earlier edition of Tennyson's poems had featured art by the Pre-Raphaelites) commissioned Daniel Maclise to illustrate a Christmas gift book edition of *The Princess*. It was an immediate hit and remained "the *ne plus ultra* of the seasonal gift book" throughout the 1860s. Maclise's illustrated edition of *The Princess* was one of the most popular books during a decade known as the "Golden Age of Illustration."[121] Maclise painted a famous portrait of Dickens in 1839 (the year *Nicholas Nickleby* appeared), and by the 1850s he was a popular artist known for his medieval themes. His illustrations interpret *The Princess* as a story of chivalry and masculine power, associating Ida's story with medieval romance and the gender ideologies that come along with it.

A quarter-century later, Gilbert and Sullivan's comic opera *Princess Ida* (1884) similarly undercut Tennyson's potentially feminist poem by ridiculing the very idea of higher education for women. Their ridicule registers "male worry about the increasingly intense feminist activity" that had characterized the years between Tennyson's poem and Gilbert and Sullivan's parody.[122] W. S. Gilbert had written a farcical adaptation of *The Princess* in 1870, much of which was incorporated into *Princess Ida* in 1884. Several universities for women opened in the intervening fourteen years,[123] and *Princess Ida* has been read as a mean-spirited defense of a misogynist lost cause.[124] *Princess Ida*, like Maclise's illustrations, silences the "feminist aspirations" of Tennyson's poem.[125]

To be sure, these anti-feminist adaptations have some basis in Tennyson's poem. Some scholars would take issue with the summary I offered above, which omits important details. Lilia's comment about education is initially dismissed by the group of male friends. "Petulant she spoke," says the narrator, "and at herself she laugh'd."[126] One friend patronizingly replies that men would surely break into such any school that excluded them, if the students were as pretty as Lilia. When Walter suggests that the narrator "take Lilia, then, for heroine . . . make her some great princess," he adds an element that fundamentally changes the tale: "And be you," he suggests, "The prince to win her."[127] For Lilia, the princess is an image of power, able to conjure up a school for women that will correct the biases resulting from unequal education. For Walter, the princess is a prize to be won.

There is good reason to believe that Tennyson agrees more with Walter than with Lilia. After all, the story of Ida is ultimately a tale about convincing a princess to submit to a marriage contract established without her consent.[128] Only the male narrator and his friends get to speak; Lilia does not participate, even though she had previously expressed a desire to tell her own story: "I wish I were / Some mighty poetess, I would shame you then."[129] The men usurp Lilia's idea, never allowing her to speak for herself, making *The Princess* "a grand exercise in the silencing of women."[130] In this view, the prince's marriage to Ida merely reinforces the ideology that his father the king had espoused: "Man to command, and woman to obey."[131]

So while some readers interpret *The Princess* as a proto-feminist poem that helped prepare the public to accept women's entry into university, others see it as a mockery of women's abilities. These two critical views are difficult to reconcile. Can a single poem can dramatize both gender equality and the "harsh and relentless oppression of women"?[132] Tennyson himself seems ambivalent. After *The Princess* returns to the frame narrative, the narrator, perhaps a proxy for Tennyson himself, must decide between two different styles. The men encourage him to make it a "mock-heroic giantesque": they read the story as a farce, a joke at Lilia's expense. But the women "wish'd for something real, / A gallant fight, a noble princess."[133] For them, Ida's tale is something to take seriously.

Tennyson's narrator chooses a middle ground, or as he puts it, "a strange diagonal."[134] Unlike the poem's Victorian audience, twenty-first century readers have a vocabulary for interpreting that "strange diagonal." Scholars today recognize gender as performative, a series of actions rather than a fixed, biological identity. The gender one is assigned at birth may or may not be the gender they feel most comfortable expressing. And indeed, critics often recognize a "feminine sensibility" in Tennyson's poems, which frequently eclipse the masculine self in order "to make the text a medium for an imagined female self-expression."[135] The male poet, in other words, often expressed himself in feminine terms. Read in this way, *The Princess* could be seen to balance male and female expectations and ultimately to reject the differences between the genders.

When the prince first expresses his agreement with Ida's mission, he does so in political terms. "[B]arbarous laws," he tells her, "were the rough ways of the world till now. / Henceforth thou has a helper, me, that know / The woman's cause is man's."[136] Speaking in terms of "laws," "ways of the world," and a "cause" implies a public issue, solved with legislation and institutions. Later in the same speech, however, the prince shifts to something more personal. Men and women are

> not like to like, but like in difference.
> Yet in the long years liker must they grow;
> The man be more of woman, she of man;
> He gain in sweetness and in moral height,
> Nor lose the wrestling thews that throw the world;
> She mental breadth, nor fail in childward care.[137]

The prince accepts the tenets of separate spheres. The man "wrestles" with the world and has "mental breadth," while women thrive in "childcare care" and "in sweetness and in moral height." But these are not essential characteristics. They are socially imposed, and the ideal will take the best aspects of both: "The man be more of woman, she of man."

Tennyson chooses the singular rather than the plural: "The man be more of woman, she of man" rather than "men be more of women, they of men." The phrasing makes the issue as much personal as political. A married couple, says the prince, sits "side by side, full-summed in all their powers, / Dispensing harvest, sowing the to-be."[138] The partnership and the prophecy ("sowing the to-be") echo the ideal future that Ida's curriculum had hoped to achieve: "two heads in council, two beside the hearth, / Two in the tangled business of the world."[139] For Ida, a balance of power requires two rulers, male and female, in collaboration. But for the prince, "either sex alone / Is half itself. . . . Each fulfills defect in each . . . they grow, / The single pure and perfect animal, / The two-cell'd heart beating."[140] What the prince describes is not a partnership between two people of opposite genders but an elision of sexual distinction, a "single pure and perfect animal" encompassing the ideal characteristics associated with each gender. Gender and power are so intertwined that achieving true equality requires rejecting the very idea of gender.[141]

Ironically, a poem that purports to engage with debates about gender roles ends up erasing the very distinction on which those debates hinge. That is the ultimate lesson of *The Princess*—and, perhaps, of the Disney Princess brand. The association of girlhood with princesses rests the construction on performance. The particulars of that performance shift over time. The heroines of *Snow White* and *Cinderella* are passive beings dependent on princes to find them attractive. Ariel, in *The Little Mermaid*, takes active steps to get what she, but what she wants is still a heteronormative marriage, and she sacrifices her voice to get it. Criticism of Ariel factored into the characterization of Belle in *Beauty and the Beast* (1991). Screenwriter Linda Woolverton (the first woman to write an animated feature for Disney) gave Belle a more active role to counter what critics had called the "cloyingly sexist" aspects of Ariel.[142] Still, Belle winds up with a husband. More recently, Merida (in *Brave*), Elsa (in *Frozen*), and Moana find fulfillment elsewhere; princes and husbands are irrelevant to their stories.

Disney's marketing campaign absorbs each of these narratives. Rather than a regressive image to which young girls much conform, Disney Princess is a brand aiming to make a profit. What makes the brand interesting, as a gender ideology, is that it reaches its full potential only by making its criteria as open as possible, expanding its reach to include girls who don't conform to its original norms. And not just girls. Nothing prevents boys from embracing the princess brand, too. And the pirate, Disney's masculine alternative to the princess, similarly destabilizes the norms it supposedly reinforces.

PIRATE MASCULINITY: HISTORICAL AND THEATRICAL

Piratical imagery, including hooks, parrots, peg-legs, and a vocabulary peppered with "arrs" and "yo-hos," pervades children's media from picture books like Claire Freedman's *Pirates Love Underpants* (2012) and Neil Gaiman's *Pirate Stew* (2020) to the television series *Jake and the Neverland Pirates* (2011–16). Disney's *Pirates of the Caribbean* franchise both draws on and contributes to the popularity of the pirate figure. The multi-billion-dollar franchise includes five films about Jack Sparrow, the pirate captain Johnny Depp debuted in *Pirates of the Caribbean: The Curse of the Black Pearl* (2003). The films themselves were based on the Pirates of the Caribbean boat ride, which opened at Disneyland in 1967, a few months before Walt Disney's death, and can now be found at several Disney parks, accompanied, of course, by gift shops offering pirate toys and other souvenirs.

The Pirates of the Caribbean attraction was originally intended to be a walk-through wax exhibit,[143] a form of entertainment that has Victorian roots (as I explain in chapter one). The 1964 World's Fair, however, proved both the feasibility of Audio-Animatronics figures (with Abraham Lincoln) and the popularity of boat rides (with It's a Small World). Today the ride is marketed as "one of the most immersive attractions ever created for a theme park," and invites riders to "behold brazen buccaneers drunk on pillaged plunder," "sing along as sea roving scalawags serenade you with their classic shanty, 'Yo Ho (A Pirate's Life for Me),'" and "skulk past the well-armed lass who commands a colorful auction of villagers' goods."[144] The marketing captures the spirit of the ride, which manages to portray violence, theft, and drunkenness in a humorous, family friendly manner.

Pirates of the Caribbean captures the paradox of the pirate figure, which is simultaneously fun and frightening, playful and transgressive. The paradox depends on historical distance: the pirate is confined to a past that is markedly different from our own time. Historical pirates are further mediated by two centuries of fictional portrayals in poems, novels, and plays, and, later, in movies and on television. Each generation remakes the pirate in its own image, and in the last decade several works have unearthed a history of both real and legendary pirate women.[145] Changing ideas of gender have led Disney to revise its own pirates, too. The "well-armed lass" referred to above is one such revision: until 2018, she was part of the auction itself, alongside a sign reading "Take a Wench for a Bride."[146] Despite this recent re-gendering, however, the pirate remains a masculine image. At Disney's theme parks, girls can choose to be a princess, a mermaid, or an empress, but the primary dress-up option marketed to boys is the pirate.[147] Yet because the pirate is by nature performative, he pushes the boundaries of gender and sexuality. The history of the fictional pirate reveals just how fluid that masculinity is. And although the pirate figure predates the nineteenth century, the familiar, fictionalized pirate emerged during the Victorian period.

Many familiar pirate tropes can be traced to Captain Charles Johnson's *A General History of the Pyrates*. The book was published in the 1720s, at the end of the so-called "golden age" of piracy that stretched from the mid-seventeenth century through the first quarter of the eighteenth century. The pirates of this era operated primarily in the Caribbean, providing the historical basis for Disney's attraction. But the historical pirates of the Caribbean depended on an economy that Disney's parks elide. The ships that pirate crews would have been robbing, the farms and colonies that the British navy would have been protecting, and in fact, the whole economic reason for white Europeans' presence in the Caribbean depended on the forced labor and enslavement of Africans.[148]

By the Victorian period, the British liked to think of themselves as enemies to slavery. Britain outlawed the slave trade in 1807 and abolished slavery in its colonies in 1833, three decades before Lincoln's Emancipation Proclamation in the United States. After 1839, the British and Foreign Anti-Slavery Society sought to end slavery worldwide, devoting huge naval resources to fighting the slave trade and relocating enslaved persons to the colony of Sierra Leone. Poets took up the cause, too. The speaker of Elizabeth Barrett Browning's "The Runaway Slave at Pilgrim's Point" (1848) stands at Plymouth Rock, addressing America's origin story: "O pilgrims, I have gasped and run / All night long from the whips of one / Who in your names works sin and woe!"[149] Later she remarks, "this land is the free America, / And this mark on my wrist—(I prove what I say) / Ropes tied me up here to the flogging place."[150] Barrett Browning's poem was first published in the *Liberty Bell*, an American abolitionist gift book. She chastises the hypocrisy of American slavery, speaking as a citizen of a nation that had already made the moral choice to abolish it.

But for Barrett Browning herself, and for Britain as a nation, taking that position required some convenient historical revision. Barrett Browning came from a family that not only benefitted from slavery but actively enslaved hundreds of people: the Barrett family made its fortune from sugar plantations in Jamaica, dating back to the seventeenth century. Her family was far from unique in this regard. Novelists like Jane Austen depict the English aristocracy on their country estates, but as Edward Said famously put it, "no matter how isolated and insulated" an English estate might seem, it depends on wealth directly connected to the empire and the slave trade.[151] Tellingly, when Britain abolished slavery in 1833 they compensated not the formerly enslaved people but the enslavers, incurring a national debt that was not fully paid off until 2015. The Centre for the Legacies of British Slave-ownership has tracked the commercial and cultural impact of that payoff, which filtered through every part of English society.[152]

For England to see itself as heroically opposed to global slavery, it needed to revise its history. Pirates played a role in this revision. Johnson's *A General History of the Pyrates* makes clear both the link to the slave trade and the racial diversity of pirate crews. Familiar elements of pirate mythology, such as walking the plank and the trope of the "reluctant pirate," can be traced directly to slave traders.[153] These elements are not typically reflected in English stories about pirates. As the Victorians downplayed their own role in the slave trade, they romanticized the pirate. In the Caribbean during the golden age of piracy, a quarter of a pirate ship's crew was likely to have been Black, and "pirate crews were multinational and multiracial, often stunningly diverse."[154] But from naval melodramas to *Treasure Island*, from Captain Hook to Captain Jack Sparrow, pirate heroes are nearly always white.

Pirate sexuality was also portrayed as ahistorically normative. Actual pirates were "rebelliously masculine," valuing traits like strength, courage, and assertiveness, but they did not necessarily define that masculinity through sexual activity.[155] In the seventeenth and eighteenth centuries (the golden age of piracy), sexual acts would not necessarily have coalesced into a sexual identity.[156] Spending most of their time at sea among all-male crews, pirates not only lived in a homosocial world but probably practiced a fluid sexuality.[157] Depp's Jack Sparrow, whose "dashing and dangerous sex appeal" typifies the pirate, breaks from that historical reality.[158] In terms of both race and sexuality, historical pirates were more diverse than the fictional tradition presents them to be.

Disney's theme parks prominently feature many aspects of American history, and the company once considered building a historical theme park in Virginia.[159] But the slave trade is conspicuously absent from the parks, and the Pirates of the Caribbean ride does not reflect the diversity of historical pirates. Of course, the elision of the historical contexts and the economic realities of piracy is by no means unique to Disney. Pirates of the Caribbean evokes a long cultural history of the pirate, including once popular but now forgotten genres that had divorced the pirate from his historical origins long before

Disneyland. "Yo Ho (A Pirate's Life for Me)," the song that plays during the Pirates of the Caribbean ride, owes its origins to nautical melodramas, a Victorian stage genre that typically featured an opening song about "the jollity of a pirate's life."[160] Nautical melodramas were the most popular theatrical genre in the 1820s and 1830s. Plays like Douglas Jerrold's *Black Ey'd Susan* (1829) promoted the heroism of the British navy, often referencing recent naval battles like the victory over Napoleon's forces at Trafalgar.[161] They established both the nautical setting and the masculine conventions that would soon be applied to pirates. The pirate became a mainstay of fiction and drama over the course of the nineteenth century and by the end of the Victorian period was not only heroic but also quintessentially straight, white, and English.[162] This was the image that the Walt Disney Company inherited in the twentieth century and reflected in the Pirates of the Caribbean attraction.

The nautical melodrama espoused its own ideal of manliness through the very language that characters spoke. Naval heroes' speech was peppered with nautical jargon (and profanity), but their martial prowess and duty to the nation were balanced by their domestic affections and familial responsibilities. When speaking of his feelings, or appearing in domestic scenes, the naval hero's speech would drop all slang and rise to a manly, sentimental eloquence.[163] Later playwrights adopted the same language for pirate characters. First a stock villain of nautical melodramas about the British navy, the pirate soon became a heroic figure in poems and novels by Byron, Walter Scott, and James Fenimore Cooper, all of which were adapted for the stage. Two productions of *Red Rover*, based on a Cooper novel, ran simultaneously at competing theaters (the productions later influenced Stevenson's *Treasure Island*).[164] Scott's trademark blending of fact and fiction mixed with the stage conventions of the nautical melodrama and the popularity of the Byronic antihero into a style Mel Campbell has termed "pirate chic." Like the hero of the nautical melodrama, the stage pirate was typically "a hyper masculine figure using an aesthetic vocabulary that at the time was decidedly feminized."[165] The stage pirate represented a bifurcated masculine ideal, complicating the gender binary by intertwining masculine heroism with feminine sensibilities.

Children could recreate stage pirates at home. Toy theaters, which came with paper characters and scenery, reached their apex in the 1830s and 1840s, contemporaneously with nautical melodramas. These toys were fondly recalled by writers like Charles Dickens, G. K. Chesterton, and Robert Louis Stevenson; painters like John Everett Millais; and actresses like Ellen Terry.[166] When Edwin J. Brett launched his periodical *Boys of England* in 1866, he included a toy theater version of *Alone in the Pirates Lair*, a "commercial crossover" that used established forms (fiction and the toy theater) to help launch a new endeavor, the juvenile magazine.[167] *Boys of England* was just one among many juvenile magazines that took off in the second half of the century, and pirate stories were common fare. Rather than being confined to the stage, theatrical pirates moved into the home, becoming a staple of childhood games. Stevenson's "Pirate Story," included in *A Child's Garden of Verses* (1885), imagines one such game: "Three of us afloat in the meadow by the swing, / Three of us aboard the basket on the lea. . . . The wicket is the harbor and the garden is the shore."[168]

As Britain's most famous naval victories faded from memory, the nautical melodrama moved from the center of theatrical culture to the margins. William Gilbert and Arthur Sullivan's hit play *H. M. S. Pinafore* (1878) parodies the genre, which audiences in the 1870s would have considered old-fashioned.[169] And their next play, *The Pirates of Penzance* (1879), would go even further. *The Pirates of Penzance*, which a century and a half later is still among the best-known pirate stories, features Frederic, an orphan whose nurse, Ruth, is supposed to secure him an apprenticeship as a ship's pilot. But she mishears the word, and he is instead apprenticed to a pirate crew until his twenty-first birthday. When he turns twenty-one he is released, and falls in love with Mabel, the daughter of Major-General Stanley. Because he was born on February 29, however, Frederic has not yet fulfilled his contract, which states twenty-one birthdays, rather than twenty-one years. His sense of duty compels him to remain with the pirates. The pirates eventually capture the Major-General, but yield when it is demanded they surrender "in Queen Victoria's name." After this show of loyalty to the queen, it is revealed that the pirates are all "noblemen who have gone wrong," and the play ends happily.

This brief summary captures the general parodic mode of *The Pirates of Penzance*, but not the extent to which the comic opera challenges Victorian norms of gender and sexuality. Gilbert and Sullivan famously renounced cross-dressing (which had been a stage staple for centuries), and Carolyn Williams has argued that the choice allows their oeuvre "simultaneously to imitate and to criticize the standards of bourgeois respectability, as they are expressed in the roles and rules of separate spheres."[170] *The Pirates of Penzance* depicts several challenges to normative sexuality, including the sexual indiscretions implied by the preponderance of orphans, the wards' assumed sexual attraction to the pirates, and the comic figure of Ruth, the middle-aged nursemaid who becomes the butt of misogynist jokes about female desire.[171] In this sense *The Pirates of Penzance* might be seen as a culmination of the stage pirate, whose complicated history runs counter to normative masculinity.

Gilbert and Sullivan maintained their cultural cachet well into the twentieth century. In 1938, the Disney storywriter Al Perkins thought the croquet scene in the *Alice* books, "a Gilbert-and-Sullivan situation that might get a polite laugh from the elite but would never go over with the boys in the balcony."[172] But the legacy of the Victorian stage is more than a highbrow humorous style. Over the course of the period, dramatic audiences became accustomed to a particular kind of pirate, one far different from the historical pirate on whom he was supposedly based. With origins closely aligned to the British navy, the stage pirate was quintessentially English and nearly always white.

Disney inherited and built on the pirate image that had emerged on the Victorian stage. But when Walt Disney designed the Pirates of the Caribbean attraction, he was probably thinking not of the general type but of two specific texts: Robert Louis Stevenson's *Treasure Island* and J. M. Barrie's *Peter Pan*. Both were mainstays of children's culture during Walt Disney's childhood, and the studio's adaptations appeared close together (*Treasure Island* in 1950 and *Peter Pan* in 1953). Each has a unique history with the company, and those histories show how the pirate transitioned from the nautical melodramas of the early nineteenth century to Disney's theme parks and films.

DISNEY'S VICTORIAN PIRATES

Disney had begun garnering a worldwide audience in the 1930s, and at the outset of World War II, the company depended on foreign markets for a profit. The war closed those markets, and the problem was not entirely solved even at the war's end. Several European nations restricted profits made by American film studios, insisting that those profits be spent in the countries where they were earned. Disney and its distribution company, RKO, had millions of dollars restricted in Europe.[173] Animation is an expensive form, and it was not financially feasible to set up an animation studio abroad. To make use of the funds frozen, Disney decided to produce its first live-action feature film. It would be financed and produced in Great Britain and based on a British novel, Robert Louis Stevenson's *Treasure Island*.

Set in the eighteenth century, towards the end of the golden age of piracy, *Treasure Island* consolidates the pirate fictions from earlier in the century. Stevenson bragged about plagiarizing other pirate stories,[174] and *Treasure Island*'s illustrators also cribbed images from earlier texts about pirates (and from each other).[175] Disney's *Treasure Island* was the first of sixty-three live-actions films that Walt Disney produced before his death in 1966.[176] It established the pirate image that would soon be incorporated into *Pirates of the Caribbean*, and its English origins left a mark on the company. *Treasure Island* was immediately followed by several live-action films based on English stories and texts: *The Story of Robin Hood and His Merrie Men* (1952); *The Sword and the Rose* (1953), a story of English knights; and *Rob Roy, the Highland Rogue* (1954), based on Walter Scott's 1817 novel. This Anglophilia became evident in the animated features as well. *Alice in Wonderland* (1951) was the first animated musical to follow *Treasure Island*. The next was a story that, like Alice, had been in production since before the war. It too was based on an English text, one that was directly influenced by Stevenson's novel: J. M. Barrie's *Peter Pan*.

Peter Pan was among the many texts to which Disney had acquired the rights in a "post-*Snow White* buying spree."[177] The company secured the animation rights from the Great Ormond Street Hospital, to whom Barrie had gifted the copyright to *Peter Pan* in 1929. Like *Alice in Wonderland*, *Peter Pan* went through several stages of pre-production at the studio, and at different stages Disney considered Mary Martin to play Peter and Cary Grant to play Hook.[178] When it finally reached fruition in 1953 it was only marginally more successful than *Alice in Wonderland*. But like *Alice in Wonderland*, it later become a valuable Disney franchise. Peter Pan's Flight was among the original Disneyland attractions, and it remains one of the most popular. Tinker Bell was initially included among the Disney Princesses, before being spun off into her own franchise, Disney Fairies.[179] Disney has shaped the popular image of *Peter Pan* almost as much as *Alice in Wonderland*.

In chapter two, I described Disney's decades-long journey to adapt the *Alice* books, tracing the story from the original texts and illustrations through stage plays, films, and theme-park attractions. A similar story might be told about Disney and *Peter Pan*. Barrie's story originated in a privately printed photo album, *The Boy Castaways of Black Lake Island* (1901), which Barrie produced for the Llewyn Davies children, based on games they had invented together. The character of Peter first appeared in Barrie's 1902 novel *The Little White Bird*, and the play *Peter Pan* was first staged in 1904. It was an immediate hit and became a staple performance during holiday season for the next decade.[180] Barrie took advantage of the popularity to reissue the relevant chapters from *The Little White Bird* as an illustrated book, *Peter Pan in Kensington Gardens* (1906). He later published the story as a novel, *Peter and Wendy* in 1911, and the text of the play (its stage directions clearly influenced by the novel) in 1928. Souvenir programs and prose retellings of the story (some but not all authorized by Barrie) proliferated, and *Peter Pan* became a "public phenomenon."[181]

Much has been written about this fascinating history[182] and about Peter Pan's relationship to masculinity.[183] The two male adults—Mr. Darling and Captain Hook, in many productions played by the same actor—are often seen to represent adulthood, the "growing up" inevitable for all children (except one). Barrie blends together different genres of children's literature, from domestic fiction to adventure stories, and he was certainly aware of the allure that pirates held for children by the turn of the twentieth century. Like Stevenson, he openly acknowledged the rich history of pirates from which he borrowed. Hook is said to be "the only man that the Sea-Cook feared," a reference to Long John Silver in *Treasure Island*.[184] The play's first season featured a scene titled "Davey Jones's Locker," in which Captain Hook is visited by ghosts of famous pirates.[185] But Hook soon eclipsed his predecessors. Shortly after the play premiered the English writer Alfred Noyes called *Peter Pan* "the last word on pirates."[186] Hook remains probably the most famous fictional pirate. He is not like the pirates in *Treasure Island*. Long John Silver may be able to "speak like a book when so minded,"[187] but in *Treasure Island* he is the quintessential ragged, one-legged pirate, complete with a parrot. The image persists in film adaptations, and Silver culminates one of the "two major competing paradigms for pirate appearance."[188] Hook, the gentleman pirate captain, represents the other.

In Barrie's texts, Hook is a sinister figure. When he first appears in the novel Barrie has him kill another pirate, just to "show Hook's method": "the hook shoots forth, there is a tearing sound and one screech, then the body is kicked aside, and the pirates pass on. He has not even taken the cigars from his mouth."[189] This violence notwithstanding, what makes Hook especially villainous is his upper-crust background. Hook is "of a different caste from his crew," having attended "a famous public school."[190] In the published script, Hook's dying words are "Floreat Etona," connecting him to Eton College,[191] and in 1923 Barrie delivered a speech titled "Captain Hook at Eton." Hook's background and diction signal the same respectability that makes Trelawney and Livesey such upstanding Englishmen in *Treasure Island*. The implication (coupled with the fact that the same actor often played both Hook and Mr. Darling) is that all grown men are essentially pirates, making Hook doubly threatening.

Barrie seems to have intended Hook seriously, as evidenced by the novel and the published play script. But those intentions were contradicted from the very start. Barrie told stage designer William Nicholson to distinguish his pirates from *The Pirates of Penzance*: he wanted serious pirates, not farcical ones. This intention was immediately undermined by Gerald du Maurier, the actor who first played Hook on stage. Famous for his impersonations, du Maurier provided time for a complicated scene change with parodies of well-known contemporary actors like Henry Irving and Beerbohm Tree.[192] Archival reports indicate that Disney initially considered serious actors like Basil Rathbone and John Barrymore for the part of Hook,[193] but ultimately Disney's Captain Hook would be truer to the comic tradition than to the darkly sinister Hook of Barrie's texts.

Materials in the Walt Disney Archives show other insights into the development of Disney's *Peter Pan*. Around the same time that Al Perkins prepared his memos about the *Alice* books, Dorothy Ann Blank researched *Peter Pan* (the earliest memo is dated October 20, 1938). Perkins had begun with the books themselves, but Blank began with secondary scholarship, reproducing sections of works by Patrick Braybrooke, James A. Roy, H. M. Walbrook, and F. J. Harvey Darton.[194] Blank found herself appropriately flummoxed by the story's textual history. "It's a swell story," she wrote in an inter-office memo, "but Mr. Barrie has scattered it around and made it as confusing as possible."[195] She concluded that *Peter Pan* is "quite free from the limits which seem to restrict some literary properties," perhaps because Barrie "was never quite satisfied with his telling of the story."[196] The extent to which Disney's film might owe fidelity to its textual sources came up regularly in subsequent meetings, but it was never as much of a concern as it was for the *Alice* books. Disney never seems to have considered a *Peter Pan* consultant, analogous to Aldous Huxley's role with Alice.

Blank and others from the studio attended a production of *Peter Pan* at the Wilshire Ebell theater, and like Perkins's *Alice* report, her memos reference stage and film versions, not just textual ones. She recognizes the primacy of the stage versions, referring to the novel *Peter and Wendy* as a "fictionalized version of the Maude Adams play."[197] Maude Adams had been the first actress to play Peter Pan on Broadway, in 1905, and Blank suggests that she had become synonymous with the role, at least in America. She reproduces a 1925 review in *Literary Digest* indicating that "America has seemed to have a set belief that Peter Pan was Maude Adams and Maude Adams, Peter Pan."[198] Blank notes the tradition of women playing Peter Pan on stage, but also that critics favor a more "robust" portrayal. She suggests that an animated *Peter Pan* be "<u>all boy</u>—funny, fierce, brave, even a little tough."[199] From the start, it seems, masculinity was a primary concern.

By October 3, 1939, Earl Hurd had sketched out a story beginning in Kensington Gardens, and Walt Disney attended a story meeting a few weeks later.[200] Meetings about *Peter Pan* continued into the 1940s (notes from a 1943 meeting indicate that production continued even as most of the Disney studio was working on the war effort).[201] A complete script was drafted by March 1946, and by January 1947, it was determined that the film would be

To American audiences in the 1920s, "Peter Pan was Maude Adams and Maude Adams, Peter Pan."

an integrated musical, with the songs carrying the plot.[202] The decision was consistent with the earliest reports, which had assumed an animated musical. Blank wrote the words "chance for a rousing musical number" next to

Barrie's reference to a "pirate chorus,"[203] and she would certainly have noted that the Neverland pirates are often singing. When they first appear in the novel they sing, "Avast, belay, yo ho, heave to, / A-pirating we go" and "Yo ho, yo ho, the pirate life / The flag o'skull and bones."[204] Pirate tunes similarly feature in *Treasure Island*. Jim Hawkins recalls the Admiral Benbow often "shaking with 'Yo-ho-ho, and a bottle of rum,'" and when he first comes onboard the ship he notes the crew "yo-ho-ing at their work."[205] Such songs are a holdover from the nautical melodramas and pirate plays with which both Barrie and Stevenson were familiar, but it was probably these specific texts that sparked the imagination of Ed Penner and X Atencio, who wrote the lyrics for, respectively, "A Pirate's Life" (in *Peter Pan*) and "Yo ho (A Pirate's Life)" (which plays during the Pirates of the Caribbean ride).

Disney's history with *Treasure Island* and *Peter Pan* reveals how those texts distilled the Victorian tradition into the pirates portrayed in the Pirates of the Caribbean boat ride. Three and a half decades after the ride opened, Disney returned to Stevenson's text. Partly to placate star animators John Musker and Ron Clements, who were unhappy with the direction they saw the company taking, Michael Eisner greenlit a project the pair had wanted to do for a while: *Treasure Island* in space.[206] The result, *Treasure Planet* (2002), was widely panned by reviewers, but does present an updated take on pirate masculinity. Sonya Sawyer Fritz argues that the film engages a modern discourse on boyhood, focused less on physical competition and more on boys' emotional and psychological needs, especially their need to connect with others.[207] In this adaptation, Silver remains the mentor figure he is in Stevenson's novel, but that mentorship takes the form of sympathy and tenderness. Fritz partially attributes the film's failure to this change in Silver's character: the gentle father figure has less potential to inspire imaginative play than the romantic pirate.[208]

Despite *Treasure Planet*'s unpopularity, the reimagined pirate masculinity helped establish the pirate as a masculine alternative to the princess. But by this time another (much more popular) franchise was taking shape. The origins of Johnny Depp's Jack Sparrow can be traced not just to the twentieth-century "flamboyant impersonations of Tyrone Power and Errol Flynn" and Howard Pyle's illustrations in *Scribner's* and *Harper's Monthly*,[209] but further back to the Victorian stage.[210] It was this image that Disney chose as the masculine alternative to the princess. The Disney Princess and Disney Pirate brands owe a debt to the Victorian period. And both franchises show how corporate brands, often condemned for promoting regressive ideologies, maintain a flexibility that allows for a fluid understanding of gender and sexuality.

Conclusion

Post-Corporate Art and Criticism

When I first began this project, I envisioned writing about several Victorian texts that Disney has adapted. Some of them are barely mentioned in the preceding chapters. I planned a chapter on European Victorianism, which would have included Jules Verne's *20,000 Leagues Under the Sea* (1870; adapted by Disney in 1954) and Carlo Collodi's *Pinocchio* (1887; adapted by Disney in 1940).[1] I chose instead to focus on a single author, Hans Christian Andersen. Dickens features prominently in chapter one, but I didn't have anything new to say about Dickensian legacies in *Mickey's Christmas Carol* (1983) or Scrooge McDuck.[2] And while the Walt Disney Archives hold some fascinating materials about *Peter Pan*, I discuss them only briefly, since my conclusions about that work are similar to what I say about *Alice in Wonderland* in chapter two.

The Disney film about which I tried hardest to write is *The Jungle Book* (1967). This film, the last animated feature produced during Walt Disney's lifetime, is based on Rudyard Kipling's short stories. Born in 1865, Kipling lived until 1936, long enough to have seen a Mickey Mouse cartoon (though I haven't found evidence that he ever did). When he won the Nobel Prize for Literature in 1907, Kipling was the first English-language writer to do so. His modern reputation today is decidedly mixed. Kipling grew up in British India, which is the subject of many of his best-known works, including *The Jungle Book* (1894). Later poems like "The White Man's Burden" overtly promote an imperialist agenda. As Edward Said puts it, Kipling has "great

POST-CORPORATE ART AND CRITICISM   151

aesthetic merit" but his novels are "deeply antithetical" to modern sensibilities.[3] Modern readers find Kipling's racism and imperialism hard to ignore, and he features prominently in postcolonial scholarship, a field that in the last few decades has profoundly reshaped literary criticism in general and Victorian studies in particular.[4]

The British Empire reached its apex under Queen Victoria, whose image presided over government offices across the globe. Inevitably, anti-imperialist scholars in the twentieth century put the Victorians at the center of their critique. Victorian writers feature prominently in groundbreaking works of postcolonial theory by writers like Homi Bhabha, Gayatri Spivak, Gauri Viswanathan, and Edward Said.[5] After interventions by Said, Spivak, Julia Sun-Joo Lee, and Chinua Achebe, teachers and students can no longer ignore the imperial underpinnings even of seemingly provincial novels like Jane Austen's *Mansfield Park* (1814), Charlotte Brontë's *Jane Eyre* (1847) and Elizabeth Gaskell's *North and South* (1854), let alone overly imperialist works like Kipling's *Kim* (1901) or Joseph Conrad's *Heart of Darkness* (1899).[6]

International corporations like the East India Company and United Fruit were closely intertwined with the imperial powers that postcolonial scholarship brought to the fore. Only in 1801 did the British government establish a single office to oversee its colonies, and it was not until the 1850s that the Colonial Office separated from the Home Office and the Board of Trade. For centuries the British government relied on private ventures like the Hudson Bay Company and the East India Company, "commercial enterprises that wielded quite a lot of control over foreign territory."[7] This link between capitalism and colonialism, and the concurrent rise of cultural studies alongside postcolonial studies, inevitably shaped critiques of the Walt Disney Company, which has been described as "an empire that conquers, colonises, and capitalises upon its textual sources."[8] Other critiques extend well beyond claims about textual appropriation. Written in the middle of the Chilean revolution, Ariel Dorfman and Armand Mattelart's *How to Read Donald Duck* (1971) argues that American media in general, and Disney in particular, provided a blueprint for Augusto Pinochet's "arsenal of psychological warfare."[9] Borrowing the language of the Victorian critic Matthew Arnold, Dorfman and Mattelart argue that the "sweetness and light" surrounding Disney elide the company's cultural imperialism and capitalist ideology.[10]

Dorfman and Mattelart attempt to do for Disney what Said, Spivak, and others had done for Victorian literature: make it impossible to engage with its works without considering imperialism. Unlike earlier critiques of Walt Disney himself, or of individual texts, *How to Read Donald Duck* approaches the Walt Disney Company as an ideological force. The argument derives its power largely because the company was (nearly) universally loved. Criticism of Disney, write Dorfman and Mattelart, is often "interpreted as an affront to morality and civilization at large."[11] That criticism had begun a few years earlier, with Schickel's *The Disney Version*. *How to Read Donald Duck*, which draws substantially on Schickel's critique, became a bestseller in Latin America and remains influential. Eleanor Byrne and Martin McQuillan's *Deconstructing Disney* (1999) begins with a quotation from Dorfman and Mattelart and the premise that the association of Disney with cultural imperialism is now taken for granted.[12] Numerous other critiques of the company on racial and imperial grounds have been published over the last few decades.[13]

In the last few years, Disney has responded to these critiques. On Disney's streaming service, Disney+, films like *Peter Pan* and *The Jungle Book* include a warning about "outdated cultural depictions," and *Song of the South* is not included at all.[14] The "Reimagine Tomorrow" initiative both accepts criticisms of the company's past works and attempts to chart a more inclusive future.[15] As I was thinking about Disney's adaptation of Kipling's stories, I kept returning to that idea: the future rather the past. My planned critique of Disney's global media empire, using *The Jungle Book* as a starting point, began to seem both redundant and short-sighted.

My teaching also shaped my thinking. Every year I taught a two-semester British literature survey, which began in the Middle Ages and ended with contemporary writers. The authors we read during the first semester, and for most of the second semester, were nearly all white. But I taught almost no white authors born in the twentieth century: the contemporary writers that my students and I found most interesting were nearly all immigrants from, or still living in, British colonies. These postcolonial writers fit into the syllabus quite well, engaging directly with works that students had read earlier in the course. They also reminded me that postcolonialism is not merely a method of critique but also a creative cultural movement.

As the British Empire shrank in the twentieth century and new nations declared their independence, postcolonial writers debated the appropriateness of writing in English, the language of the colonizer. Ngũgĩ wa Thiong'o led a successful movement to abolish the English department at University College in Nairobi, Kenya, replacing it with a Department of African Literature and Language. Thiong'o had built his reputation as a novelist writing in English, but in *Decolonizing the Mind* (1986) he rejected English as a tool of colonial oppression, choosing instead to write in native Kenyan languages.[16] Around the same time, Salman Rushdie asserted that the "English language ceased to be the sole possession of the English some time ago."[17] Rushdie registers concerns like Thiong'o's but also argues that English is a world language. By writing in English, says Rushdie, pragmatic artists can not only extend their reach but also remake the language for their own purposes.

Rushdie's view seems to have won out, evidenced by a rich tradition of postcolonial literature in English, from poets like Louise Bennett and Grace Nichols to novelists like Chinua Achebe, Mohsin Hamid, and Amitav Ghosh. Just as postcolonial critics made the Victorians central to their arguments, many postcolonial writers adapted Victorian texts. Jean Rhys's *Wide Sargasso Sea* (1966) imagines a Caribbean backstory for Bertha Mason, Mr. Rochester's first wife in Charlotte Brontë's *Jane Eyre* (1847).[18] Timothy Greene's film *Boy Called Twist* (2004) sets Dickens's *Oliver Twist* in post-apartheid South Africa, while Tanika Gupta's play sets *Great Expectations* in Calcutta.[19] English writers who trace their roots to former colonies similarly draw on Victorian texts to imagine the experience of immigration. One of my favorite poets, Daljit Nagra, riffs on Matthew Arnold's poem "Dover Beach" in "Look, We Have Coming to Dover!" Arnold's lyric is set at Dover, the entry point back into England from Europe. Returning from his honeymoon on the continent, Arnold gazes across the English channel, listening to "the grating roar / Of pebbles which the waves draw back."[20] Nagra repurposes that setting as a place of immigration, and he hears a different sound. He imagines "swarms of us . . . babbling our lingoes, flecked by the chalk of Britannia!"[21] Another poem by Nagra, "The Man Who Would Be English," alludes to Kipling's "The Man Who Would Be King." Nagra locates his speaker in an English pub during a football match, feeling "all in with the English race" until he returns home to his wife, who is less happy in their new nation.[22]

Rhys, Greene, Gupta, and Nagra treat these Victorian texts not as evidence of a hegemony to be spurned but as a tradition with which to actively engage. Inspired by these writers, I began to wonder what a post-corporate literature might look like. Instead of using *The Jungle Book* to offer yet another critique of capitalism, I became interested in works that creatively engage with the legacy and ubiquity of Disney, such as Cory Doctorow's novel *Down and Out in the Magic Kingdom* (2003) and Banksy's installation Dismaland (2015).

Cory Doctorow (no relation to the novelist E. L. Doctorow) has emerged as one the leaders of the "cypherpunk" genre. Today he is best known for writing about technology culture and for his *Little Brother* trilogy.[23] But his first novel was a futuristic dystopia set in a Disney theme park. *Down and Out in the Magic Kingdom* was positively reviewed in the *New York Times* when it first appeared, its "clumsy" characterization and plotting balanced by "a knowing, gently satiric view of an ascendant digital culture" and a plethora of interesting technologies.[24] At the time, Doctorow was working for the Electronic Frontier Foundation, a nonprofit digital rights group, and he released *Down and Out in the Magic Kingdom* under a creative commons license.[25] He was the first novelist to publish a book in this way.[26] In this sense, Doctorow stands in contrast to the Walt Disney Company. Under CEO Michael Eisner, Disney developed a reputation for fiercely defending its intellectual property. Nevertheless, *Down and Out in the Magic Kingdom* evinces a clear fondness for Disney. Doctorow visited Disney World regularly as a child and recalls discussing with his father "the techno-utopia elements of the Disney parks."[27] Much of the plot revolves around the protagonist's attempt to forestall a new technology that imprints memories, replacing real experiences with falsely implanted memories of them. The fictional technology has already replaced the Audio-Animatronics figures in the Hall of Presidents, and the protagonist tries to keep it out of the Haunted Mansion.[28] The novel reads like a paean to Disney, even while its publication context and some of its plot critique the corporate structures through which the company has thrived.

When asked how he reconciles his obsession with Disney with his work reforming copyright legislation, Doctorow remarked that popular entertainment, even when produced by global media companies, is "our shared cultural heritage," and shouldn't be cast aside to serve an ideological agenda.[29] While Dorfman and Mattelart find Disney's stories and characters ineluctably tied to a corporate ethos, Doctorow separates the two. He is comfortable celebrating Disney's attractions while resisting its profit-centered litigiousness. I see this stance as something analogous to postcolonial writers who critique the imperialist context of canonical writers without denying those writers' cultural importance and aesthetic value.

A more recent example of post-Disney art is Banksy's Dismaland. Banksy built his reputation as a street artist, and his political-themed graffiti has made him one of the most famous contemporary artists. Much of Banksy's work is anti-capitalist, and in 2006 he managed to smuggle into Disneyland a life-size inflatable doll dressed as a Guantanamo Bay detainee and to display it in the Big Thunder Mountain Railroad.[30] Located near Bristol, where Banksy began his career, Dismaland was a collaborative effort among nearly sixty artists.[31] The pop-up art exhibition billed itself as "bemusement park," and remained open for five weeks.[32] Parts of Dismaland target Disney directly. Like Disney's parks, Dismaland features a castle at its center, though Dismaland's is deliberately decrepit, with the scaffolding exposed and a distorted caricature of *The Little Mermaid*'s Ariel perched in front of it. Photos on the exhibition's website show employees in oversize Mickey Mouse ears, their surly demeanor a deliberate contrast to the "cast members" who put into practice Disney's famous customer service.[33] One exhibit portrays

Cinderella's carriage overturned, the princess's body hanging lifeless through the window while surrounding paparazzi take pictures.

But most of the art exhibited at Dismaland has little to do with Disney. Several well-established artists were among the collaborators. Mike Ross displayed his sculpture "Big Rig Jig," which had premiered at Burning Man in 2007, and Jenny Holzer included excerpts from her *Truisms* series, begun in the late 1970s.[34] Primarily, Dismaland alludes to Disney not with its content but with its form. The exhibition parodies a theme park. Parody, whether as lighthearted as John Cozart's YouTube parodies of Disney princesses[35] or as scathing as Dismaland, relies on its audience's prior knowledge. Parody "always looks and sounds like what it criticizes."[36] Rhys's *Wide Sargasso Sea* and Nagra's "Look, We Have Coming to Dover!" depend not only on readers' familiarity with *Jane Eyre* or "Dover Beach," but also on the genre expectations of (respectively) a novel and a poem. Similarly, Dismaland is built on the conventions of the theme park. It is built around a highly visible central icon (what Walt Disney called a "wienie")[37] and offers a participatory experience. Banksy told the BBC that many of the works rely on audience participation. The crashed Cinderella carriage, for example, "is only complete when surrounded by gawping crowds with their cameras out."[38] The term "theme park" was coined to describe Disneyland, and the Disney did so much to define the theme-park aesthetic that the company is inevitably tied to the form. Dismaland's parody is as much an homage to what Disney has created as it is a critique of the company itself.

The two subjects of this book—Victorian literature and the Walt Disney Company—have, rightly, been subjected to criticism and revision. Yet they have also evolved. Neither Victorian studies nor Disney's films and attractions are the same today as they were when they emerged in the first half of the twentieth century. Under Robert Iger, Disney has not only grown is size and profitability, but has also become more diverse and less litigious than it had been. In the 2020s, Disney has faced criticism for being *too* welcoming of racial and sexual differences, or too "woke." Similarly, V21 and the "Undisciplining Victorians" special issue of *Victorian Studies* offer much-needed revisions to how scholars approach Victorian literature and culture.[39]

Disney and the Victorians are part of our cultural heritage, and passing on that heritage is a complicated business. Even the most critical scholars don't suggest that either should be jettisoned entirely. Trying uncritically to ignore or to refuse the prominence of Disney and the Victorians is as damaging as uncritically accepting the values of generations past. We have the power to choose not only the texts we privilege but also the way we interpret them.

Literary studies provides tools both of appreciation and of critique, and this book applies some of those tools to the corporate products that later generations will inherit.

Appendix

Disney Studies and Victorian Studies

When I first proposed to teach a seminar about "Disney's Victorians," I justified the course simply by the plurality of Victorian texts that Disney had adapted and by the proximity of Disney World to the college where I was teaching. I thought the title would attract students. But as I prepared the class, and especially after visiting the Walt Disney Archives, I came to see connections between Disney and the Victorians, and also, more broadly, connections between corporate productions and literary history. This book is the result of thinking more deeply about those connections, especially as they relate to scholarship in Victorian studies, media studies, children's literature, and adaptation studies. The preceding chapters are shaped by that scholarship and by conversations with colleagues in those fields.

Scholars reading this book will (rightfully) expect an engagement with the scholars whose work undergirds my thinking. That engagement typically comes in a monograph's introduction. While writing this book, however, and reading other scholarship about the Walt Disney Company, I began to envision another reader, someone interested in the history of the Walt Disney Company and willing to see how Victorian studies might inform that history, but less invested in theoretical methods or how this book responds to specific scholarship. And so I chose instead to move the research review to this appendix. I've structured it with three questions, each linked, generally, to a different discipline: Why Disney? Why the Victorians? And why the two together?

WHY DISNEY?

Academic study of Disney's adaptations can be traced to two landmark texts in the 1960s: Frances Clarke Sayers's letter to the *Los Angeles Times*, "Walt Disney Accused" (1965), and Richard Schickel's *The Disney Version* (1968). Sayers was a senior lecturer in English and Library Science at UCLA, and she later succeeded Anne Carroll Moore as head of the children's section of the New York Public Library. Moore had helped establish children's libraries as a fixture in the United States, and Sayers continued her legacy.[1] "Walt Disney Accused" was "the first widely heard salvo" that "the conscious custodians of children's culture" launched against Disney.[2] Sayers objected more to Disney's retellings of its films in book form than to the films themselves, but she made it clear that establishment children's literature scholars didn't buy into the Disney ideology. She positioned herself as a defender of children's classics and argued that Disney's versions too often sanitize and oversimplify the original. "If you read *Treasure Island*, *Alice in Wonderland*, and *The Wind in the Willows*," Sayers writes, "you will see for yourself how Disney has destroyed something which was delightful."[3]

Richard Schickel was a film historian who also wrote biographies of Hollywood luminaries D. W. Griffith, Cary Grant, and Clint Eastwood. Schickel praises Disney for his early contributions to the film medium, but accuses him of abandoning any artistic pretentions in favor of making money. "As capitalism," writes Schickel, the Walt Disney Company "is a work of genius; as culture, it is mostly a horror."[4] If Sayers turned children's literature scholars against Disney, Schickel did the same for film scholars. To Sayers's accusations of oversimplification and sanitization, Schickel adds a capitalist motivation and a push toward homogeneity. Together, these traits sum up what most critics mean by the word "Disneyfication."[5]

The culture wars of the 1990s raised the stakes of literary criticism. Literary theory provided new tools to engage in debates about representation while cultural studies scholars turned their attention to popular film. These academic debates corresponded with the Disney Renaissance, and Disney's success made the company a target for academic critique like Henry Giroux's *The Mouse that Roared* (1999) and the essay collection *From Mouse to Mermaid* (1995). Giroux's book is in line with Schickel's argument, but while Schickel is primarily a film critic, Giroux sees Disney as a public pedagogue. According to Giroux, Disney's lessons about identity-formation (including who gets to be "American") and consumerism are at odds with public culture's democratic goals.[6]

The essays in *From Mouse to Mermaid* draw heavily from feminist scholarship. In "Somatexts at the Disney Shop," Elizabeth Bell connects Disney's feminine stereotypes, in films from *Snow White* (1937) to *Aladdin* (1992), to the material production of Disney animation.[7] Laura Sells focuses on *The Little Mermaid*, whose message is "more insidious and also more liberatory" than simply that a princess should have "little ambition beyond getting her prince."[8] It is insidious, Sells argues, because it "sanitizes the costs of women's access to the 'male sphere'" but liberatory because "the camp character of Ursula the Sea Witch" challenges that sanitization and because the film ends by bestowing on Ariel "both access *and* voice."[9] Susan Jeffords's essay is also notable in the collection. Jeffords draws on masculinity studies and interprets Disney's Beast as the "new man" of the 1990s, a figure that extends the hyper-masculine hero of the 1980s films by adding unwanted emotional baggage. Unlike his double, the chauvinist Gaston, the Beast is not innately wicked, and so allows Belle to be a teacher as well as a lover.[10] These essays, and Giroux's book, provide a representative sample of late twentieth-century scholars' general approach to Disney.

In the introduction to *From Mouse to Mermaid*, Elizabeth Bell, Lynda Haas, and Laura Sells describe their students as "extremely resistant to critique of Disney films," which seemed to the students beyond reproach: their students accused them of reading too much into media for children.[11] Like *How to Read Donald Duck* (which I discuss in the conclusion),[12] *From Mouse to Mermaid* positions itself as a minority opinion, critiquing Disney when few others will. Thanks in part to the success of these arguments, my own experience teaching Disney films to college students, two decades later, was almost the opposite. Stripped of their nuance, the arguments in *From Mouse to Mermaid* float freely online. My students, who came of age with social media, already assumed that Disney princesses are sexist stereotypes: they'd seen the memes, Reddit threads, and YouTube parodies. Even Disney is in on the joke, as shown in the Disney Princess scene in *Wreck It Ralph 2: Ralph Breaks the Internet* (2018).[13]

As critique of Disney became mainstream, and the hegemony of high theory began to wane, Disney scholarship became more nuanced. Disney's ideological investitures could be assumed, allowing scholars freedom to make other arguments. Like Giroux, Deborah Ross contrasts Disney's corporate goals with its films' messages. But Ross sees the company as conflicted. On the one hand, "Disney the man and the corporation are known for a belief in control," but on the other hand the company's "major commodity" is imagination, which "does not easily lend itself to a program of control."[14] While she accepts that market forces can be dangerous, Ross ultimately sees the conflict as a productive one. Because Disney's "overriding goal is self-promotion," rather than ideology, "the movies lack the philosophical consistency of propaganda."[15] Scholars today worry less about the ideological implications of specific films than the homogeneity created by a company with Disney's global reach.

Disney also features regularly on college syllabi. Christopher Tremblay notes an "emerging practice of creating single college courses focused on a Disney theme," finding such courses at seventy colleges and universities in fields like American history, business and marketing, and media studies.[16] Several books provide advice about using Disney in the classroom,[17] and scholarly studies have similarly proliferated in the past decade.[18] An academic journal, the *International Journal of Disney Studies*, is scheduled to publish its first issue in 2025. These works offer a more nuanced view of the company than the myriad histories, fan sites, and guidebooks for popular audiences, but few present critiques as stringent as those in *From Mouse to Mermaid*. Moreover, the Walt Disney Company publicly recognizes that its values and objectives shift over time and that some of its past products are out of step with modern values. Disney's "Reimagine Tomorrow" initiative states, "we haven't always gotten it right," and aims to amplify "underrepresented voices and untold stories" and to champion "the importance of accurate representation in media and entertainment."[19]

The Walt Disney Company is not a nefarious purveyor of sexist stereotypes but rather an institution with a complex history. Disney preserves that history in a private company archive, which I had the privilege to visit in 2014 (the Walt Disney Archives are not typically open to the public). Even something as simple as a production list provides insight into Disney's process. For example, following the success of *Snow White* (1937), Disney animators began by brainstorming potential titles. Their initial list includes several texts from the Victorian period: William Thackeray's *The Rose and the Ring* (1854), Anna Sewell's *Black Beauty* (1877), Alfred Tennyson's *Idylls of the King* (1859), Charles Kingsley's *The Water Babies* (1862–63), and John Ruskin's *King of the Golden River* (1841). Each title was assigned a "story number," and a title would be "written off" if the studio decided not to make it. Though the list doesn't record when titles were assigned story numbers, handwritten notes indicate when several of them were written off. Since story numbers indicate the order in which the titles were added, we can deduce roughly how long they were under consideration. Walter Scott's *Ivanhoe* (1820), story number 1010, was written off on September 30, 1939, while *Idylls of the King* (story number 1115) and *The Water Babies* (number 1120) were both nixed on June 21, 1941. But *Black Beauty* (number 1108) and *The King of the Golden River* (number 1224) were not written off until October 2, 1943.[20] At the very least, then, *Black Beauty* was under consideration for more than two years, since its story number puts it before *Idylls of the King* but it was not written off until two years later.[21]

The Walt Disney Archives were established in 1970, almost a half-century after the company's founding, and many early materials were not preserved.[22] For most of the titles, it's impossible to say precisely what being "under consideration" meant, and one can only speculate about why these titles were added or deleted. Other sources must be used to fill in the context. Certainly the studio's support of the war effort limited the time and resources that could be devoted to other projects. Disney was actively pursuing war-related films as early as March 1941, and for the fiscal year ending October 1943, 94 percent of Disney's film footage was made for the government.[23] But writers and animators knew that the war would not last forever, and they preserved reports and drafts from the 1930s so that they could return to them later. As I argue in chapter two, internal reports about *Alice in Wonderland* provide insight into both the inner workings of the studio and Lewis Carroll's place in American culture both before and after the war.

Cultural products, including the works of luminaries like Shakespeare and the Romantic poets, emerge in specific historical circumstances and are shaped by seemingly minor, local, and personal events.[24] This fact is no less true when the subject of inquiry is a corporation rather than an individual. But scholars writing about Disney too often see an ideological continuity in Disney's films, reinforcing a "mythical center and its ethos" and ignoring changes both in the company's ethos and in how the films are received.[25] Chapters two and three trace Disney's production of the *Alice* books and Andersen's tales across several decades, paying close attention to historically contextualized decisions and to the state of the movie industry and the Walt Disney Company at particular moments. This approach to Disney differs from most prior works, which tend either to consider a single era of Disney animation or to claim a single ideology over a long period of the company's history. My approach emerges from my training in Victorian studies, which has always been invested in historicizing texts.

WHY THE VICTORIANS?

As I explain in the introduction, the field of Victorian studies emerged alongside the Walt Disney Company. While I hope that readers come away from this book with the belief that the Walt Disney Company owes an important debt to Victorian culture, I also hope that scholars in Victorian studies come away thinking that Disney might have something to offer them and their students as well. Nobody approaches Victorian literature without preconceptions, and those preconceptions are shaped not only in classrooms but also at movie theaters and theme parks.

It may seem an odd choice to link an American company to British literary history. Shouldn't this book instead have been about Americans like P. T. Barnum or Mark Twain? Walt Disney and his eponymous company were certainly influenced by American culture, but that influence, and the influence Disney excerpted in the other direction, is fairly well established.[26] It is also well-known that the Walt Disney Company has always found inspiration from texts outside America, especially in Europe.[27] This book takes a different approach. I connect the Walt Disney Company not only to Victorian culture itself but also, crucially, to the institutions that mediate that culture for American audiences.

Individual chapters build on particular subfields in Victorian studies. One reason why Disney adapted so many Victorian texts is that the period corresponds to the first "golden age" of children's literature, about which there is a rich body of scholarship by writers like Claudia Nelson, Marah Gubar, and Victoria Ford Smith.[28] Chapter one relies on scholarship about Victorian theater, especially Carolyn Williams's *Gilbert and Sullivan: Gender, Genre, Parody* (2011), and about non-theatrical entertainments, especially Richard Altick's classic study *The Shows of London* (1978) and Lee Jackson's more recent *Palaces of Pleasure* (2019). Chapter four builds on feminist scholarship and masculinity studies, while queer theory in general, and the works of Eve Kosofsky Sedgwick in particular, undergird chapters three and four.

In broader sense, however, this book's argument hinges on theorizations of the Victorian period and of periodization in general. The period is named for Queen Victoria, who ruled from 1837 until her death in 1901, the year Walt Disney was born. But the adjective "Victorian" also connotes family values, sexual prudishness, and moral high-mindedness—connotations also associated with "Disneyfied." Just as "Disneyfication" may not match the historical reality of Disney's adaptation practices at any given moment, the Victorian period also contains multitudes. Even the idea of dividing literary history into periods is a controversial one. Periodization structures university English departments (see the introduction to this book), but for all its utility and ubiquity it remains a contentious concept. The Association of Departments of English reports a nationwide trend in revisions to universities' English majors "toward contracting or reconciling the requirements in literary history."[29] The Victorian period is especially vulnerable to contraction, absorbed into a long nineteenth century, or even into early modernism. When hiring in tenure track positions declined drastically in 2008, the proportion of professors held constant for most literary periods but declined for the Victorians.[30]

Efforts to revise literary-historical curricula in general, and the Victorian period in particular, come from different directions. Scholars disagree even about the period's boundaries. I stated above that the Victorian period begins in 1837, when Victoria ascended to the throne. Others might instead choose 1832, the year the first Reform Bill expanded voting rights in England. Doing so distinguishes the Victorian period not for its monarch but for the progressive social reforms that characterize the era: the 1829 Catholic Emancipation Act first allowed members of parliament from outside the Church of England, and the 1833 Slavery Abolition Act abolished slavery in most British colonies. Victoria lived until 1901, so the Victorian period stretched well beyond this half-decade of progressive legislation. While some scholars see Reform as a unifying Victorian idea, others argue that the Victorian period is less culturally and ideologically coherent than other literary periods, and therefore less useful conceptually.[31]

Other critics highlight the political implications of literary periodization. Tying the Victorian period to the English monarchy or to English politics means accepting England as a master concept. "Literature and nationalism were born twins," writes Kwame Anthony Appiah, who describes how modern concepts of literature emerged simultaneously with the nation state in the late eighteenth and early nineteenth century.[32] Appiah and other postcolonial, transnational, and global scholars critique or refuse nationalist frameworks. The Reform Act expanded the right to vote, but it still excluded women and colonial subjects. Ronjaunee Chatterjee, Alicia Mireles Christoff, and Amy R. Wong argue that the failure of Victorian studies to fully engage with scholarship about race and racial difference belies claims about the era's supposedly progressive politics.[33]

The concept of periodization itself emerged in response to Victorian values. Universities began offering courses in English literature in the mid-nineteenth century, as England sought in its past a justification for its national and imperial future. F. D. Maurice introduced the period survey at King's College in the 1840s, believing that the study of "discrete moments of the national past would give the middle classes a sense of national pride equivalent to aristocratic inheritance."[34] Modern literary scholars like Appiah resist nationalist pressures, but it was those pressures that created the discipline in the first place, both domestically and abroad. Years before Maurice began teaching literary periods at King's College, literature was used to establish

British superiority in the colonies. In the 1830s, Thomas Babington Macaulay argued that English should be the primary language in Indian schools,[35] and Gauri Viswanathan has described the centrality of English literature to colonial curricula.[36]

Over the course of the nineteenth century it became increasingly less clear who might be included in the category of "British literature." The British Empire had spread the English language across the globe, and it spread further as America expanded. Ideological and economic changes altered national relations, and inventions like steam travel and the telegraph increased the speed at which new ideas circulated.[37] Mark Twain's *The Adventures of Tom Sawyer* (1876), a touchstone of American literature, was first published in England (to secure the copyright). The novelist Henry James was born in America but moved to Britain later in life. Frances Hodgson Burnett was born in England, moved to America as a teenager, and lived in England for a decade as an adult. The problem compounds as the canon diversifies. Frederick Douglass spent years in England escaping the Fugitive Slave Law, briefly sharing a house with Hans Christian Andersen.[38] Both Douglass and Andersen were best-selling authors in England, where they remain popular today, but neither would typically be included on a Victorian literature syllabus.

For the moment, most Victorian scholarship still "goes on confining itself to the study of British writers without justifying this choice."[39] But recent work in transnational Victorian studies is changing the shape of the field. A decade ago, Jon Mee and Adela Pinch noted trends towards, respectively, the "internationalization of nineteenth-century literary studies beyond narrowly construed national boundaries" and a "new internationalism" in nineteenth-century studies.[40] Daniel Hack's *Reaping Something New* (2016) connects Victorian literature and African American literature.[41] This general trend towards a global Victorian period helps justify my chapter on Hans Christian Andersen and, more generally, helped me not to take the period's boundaries for granted.

If the Victorian period specifically, and literary periods in general, are vague, historically untenable, and nationalist, why do they remain so ubiquitous? It's not for a lack of alternatives. Scholars identify "a variety of competing concepts, including transperiodizing ones, for the study of literary history."[42] But institutions, including universities, survive because "participants actively reproduce their rules and practices," and it is difficult to break from those rhythms.[43] Scholars like Sarah Brouillette, Mark McGurl, and Sara Ahmed have shown how institutions as different as UNESCO, MFA programs, and diversity committees shape cultural production.[44] Rachel Ablow and Daniel Hack defend not only the Victorian period's "descriptive and heuristic value" but also its "institutional reality."[45] Victorian studies persists because universities hire Victorianist scholars to teach courses in Victorian literature and culture, and those scholars read and publish in journals like *Victorian Studies* and attend conferences like the North American Victorian Studies Association (NAVSA).

In this sense, a university is not so different from a corporation. Both the Victorian period and the Walt Disney Company are institutions. Just as the Walt Disney Company is greater than the sum of the individuals who work there, so the Victorian period is beyond the control of the individuals who study it. The fluidity of the term "Victorian" and its reliance on institutional structures rather than hard-and-fast definitions are essential to the argument this book makes; so is the notion that the Victorians have an appeal that transcends the academic discipline of Victorian studies. Recent scholars find Victorian legacies not just in twenty-first-century children's literature[46] but also in unexpected places like pornography and Broadway musicals.[47] By connecting the Victorians to the world's largest global media company, I hope also to take a modest step in that direction. Chapters two and four, in particular, are as much about the legacy of the Victorians—the way in which we remember the period—as they are about the Victorians themselves.

WHY "DISNEY'S VICTORIANS"?

The popularity of the Victorians is especially in evident in film and television. Recent Victorian film adaptations include *David Copperfield* (2019), several Sherlock Holmes adaptations, and *Jane Eyre* (2011). Television adaptations include *Victoria* (2016), still further Sherlock Holmes adaptations, and *Penny Dreadful* (2014). Victorianists have taken notice.[48] Scholarship about Victorian adaptation sits within, and in many cases has contributed substantially to, the thriving and relatively new field of adaptation studies.[49] The field established itself by rejecting the idea that an adaptation should be evaluated based on its fidelity to an original. Comparison between a film and its source has always been (and remains) a common critical move. Jack Zipes, for example, argues that Walt Disney imposes his own rags-to-riches story onto European fairy tales, "stamping his signature as owner on the title frame of the film."[50] In this view, Disney's films are mere variations on the same homogenized theme, and studying fairy tales after Disney's intervention necessitates, in Zipes's title, "Breaking the Disney Spell." Zipes focuses on Disney's appropriation of the fairy tale, an appropriation that makes sense only in the context of the history of fairy tales that Zipes provides.

Comparing an adaptation to a source text can yield valuable insights; Zipes's essay is a classic one, for good reason. But scholars who study adaptations find fidelity "a hopelessly fallacious measure of a given adaptation's value."[51] Focusing on fidelity too often leads to value judgments—typically, "the book is better"—rather than "analyzing process, ideology, and methodology," which are the goals of modern scholarship.[52] Such an approach also "ignores the wider question: Fidelity to what?"[53] As the preceding chapters demonstrate, Disney's films never adapt just a single text. They incorporate multiple intervening adaptations across media, as well as contemporary styles and trends. Leitch cites "a rupture between the theory and the practice of adaptation studies,"[54] and this book (especially chapters two and three) helps to bridge the gap between the two. Critics are too apt to draw a straight line to a single source. Zipes (in a footnote) acknowledges that a theatrical version of *Snow White* might have been Disney's source for the narrative, but mostly compares Disney's films to the Grimms' tale.[55] And even though, as I discuss in chapter three, the artist Kay Nielson had produced concept paintings about "The Little Mermaid" as early as 1939 and Disney had plans to collaborate with Samuel Goldwyn on a biographical feature about Andersen, Waller Hastings takes Andersen's tale as the "original" in his excellent essay about Disney's *The Little Mermaid*.[56] In practice, Disney was more likely to eschew one-to-one comparisons than to encourage them. During the production of *The Jungle Book*, Walt Disney reportedly gave a copy of Kipling's stories to gag writer Larry Clemmons with an injunction not to read them.[57]

A commitment to fidelity also peremptorily elevates the literary original over the cinematic adaptation, precisely the elevation that Schickel complains of when he faults Disney for the "depressing tendency" to base his films on literary texts.[58] Kamilla Elliott historicizes this tendency. While early critics "perceived film to be an impressive combination of art forms," filmmakers carved out a space for their own unique art form by eliding its combinatory past: they first claimed and then rejected literary forebears, especially the Victorian novel.[59] The pioneering Russian filmmaker Sergei Eisenstein claimed that "from Dickens, from the Victorian novel, stem the first shoots of American film aesthetic."[60] (Not incidentally, Eisenstein also called Disney's works "the greatest contribution of the American people to art"; Walt Disney owned a copy of Eisenstein's *The Film Sense*.)[61] Claims like Eisenstein's, that film has its roots in the novel, imply "not simply that the nineteenth-century novel influenced western film, but that it in some sense *became* film."[62] These claims disregard other art forms, especially illustration and the theater, that had more obviously influenced film's emergence in the early twentieth century. That disregard was a political move. "Quite apart from the prestige and interest early film derived from crediting celebrated popular novelists like Dickens," writes Elliott, "a debt to the invisible visualities of prose is far easier to cast off than debts to tangible visual arts in a bid to declare film a unique art."[63] As I demonstrate in chapters one and two, Victorian theater excerpted a strong influence on Disney's films, and Disney's *Alice in Wonderland* draws as much on Tenniel's illustrations and the story's cultural resonance as on Carroll's prose.

Linda Hutcheon helped move the field of adaptation studies beyond novel-film comparisons, including adaptations in media such as opera, video games, and theme parks. As Hutcheon points out, "expensive collaborative art forms" like film and theater tend to select "safe bets with a ready audience—and that usually means adaptations."[64] Animation is an especially expensive, laborious, and collaborative form. *Snow White and the Seven Dwarfs* (1937) was referred to as "Disney's folly," as most Hollywood executives questioned whether audiences would sit through an animated feature, even one adapting a familiar tale.[65] It is no wonder that Disney's animated films are nearly all adaptations, or that most Disney theme-park attractions draw on existing films. As Simone Murray has argued, in the age of global media the adaptation industry is "a cultural ecosystem" whose components are "complexly interdependent and dynamic."[66]

My first chapter reveals the Victorian public entertainment industry that helped establish that ecosystem and throughout the book I draw many comparisons between Disney's films and the works on which they are based. But by rejecting such comparisons as the only method, adaptation scholars open other interpretive possibilities. Literary studies and individual corporations represent two of those components, and this book explores their interdependence.

Notes

INTRODUCTION: DISNEY AND THE VICTORIANS

1. Leavis, *The Great Tradition*, 1.

2. Leavis, 1–2.

3. Disney, *The Official Walt Disney Quote Book*; see also Schickel, *The Disney Version*, 151–52.

4. Churchill, "Now Mickey Mouse Enters Art's Temple."

5. Arnold, "The Function of Criticism at the Present Time," 1405–1406.

6. Leavis, *The Great Tradition*, 1. See also Sadoff, *Victorian Vogue*.

7. Watts, "Walt Disney," 85–87.

8. This fraction requires stretching "Victorian" only slightly. Disney's features included adaptations of Lewis Carroll's *Alice* books (1865 and 1871), Robert Louis Stevenson's *Treasure Island* (1887), and Kenneth Grahame's "The Reluctant Dragon" (1898). These English texts fall squarely within the reign of Queen Victoria (1837–1901). J. M. Barrie's *Peter Pan* is more tentatively Victorian: the play was first performed in 1904, and the novel *Peter and Wendy* appeared only 1911. But Peter himself had first appeared in *The Little White Bird* (1902), and Barrie's plays were popular throughout the 1880s. If it missed Victoria's life by a few years, *Peter Pan* was certainly shaped by the Victorian ethos.

Extending the Victorian period to Europe captures the Italian Carlo Collodi's *Pinocchio* (1887) and the French Jules Verne's *20,000 Leagues Under the Sea* (1870). Including America adds *Song of the South*, based on Joel Chandler Harris's *Uncle Remus* (1880). *The Sword and the Rose* (1953) is based on a novel by Charles Major, *When Knighthood was in Flower* (1898). The live-action movies have a particularly English flavor, since they were produced in England to make use of funds restricted after World War II. *Treasure Island* was the first, and Disney also adapted Walter Scott's *Rob Roy* (1817). Scott precedes the Victorian period, though his novels were bestsellers throughout the century. (During his lifetime, Scott outsold all contemporary novelists *combined*, and he remained a household name through the 1890s.) Rounding out my list of Victorian Disney features, *The Adventures of Ichabod and Mr. Toad* features characters from Kenneth Grahame's *The Wind in the Willows* (1916) and Washington Irving's *Sketch-Book* (1820). These works are just outside Victoria's life, but both authors lived during her reign.

9. To take just one example: since its first publication in 1962, the *Norton Anthology of English Literature* has become ubiquitous and exerts a strong influence on how literature is taught and studied (Shesgreen, "Canonizing the Canonizer," 294). The most recent edition of the *Norton Anthology* divides English literary history into the Middle Ages, the sixteenth and early seventeenth centuries, the Restoration and the eighteenth century, the Romantic period, the Victorian age, and the twentieth and twenty-first centuries. American literature is considered separately and divided into two periods, before and after 1865.

10. Cartwright, Chin, and Stanley, "A Changing Major," 5; for critiques of periodization, 15.

11. See the appendix to this book for a larger discussion of periodization and its institutional role in higher education.

12. For example, linguists Carmen Fought and Karen Eisenhauer compare Disney princesses from three periods, which they term "classics" (during Walt's life), "Renaissance" (1989–1998) and "New Age" (post-2009). Chris Pallant divides his *Demystifying Disney* into sections on early and middle Disney, the Disney renaissance, and "Neo-Disney." Michelle Anya Anjirbag compares *Mulan* (1998) to *Moana* (2016), contrasting the different marketing approaches to films that adapt stories from other cultures, and Peter C. Kunze broadens the context of the Disney Renaissance (Eisenhauer, "A Quantitative Analysis"; Guo, "Researchers Have Found a Major Problem with 'The Little Mermaid' and Other Disney Movies"; Pallant, *Demystifying Disney*, xi; Anjirbag, "Reforming Borders of the Imagination Kunze, "Don Bluth").

13. Unofficial sites like Disneyavenue.com, JustDisney.com, and Wikipedia split their detailed histories of the company into stages

14. "Disney History."

15. The post-Iger period remains to be seen: he retired in 2020 and then returned in late 2022, replacing the short-tenured and unpopular Bob Chapek.

16. Pykett, "The Changing Faces and Spaces of Victorian Studies," 11.

17. Wyland, "Public Funding and the 'Untamed Wilderness' of Victorian Studies," para 1.

18. "Prefatory Note," 3.

19. Houghton, *The Victorian Frame of Mind, 1830–1870*, xv.

20. Graff, "How Periods Erase History."

21. Jay Clayton notes the prominence of Victorian texts in the works of Marxist scholars like Raymond Williams, Terry Eagleton, and Fredric Jameson; feminist scholars like Elaine Showalter, Sandra Gilbert and Sarah Gubar, and Mary Poovey; postcolonial theorists like Gayatri Spivak; and queer theorists like Eve Sedgwick (Clayton, "The Future of Victorian Literature," 715).

22. See, for example, Felluga, "BRANCHing Out"; Babb, "Victorian Roots and Branches"; Taylor, "Where Is Victorian Ecocriticism?" and *The Sky of Our Manufacture*.

23. This is not to say that Victorian scholars always agree with one another. In 2015, the V21 manifesto accused the field of being too historicist, and called for a "strategic presentism" ("Manifesto of the V21 Collective.") And in 2020, Ronjaunee Chatterjee, Alicia Mireles Christoff, and Amy R. Wong lamented the field's persistent Eurocentrism and colonial ideologies (Chatterjee et al., "Undisciplining Victorian Studies"). For more about debates within the Victorian studies, see the conclusion and the appendix, "Why the Victorians?"

24. Felski, "Context Stinks!," 580. See also Guillory, *Cultural Capital*; Stevenson, "Sentiment and Significance."

25. Gilbert and Gubar, *The Madwoman in the Attic*; Baudrillard, *Simulacra and Simulation*.

26. Tremblay, "Disney in the Academy"; Sandlin and Garlen, *Disney, Culture, and Curriculum*; Brode and Brode, *Debating Disney*.

27. See the appendix, "Why Disney?"

28. My earlier article about *Oliver & Company*, which appears in a revised form in chapter one, is based on early drafts of that film. David Leon Higdon and Phill Lehrman describe Aldous Huxley's draft of *Alice in Wonderland*, but do not refer to the archival materials about that film that I discuss in chapter two; the ones I describe are from an earlier date. I rely on Higdon and Lehrman's reproduction of Huxley's script. I also refer, throughout, to story notes about *Peter Pan*, which I have not seen mentioned elsewhere.

CHAPTER ONE: DISNEY AND THE VICTORIAN TRADITION

1. Dettmar, "A Hundred Years of T. S. Eliot's 'Tradition and the Individual Talent.'"

2. Eliot, "Tradition and the Individual Talent," 2555.

3. Disney Institute and Kinni, *Be Our Guest*, 66–68.

4. Miller, "A Conversation with Diane Disney Miller."

5. Gabler, *Walt Disney*, 487–88.

6. The exhibits were the People Mover for Ford, Progressland for GE (later renamed the Carousel of Progress), It's a Small World for Pepsi, and the Audio-Animatronics Abraham Lincoln for the state of Illinois.

7. Arnold, "The Function of Criticism at the Present Time," 1405–6.

8. Zipes, "Breaking the Disney Spell."

9. Cullen, "For Whom the Shoe Fits," 62, 69.

10. Hillard, *Spellbound*, 79–81.

11. Smith and Rozario, 37.

12. Miller and Martin, "My Dad, Walt Disney," part 8, 82.

13. See Pickering, *John Locke and Children's Books in Eighteenth-Century England*; Jackson, *Engines of Instruction, Mischief, and Magic*; Summerfield, *Fantasy and Reason*; Plotz, *Romanticism and the Vocation of Chidhood*; O'Malley, *The Making of the Modern Child*.

14. Nelson, "Writing for Children," 314.

15. Flint, "The Victorian Novel and Its Readers," 24.

16. James, *The Victorian Novel*, 17; Eliot, "The Business of Victorian Publishing," 40; Gilbert, *Better Left Unsaid*.

17. See Gilbert, *Better Left Unsaid*. Other publishers flouted Mudie's morality and sought other venues of distribution: Victorian erotica and pornography is typically seen as outside the boundaries of "literature," but it was widespread. For a classic study of Victorian pornography, see Marcus, *The Other Victorians*.

18. Gilbert, *Better Left Unsaid*, 3.

19. Krämer, "The Walt Disney Company," 578–80.

20. Kunze, "Don Bluth," 635.

21. Birch, "Education," 331–32.

22. *Culturing the Child, 1690–1914*; Richardson, *Literature, Education, and Romanticism*; Carpenter, *Secret Gardens*; Gubar, *Artful Dodgers*; Smith, *Between Generations*.

23. Salmon, Juvenile Literature, 158.

24. Pallant, *Demystifying Disney*, 84–85.

25. Smith, "Episode 662."

26. de Kosnik, "2021 Will Launch the Platinum Age of Piracy."

27. Miller and Martin, "My Dad, Walt Disney," part 4, 78.

28. Schickel, *The Disney Version*, 340.

29. Lethem, "The Ecstasy of Influence."

30. Sayers, "Walt Disney Accused."

31. Schickel, *The Disney Version*, 110.

32. Dickens, *Nicholas Nickleby*, 633.

33. Dickens, 633.

34. Dickens, *Nicholas Nickleby*, 633.

35. St Clair, *The Reading Nation in the Romantic Period*, 43.

36. Eliot, "The Business of Victorian Publishing," 55.

37. Abraham, *Plagiarizing the Victorian Novel*, 7–14.

38. Cohen, *Pirating Fictions*, 124.

39. Cohen, 124.

40. Williams, *Gilbert and Sullivan*, 122–23.

41. Williams, 123.

42. Williams, 124.

43. Williams, 124–25.

44. Rezek, *London and the Making of Provincial Literature*, 33.

45. Whipple, "Dickens's American Notes."

46. Quoted in Westover, "How America 'Inherited' Literary Tourism," 185–86.

47. Robson, *Heart Beats*, 65.

48. Cohen, *Pirating Fictions*, 216.

49. Quoted in Stewart, *DisneyWar*, 32.

50. Quoted in Houghton, *The Victorian Frame of Mind, 1830–1870*, 183.

51. Carlyle, "Past and Present," 1073.

52. Adams, *Dandies and Desert Saints*, 6.

53. Eliot, *Middlemarch*, 399.

54. Smiles, 222.

55. Smiles, *Self-Help*, 4.

56. Smiles, 270.

57. Huxley's grandson, Aldous Huxley, wrote a script for Disney's *Alice in Wonderland*. See chapter 2.

NOTES

58. Arnold, "Literature and Science." Arnold was no fan of Smiles, either. He elsewhere condemns "the absorbing and brutalizing influences of our passionate material progress" (Arnold, "The Function of Criticism at the Present Time," 1411).

59. Huxley, "Science and Culture," 1451.

60. Huxley, 1451.

61. Walt Disney World Resort, "Walt Disney's Carousel of Progress."

62. Barrier, *Hollywood Cartoons*, 55.

63. Dickens, *American Notes for General Circulation*, 9.

64. Dickens, *Hard Times*, 26.

65. Wordsworth, "Tintern Abbey," ll. 25–26 and 122–23.

66. Wordsworth, "Steamboats, Viaducts, and Railways," ll. 10–11.

67. Quoted in Fyfe, "On the Opening of the Liverpool and Manchester Railway, 1830."

68. Grossman, *Charles Dickens's Networks*.

69. Donovan, "How the Post Office and Postal Products Shaped Mid-Nineteenth-Century Letter-Writing"; Golden, *Posting It*.

70. Eliot, "The Business of Victorian Publishing," 51.

71. Ferguson, *Victorian Time*, 1–2; Zemka, *Time and the Moment in Victorian Literature and Society*, 2–7.

72. Woolf, "Mrs. Dalloway."

73. Taylor, *The Sky of Our Manufacture*, 1.

74. Dickens, *Dombey and Son*, 62.

75. Dickens, 211.

76. Armstrong, *Fiction in the Age of Photography*, 77.

77. Dickens, *Great Expectations*, 1.

78. Teukolsky, *Picture World*.

79. Petzold, "Victorian Gendered Photography."

80. Stevenson, "The Strange Case of Dr. Jekyll and Mr. Hyde," 1690.

81. Novak, *Realism, Photography and Nineteenth-Century Fiction*, 5.

82. Bak, *Playful Visions*, 1, 4.

83. Stewart, "Curtain Up."

84. Camlot, "The First Phonogramic Poem."

85. The American industry thrived during the period, too, of course. Thomas Edison invented the technology for recording both sound and moving pictures, and P. T. Barnum's influence on public entertainment is as important as those described in this chapter. Other scholars have situated Disney among his American precursors (see Watts, *The Magic Kingdom*; Gabler, *Walt Disney*; Barrier, *Hollywood Cartoons*). In this book I focus primarily on British Victorian culture.

86. Pallant, *Demystifying Disney*, 21–23.

87. Snow, *Disney's Land*.

88. Iger, *The Ride of a Lifetime*.

89. Bohas, *The Political Economy of Disney*, 2.

90. Byerly, "Media," 759. See also Szwydky, *Transmedia Adaptation in the Nineteenth Century*.

91. Abraham, *Plagiarizing the Victorian Novel*, 23.

92. Hutcheon, *A Theory of Adaptation*, xiii.

93. Eisenstein, "Dickens, Griffith, and Film Today," 195.

94. Altman, "Dickens, Griffith, and Film Theory Today," 148.

95. Perkins, "Research Report for Alice in Wonderland (Sept)," 1.

96. Perkins, 85.

97. Corry, "Eva Le Gallienne to Return in 'Alice in Wonderland.'"

98. Patterson, *Maude Adams*.

99. Blank, "Research Report for Peter Pan (Nov 23)."

100. Blank.

101. Blank.

102. Blank, 2.

103. Blank, 1.

104. Barnes, "Not Streaming."

105. Ramirez, "New Adventures with Princess Tiana."

106. Brode, *Multiculturalism and the Mouse*, 53–55.

107. Miller and Rode, "The Movie You See, The Movie You Don't," 88–90; Barrier, *Hollywood Cartoons*, 392; Korkis, *The Vault of Walt*, 145–54.

108. Bernstein, *Racial Innocence*, 7.

109. Sammond, *Birth of an Industry*, 3. Blackface is not, of course, Mickey's *only* precedent: he has been called "an amalgam of existing visual styles." See Barrier, *Hollywood Cartoons*; Abate, "Mickey Mouse as Teddy's Bear."

110. Sammond, *Birth of an Industry*.

111. Jackson, *Mickey's Mellerdrammer*. The cartoon short also features "My Old Kentucky Home," a song that originated with stage adaptations of *Uncle Tom's Cabin*.

112. Flint, "The Victorian Novel and Its Readers," 31. Besides her literary legacy, Stowe's "dogged promotion of Florida as an antidote to the frigid North" helped establish the state as a tourist destination, and ultimately a feasible site for Disney's Magic Kingdom (Roberts, "Harriet Beecher Stowe and Florida Tourism," 198).

113. Bernstein, *Racial Innocence*, 112.

114. Railton, "The Howard Family & Uncle Tom's Cabin."

115. Bernstein, *Racial Innocence*, 34–35.

116. Bernstein, 53.

117. Moody, *Illegitimate Theatre in London, 1770–1840*, 10.

118. Altick, *The Shows of London*, 176.

119. Pollack-Pelzner, "Shakespeare Burlesque and the Performing Self," 402.

120. Williams, "Melodrama," 193.

121. Williams, 208.

122. Williams, 210. See also Teukolsky, *Picture World*.

123. Meisel, *Realizations*.

124. Mattacks, "Acts of Piracy," 133.

125. Williams, "Melodrama," 218.

126. Bratton, *The Making of the West End Stage*, 170.

127. Williams, *Gilbert and Sullivan*, 49, 53.

128. Leitch, *Film Adaptation and Its Discontents*, 247.

129. Disney, *The Official Walt Disney Quote Book*.

130. Marcus, "Victorian Theatrics," 439.

131. Contemporary theater also demonstrates the combined legacy of both Disney and the Victorians. The twenty-first century evinces "a phenomenal interest in portraying the Victorians on stage" (Weltman, "Victorians on the Contemporary Stage," 303; see also Weltman's *Victorians on Broadway*). As was the case in the 1930s, when Disney's storywriters read theatrical reviews of works they considered adapting, a text's popularity on stage increases its likelihood of becoming a Disney movie. The popularity of *Oliver!* in school and community theaters influenced Disney's *Oliver & Company*, and the studio's release of a star-studded film version of *Into the Woods* (2014) probably owes something to that play's popularity as a high-school production: it ranked thirteenth in the 1990s, seventh in the 2000s, and fourth in the 2010s ("The Most Popular High School Plays and Musicals").

Today the influence goes both directions, as Disney's animated musicals are also adapted for the stage. However much we associate theater with Broadway and the West End, the vast majority of theatrical productions take place in schools and community theaters. A little under 14 million people saw a Broadway show in the 2017–18 season ("Statistics—Broadway in NYC") compared to 50 million who attended high school productions—and that number represents only the 3,000 schools that responded to the Educational Theater Association's survey (there are four times that many high schools in the US) ("The Most Popular High School Plays and Musicals"). Founded under Eisner's leadership in 1993, Disney Theatrical Productions licenses stage versions of its plays, and since 2010 the Disney Musicals in Schools program has helped elementary schools develop musical theater programs ("Disney Musicals in Schools"). The company exerts a profound influence on American theater. In 2019, Disney musicals held three of the top five spots on the list of top-performed high school musicals ("The Most Popular High School Plays and Musicals"). See also Kunze, *Staging a Comeback*.

132. For more on Victorian children and theater, see Varty, *Children and Theatre in Victorian Britain*; Gubar, *Artful Dodgers*, chapters five and six; and the entry on "Children's theater and public entertainment" in Fleming, *Nineteenth-Century British Children's Literature: A Companion*.

133. Lovett, 12.

134. Gubar, *Artful Dodgers*, 193–94.

135. Gubar, 189.

136. See Brown, "Introduction" in *Oxford Handbook of Children's Film*, 1.

137. Knoepflmacher, "*Little Lord Fauntleroy*: The Afterlife of a Best-Seller," 187.

138. Dickens, *Hard Times*, 7.

139. Dickens, 269.

140. Jackson, *Palaces of Pleasure*, 2.

141. Altick, *The Shows of London*, 4.

142. Burney, *Evelina*.

143. Thackeray, *Vanity Fair*, 63.

144. Altick, *The Shows of London*, 320.

145. Jackson, *Palaces of Pleasure*, 122.

146. Faulk, *Music Hall and Modernity*, 1.

147. Jackson, *Palaces of Pleasure*, 56.

148. Jackson, 58.

149. Faulk, *Music Hall and Modernity*, 1.

150. Faulk, 23–24.

151. Altick, 333.

152. "Our History."

153. Nesbit, *The Railway Children*.

154. "Our History."

155. Carroll, *Alice in Wonderland*, 135.

156. "Pirates of the Caribbean."

157. Altick, *The Shows of London*, 335.

158. Altick, 333.

159. Altick, 54, 342.

160. Pearce, *Madame Vestris and Her Times*.

161. Shannon, *Dickens, Reynolds, and Mayhew on Wellington Street*, 117–18.

162. Bredsdorff, *Hans Andersen and Charles Dickens*, 54, 84.

163. Williams, *Gilbert and Sullivan*, 3.

164. Young, "Henry Irving's Hamlet," 3.

165. Pollack-Pelzner, "Shakespeare Burlesque and the Performing Self," 405–6.

166. Jaques and Giddens, *Lewis Carroll's Alice's Adventures in Wonderland and Through the Looking-Glass*, 219; Lovett, *Alice on Stage*, 110.

167. Altick, *The Shows of London*, 128–62, 208–9.

168. Eliot, *Middlemarch*, 782.

169. Altick, *The Shows of London*, 163.

170. Otto, "Artificial Environments, Virtual Realities, and the Cultivation of Propensity in the London Colosseum," 178.

171. Altick, *The Shows of London*, 504.

172. Dickens, *American Notes for General Circulation*, 98.

173. Altick, *The Shows of London*, 132, 229.

174. Buzard, Childers, and Gillooly, "Introduction," 1.

175. Collins, *The Woman in White*, 376.

176. Jackson, *Palaces of Pleasure*, 149.

177. Jackson, 149.

178. Jackson, 155.

179. Jackson, 151.

180. Jackson, 153.

181. Jackson, 155–56.

182. Jackson, 1–2.

183. Bratton, *The Making of the West End Stage*, 13.

184. Davis and Emeljanow, *Reflecting the Audience*, 246.

185. Krutnik, "A Spanner in the Works?," 23.

NOTES

186. McKernan, "The Familiarity of the New," 34.

187. Gunning, "The Cinema of Attraction," 65.

188. McKernan, "The Familiarity of the New," 35.

189. McKernan, 39–40.

190. Queen Victoria's Journals, October 3, 1896.

191. McKernan, 39–40.

192. Disney Institute and Kinni, *Be Our Guest*, 101–2.

193. Disney Institute and Kinni, *Be Our Guest*; Snow, *Disney's Land*.

194. Lydall, "Forget Disneyland, Try Dickens World."

195. Swift, "What the Dickens?"

196. O'Neill, "Bemusement Park."

197. John, *Dickens and Mass Culture*, 275–76, 284.

198. John, 239.

199. Gould and Mitchell, "It Was the Worst of Times," 292.

200. Marsh, "Dickens and Film," 67.

201. John, 285.

202. John, 284.

203. James, "The Limitations of Dickens," 53.

204. Orwell, "Charles Dickens."

205. Leavis, *The Great Tradition*, 19.

206. Watts, "Walt Disney," 89.

207. Gabler, *Walt Disney*, 415.

208. Pallant, *Demystifying Disney*, 39.

209. Miller and Martin, "My Dad, Walt Disney," part 8, 82.

210. Fleming, "After Dickens World."

211. Pallant, *Demystifying Disney*, 79–80; Wells, *Animation and America*, 129; Kunze, "Don Bluth."

212. Stewart, *Disney War*, 71–72.

213. As Martin Meisel insightfully notes, the experience of reading Dickens as he was published was doubly divided: Victorian readers were accustomed both to alternating between text an image and to waiting for the next serial part. Meisel, *Realizations*, 53.

214. Hadley, *Melodramatic Tactics*, 77.

215. Ford, "Review of Oliver Twist. *Quarterly Review*, 1839," 407.

216. Jackson, *Walt Disney, a Bio-Bibliography*, 88.

217. Slater, *Charles Dickens*, 591.

218. Slater, 591.

219. Dickens, *Oliver Twist*, 117.

220. Forster, *The Life of Charles Dickens*, 152.

221. Barreca, "'The Mimic Life of Theatre': The 1838 Adaptation of *Oliver Twist*," 89.

222. Barreca, 91.

223. Barnett, *Oliver Twist, Or, the Parish Boys Progress*, 4, 20.

224. John, *Dickens and Mass Culture*, 212.

225. Barnett, *Oliver Twist, Or, the Parish Boys Progress*, 7.

226. John, *Dickens and Mass Culture*, 230.

227. Napolitano, *Oliver!*, 11.

228. Napolitano, 16.

229. John, *Dickens and Mass Culture*, 219–26.

230. Napolitano, *Oliver!*, 47.

231. Weltman, "'Can a Fellow Be a Villain All His Life?,'" 382. Bart changes the spelling from "Sikes" to "Sykes," perhaps as an homage to earlier adaptations. Disney would adopt the same spelling.

232. Napolitano, *Oliver!*, 135.

233. Napolitano, 106.

234. Culhane.

235. Weltman, "Can a Fellow Be a Villain All His Life?," 383.

236. Culhane, "'Oliver & Company' Gives Dickens A Disney Twist."

237. For more about Disney and Broadway, see Kunze, *Staging a Comeback*. Kunze argues that *Oliver & Company* does not follow the integrated musical tradition that Ashman promoted.

238. "'Oliver Twist' Musical (Untitled Memo) (Sept 24)."

239. "'Oliver Twist' Musical Feature. Character Descriptions."

240. "'Oliver.' Prod. #0421 Rough Working Copy," The panda plot may have been inspired by the National Zoo in Washington, DC. The Pandas Ling-Ling and Hsing-Hsing had four cubs between 1983 and 1987, though none survived more than a day ("A Brief History of Giant Pandas at the Zoo").

241. "'Oliver Twist' Musical (Untitled Memo) (Sept 24)," 1–2.

242. Scribner, *Oliver and Company.*

243. "'Oliver Twist' Musical (Untitled Memo) (Sept 24)," cover sheet.

244. "'Oliver Twist' Musical (Untitled Memo) (Sept 24)," 4.

245. "'Oliver Twist' Musical (Untitled Memo) (Sept 24)," 11.

246. "'Oliver Twist' Musical (Untitled Memo) (Sept 24)," 13.

247. "'Oliver Twist' Musical (Untitled Memo) (Sept 24)," 13.

248. "'Oliver Twist' Musical (Untitled Memo) (Sept 26)," 4.

249. "'Oliver Twist' Musical Feature. Story Outline, Rough," 6.

250. "Story Outline," 7.

251. "Story Outline," 3.

252. "Rough Working Copy," 11, 17.

253. Culhane, "'Oliver & Company' Gives Dickens A Disney Twist."

254. Napolitano, *Oliver!*, 106.

255. "'Oliver Twist' Musical (Untitled Memo) (Sept 24)," cover sheet; "'Oliver Twist' Musical. One Additional Story Concept."

256. Davis, "Retelling *A Christmas Carol.*"

CHAPTER TWO: ALICE FROM GAG TO FRANCHISE

1. Disney, "Walt Disney's Alice in Wonderland," 16.

2. Seldes.

NOTES   179

3. See Murray, "Phantom Adaptations."

4. Miller and Martin, "My Dad, Walt Disney," part 8, 80–81.

5. Murray, "Phantom Adaptations," 6. Murray's approach to adaptation informs much of this chapter.

6. Carroll, *Alice in Wonderland*, 3.

7. Disney, "Walt Disney's Alice in Wonderland," 16. Dodgson had a falling out with the Liddell family shortly after the river trip, and destroyed the pages of his diary that refer to its cause. In the 1940s, scholars had just begun to suggest he might have been a pedophile. In addition to a mathematician and author, Dodgson was a prolific amateur photographer. Many of his photographs are of little girls, a few of them nudes. Critics remain divided as to what this might mean, and today Dodgson's sexuality is an unavoidable part of his biography. For the first half of the century, though, this would have been something of a fringe idea, even in academic circles, and it's not surprising that it doesn't come up in the archival materials (let alone the publicity materials).

8. See, for example, Elliott, *Rethinking the Novel/Film Debate*, chapter 6; Brooker, *Alice's Adventures*; Siemann, "But I'm Grown up Now."

9. Jaques and Giddens, *Lewis Carroll's Alice's Adventures in Wonderland and Through the Looking-Glass*, 34.

10. Susina, *The Place of Lewis Carroll* 4, 8.

11. Jaques and Giddens, 34.

12. Jaques and Giddens, 94.

13. Susina, 67–68.

14. Lovett, *Alice on Stage*, 20–21. Thomas Coe, at the Haymarket, thought it too much for a pantomime, but a good candidate for an extravaganza; Arthur Sullivan thought it would make a great "fairy piece" (28).

15. Susina, *The Place of Lewis Carroll*, 66.

16. Lovett, *Alice on Stage*, 36–37. Lovett points out that Carroll himself suggested the operetta as more appropriate than a pantomime, objecting specifically to the harlequinade that typically accompanied the latter genre.

17. Lovett, 47–48.

18. Lovett, 108.

19. Lovett, 108.

20. Paramount's *Alice in Wonderland* was mostly live-action, but included one animated sequence, the Walrus and the Carpenter, produced by the Harman-Ising studio. Hugh Harman and Rudolph Ising had been among Disney's earliest collaborators, working on the early Laugh-O-grams in Kansas City before coming to Los Angeles with Disney. They were among the animators who left Disney and signed with Charles Mintz when he secured the rights to Oswald the Rabbit.

21. Disney, "Walt Disney's Alice in Wonderland," 17.

22. Jaques and Giddens, *Lewis Carroll's Alice's Adventures in Wonderland and Through the Looking-Glass*, 161.

23. For many examples, see St Clair, *The Reading Nation in the Romantic Period*.

24. Leitch, *Film Adaptation and Its Discontents*, 182–85.

25. Leitch, 185.

26. Carroll, *Alice in Wonderland*, 52–55.

27. Carroll, 73–75.

28. See Crafton, "Pie and Chase"; Gunning, "Crazy Machines in the Garden of Forking Paths"; Jenkins and Karnick, *Classical Hollywood Comedy*, 80–85.

29. Miller and Martin, "My Dad, Walt Disney," part 6.

30. See Barrier, *Hollywood Cartoons*.

31. Disney, "Walt Disney's Alice in Wonderland," 16.

32. Gabler, *Walt Disney*, 55.

33. Lutz, *Animated Cartoons*, 245.

34. Lutz, 246.

35. Susanin, *Walt before Mickey*, 64.

36. Churchill, "Now Mickey Mouse Enter's Art's Temple."

37. Susanin, *Walt before Mickey*, 30–32.

38. Barrier, *Hollywood Cartoons*, 35.

39. Barrier, 39.

40. Sammond, *Birth of an Industry*, 47.

41. Sammond, 3.

42. Barrier, 12.

43. Susanin, *Walt before Mickey*, 19.

44. Susanin, 22.

45. Disney, Harman, and Maxwell, *Alice's Wonderland*.

46. Disney, Harman, and Maxwell.

47. Susanin, *Walt before Mickey*, 64–65.

48. Merritt and Kaufman, *Walt in Wonderland*, 12.

49. Merritt and Kaufman, 15.

50. Disney, Harman, and Maxwell, *Alice's Wonderland*.

51. Carroll, *Alice in Wonderland*, 8.

52. Susanin, *Walt before Mickey*, 66, 83.

53. Susanin, 70.

54. Susanin, 82–87.

55. Susanin, 91.

56. Susanin, 110.

57. Susanin, 128.

58. Susanin, 99.

59. Barrier, *Hollywood Cartoons*, 40.

60. Susanin, *Walt before Mickey*, 119.

61. Merritt and Kaufman, *Walt in Wonderland*, 16.

62. Susanin, *Walt before Mickey*, 137, 153.

63. Barrier, *Hollywood Cartoons*, 46.

64. Susanin, *Walt before Mickey*, 156.

65. Barrier, *Hollywood Cartoons*, 50.

66. Bakewell, *Lewis Carroll*, 340.

67. Allan, *Walt Disney and Europe*, 211.

68. Bakewell, *Lewis Carroll*, 342.

NOTES

69. Korkis, *The Vault of Walt*, 158.

70. Disney, "Walt Disney's Alice in Wonderland."

71. Seldes.

72. Gabler, *Walt Disney*, 215.

73. Barrier, *Hollywood Cartoons*, 91.

74. Barrier, 91–92.

75. Barrier, 69.

76. Churchill, "Now Mickey Mouse Enter's Art's Temple."

77. Barrier, *Hollywood Cartoons*, 98.

78. Lang was a late-Victorian writer and editor, and so prolific that he has been called "the vanished mediator of the late-Victorian mediascape" (Hensley, "What Is A Network?").

79. Barrier, *Hollywood Cartoons*, 100.

80. Gabler, *Walt Disney*, 215.

81. Barrier, *Hollywood Cartoons*, 85.

82. "Mary Pickford Back from Europe."

83. "Mickey Mouse's New Affiliation."

84. Gabler, *Walt Disney*, 215.

85. Quoted in Gabler, 214.

86. Barrier, *Hollywood Cartoons*, 367.

87. Churchill, "Now Mickey Mouse Enter's Art's Temple."

88. Gabler, *Walt Disney*, 215.

89. "Activities on the Hollywood Front."

90. Hand, *Thru the Mirror*.

91. Barrier, *Hollywood Cartoons*, 109

92. Gabler, *Walt Disney*, 276.

93. Gabler, 283.

94. "Disney Plans to Film 'Alice in Wonderland.'"

95. Perkins, "Research Report for Alice in Wonderland (May)"

96. Disney's early feature films, including the very first, *Snow White and the Seven Dwarfs* (1937), often begin with the image of a book containing the story on which the film is based. Fairy tales like *Snow White* are oral tales belonging to popular culture, but even in the case of original works, the author's name does not appear on the title. Carlo Collodi's name is absent from the *Pinocchio* sequence, as are J. M. Barrie's and Lewis Carroll's, in the background.

97. Altman, "Dickens, Griffith, and Film Theory Today," 148.

98. Blank, "Research Report for Peter Pan (Oct 20)."

99. Perkins, "Research Report for Alice in Wonderland (Sept)" 8, 14.

100. Perkins, 11.

101. Disney, "Walt Disney's Alice in Wonderland."

102. See, for example, Stam, "Beyond Fidelity: The Dialogics of Adaptation"; Leitch, *Film Adaptation and Its Discontents*; Sadoff, *Victorian Vogue*; Albrecht-Crane and Cutchins, *Adaptation Studies*. For more recent works on adaptation theory see Leitch, *Oxford Handbook* and Elliott, *Theorizing Adaptation*.

103. Hutcheon, *A Theory of Adaptation*, 120.

104. Perkins, "Research Report for Alice in Wonderland (Sept)," 15.

105. Perkins, 14.

106. Perkins, 116–17.

107. Perkins, 40.

108. Perkins, "Research Report for Alice in Wonderland (May)," 1.

109. Perkins, 10.

110. Disney, "Walt Disney's Alice in Wonderland."

111. Perkins, "Research Report for Alice in Wonderland (Sept)," 29.

112. Perkins, 45.

113. Perkins, 75, 80.

114. Perkins, 85.

115. Perkins, 90.

116. Perkins, 133.

117. Perkins, 97, 103.

118. Perkins, "Research Report for Alice in Wonderland (May)," 4.

119. Perkins, "Research Report for Alice in Wonderland (Sept)," 115.

120. Perkins, 148.

121. Jaques and Giddens, *Lewis Carroll's Alice's Adventures in Wonderland and Through the Looking-Glass*, 204.

122. Disney, "How I Cartooned Alice," 7.

123. Higdon and Lehrman, "Huxley's 'Deep Jam' and the Adaptation of *Alice in Wonderland*," 58–59.

124. Korkis, *The Vault of Walt*, 160.

125. Loos, "Aldous Huxley in California," 55.

126. Gabler, *Walt Disney*, 459.

127. Huxley, "Letter to Anita Loos."

128. Higdon and Lehrman, "Huxley's 'Deep Jam' and the Adaptation of *Alice in Wonderland*," 59–60.

129. Huxley, "Letter to Anita Loos."

130. Huxley, "Synopsis."

131. "I take this opportunity of giving what publicity I can to my contradiction of a silly story, which has been going the round of the papers, about my having presented certain books to Her Majesty the Queen. It is so constantly repeated, and is such absolute fiction, that I think it worth while to state, once for all, that it is utterly false in every particular: nothing even resembling it has occurred" (Carroll, *Symbolic Logic*, vi).

132. Moses, *Lewis Carroll in Wonderland and at Home*, 95.

133. Perkins, "Research Report for Alice in Wonderland (Sept)," 11.

134. Huxley, "Synopsis," 67.

135. Collingwood, *Life and Letters*, 68.

136. Collingwood, 184.

137. Huxley, "Synopsis," 69.

138. Huxley, 67.

139. Huxley, 67–68.

NOTES

140. Huxley, 68. *Tom Brown at Oxford* is a sequel to *Tom Brown's Schooldays*, which is based on Thomas Hughes's time at Rugby School under the tutelage of Huxley's great uncle, Thomas Arnold.

141. Huxley, 68.

142. Carroll, *Alice in Wonderland*, 16.

143. Huxley, "Synopsis," 71–72.

144. Higdon and Lehrman, "Huxley's 'Deep Jam' and the Adaptation of *Alice in Wonderland*," 65–66.

145. Higdon and Lehrman, 64.

146. Gabler, *Walt Disney*, 486.

147. Disney, 16.

148. Jaques and Giddens, *Lewis Carroll's Alice's Adventures in Wonderland and Through the Looking-Glass*, 205.

149. Gabler, *Walt Disney*, 486–87.

150. Jackson, *Walt Disney, a Bio-Bibliography*, 52.

151. Miller and Martin, "My Dad, Walt Disney," part 8, 80–81.

152. Wells, *Animation and America*, 128.

153. Gopnik, "Who Can Be Finished With Alice?"

154. Perkins, "Research Report for Alice in Wonderland (Sept)," 128.

155. Jaques and Giddens, *Lewis Carroll's Alice's Adventures in Wonderland and Through the Looking-Glass*. See also Clark, *Kiddie Lit*, 155.

156. See, for example, Siemann, "But I'm Grown up Now"; Day and Fritz, *The Victorian Period in Twenty-First Century Children's and Adolescent Literature and Culture*, introduction.

157. Disney, "How I Cartooned Alice," 7.

158. Disney, 8.

159. Gubar, *Artful Dodgers*, 111.

160. Ross, "Escape from Wonderland," 56.

161. Carroll, *Alice in Wonderland*, 95.

162. For a similar argument about the ending to Disney's *Alice in Wonderland*, see Leitch, *Film Adaptation and Its Discontents*, 186.

163. Perkins, "Research Report for Alice in Wonderland (Sept)," 4.

164. Elliott, *Rethinking the Novel/Film Debate*, 223.

165. Geronimi et al., *Alice in Wonderland*.

166. Elliott, *Rethinking the Novel/Film Debate*, 223.

167. Parody, "Franchising/Adaptation," 211.

168. Meikle, *Adaptations in the Franchise Era*, 8.

169. Seldes.

170. Pallant, *Demystifying Disney*, 21–23; Wasko, *Understanding Disney*.

171. Rodriguez, "Disney, Built on Franchises, Says Not Everything Needs to Be a Franchise."

172. Jackson, *Walt Disney, a Bio-Bibliography*, 145.

173. Snow, *Disney's Land*.

174. King and O'Boyle, "The Theme Park," 5–7.

184 NOTES

175. King and O'Boyle, 7.

176. Florey and Jackson, "The Disneyland Story."

177. Geronimi, Jackson, and Luske, "Alice in Wonderland."

178. "Mad Tea Party."

179. "Alice in Wonderland (Ride)."

180. Rahn, "The Dark Ride of Snow White," 88.

181. Rahn, 89.

182. Disney, "How I Cartooned Alice," 8.

183. Leitch, *Film Adaptation and Its Discontents*, 186; Ross, "Escape from Wonderland."

184. Brooker, *Alice's Adventures*, 309; "Alice's Labyrinth."

185. Disney, "How I Cartooned Alice," 9.

186. Lovett, *Alice on Stage*, 133.

187. Burton, *Alice in Wonderland*.

188. Elliott, "Adaptation as Compendium," 194.

189. Elliott, 194.

190. Burton, *Alice in Wonderland*.

191. See Siemann, "But I'm Grown up Now." One might also link these darker adaptations to arguments about Carroll's pedophilia.

192. Elliott, "Adaptation as Compendium," 193.

193. Hutcheon, *A Theory of Adaptation*, 4.

194. Elliott, "Tie-Intertextuality," 202.

CHAPTER THREE: ANIMATING HANS CHRISTIAN ANDERSEN

1. Zipes, *Hans Christian Andersen*, 49.

2. Zipes, 50.

3. Andersen, *Hans Christian Andersen*, 14. Even the travel writer Michael Booth dwells on Andersen's sexuality as he follows the itinerary of Andersen's 1840 travelogue, *A Poet's Bazaar*. See Booth, *Just As Well I'm Leaving*.

4. Recordings of "Celebrate the Magic" can be found on YouTube.

5. Stewart, *DisneyWar*, 24.

6. Stewart, 473.

7. *LIFE Walt Disney*.

8. Seldes, "Mickey-Mouse Maker."

9. Seldes.

10. See, for example, D23, "About Walt Disney."

11. Seldes.

12. Heide, *Mickey Mouse*, 22.

13. Heide, 27.

14. Walt is the clear protagonist of *Be Our Guest: Perfecting the Art of Customer Service*, which is published by the Disney Institute, the arm of the company that has offered professional development and business training since 1996. Just as the corporate version of Walt Disney competes with other biographies, this official training manual competes

NOTES   185

with numerous business textbooks. The best-known, perhaps, is Bill Capodagli and Lynn Jacksons's *The Disney Way: Harnessing the Management Secrets of Disney in Your Company*, first published in 1999 and rereleased in a third edition in 2016. Other examples, just in the last few years, include Sichol, *From an Idea to Disney*; Goldsby and Mathews, *Entrepreneurship the Disney Way*; and Linetsky, *The Business of Walt Disney and the Nine Principles of His Success*.

15. Miller and Martin, "My Dad, Walt Disney." On being prearranged to forestall another biography, Schickel 142.

16. Schickel, *The Disney Version*, 18.

17. Schickel, 72–73.

18. Schickel, 43.

19. Wells, *Animation and America*, 12.

20. Gabler, *Walt Disney*, xix.

21. Dickens's friend Charles Forster penned the novelist's first biography, and Claire Tomalin's 2011 book is among the most critical.

22. Wullschlager, *Hans Christian Andersen*, 239.

23. Wullschlager, 151.

24. Sumpter, Victorian Press 6.

25. Bredsdorff, *Hans Andersen and Charles Dickens*, 14–15.

26. Salmon, *Juvenile Literature*, 156–57

27. Bredsdorff, *Hans Andersen and Charles Dickens*, 20–21, 26–27.

28. Bredsdorff, 40.

29. Slater, *Charles Dickens*, 429.

30. Bredsdorff, *Hans Andersen and Charles Dickens*, 115.

31. A July 3, 1857, letter to Miss Burdett-Coutts, quoted in Bredsdorff, 112.

32. Bredsdorff, 112–13.

33. Prince, *Hans Christian Andersen*, 243.

34. Wullschlager, *Hans Christian Andersen*, 301. See also Prince, *Hans Christian Andersen*, 250.

35. Wullschlager, *Hans Christian Andersen*, 302.

36. Andersen, *Diaries*, 78.

37. Bredsdorff, *Hans Andersen and Charles Dickens*, 60.

38. Andersen, *Diaries*, 80.

39. James, *William Wetmore Story and His Friends*, 285–86. The gifts would have been prompted by Andersen's tale "The Steadfast Tin Soldier," whose eponymous soldier has one leg.

40. Andersen, *Diaries*, 279.

41. Wullschlager, *Hans Christian Andersen*, 374–75.

42. Andersen, *Diaries*, 281.

43. Byron, *Don Juan*, 683. In Lynch and Stillinger, *Norton Anthology, Vol. D*.

44. Carlyle, from *Past and Present*, 1076. In Robson and Christ, *Norton Anthology, Vol. E*.

45. Ruskin, *Stones of Venice*, 364.

46. Browning, *Poetical Works*, 532–33.

47. Andersen, *Diaries*, 307.

186 NOTES

48. Eliot, *Middlemarch*, 4.

49. Eliot, 4.

50. Yonge, "Children's Literature of the Last Century," 452.

51. Lovett, *Alice on Stage*, 78.

52. Wullschlager, *Hans Christian Andersen*, 293.

53. Julia Briggs argues that the Danish "*eventyr*" or German "*märchen*" are more precise terms than the English "fairy tale," and their failure to catch on in England contributed to Andersen's relegation to children's literature. See Briggs, "A Liberating Imagination."

54. Briggs, 183.

55. Yonge, "Children's Literature of the Last Century," 452.

56. Wullschlager, *Hans Christian Andersen*, 144.

57. Wullschlager, 222.

58. Porsdam, *Copyright And Other Fairy Tales*, 6.

59. Andersen, *Diaries*, 422.

60. Briggs, "A Liberating Imagination," 186.

61. The Disney adaptations are of Barrie, *Peter Pan* (1953); Kipling, *The Jungle Book* (1968); Grahame, *The Reluctant Dragon* (1941) and *The Adventures of Ichabod and Mr. Toad* (1949); Carroll, *Alice in Wonderland* (1951); and Milne, *The Many Adventures of Winnie the Pooh* (1977). All but the last were based on Victorian texts and produced during Walt's lifetime. Milne's *Winnie the Pooh* was published in 1926, and the film released a few years after Walt's death.

Briggs also finds the legacy of "The Snow Queen" in MacDonald's North Wind, C. S. Lewis's White Witch, and Philip Pullman's Lyra Silvertongue (Briggs, 190). Wilfred Owen, best known for his World War I poetry, produced two verse versions of Andersen's tales, including "The Little Mermaid" (Butts, "Anthems for (Un)Doomed Youth?").

62. Wullschlager, *Hans Christian Andersen*, 20.

63. Prince, *Hans Christian Andersen*, 18.

64. Andersen, *Hans Christian Andersen*, 35.

65. Wullschlager, *Hans Christian Andersen*, 172.

66. Wullschlager, 194.

67. Andersen, *Hans Christian Andersen*, 133.

68. Andersen, *Diaries*, 169.

69. Andersen, *Hans Christian Andersen*, 438.

70. Rowland, *More Than Meets the Eye*, 57.

71. Rowland, 78.

72. Rowland, 78.

73. Rowland, 79.

74. Andersen, *Diaries*, 167.

75. Andersen, 155.

76. Andersen, *Hans Christian Andersen*, 287.

77. Andersen, 327–28.

78. Andersen, 215–16.

79. Prince, *Hans Christian Andersen*, 274.

80. Andersen, *Diaries*, 373.

81. Andersen, 399.

82. Andersen, 412.

83. Quoted in Andersen, *Hans Christian Andersen*, 228.

84. Bredsdorff, *Hans Andersen and Charles Dickens*, 27.

85. Bredsdorff, 28.

86. Andersen, *Hans Christian Andersen*, 155.

87. Andersen, 80–81.

88. Andersen, *Diaries*, 245.

89. Zipes, *Hans Christian Andersen*, 90.

90. Andersen, xvii.

91. Andersen, 80.

92. Andersen, xvii.

93. Prince, *Hans Christian Andersen*, 212.

94. Prince, 340.

95. Prince, 341.

96. Wullschlager, *Hans Christian Andersen*, 382.

97. Wullschlager, 382.

98. Andersen, *Hans Christian Andersen*, 254; Wullschlager, *Hans Christian Andersen*, 175.

99. Prince, *Hans Christian Andersen*, 211–12.

100. Binding, "Review."

101. "Hans Christian Andersen—FAQ."

102. Booth, *Just As Well I'm Leaving*, 2.

103. Booth, 149.

104. Wullschlager, *Hans Christian Andersen*, 427.

105. Andersen, *Hans Christian Andersen*, 171–72.

106. Wullschlager, *Hans Christian Andersen*, 88.

107. Wullschlager, 106; Andersen, *Hans Christian Andersen*, 167; Prince, *Hans Christian Andersen*, 111–14.

108. Andersen, *Diaries*, 96.

109. Zipes, *Hans Christian Andersen*, 42.

110. Zipes, 10.

111. Wullschlager, *Hans Christian Andersen*, 111.

112. Andersen, *Hans Christian Andersen*, 163.

113. Wullschlager, *Hans Christian Andersen*, 379.

114. Andersen, *Diaries*, 305.

115. Andersen, 343, 350, 372, 378.

116. Andersen, *Hans Christian Andersen*, 474.

117. Andersen, 475.

118. Andersen, 477.

119. Andersen, 525–26.

120. Andersen, 141.

121. Wullschlager, *Hans Christian Andersen*, 94.

122. Wullschlager, 220–22.

123. Andersen, *Hans Christian Andersen*, 314.

124. Andersen, *Diaries*, 488.

125. Andersen, *Hans Christian Andersen*, 490–91.

126. Andersen, 525–26.

127. Sedgwick, "Jane Austen and the Masturbating Girl."

128. Andersen, *Hans Christian Andersen*, 231.

129. Andersen, 332.

130. *The Ugly Duckling* (1931).

131. *The Ugly Duckling* (1939). Disney had won the Oscar in this category every year since its creation in 1932. In 1937, Disney's *The Old Mill* had beaten another Andersen adaptation, Charles Mintz's *The Little Match Girl*. As I discuss in chapter one, Mintz distributed Disney's Alice comedies, and had wrested control of Oswald the Lucky Rabbit the previous decade. *The Little Match Girl* was part of Mintz's *Color Rhapsody* series, launched in 1934 to compete with Disney's *Silly Symphonies* and Warner Bros.' *Merrie Melodies*. Arthur Davis and Sid Marcus, who worked on the film, would later have successful careers with Warner Bros.

132. Andersen, *Hans Christian Andersen*, 333–35.

133. Zipes, *Hans Christian Andersen*, 39.

134. Wullschlager, *Hans Christian Andersen*, 223–25; Andersen, *Hans Christian Andersen*, 329–31.

135. Andersen, "The Ugly Duckling." Quotations from Andersen's tales are from Jean Hersholt's translation, reprinted at the Hans Christian Andersen Centre.

136. Andersen, "The Ugly Duckling."

137. Andersen, "The Ugly Duckling."

138. Andersen, "The Ugly Duckling."

139. Eliot, 4.

140. Andersen, "In the Duckyard."

141. Hersholt's translations are available through the Hans Christian Andersen Centre at Southern Denmark University: https://andersen.sdu.dk/vaerk/hersholt/om_e.html.

142. Jackson, "Walt Disney as Reader and Storyteller: The Books in His Library and What They Mean," 11.

143. "Jean Hersholt Humanitarian Award."

144. Solomon, *The Disney That Never Was*, 73. Solomon states that the Lady Mabel Dunn first suggested the idea for an Andersen biopic, after a visit to Disney's studio.

145. Solomon, 73, 76.

146. Solomon, 76–77.

147. I haven't been able to determine the extent to which Ub Iwerks was involved in the collaboration, though circumstantial evidence suggests he may have played a role. Iwerks had been Disney's friend and collaborator since he started out in Kansas City. He had worked on the Alice comedies and Oswald the Lucky Rabbit, and was among the few animators who stuck with Disney after Mintz took control of Oswald. Iwerks is credited with transforming Disney's vague notion of a cartoon mouse into a full-fledged cartoon character, and never felt he received sufficient credit for his work on Mickey Mouse. He resigned from the Disney studio in 1930 and started his own company, Iwerks Studio, which contracted with Metro-Goldwyn-Mayer. Iwerks made a version of Andersen's "The Brave Tin Soldier" for MGM in 1934, but his studio folded soon after. He worked

briefly on Looney Tunes and *Color Rhapsody* cartoons before returning to Disney in 1940, around the time Disney began collaborating with Goldwyn.

148. Solomon, 66.

149. Solomon, 70.

150. Solomon, 70.

151. Solomon, 73.

152. Allan, *Walt Disney and Europe*, 254.

153. Barrier, *Hollywood Cartoons*, 392.

154. Solomon, *The Disney That Never Was*, 70.

155. For Disney as auteur, see Leitch, *Film Adaptation and Its Discontents*, 245–56.

156. Vidor, *Hans Christian Andersen*.

157. Babington, "Danny Kaye," 386.

158. Mackrell, "Hans Christian Andersen's Failed Career as a Dancer."

159. Mackrell.

160. Mackrell.

161. Ames, "Just The Way Walt Made 'Em."

162. Sanders and DeBlois, *Lilo & Stitch*.

163. Andersen, "The Steadfast Tin Soldier."

164. Wullschlager, *Hans Christian Andersen*, 178–81.

165. Andersen, "The Steadfast Tin Soldier."

166. Wullschlager, *Hans Christian Andersen*, 258–59.

167. Andersen, "The Little Match Girl."

168. Allers, *The Little Matchgirl*.

169. Stewart, *DisneyWar*, 473.

170. Stewart, 71–72.

171. Ebert, "The Little Mermaid Movie Review."

172. Hastings, "Moral Simplification in Disney's *The Little Mermaid*."

173. Aldrich and Wotherspoon, *Who's Who in Gay and Lesbian History*, 23; see also Prince, *Hans Christian Andersen*, 172; Wullschlager, *Hans Christian Andersen*, 401.

174. Griffin, *Tinker Belles and Evil Queens*, 97–104.

175. Griffin, 12.

176. Griffin, 109.

177. Cleto, *Camp*, 1.

178. Griffin, *Tinker Belles and Evil Queens*, 98.

179. Malcolm, "Busby Berkeley, Patron Saint of Movie Camp."

180. Griffin, *Tinker Belles and Evil Queens*, 90.

181. Griffin, 90.

182. Griffin, 90.

183. Rather, "The AIDS Metaphor in 'Beauty and the Beast.'"

184. Griffin, *Tinker Belles and Evil Queens*, 86.

185. Griffin, 93.

186. Griffin, 94.

187. Erb, "Another World or the World of an Other?," 61.

188. Griffin, *Tinker Belles and Evil Queens*, 95–96.

189. See, for example, Hastings, "Moral Simplification"; Giroux, *The Mouse that Roared*; and Bell, Haas, and Sells, "Introduction."

190. Sedgwick, *Tendencies*, 3.

191. Cloud.

192. Nikolas, "The Pro-Gay Message Hidden In Every Disney Film."

193. Johnson, "Disney, Marvel to Boycott Georgia if Religious Liberty Bill Is Passed."

194. Finnegan, "After Criticism over Silence, Disney CEO Opposes Florida Bill Restricting LGBTQ Topics in Schools."

195. Griffin, *Tinker Belles and Evil Queens*, 10.

196. Cloud, "How Gay Days Made a Home at Disney World."

197. Romano, "The Racist Backlash."

198. Di Placido.

199. Konnikova, "How 'Frozen' Took Over the World."

200. Andersen, "The Snow Queen."

201. Andersen, "The Snow Queen."

202. Andersen, "The Snow Queen."

203. Hill, "Countdown to Disney 'Frozen.'"

204. Connelly, "Inside the Research"; "Frozen: The Disney Princess Comes in from the Cold."

205. Rosenstein, "Disney Animation Reveals."

206. Hill, "Countdown to Disney 'Frozen.'"

207. Hill.

208. Andersen, "The Snow Queen."

209. Stewart, *DisneyWar*, 436–37.

210. Connelly, "Inside the Research."

211. Connelly.

212. Andersen, "The Snow Man."

213. Andersen, "The Snow Man."

214. Buck and Lee, *Frozen*.

215. Andersen, "The Snow Man."

216. Wullschlager, *Hans Christian Andersen*, 370; see also Miller, "'Worth Melting For,'" 163; Prince, *Hans Christian Andersen*, 339.

217. Andersen, "The Snow Queen."

218. Mendelson, "Review"; Stevens, "'Let It Go' Leaves Me Cold"; "Frozen: The Disney Princess Comes in from the Cold."

219. Pulver, "Frozen Lambasted as Pro-Gay Propaganda by Christian Pastor"; Petersen, "Disney's Frozen and the 'Gay Agenda.'"

220. Matos, "Conceal, Don't Feel."

221. Mendelson, "Review."

222. Nikolas, "The Pro-Gay Message Hidden In Every Disney Film."

223. "Top Comments"; Salvatore, "Disney's Frozen"; Faraci, "FROZEN Movie Review"; Linde, "My Ice Gown Is in the Closet."

224. Allen, "Is Elsa Really Getting a Girlfriend?"

225. VanDerWerff, "Why Elsa from Frozen Is a Queer Icon—and Why Disney Won't Embrace That Idea"; Renfro, "Why Elsa Doesn't Have a Love Story."

NOTES 191

226. Davis, "On 'Love Experts,'" 667.

227. Wullschlager, *Hans Christian Andersen*, 245, 247.

228. Andersen, *Hans Christian Andersen*, 536–37.

229. The 1843 visit inspired "The Nightingale," and he returned to Tivoli Gardens in 1872, with Harald Scharff. Tivoli Gardens is still open, and its publicity features the connection to Andersen; plans for an HC Andersen hotel were announced in June 2019. Miller, "'Worth Melting For,'" 167; "About Tivoli Gardens"; Crook, "H C Andersen Hotel."

CHAPTER FOUR: PRINCESSES AND PIRATES

1. Orenstein, *Cinderella Ate My Daughter*, 13–14.

2. "Disney Princess." See also Sweeney, "'Where Happily Ever After Happens Every Day.'"

3. Jones, "The World's 25 Most Successful Media Franchises, and How They Stay Relevant."

4. Stewart, *DisneyWar*, 355.

5. Orenstein, *Cinderella Ate My Daughter*.

6. See for example the essays in Sells, Haas, and Bell, *From Mouse to Mermaid*. The Disney Princess brand continues to attract feminist scholarship, including Robin Muir's recent *The Disney Princess Phenomenon: A Feminist Analysis* (2023).

7. "Bibbidi Bobbidi Boutique."

8. Cendrowski, *The Contractual Obligation Implementation*.

9. Ruskin, "Of Queen's Gardens," 1615.

10. Woolf, "Professions for Women," 2273.

11. Bell, "Somatexts at the Disney Shop," 108.

12. Anderson, *Tainted Souls and Painted Faces*, 2.

13. Auerbach, *Woman and the Demon*, 63.

14. Caine, *English Feminism, 1780–1980*, 92.

15. Butler, *Woman's Work and Woman's Culture*, xxv.

16. Butler, xxx.

17. Browning, "Aurora Leigh," ll. 427, 430–32.

18. Browning, ll. 403–4, 455.

19. Schwartzel, "Beauty and the Backlash."

20. Johnston and Moore, *Ralph Breaks the Internet*.

21. Psychologist Sarah M. Coyne interviewed over 300 preschool-aged children about their engagement with Disney princesses, and found that higher engagement indeed correlated with stereotypically female play (Coyne et al., "Pretty as a Princess"). A follow-up study with the same children five years later, however, found that those who engaged with Disney princesses actually had slightly more egalitarian views of gender (Coyne et al., "Princess Power"). Coyne attributes the difference to the secondary roles male characters typically play in princess films.

22. Wills, *Disney Culture*, 123.

23. "Dream Big, Princess."

24. Butler, "Performative Acts and Gender Constitution," 520.

25. Sedgwick, *Epistemology of the Closet*, 68.

26. Orenstein, *Cinderella Ate My Daughter*, 14.

27. Wells, *Animation and America*, 107.

28. Hone, "The Political House That Jack Built."

29. Shelley, "England in 1819."

30. Nadel, "Portraits of the Queen," 189.

31. Williams, *Becoming Queen Victoria*, 51.

32. Zipes, *Victorian Fairy Tales*, xiii–iv.

33. Williams, *Becoming Queen Victoria*, 101.

34. Quoted in Williams, 65.

35. Williams, 70.

36. Rowell, *The Old Vic Theatre*, 4–5.

37. Williams, *Becoming Queen Victoria*, 136–37.

38. Strachey, *Queen Victoria*, 9.

39. Plunkett, *Queen Victoria*, 3.

40. Brown, "The Influence of Queen Victoria on England's Literary Fairy Tale," 35.

41. Vallone, *Becoming Victoria*, 109.

42. Nadel, "Portraits of the Queen," 173–75; Vallone, *Becoming Victoria*, 111.

43. Plunkett, *Queen Victoria*, 13–14.

44. Nadel, "Portraits of the Queen," 170.

45. Plunkett, *Queen Victoria*, 13.

46. Strachey, *Queen Victoria*, 404.

47. Lee, *Queen Victoria*, 353, 334.

48. Longford, *Queen Victoria*.

49. Lee, *Queen Victoria*, 354.

50. Lee, 357.

51. Lee, 416.

52. Strachey, *Queen Victoria*, 342.

53. Strachey, 375.

54. Nadel, "Portraits of the Queen," 179.

55. Kuhn, "Queen Victoria's Jubilees and the Invention of Tradition," 107–8, 112.

56. Richards, "The Image of Victoria in the Year of Jubilee," 11, 27.

57. Hawksley, *Queen Victoria's Mysterious Daughter*, 110.

58. Strachey, *Queen Victoria*, 258.

59. Hawksley, *Queen Victoria's Mysterious Daughter*, 7.

60. Hawksley, 7.

61. Hawksley, 2–3.

62. Packard, *Victoria's Daughters*, 124.

63. Hawksley, *Queen Victoria's Mysterious Daughter*, 109–10.

64. Ruskin, "Pre-Raphaelitism," 1468.

65. Dickens, "New Lamps for Old Ones," 1465.

66. Hawksley, *Queen Victoria's Mysterious Daughter*, 20.

67. Hawksley, 111.

68. Caine, *English Feminism, 1780–1980*, 88.

69. Quoted in Strachey, *Queen Victoria*, 409.

70. Packard, *Victoria's Daughters*.

NOTES

71. "Princess Louise to Josephine Butler," March 27, 1869.

72. Walkowitz, *Prostitution and Victorian Society*, 91.

73. Walkowitz, 93.

74. Butler, *Personal Reminiscences of a Great Crusade*, 1.

75. Walkowitz, *Prostitution and Victorian Society*, 113, 93.

76. Hawksley, *Queen Victoria's Mysterious Daughter*, 111–12.

77. Hawksley, 112.

78. Hawksley, 113.

79. Hawksley, 113–14.

80. Butler, *Woman's Work and Woman's Culture*, xiii.

81. Hawksley, *Queen Victoria's Mysterious Daughter*, 118.

82. Hawksley, 119–20.

83. Among the guests at Louise's wedding was the thirteen-year-old Frances Campbell, Lorne's younger sister. She shared her sister-in-law's passion for women's emancipation. In the 1880s, she became involved in the suffragist movement, where both her rank and her public speaking talent made her "the most exciting advocate for women's enfranchisement." When, in the 1890s, the National Society for Women's Suffrage consolidated various suffrage societies into a single organization, she was named to the executive board, a role she served for two decades. She was the only noblewoman to take a leadership role in the suffrage movement. Huffman, *Lady Frances*.

84. Strachey, *Queen Victoria*, 339–40.

85. Quoted in Strachey, 409–10.

86. Tennyson, *The Princess*, Part V, ll. 437–41.

87. Stone, "Genre Subversion and Gender Inversion," 107.

88. Peterson, "Tennyson and the Ladies," 27.

89. Ricks, "*The Princess* and the Queen," 133.

90. Ricks, 138.

91. Hall, "The Anti-Feminist Ideology of Tennyson's *The Princess*," 50.

92. Tennyson, "*In Memoriam A. H. H.*," no. 27, ll. 15–16.

93. Banerjee, "Queen's College and the 'Ladies' College.'"

94. Quoted in Hall, "The Anti-Feminist Ideology of Tennyson's *The Princess*," 49.

95. Wolstenholme, "The Education of Girls, Its Present and Its Future," 294.

96. Banerjee, "The University of London and Women Students."

97. Batchelor, *Tennyson*, 4.

98. Ledbetter, *Tennyson and Victorian Periodicals*, 2.

99. Kooistra, "The Moxon Tennyson."

100. Tennyson, *The Princess*, Prologue, ll. 29–30, 32–34.

101. Tennyson, Prologue, ll. 126–29.

102. Tennyson, Prologue, ll. 133–36.

103. Tennyson, Prologue, ll. 217–19.

104. *The Princess* also includes several "interludes," short lyrics attributed to the women at the party. Many scholars have written about them, but since they are ancillary to the point I'm making in this chapter, I omit them from the summary.

105. Tennyson, *The Princess*, Part I, ll. 48–49.

106. Tennyson, Part I, ll. 128–30.

107. Tennyson, Part I, ll. 149–50.

108. Tennyson, Part II, l. 130.

109. Tennyson, Part II, ll. 45–47.

110. Tennyson, Part IV, ll. 492–94.

111. Tennyson, Part V, ll. 193–96.

112. Tennyson, Part V, ll. 440–41.

113. Tennyson, Part VII, ll. 134–35.

114. Tennyson, Part VII, ll. 144–46.

115. Stone, "Genre Subversion and Gender Inversion," 108.

116. Tennyson, *The Princess*, Part VII, l. 243.

117. Tennyson, Part II, ll. 154–57.

118. Tennyson, Conclusion, ll. 72–73.

119. Johnston, "This Were a Medley," 560. See also Collins, "The Education of the Prince"; Joseph, "Tennyson's Three Women"; Watson, "Tennyson's 'The Princess.'"

120. Clapp-Itnyre, "Marginalized Musical Interludes," 229. See also Buchanan, "Doing Battle with Forgotten Ghosts."

121. Kooistra, "Poetry in the Victorian Marketplace," 49.

122. Gilbert and Gubar, *No Man's Land*, 15.

123. Banerjee, "The University of London and Women Students."

124. Williams, *Gilbert and Sullivan*, 244.

125. Kooistra, "Poetry in the Victorian Marketplace," 56–57, 69–71.

126. Tennyson, *The Princess*, Prologue, l. 152.

127. Tennyson, Prologue, ll. 217–20.

128. Kooistra, "Poetry in the Victorian Marketplace," 72.

129. Tennyson, *The Princess*, Prologue, ll. 131–32.

130. Hall, "The Anti-Feminist Ideology of Tennyson's *The Princess*," 55.

131. Tennyson, *The Princess*, Part V, l. 440. For *The Princess* as asserting male dominance, Gilbert and Gubar, *No Man's Land*, 10.

132. Collins, "The Education of the Prince"; Hall, "The Anti-Feminist Ideology of Tennyson's *The Princess*," 49.

133. Tennyson, *The Princess*, Conclusion, ll. 11, 18–19.

134. Tennyson, Conclusion, ll. 27–28.

135. Hughes, "Hang There like Fruit, My Soul," 96–97; Adams, *Dandies and Desert Saints*.

136. Tennyson, *The Princess*, Part VII, ll. 240–43.

137. Tennyson, Part VII, ll. 262–67.

138. Tennyson, Part VII, ll. 272–73.

139. Tennyson, Part II, ll. 154–57.

140. Tennyson, Part VII, ll. 284–89.

141. For a similar interpretation of *The Princess*, see Hughes, "Hang There like Fruit, My Soul," 97.

142. Ames, "Just The Way Walt Made 'Em."

143. "Pirates of the Caribbean."

144. "Pirates of the Caribbean."

145. Yolen, *Sea Queens*; Tucker, *Anne Bonny the Famous Female Pirate*; Duncombe, *Pirate Women*.

146. McNary, "Disney World Updates Controversial 'Pirates of the Caribbean' Ride Bride Auction Scene."

147. "The Pirates League"; see also "The Bibbidi Bobbidi Boutique."

148. Sutton, *Pirates of the Slave Trade*; Lowe, *The Intimacies of Four Continents*.

149. Browning, "The Runaway Slave at Pilgrim's Point," ll. 12–14.

150. Browning, ll. 223–24.

151. Said, *Culture and Imperialism*, 89.

152. "Legacies of British Slave-Ownership."

153. Powell, *British Pirates in Print and Performance*, 155.

154. Powell, 22.

155. Powell, 102.

156. Only in the nineteenth century would men begin to distinguish "homosocial" masculine desire from homosexuality (Sedgwick, *Between Men*, 1).

157. Turley, *Rum, Sodomy, and the Lash*; Burg, *Sodomy and the Pirate Tradition*.

158. Williams, *Gilbert and Sullivan*, 130.

159. For Disney's investment in portraying American history see Watts, "Walt Disney"; Francaviglia, "History after Disney"; and Schaffer, "Disney and the Imagineering of Histories."

160. Emeljanow, "Staging the Pirate," 231. For a discussion of the melodrama's conventions and popularity, see chapter one.

161. Williams, *Gilbert and Sullivan*, 98; Kaiser, *The World in Play*, 54. Jerrold is the playwright for whose widow Dickens produced *The Frozen Deep*; see chapter 1.

162. Nonwhite pirates still made convenient villains, especially as imperial fiction became a common genre. R. M. Ballantyne's *The Pirate City* (1874) is set in Algiers, and G. A. Henty's *Among Malay Pirates* (1899) takes place along the Suez Canal. In these works, however, the Middle Eastern or Asian pirates contrast with the heroes' whiteness.

163. Williams, *Gilbert and Sullivan*, 99–100, 107.

164. Emeljanow, "Staging the Pirate," 226–28.

165. Campbell, "Pirate Chic," 12.

166. Farr, "Paper Dreams," 46.

167. Emeljanow, "Staging the Pirate," 225.

168. Stevenson, *A Child's Garden of Verses*, 1182. See also Deane, "Imperial Boyhood."

169. Williams, *Gilbert and Sullivan*, 102.

170. Williams, 20.

171. Williams, 136–48.

172. Perkins, "Research Report for Alice in Wonderland (Sept)," 127–28.

173. Jackson, *Walt Disney, a Bio-Bibliography*, 46–47; Gabler, *Walt Disney*, 470.

174. Cohen, *Pirating Fictions*, 183.

175. Eidam, "Reexamining Illustration's Role in Treasure Island," 45.

176. Jackson, *Walt Disney, a Bio-Bibliography*, 46–47.

177. Gabler, *Walt Disney*, 490–91.

178. Gabler, 490–91.

179. "Disney Fairies."

180. Cohen, *Pirating Fictions*, 219.

181. Carpenter, *Secret Gardens*, 170; Cohen, *Pirating Fictions*, 217–23; Rose, *The Case of Peter Pan*, 66.

182. See for example Green, *Fifty Years of Peter Pan*; Gubar, "Peter Pan as Children's Theatre: The Issue of Audience"; Gubar, *Artful Dodgers*; Hanson, *Peter Pan on Stage and Screen, 1904-2010*; Han, "Co-Narrating Like a Child."

183. Gryctko, "The Romance of the Nursery."

184. Barrie, *Peter and Wendy*, 49, 63. *Peter Pan* quotations are from this novel unless otherwise specified.

185. Cohen, *Pirating Fictions*, 227. The scene was cut and replaced with what became one of the most iconic moments in the play, the Mermaid's Lagoon.

186. Quoted in Emeljanow, "Staging the Pirate," 241.

187. Stevenson, *Treasure Island*, 58.

188. Powell, *British Pirates in Print and Performance*, 143.

189. Barrie, *Peter and Wendy*, 50.

190. Barrie, 49, 117.

191. Barrie, *Peter Pan* (play), 146.

192. Emeljanow, "Staging the Pirate," 236–38.

193. Blank, "Research Report for Peter Pan (Dec 1)."

194. Blank, "Research Report for Peter Pan (Oct 20)."

195. Blank, "Research Report for Peter Pan (Nov 7)."

196. Blank.

197. Blank.

198. Blank, "Research Report for Peter Pan (Nov 23)."

199. Blank, "Research Report for Peter Pan (Nov 1)."

200. Hurd, "Peter Pan Notes"; "Peter Pan Meeting Notes, 1939."

201. "Peter Pan Meeting Notes, 1943."

202. "Summary of the Most Recent Discussions of Peter Pan Musical Feature."

203. Blank, "Research Report for Peter Pan (Nov 7)."

204. Barrie, *Peter and Wendy*, 47–48, 53.

205. Stevenson, *Treasure Island*, 5, 54.

206. Stewart, *DisneyWar*, 233.

207. Fritz, "Late Victorian Adventure."

208. Fritz.

209. Merle Johnson wrote that the popular image of the pirate exists "in great degree as drawn by the pen and pencil of Howard Pyle" (Pyle and Johnson, *Howard Pyle's Book of Pirates*, xi).

210. Emeljanow, "Staging the Pirate," 223.

NOTES

CONCLUSION: POST-CORPORATE ART AND CRITICISM

1. For a wonderful cultural history of *Pinocchio*, see Wunderlich and Morrissey's *Pinocchio Goes Postmodern*.

2. For an excellent reading of adaptations of *A Christmas Carol*, including Disney's and also the Muppets (a Disney-owned franchise), see Leitch's chapter on "entry level Dickens" in *Film Adaptation and Its Discontents*.

3. Said, *Culture and Imperialism*, 148, 32.

4. In the last decade, Victorian studies has faced pressure to make its analysis more relevant to the modern world. In 2014, the V21 Manifesto promised a "presentist" analysis, favoring topics like capitalism and environmental degradation, which took root in the Victorian period but remain important today. The Spring 2020 issue of *Victorian Studies* emphasizes race and racial difference, and argues that Victorian studies has not sufficiently engaged with those concepts ("Manifesto of the V21 Collective"; Chatterjee, Christoff, and Wong, "Introduction").

5. Bhabha, *The Location of Culture*; Spivak, "Three Women's Texts and a Critique of Imperialism"; Viswanathan, *Masks of Conquest*; Said, *Culture and Imperialism*.

6. Spivak, "Three Women's Texts and a Critique of Imperialism"; Lee, "The Return of the 'Unnative'"; Said, *Culture and Imperialism*, 133–56; Achebe, "Image of Africa: Racism in Conrad's *Heart of Darkness*."

7. Kutzer, *Empire's Children*, xviii

8. Napolitano, "Of Mice and Men."

9. Dorfman and Mattelart, *How to Read Donald Duck*, 9.

10. Dorfman and Mattelart, 28.

11. Dorfman and Mattelart, 98, 28.

12. Byrne and McQuillan, *Deconstructing Disney*, 1.

13. See, for example, Hurley, "Seeing White"; Wojcik-Andrews and Phillips, "Telling Tales to Children"; Mauro, "Disney's Splash Mountain"; Szumsky, "All That Is Solid Melts into the Air"; Anjirbag, "Mulan and Moana."

14. Countryman, "Disney Plus Adds Content Warning."

15. "Disney Launches Reimagine Tomorrow Amplifying Underrepresented Voices."

16. Thiong'O, "Decolonising the Mind."

17. Rushdie, "Imaginary Homelands," 2751.

18. Rhys, *Wide Sargasso Sea*.

19. Greene, *Boy Called Twist*; Gupta and Dickens, *Great Expectations*.

20. Arnold, "Dover Beach," ll. 9–10.

21. Nagra, "Look We Have Coming to Dover!

22. Nagra.

23. Greenberg, "His Writing Radicalized Hackers. Now He Wants to Redeem Them."

24. Antrim, "Does That Mean We Can Defrost Walt?"

25. Pond and Doctorow, "Interview with Cory Doctorow."

26. wmfrank, "Creative Fiction, or CC SF."

27. Pond and Doctorow, "Interview with Cory Doctorow," 746.

28. Doctorow, *Down and Out in the Magic Kingdom*.

198   NOTES

29. Pond and Doctorow, 746.

30. Levy, "Upcoming."

31. Jobson, "Welcome to Dismaland."

32. "Dismaland."

33. "Dismaland."

34. Levy, "Upcoming."

35. Cozart, *After Ever After—DISNEY Parody*.

36. Williams, *Gilbert and Sullivan*, 6.

37. Korkis, "The Origin of the Disneyland Wienie"; Snow, *Disney's Land*.

38. Kelly, "Banksy Dismaland Show Revealed at Weston's Tropicana."

39. "Manifesto of the V21 Collective"; Chatterjee, Christoff, and Wong, "Introduction."

APPENDIX: DISNEY STUDIES AND VICTORIAN STUDIES

1. Lepore, "The Lion and the Mouse: The Battle That Reshaped Children's Literature."

2. Clark, *Kiddie Lit*, 177.

3. Sayers, "Walt Disney Accused."

4. Schickel, *The Disney Version*, 18.

5. The pejorative actually predates Sayers by a few years; the *OED Online* gives the first usage as Lawrence Lipton's *The Holy Barbarians* (1959), referring to "the neon chrome artyfake Disneyfication of America" ("Disneyfication, n.")

6. Giroux, *The Mouse That Roared*, 10.

7. Bell, "Somatexts at the Disney Shop," 108.

8. Sells, "Where Do the Mermaids Stand?," 176.

9. Sells, 176–77.

10. Jeffords, "Where Do the Mermaids Stand?," 168–70.

11. Bell, Haas, and Sells, "Introduction," 4.

12. As I discuss in the conclusion, Dofrman and Mattelart point out that Walt Disney "has been exalted as the inviolable common cultural heritage of contemporary man" (Dorfman and Mattelart, *How to Read Donald Duck*, 28).

13. See chapter 4.

14. Ross, "Escape from Wonderland," 53–54.

15. Ross, 63.

16. Tremblay, "Disney in the Academy."

17. Wasko, *Understanding Disney*; Sandlin and Garlen, *Disney, Culture, and Curriculum*; Brode and Brode, *Debating Disney*.

18. For example, Jackson and West, *Disneyland and Culture*; Pallant, *Demystifying Disney*; Jackson and West, *Walt Disney, from Reader to Storyteller*; Apgar, *A Mickey Mouse Reader*; Rodosthenous, *The Disney Musical on Stage and Screen*; Bohn, *Music in Disney's Animated Features*; Wills, *Disney Culture*; Davis, *Discussing Disney*; Burchard, *Inspiring Walt Disney*; Kapurch, "Something Else Besides a Daughter"; Kunze, *Staging a Comeback*. Recent handbooks like in Brown's *The Oxford Handbook of Children's Film* and Hermansson and Zepernikck's *The Palgrave Handbook of Children's Film and Television* include essays about

Disney, and the company's prominence is implied in works like *Family Films in Global Cinema: The World beyond Disney*.

19. "Disney launches Reimagine Tomorrow amplifying underrepresented voices."

20. I first learned of the list through a partial reproduction in Allan, *Walt Disney and Europe*, 268–69. I did not see the list myself, but Steven Vagnini (at the time, a Disney archivist) was able to answer some questions about it via email, after my visit (Vagnini, "Disney Archives," July 28, 2014).

21. I'll leave it to someone else to see if Disney still has the research from the early 1940s, and if it was used in Disney's recent *Black Beauty* (2020).

22. Smith, "Comics and Cels: The Walt Disney Archives."

23. Barrier, *Hollywood Cartoons*, 368, 372.

24. For foundational works in New Historicism, see Greenblatt, *Will in the World* and McGann, *The Romantic Ideology*.

25. Wells, *Animation and America*, 123.

26. See for example Abate, "Mickey Mouse as Teddy's Bear"; Barrier, *Hollywood Cartoons*; Clark, *Kiddie Lit*; Gabler, *Walt Disney: Triumph of the American Imagination*; Shortsleeve, "The Wonderful World of the Depression"; Watts, *The Magic Kingdom: Walt Disney and the American Way of Life*; Wells, *Animation and America*.

27. See, for example, Allan, *Walt Disney and Europe*; Burchard, *Inspiring Walt Disney*.

28. Gubar, *Artful Dodgers*; Nelson, *Precocious Children and Childish Adults*; Smith, *Between Generations*. See also Shuttleworth, *The Mind of the Child*; Kincaid, *Child-Loving*; Knoepflmacher, *Ventures Into Childland*; and Fleming, *Nineteenth-Century English Children's Literature: A Companion*.

29. Cartwright, Chin, and Stanley, "A Changing Major," 15.

30. Kramnick, "What We Hire in Now."

31. McGann, "The Crisis in the Humanities," 7.

32. Appiah, "Boundaries of Culture," 514.

33. Chatterjee, Christoff, and Wong, "Introduction."

34. Underwood, 6.

35. Macaulay, "A Minute on Indian Education."

36. Viswanathan, *Masks of Conquest*.

37. Hughes, "Transatlanticism," 917.

38. Levine, "From Nation to Network," 661.

39. Levine, 668.

40. Mee, "Recent Studies," 914; Pinch, "Recent Studies," 956.

41. Hack, *Reaping Something New*.

42. Hayot, "Against Periodization; or, On Institutional Time," 741–43.

43. Levine, *Forms*, 57–58.

44. Brouillette, *UNESCO and the Fate of the Literary*; McGurl, *The Program Era*; Ahmed, *On Being Included*.

45. Ablow and Hack, "Keywords," 547.

46. Day and Fritz, *The Victorian Period in Twenty-First Century Children's and Adolescent Literature and Culture*.

47. Marks, *Alice in Pornoland*; Weltman, *Victorians on Broadway*.

48. See, for example, Elliott, *Rethinking the Novel/Film Debate*; Sadoff, *Victorian Vogue*; Laird, *The Art of Adapting Victorian Literature, 1848–1920*.

49. The journal *Adaptation* launched in 2008, and recent works include Leitch, *The Oxford Handbook of Adaptation Studies* and Meikle, *Adaptations in the Franchise Era*.

50. Zipes, "Breaking the Disney Spell," 38.

51. Leitch, "Twelve Fallacies in Contemporary Adaptation Theory," 161.

52. Sanders, *Adaptation and Appropriation*, 20.

53. Stam, "Beyond Fidelity: The Dialogics of Adaptation," 57.

54. Leitch, *Film Adaptation and Its Discontents*, 1.

55. Zipes, "Breaking the Disney Spell," 41.

56. Hastings, "Moral Simplification in Disney's *The Little Mermaid*."

57. Jackson, "Walt Disney as Reader and Storyteller: The Books in His Library and What They Mean," 18; Allan, *Walt Disney and Europe*, 243.

58. Schickel, *The Disney Version*, 273.

59. Elliott, *Rethinking the Novel/Film Debate*, 114.

60. Eisenstein, "Dickens, Griffith, and Film Today," 195.

61. Quoted in Clark, *Kiddie Lit*, 169. For Disney's library, see Jackson, "Walt Disney as Reader and Storyteller: The Books in His Library and What They Mean," 12. Eisenstein's assessment was sufficiently well-known that it was quoted in a *New Yorker* profile of Walt Disney, less than three years after Mickey's debut. See Seldes.

62. Elliott, *Rethinking the Novel/Film Debate*, 3. Emphasis original.

63. Elliott, 123.

64. Hutcheon, *A Theory of Adaptation*, 86–88.

65. Miller and Martin, "My Dad, Walt Disney."

66. Murray, *The Adaptation Industry*, 73.

Works Cited

Abate, Michelle Ann. "Mickey Mouse as Teddy's Bear: The Political Cartoons of Clifford Berryman and the Origins of Disney's Iconic Character." *Children's Literature Association Quarterly* 42, no. 4 (November 10, 2017): 396–416. https://doi.org/10.1353/chq.2017.0041.

Ablow, Rachel, and Daniel Hack. "Keywords." *Victorian Literature and Culture* 46, no. 3–4 (2018): 547–50. https://doi.org/10.1017/S1060150318000177.

"About Tivoli Gardens." Accessed November 25, 2020. https://www.tivoligardens.com:443/en/om/tivolis+historie.

Abraham, Adam. *Plagiarizing the Victorian Novel.* Cambridge University Press, 2019.

Achebe, Chinua. "Image of Africa: Racism in Conrad's *Heart of Darkness.*" *Massachusetts Review*, no. 18 (1977).

"Activities on the Hollywood Front." *New York Times*, May 21, 1933, sec. Archives.

Adams, James Eli. *Dandies and Desert Saints: Styles of Victorian Masculinity.* Cornell University Press, 1995.

Ahmed, Sara. *On Being Included: Racism and Diversity in Institutional Life.* Duke University Press, 2012.

Albrecht-Crane, Christa, and Dennis Ray Cutchins. *Adaptation Studies: New Approaches.* Fairleigh Dickinson University Press, 2010.

Aldrich, Robert, and Garry Wotherspoon. *Who's Who in Gay and Lesbian History: From Antiquity to the Mid-Twentieth Century.* Routledge, 2020.

"Alice in Wonderland | Rides & Attractions | Disneyland Park." Disneyland Resort. Accessed December 3, 2020. https://disneyland.disney.go.com/attractions/disneyland/alice-in-wonderland/.

"Alice's Curious Labyrinth | Rides & Attractions | Disneyland Paris." Accessed November 19, 2021. https://www.disneylandparis.com/en-us/attractions/disneyland-park/alices-curious-labyrinth/

Allan, Robin R. *Walt Disney and Europe: European Influences on the Animated Feature Films of Walt Disney.* London: John Libbey Publishing, 1999.

Allen, Samantha. "Is Elsa Really Getting a Girlfriend in 'Frozen 2?' Dream On, Disney Fans." *Daily Beast*, March 2, 2018. https://www.thedailybeast.com/is-elsa-really-getting-a-girlfriend-in-frozen-2-dream-on-disney-fans.

Allers, Roger. *The Little Matchgirl.* Buena Vista Home Video, n.d. Accessed November 24, 2020.

Altick, Richard Daniel. *The Shows of London*. Harvard University Press, 1978.

Altman, Rick. "Dickens, Griffith, and Film Theory Today." In *Silent Film*, edited by Richard Abel, 145–62. New Brunswick: Rutgers University Press, 1996.

Ames, Katrine. "Just The Way Walt Made 'Em." *Newsweek*, November 17, 1991. https://www.newsweek.com/just-way-walt-made-em-202018.

Andersen, Hans Christian. *The Diaries of Hans Christian Andersen*. Edited by Sven Hakon Rossel and Patricia Conroy. University of Washington Press, 1990.

Andersen, Hans Christian. "In the Duckyard." Translated by Jean Hersholt. Hans Christian Andersen Center. Accessed November 23, 2020. https://andersen.sdu.dk/vaerk/hersholt/InTheDuckYard_e.html.

Andersen, Hans Christian. "The Little Match Girl." Translated by Jean Hersholt. Hans Christian Andersen Center. Accessed November 23, 2020. https://andersen.sdu.dk/vaerk/hersholt/TheLittleMatchGirl_e.html.

Andersen, Hans Christian. "The Snow Man." Translated by Jean Hersholt. Hans Christian Andersen Center. Accessed November 23, 2020. https://andersen.sdu.dk/vaerk/hersholt/TheSnowMan_e.html.

Andersen, Hans Christian. "The Snow Queen." Translated by Jean Hersholt. Hans Christian Andersen Center. Accessed November 23, 2020. https://andersen.sdu.dk/vaerk/hersholt/TheSnowQueen_e.html.

Andersen, Hans Christian. "The Steadfast Tin Soldier." Translated by Jean Hersholt. Accessed November 24, 2020. https://andersen.sdu.dk/vaerk/hersholt/TheSteadfastTinSoldier_e.html.

Andersen, Hans Christian. "The Ugly Duckling." Translated by Jean Hersholt. Hans Christian Andersen Center. Accessed November 23, 2020. https://andersen.sdu.dk/vaerk/hersholt/TheUglyDuckling_e.html.

Andersen, Jens. *Hans Christian Andersen: A New Life*. Harry N. Abrams, 2005.

Anderson, Amanda. *Tainted Souls and Painted Faces: The Rhetoric of Fallenness in Victorian Culture*. Cornell University Press, 2018.

Anjirbag, Michelle Anya. "Mulan and Moana: Embedded Coloniality and the Search for Authenticity in Disney Animated Film." *Social Sciences* 7, no. 11 (November 2018): 230. https://doi.org/10.3390/socsci7110230.

Anjirbag, Michelle Anya. "Reforming Borders of the Imagination: Diversity, Adaptation, Transmediation, and Incorporation in the Global Disney Film Landscape." *Jeunesse: Young People, Texts, Cultures* 11, no. 2 (2019): 151–76.

Antrim, Taylor. "Does That Mean We Can Defrost Walt?" *New York Times*, March 9, 2003, sec. Books. https://www.nytimes.com/2003/03/09/books/does-that-mean-we-can-defrost-walt.html.

Apgar, Garry. *A Mickey Mouse Reader*. University Press of Mississippi, 2014.

Appiah, Kwame Anthony. "Presidential Address 2017—Boundaries of Culture." *PMLA* 132, no. 3 (May 1, 2017): 513–25. https://doi.org/10.1632/pmla.2017.132.3.513.

Armstrong, Nancy. *Fiction in the Age of Photography*. Harvard University Press, 1999.

Arnold, Matthew. "Dover Beach." In *The Norton Anthology of English Literature*, edited by Catherine Robson and Carol T. Christ. 9th ed., vol. E: The Victorian Age: 1387–88. W. W. Norton & Company, 2012.

WORKS CITED

Arnold, Matthew. "The Function of Criticism at the Present Time." In *The Norton Anthology of English Literature*, edited by Catherine Robson and Carol T. Christ. 9th ed., vol. E: The Victorian Age, 1404–18. W. W. Norton & Company, 2012.

Auerbach, Jeffrey A. *The Great Exhibition of 1851: A Nation on Display*. Yale University Press, 1999.

Auerbach, Nina. *Woman and the Demon: The Life of a Victorian Myth*. Harvard University Press, 1982.

Babb, Genie. "Victorian Roots and Branches: 'The Statistical Century' as Foundation to the Digital Humanities." *Literature Compass* 15, no. 9 (2018): e12487. https://doi.org/10.1111/lic3.12487.

Babington, Bruce. "Danny Kaye as Children's Star." In *The Oxford Handbook of Children's Film*, edited by Noel Brown, 386–97. Oxford University Press, 2022.

Bak, Meredith A. *Playful Visions: Optical Toys and the Emergence of Children's Media Culture*. MIT Press, 2020.

Bakewell, Michael. *Lewis Carroll: A Biography*. Random House of Canada, 1996.

Banerjee, Jacqueline. "Queen's College and the 'Ladies' College.'" Victorian Web. Accessed November 27, 2020. http://www.victorianweb.org/history/education/ulondon/6.html.

Banerjee, Jacqueline. "The University of London and Women Students." Victorian Web. Accessed November 27, 2020. http://www.victorianweb.org/history/education/ulondon/3.html.

Barnes, Brooks. "Not Streaming: 'Song of the South' and Other Films Stay in the Past." *New York Times*, November 12, 2019, sec. Business. https://www.nytimes.com/2019/11/12/business/media/not-streaming-on-disney-plus.html.

Barnett, Charles Zachary. *Oliver Twist, Or, the Parish Boys Progress: A Domestic Drama in Three Acts*. J. Duncombe & Company, 1838.

Barreca, Regina. "'The Mimic Life of Theatre': The 1838 Adaptation of *Oliver Twist*." In *Dramatic Dickens*, edited by Carol Hanbery MacKay, 87–95. St. Martin's Press, 1989.

Barrie, J. M. *Peter Pan and Other Plays: The Admirable Crichton; Peter Pan; When Wendy Grew Up; What Every Woman Knows; Mary Rose*. Edited by Peter Hollindale. 1st ed. Oxford University Press, 2008.

Barrie, J. M. *Peter Pan: Peter and Wendy and Peter Pan in Kensington Gardens*. Edited by Jack Zipes. Penguin Classics, 2004. https://www.penguinrandomhouse.com/books/293680/peter-pan-by-j-m-barrie/.

Barrier, Michael. *Hollywood Cartoons: American Animation in Its Golden Age*. Oxford University Press, 2003.

Batchelor, John. *Tennyson: To Strive, to Seek, to Find*. Open Road Media, 2013.

Baudrillard, Jean. *Simulacra and Simulation*. Translated by Sheila Faria Glaser. University of Michigan Press, 1994.

Bell, Elizabeth. "Somatexts at the Disney Shop: Constructing the Pentimentos of Women's Animated Bodies." In *From Mouse to Mermaid: The Politics of Film, Gender, and Culture*, 107–24. Indiana University Press, 1995.

Bell, Elizabeth, Lynda Haas, and Laura Sells. "Introduction." In *From Mouse to Mermaid: The Politics of Film, Gender, and Culture*, 1–17. Indiana University Press, 1995.

Bernstein, Robin. *Racial Innocence: Performing American Childhood from Slavery to Civil Rights*. NYU Press, 2011.

Bhabha, Homi K. *The Location of Culture*. Routledge, 2012.

"Bibbidi Bobbidi Boutique." Accessed December 21, 2020. https://disneyworld.disney.go.com/shops/magic-kingdom/bibbidi-bobbidi-boutique-park/.

Binding, Paul. "Review: Hans Christian Andersen: The Life of a Storyteller by Jackie Wullschlager." *The Guardian*, November 18, 2000. http://www.theguardian.com/books/2000/nov/18/biography5.

Birch, Dinah. "Education." In *The Cambridge History of Victorian Literature*, edited by Kate Flint, 331–49. 1st ed. New York: Cambridge University Press, 2012.

Blank, Dorothy Ann. "Research Report for Peter Pan (Dec 1)," December 1, 1938. Walt Disney Archives.

Blank, Dorothy Ann. "Research Report for Peter Pan (Nov 1)," November 1, 1938. Walt Disney Archives.

Blank, Dorothy Ann. "Research Report for Peter Pan (Nov 7)," November 7, 1938. Walt Disney Archives.

Blank, Dorothy Ann. "Research Report for Peter Pan (Nov 23)," November 23, 1938. Walt Disney Archives.

Blank, Dorothy Ann. "Research Report for Peter Pan (Oct 20)," October 20, 1938. Walt Disney Archives.

Bohas, Alexandre. *The Political Economy of Disney: The Cultural Capitalism of Hollywood*. Springer, 2016.

Bohn, James. *Music in Disney's Animated Features: Snow White and the Seven Dwarfs to The Jungle Book*. University Press of Mississippi, 2017.

Booth, Michael. *Just as Well I'm Leaving: To the Orient with Hans Christian Andersen*. Random House, 2016.

Bratton, Jacky. *The Making of the West End Stage: Marriage, Management and the Mapping of Gender in London, 1830–1870*. Cambridge University Press, 2011.

Bredsdorff, Elias. *Hans Andersen and Charles Dickens: A Friendship and Its Dissolution*. Rosenkilde and Bagger, 1956.

"Brief History of Giant Pandas at the Zoo, A." Accessed December 20, 2020. https://nationalzoo.si.edu/animals/brief-history-giant-pandas-zoo.

Briggs, Julia. "A Liberating Imagination: Andersen in England." *Marvels & Tales* 20, no. 2 (2006): 179–92.

Bristow, Joseph. *Empire Boys: Adventures in a Man's World*. Harper Collins Academic, 1991.

Brode, Douglas. *Multiculturalism and the Mouse: Race and Sex in Disney Entertainment*. University of Texas Press, 2005.

Brode, Douglas, and Shea T. Brode. *Debating Disney: Pedagogical Perspectives on Commercial Cinema*. Rowman & Littlefield, 2016.

Brooker, Will. *Alice's Adventures: Lewis Carroll in Popular Culture*. Continuum, 2004.

Brouillette, Sarah. *UNESCO and the Fate of the Literary*. Stanford University Press, 2019.

Brown, Eric C. "The Influence of Queen Victoria on England's Literary Fairy Tale." *Marvels & Tales* 13, no. 1 (1999): 31–51.

Brown, Marshall. "The Din of Dawn." In *On Periodization: Selected Essays from the English Institute*, edited by Virginia Jackson. English Institute Publications, 2010. https://quod.lib.umich.edu/cgi/t/text/text-idx?cc=acls;c=acls;idno=heb90047.0001.001;node=heb90047.0001.001%3A9;rgn=div1;view=text.

WORKS CITED

Brown, Noel, ed. *The Oxford Handbook of Children's Film*. Oxford University Press, 2022.

Brown, Noel, and Bruce Babington, eds. *Family Films in Global Cinema: The World beyond Disney*. I. B. Tauris, 2015.

Browning, Elizabeth Barrett. "Aurora Leigh." In *The Norton Anthology of English Literature*, edited by Catherine Robson and Carol T. Christ, 1138–50. 9th ed., vol. E: The Victorian Age, 1138–50. W. W. Norton & Company, 2012.

Browning, Elizabeth Barrett. *The Poetical Works of Elizabeth Barrett Browning*. Fields, Osgood, 1871.

Browning, Elizabeth Barrett. "The Runaway Slave at Pilgrim's Point." In *The Norton Anthology of English Literature*, edited by Catherine Robson and Carol T. Christ, 1130–38. 9th ed., vol. E: The Victorian Age. W. W. Norton & Company, 2012.

Buchanan, Lindal. "'Doing Battle with Forgotten Ghosts': Carnival, Discourse, and Degradation in Tennyson's *The Princess*." *Victorian Poetry* 39, no. 4 (December 22, 2001): 573.

Buck, Chris, and Jennifer Lee. *Frozen*. Walt Disney Studios Home Entertainment, 2014.

Burchard, Wolf. *Inspiring Walt Disney: The Animation of French Decorative Arts*. Yale University Press, 2021.

Burg, B. R. *Sodomy and the Pirate Tradition: English Sea Rovers in the Seventeenth Century Caribbean*. NYU Press, 1995.

Burney, Frances. *Evelina*. Edited by Edward A. Bloom. New ed. Oxford: Oxford University Press, 2008.

Burton, Tim. *Alice in Wonderland*. Walt Disney Pictures, Roth Films, Team Todd, 2010.

Butler, Josephine. *Personal Reminiscences of a Great Crusade*. H. Marshall, 1896.

Butler, Josephine. *Woman's Work and Woman's Culture: A Series of Essays*. Cambridge University Press, 2010.

Butler, Judith. "Performative Acts and Gender Constitution: An Essay in Phenomenology and Feminist Theory." *Theatre Journal* 40, no. 4 (1988): 519–31. https://doi.org/10.2307/3207893.

Butts, Dennis. "Anthems for (Un)Doomed Youth?: The Fairy Tales of Wilfred Owen." *Children's Literature* 40, no. 1 (May 30, 2012): 218–30. https://doi.org/10.1353/chl.2012.0000.

Buzard, James, Joseph W. Childers, and Eileen Gillooly. "Introduction." In *Victorian Prism: Refractions of the Crystal Palace*, 1–22. University of Virginia Press, 2007.

Byerly, Alison. "Media." *Victorian Literature and Culture* 46, no. 3–4 (2018): 759–63. https://doi.org/10.1017/S1060150318000761.

Byrne, Eleanor, and Martin McQuillan. *Deconstructing Disney*. Pluto Press, 1999.

Caine, Barbara. *English Feminism, 1780–1980*. Oxford University Press, 1997.

Camlot, Jason. "The First Phonogramic Poem: Conceptions of Genre and Media Format, Circa 1888." In *BRANCH: Britain, Representation and Nineteenth-Century History*, edited by Dino Felluga, 2020. http://www.branchcollective.org/?ps_articles=jason-camlot-the-first-phonogramic-poem-conceptions-of-genre-and-media-format-circa-1888.

Campbell, Mel. "Pirate Chic: Tracing the Aesthetics of Literary Piracy." In *Pirates and Mutineers of the Nineteenth Century: Swashbucklers and Swindlers*, edited by Grace Moore, 11–12. Ashgate Publishing, 2011.

Cantor, Geoffrey. "Emotional Reactions to the Great Exhibition of 1851." *Journal of Victorian Culture* 20, no. 2 (April 3, 2015): 230–45. https://doi.org/10.1080/13555502.2015.1023686.

Capodagli, Bill and Lynn Jackson. *The Disney Way: Harnessing the Management Secrets of Disney in Your Company*. 3rd ed. McGraw-Hill Education, 2016.

Carlyle, Thomas. "Past and Present." In *The Norton Anthology of English Literature*, edited by Catherine Robson and Carol T. Christ, 1067–76. 9th ed., vol. E: The Victorian Age. W. W. Norton & Company, 2012.

Carpenter, Humphrey. *Secret Gardens: A Study of the Golden Age of Children's Literature*. Faber & Faber, 2012.

Carroll, Lewis. *Alice in Wonderland*. Edited by Donald J. Gray. W. W. Norton & Company, 2016.

Carroll, Lewis. *Symbolic Logic*. Macmillan, 1896.

Cartwright, Kent, Sarah Chin, and Tarshia Stanley. "A Changing Major: The Report of the 2016–17. ADE Ad Hoc Committee on the English Major," July 18, 2018. https://www.ade.mla.org/Resources/Reports-and-Other-Resources/A-Changing-Major-The-Report-of-the-2016-17-ADE-Ad-Hoc-Committee-on-the-English-Major.

Cendrowski, Mark. *The Contractual Obligation Implementation*. Chuck Lorre Productions, Warner Bros. Television, 2013.

Chatterjee, Ronjaunee, Alicia Mireles Christoff, and Amy R. Wong. "Introduction: Undisciplining Victorian Studies." *Victorian Studies* 62, no. 3 (2020): 369–91. https://doi.org/10.2979/victorianstudies.62.3.01.

Churchill, Douglas W. "Now Mickey Mouse Enters Art's Temple." *New York Times*, June 3, 1934. https://www.nytimes.com/1934/06/03/archives/now-mickey-mouse-enters-arts-temple-he-and-minnie-are-acclaimed-as.html.

Clapp-Itnyre, Alisa. "Marginalized Musical Interludes: Tennyson's Critique of Conventionality in *The Princess*." *Victorian Poetry* 38, no. 2 (2000): 227–48.

Clark, Beverly Lyon. *Kiddie Lit: The Cultural Construction of Children's Literature in America*. Johns Hopkins University Press, 2004.

Clayton, Jay. "The Future of Victorian Literature." In *The Cambridge History of Victorian Literature*, edited by Kate Flint, 712–29. 1st ed. Cambridge University Press, 2012.

Cleto, Fabio. *Camp: Queer Aesthetics and the Performing Subject: A Reader*. University of Michigan Press, 1999.

Cloud, John. "How Gay Days Made a Home at Disney World." *Time*, June 21, 2010. http://content.time.com/time/magazine/article/0,9171,1995839,00.html.

Cohen, Monica F. *Pirating Fictions: Ownership and Creativity in Nineteenth-Century Popular Culture*. University of Virginia Press, 2018.

Collingwood, Stuart Dodgson. *The Life and Letters of Lewis Carroll (Rev. C.L. Dodgson)*. T. F. Unwin, 1898.

Collins, Wilkie. *The Woman in White*. J. M. Dent, 1919.

Collins, Winston. "The 'Princess': The Education of the Prince." *Victorian Poetry* 11, no. 4 (1973): 285–94.

Connelly, Brandon. "Inside the Research, Design and Animation of Walt Disney's Frozen with Producer Peter Del Vecho." *Bleeding Cool Comic Book, Movie, TV News*,

September 25, 2013. https://bleedingcool.com/2013/09/25/inside-the-research-design
-and-animation-of-walt-disneys-frozen-with-producer-peter-del-vecho/.

Corry, John. "Eva Le Gallienne to Return in 'Alice in Wonderland.'" *New York Times*, June
4, 1982, sec. Theater. https://www.nytimes.com/1982/06/04/theater/broadway-eva-le
-gallienne-to-return-in-alice-in-wonderland.html.

Countryman, Eli. "Disney Plus Adds Content Warning to 'Dumbo,' 'Peter Pan.'" *Chicago
Tribune*, October 16, 2020. https://www.chicagotribune.com/entertainment/movies/ct
-ent-disney-plus-content-warning-20201016-ntsxaef2nbbo7bnf32oyofucry-story.html.

Coyne, Sarah M, Jennifer Ruh Linder, Eric E. Rasmussen, David A. Nelson, and Victoria
Birkbeck. "Pretty as a Princess: Longitudinal Effects of Engagement with Disney
Princesses on Gender Stereotypes, Body Esteem, and Prosocial Behavior in Children."
Child Development 87, no. 6 (November/December 2016): 1909–25.

Coyne, Sarah M, Jennifer Ruh Linder, McCall Booth, Savannah Keenan-Kroff, Jane E.
Shawcroft, and Chongming Yang. "Princess Power: Longitudinal Associations Between
Engagement with Princess Culture in Preschool and Gender Stereotypical Behavior,
Body Esteem, and Hegemonic Masculinity in Early Adolescence." *Child Development*
87–92, no. 6 (November/December 2021): 2413–30.

Cozart, John. *After Ever After—DISNEY Parody*, 2013. https://www.youtube.com/
watch?v=diU7oKshcjA.

Crafton, Donald. "Pie and Chase: Gag, Spectacle and Narrative in Slapstick Comedy." In
Classical Hollywood Comedy, edited by Kristine Brunovska Karnick and Henry Jenkins,
106–19. Psychology Press, 1995.

Crook, Lizzie. "BIG Reveals Visuals of H C Andersen Hotel for Copenhagen's Tivoli Park."
de zeen, June 18, 2019. https://www.dezeen.com/2019/06/18/big-h-c-andersen-hotel
-tivoli-copenhagen-architecture/.

Culhane, John. "'Oliver & Company' Gives Dickens a Disney Twist." *New York Times*,
November 13, 1988, sec. Movies. http://www.nytimes.com/1988/11/13/movies/film
-oliver-company-gives-dickens-disney-twist-urban-scene-appropriate-rooftop.html.

Cullen, Bonnie. "For Whom the Shoe Fits: Cinderella in the Hands of Victorian Writers and
Illustrators." *Lion and the Unicorn* 27, no. 1 (March 11, 2003): 57–82. https://doi.org/
10.1353/uni.2003.0002.

Culturing the Child, 1690–1914: Essays in Memory of Mitzi Myers. Edited by Donelle
Ruwe. Scarecrow Press, 2005.

Davis, Amy M. *Discussing Disney*. Indiana University Press, 2019.

Davis, Amy M. "On 'Love Experts,' Evil Princes, Gullible Princesses, and *Frozen*." *The
Oxford Handbook of Children's Film*, edited by Noel Brown, 649–70. Oxford University
Press, 2022.

Davis, Jim, and Victor Emeljanow. *Reflecting the Audience: London Theatregoing, 1840–
1880*. University of Iowa Press, 2005.

Davis, Paul. "Retelling *A Christmas Carol*: Text and Culture-Text." *American Scholar* 59,
no. 1 (1990): 109–15.

Day, Sara K., and Sonya Sawyer Fritz. *The Victorian Period in Twenty-First Century
Children's and Adolescent Literature and Culture*. Routledge, 2018.

Deane, Bradley. "Imperial Boyhood: Piracy and the Play Ethic." *Victorian Studies* 53, no. 4 (2011): 689–714. https://doi.org/10.2979/victorianstudies.53.4.689.

Dettmar, Kevin. "A Hundred Years of T. S. Eliot's 'Tradition and the Individual Talent.'" *New Yorker*. Accessed November 30, 2020. https://www.newyorker.com/books/page-turner/a-hundred-years-of-t-s-eliots-tradition-and-the-individual-talent.

Di Placido, Dani. "Disney's 'Little Mermaid' Backlash Has Reached Insane Heights." *Forbes*, September 14, 2022. https://www.forbes.com/sites/danidiplacido/2022/09/14/disneys-little-mermaid-backlash-has-reached-insane-heights.

Dickens, Charles. *American Notes for General Circulation*. Edited by Patricia Ingham. Reissue ed. Penguin Classics, 2001.

Dickens, Charles. *Dombey and Son*. Modern Library, 2007.

Dickens, Charles. *Great Expectations*. W. W. Norton, 2001.

Dickens, Charles. *Hard Times*. Edited by Paul Schlicke. 1st ed. Oxford University Press, 2008.

Dickens, Charles. "New Lamps for Old Ones." In *The Norton Anthology of English Literature*, edited by Catherine Robson and Carol T. Christ, 1465–66. 9th ed., vol. E: The Victorian Age. W. W. Norton & Company, 2012.

Dickens, Charles. *Nicholas Nickleby*. Edited by Paul Schlicke. 1st ed. Oxford University Press, 2009.

Dickens, Charles. *Oliver Twist*. Edited by Fred Kaplan. W. W. Norton & Company, 1992.

"Dismaland." Accessed November 25, 2020. http://dismaland.co.uk/.

Disney, Abigail. "If My Grandfather's Company Doesn't Stand for Love, What's It For?" *Washington Post*, April 8, 2022. https://www.washingtonpost.com/opinions/2022/04/08/abigail-disney-florida-dont-say-gay-backlash-stand-love/.

Disney, Walt. "How I Cartooned Alice." *Films in Review* 2, no. 5 (1951): 7–11.

Disney, Walt. "Walt Disney's Alice in Wonderland." *American Weekly*, August 11, 1946.

Disney, Walt, Hugh Harman, and Carman Maxwell. *Alice's Wonderland*. Laugh-O-gram Films, 1923.

Disney, Walter E., and Staff of the Walt Disney Archives. *The Official Walt Disney Quote Book*. Disney Book Group, 2023.

"Disney Fairies." Accessed November 28, 2020. https://fairies.disney.com/shop.

Disney Institute, and Theodore Kinni. *Be Our Guest: Perfecting the Art of Customer Service*, revised and updated edition. Disney Electronic Content, 2011.

"Disney Launches Reimagine Tomorrow Amplifying Underrepresented voices." Accessed November 15, 2021. https://reimaginetomorrow.disney.com.

"Disney Musicals in Schools Helps Build Theatrical Education Programs in Public Schools," June 15, 2018. Walt Disney Company. https://thewaltdisneycompany.com/disney-musicals-in-schools-helps-build-theatrical-education-programs-in-public-schools/.

"Disney Plans to Film 'Alice in Wonderland': Buys Rights to Lewis Carroll Book for Animated Picture." *New York Times*, May 20, 1938, sec. Archives. https://www.nytimes.com/1938/05/20/archives/disney-plans-to-film-alice-in-wonderland-buys-rights-to-lewis.html.

Disney Princess. "Disney Princess." Accessed November 27, 2020. http://princess.disney.com/.

"Disneyfication, n." In *OED Online*. Oxford University Press. Accessed April 7, 2015. http://www.oed.com/view/Entry/249855.

Doctorow, Cory. *Down and Out in the Magic Kingdom*. Macmillan, 2003.

Donovan, Susan. "How the Post Office and Postal Products Shaped Mid-Nineteenth-Century Letter-Writing." In *BRANCH: Britain, Representation and Nineteenth-Century History*, edited by Dino Felluga. Accessed November 30, 2020. https://www.branchcollective.org/?ps_articles=susan-donovan-how-the-post-office-and-postal-products-shaped-mid-nineteenth-century-letter-writing.

Dorfman, Ariel, and Armand Mattelart. *How to Read Donald Duck: Imperialist Ideology in the Disney Comic*. 2nd ed. Intl. General, 1984.

"Dream Big, Princess." Walt Disney Company and Girl Up. Accessed November 22, 2021. https://partners.disney.com/dream-big-princess-video-series

D23. "About Walt Disney." Accessed April 30, 2023. https://d23.com/about-walt-disney/.

D23. "Disney History." Accessed November 27, 2020. https://d23.com/disney-history/.

Duncombe, Laura Sook. *Pirate Women: The Princesses Prostitutes, and Privateers Who Ruled the Seven Seas*. Chicago Review Press, 2017.

Ebert, Roger. "The Little Mermaid Movie Review." rogerebert.com, November 17, 1989. https://www.rogerebert.com/reviews/the-little-mermaid-1989.

Eidam, Laura. "Reexamining Illustration's Role in Treasure Island: Do Images Pirate Texts?" *English Literature in Transition, 1880–1920* 55, no. 1 (2012): 45–68.

Eisenhauer, Karen. "A Quantitative Analysis of Directives in Disney Princess Films." masters thesis, North Carolina State University, 2017.

Eisenstein, Sergei. "Dickens, Griffith, and Film Today." In *Film Form: Essays in Film Theory*, translated by Jay Leyda, 195–255. Harcourt Brace, 1949.

Eliot, George. *Middlemarch*. Penguin Classics, 2003.

Eliot, Simon. "The Business of Victorian Publishing." In *The Cambridge Companion to the Victorian Novel*, edited by Deirdre David, 37–60. Cambridge: Cambridge University Press, 2000. http://universitypublishingonline.org/ref/id/companions/CBO9781139000093A006.

Eliot, T. S. "Tradition and the Individual Talent." In *The Norton Anthology of English Literature*, edited by Jahan Ramazani and Jon Stallworthy, 2254–60. 9th ed., vol. F: The Twentieth Century and After, 2554–60. W. W. Norton & Company, 2012.

Elliott, Kamilla. "Adaptation as Compendium: Tim Burton's *Alice in Wonderland*." *Adaptation* 3, no. 2 (September 1, 2010): 193–201. https://doi.org/10.1093/adaptation/apq009.

Elliott, Kamilla. *Rethinking the Novel/Film Debate*. Cambridge University Press, 2003.

Elliott, Kamilla. *Theorizing Adaptation*. Oxford University Press, 2020.

Elliott, Kamilla. "Tie-Intertextuality, or, Intertextuality as Incorporation in the Tie-in Merchandise to Disney's Alice in Wonderland (2010)." *Adaptation* 7, no. 2 (August 1, 2014): 191–211. https://doi.org/10.1093/adaptation/apu007.

Emeljanow, Victor. "Staging the Pirate: The Ambiguities of Representation and the Significance of Convention." In *Pirates and Mutineers of the Nineteenth Century: Swashbucklers and Swindlers*, edited by Grace Moore, 223–42. Ashgate Publishing, 2011.

Erb, Cynthia. "Another World or the World of an Other? The Space of Romance in Recent Versions of 'Beauty and the Beast.'" *Cinema Journal* 34, no. 4 (1995): 50–70. https://doi.org/10.2307/1225577.

Faraci, Devin. "Frozen Movie Review: A New Classic Disney Animated Musical." *Birth.Movies.Death.*, November 18, 2013. https://birthmoviesdeath.com/2013/11/18/frozen-movie-review-a-new-classic-disney-animated-musical.

Farr, Liz. "Paper Dreams and Romantic Projections: The Nineteenth-Century Toy Theater, Boyhood, and Aesthetic Play." *The Nineteenth-Century Child and Consumer Culture*, edited by Dennis Denisoff, 43–62. Ashgate, 2008.

Faulk, Barry J. *Music Hall and Modernity: The Late-Victorian Discovery of Popular Culture*. Ohio University Press, 2004.

Felluga, Dino Franco. "BRANCHing out: Victorian Studies and the Digital Humanities." *Critical Quarterly* 55, no. 1 (2013): 43–56. https://doi.org/10.1111/criq.12032.

Felski, Rita. "Context Stinks!" *New Literary History* 42, no. 4 (2011): 573–91. https://doi.org/10.1353/nlh.2011.0045.

Felski, Rita. *The Limits of Critique*. University of Chicago Press, 2015.

Ferguson, Trish. *Victorian Time: Technologies, Standardizations, Catastrophes*. Springer, 2013.

Finnegan, Amanda. "After Criticism over Silence, Disney CEO Opposes Florida Bill Restricting LGBTQ Topics in Schools." *Washington Post*, March 9, 2022. https://www.washingtonpost.com/travel/2022/03/09/disney-ceo-dont-say-gay-florida/

Fleming, Patrick C. "After Dickens World: Performing Victorians at the Chatham Docks." *Neo-Victorian Studies* 9, no. 1 (2016): 12–31.

Fleming, Patrick C. *The Legacy of the Moral Tale: Children's Literature and the English Novel, 1744–1859*. University of Tennessee Press, 2016.

Fleming, Patrick C. *Nineteenth-Century British Children's Literature: A Companion*. McFarland, 2023.

Flint, Kate. "The Victorian Novel and Its Readers." In *The Cambridge Companion to the Victorian Novel*, edited by Deirdre David, 17–36. Cambridge Companions to Literature. Cambridge: Cambridge University Press, 2000. https://doi.org/10.1017/CCOL0521641500.002.

Florey, Robert, and Wilfred Jackson. "The Disneyland Story." *The Magical World of Disney*. Walt Disney Productions, October 27, 1954.

Ford, Richard. "Review of Oliver Twist. *Quarterly Review*, 1839." In *Oliver Twist*, edited by Fred Kaplan. 1st ed. W. W. Norton & Company, 1992.

Forster, John. *The Life of Charles Dickens: 1812–1842*. Chapman and Hall, 1872.

Francaviglia, Richard. "History after Disney: The Significance of 'Imagineered' Historical Places." *Public Historian* 17, no. 4 (1995): 69–74. https://doi.org/10.2307/3378386.

Fritz, Sonya Sawyer. "In Space No One Can Hear You Cry: Late Victorian Adventure and Contemporary Boyhood in Disney's *Treasure Planet*." In *The Victorian Period in Twenty-First Century Children's and Adolescent Literature and Culture*, edited by Sara K. Day and Sonya Sawyer Fritz. Routledge, 2018.

"Frozen: The Disney Princess Comes in from the Cold." *The Telegraph*. Accessed November 25, 2020. https://www.telegraph.co.uk/culture/film/10484803/Frozen-the-Disney-princess-comes-in-from-the-cold.html.

Fyfe, Paul. "On the Opening of the Liverpool and Manchester Railway, 1830." In *BRANCH: Britain, Representation and Nineteenth-Century History*, edited by Dino Felluga, 2012.

WORKS CITED

http://www.branchcollective.org/?ps_articles=paul-fyfe-on-the-opening-of-the
-liverpool-and-manchester-railway-1830.

Gabler, Neal. *Walt Disney: The Triumph of the American Imagination*. New York: Vintage, 2007.

Geronimi, Clyde, Wilfred Jackson, and Hamilton Luske. "Alice in Wonderland." *The Magical World of Disney*. Walt Disney Productions, November 3, 1954.

Geronimi, Clyde, Wilfred Jackson, Hamilton Luske, and Jack Kinney. *Alice in Wonderland*. Walt Disney Animation Studios, Walt Disney Productions, 1951.

Gilbert, Nora. *Better Left Unsaid: Victorian Novels, Hays Code Films, and the Benefits of Censorship*. Stanford University Press, 2013.

Gilbert, Sandra M. *The Madwoman in the Attic: The Woman Writer and the Nineteenth-Century Literary Imagination*. Yale University Press, 2020.

Gilbert, Sandra M., and Susan Gubar. *No Man's Land: The War of the Words*. Yale University Press, 1988.

Giroux, Henry A. *The Mouse That Roared: Disney and the End of Innocence*. Rowman & Littlefield, 2001.

Golden, Catherine. *Posting It: The Victorian Revolution in Letter Writing*. University Press of Florida, 2009.

Goldsby, Michael G., and Rob Mathews. *Entrepreneurship the Disney Way*. Routledge, 2019.

Gopnik, Adam. "Who Can Be Finished with Alice?" *New Yorker*, October 11, 2015. https://www.newyorker.com/books/page-turner/who-can-be-finished-with-alice.

Gould, Marty, and Rebecca Mitchell. "It Was the Worst of Times: A Visit to Dickens World." *Victorian Literature and Culture* 38, no. 1 (2010): 287–93.

Graff, Gerald. "How Periods Erase History." In *On Periodization: Selected Essays from the English Institute*, edited by Virginia Jackson. English Institute Publications, 2010. https://quod.lib.umich.edu/cgi/t/text/text-idx?cc=acls;c=acls;idno=heb90047.0001.001;node=heb90047.0001.001%3A9;rgn=div1;view=text.

Green, Roger Lancelyn. *Fifty Years of Peter Pan*. P. Davies, 1954.

Greenberg, Andy. "His Writing Radicalized Hackers. Now He Wants to Redeem Them." *Wired*. Accessed November 25, 2020. https://www.wired.com/story/his-writing -radicalized-young-hackers-now-he-wants-to-redeem-them/.

Greenblatt, Stephen A. *Will in the World: How Shakespeare Became Shakespeare*. W. W. Norton, 2005.

Greene, Tim. *Boy Called Twist*. Monkey Films, Twisted Pictures, 2004.

Griffin, Sean P. *Tinker Belles and Evil Queens: The Walt Disney Company from the Inside Out*. NYU Press, 2000.

Grossman, Jonathan H. *Charles Dickens's Networks: Public Transport and the Novel*. Oxford University Press, 2012.

Gryctko, Mary. "'The Romance of the Nursery': Lost Boys and Deadly Femininity in *The Turn of the Screw* and *Peter Pan*." *Children's Literature Association Quarterly* 41, no. 2 (June 3, 2016): 142–57. https://doi.org/10.1353/chq.2016.0021.

Gubar, Marah. *Artful Dodgers: Reconceiving the Golden Age of Children's Literature*. Oxford University Press, 2009.

Gubar, Marah. "Peter Pan as Children's Theatre: The Issue of Audience." In *The Oxford Handbook of Children's Literature*, edited by Lynne Vallone and Julia Mickelberg, 2011. https://doi.org/10.1093/oxfordhb/9780195379785.013.0024.

Guillory, John. *Cultural Capital: The Problem of Literary Canon Formation*. University of Chicago Press, 2013.

Gunning, Tom. "The Cinema of Attraction: Early Film, Its Spectator, and the Avant-Garde." *Wide Angle* 8, no. 3 (1986): 64–70.

Gunning, Tom. "Crazy Machines in the Garden of Forking Paths: Mischief Gags and the Origins of American Film Comedy." In *Classical Hollywood Comedy*, edited by Kristine Brunovska Karnick and Henry Jenkins, 87–105. Psychology Press, 1995.

Guo, Jeff. "Researchers Have Found a Major Problem with 'The Little Mermaid' and Other Disney Movies." *Washington Post*, January 25, 2016. https://www.washingtonpost.com/news/wonk/wp/2016/01/25/researchers-have-discovered-a-major-problem-with-the-little-mermaid-and-other-disney-movies/.

Gupta, Tanika, and Charles Dickens. *Great Expectations*. Oberon Books, 2012.

Hack, Daniel. *Reaping Something New: African American Transformations of Victorian Literature*. Princeton University Press, 2016.

Hadley, Elaine. *Melodramatic Tactics: Theatricalized Dissent in the English Marketplace, 1800–1885*. Stanford: Stanford University Press, 1995.

Hall, Donald E. "The Anti-Feminist Ideology of Tennyson's *The Princess*." *Modern Language Studies* 21, no. 4 (1991): 49–62. https://doi.org/10.2307/3194982.

Han, Carrie Sickmann. "Co-Narrating Like a Child: Adding the 'Blots' and 'Interesting Bits' to Peter Pan." *Children's Literature Association Quarterly* 43, no. 2 (summer 2018): 145–63. https://doi.org/10.1353/chq.2018.0016.

Hand, David. *Thru the Mirror*. Walt Disney Productions, 1936.

Hans Christian Andersen Center. "Hans Christian Andersen—FAQ." Accessed November 23, 2020. https://andersen.sdu.dk/rundtom/faq/index_e.html?emne=homo.

Hanson, Bruce K. *Peter Pan on Stage and Screen, 1904–2010*. 2nd ed. McFarland, 2011.

Hastings, A. Waller. "Moral Simplification in Disney's *The Little Mermaid*." *Lion and the Unicorn* 17, no. 1 (1993): 83–92. https://doi.org/10.1353/uni.0.0281.

Hawksley, Lucinda. *Queen Victoria's Mysterious Daughter: A Biography of Princess Louise*. Macmillan, 2015.

Hayot, Eric. "Against Periodization; or, On Institutional Time." *New Literary History* 42, no. 4 (2011): 739–56.

Heide, Robert. *Mickey Mouse: The Evolution, the Legend, the Phenomenon!* Disney Editions, 2003

Hensley, Nathan. "What Is a Network? (And Who Is Andrew Lang?)." *Romanticism and Victorianism on the Net*, no. 64 (2013). https://doi.org/10.7202/1025668ar.

Hermansson, Cassie, and Janet Zepernick, eds. *The Palgrave Handbook of Children's Film and Television*. Palgrave Macmillan, 2019.

Higdon, David Leon, and Phill Lehrman. "Huxley's 'Deep Jam' and the Adaptation of *Alice in Wonderland*." *Review of English Studies* 43, no. 169 (1992): 57–74.

Hill, Jim. "Countdown to Disney 'Frozen': How One Simple Suggestion Broke the Ice on the 'Snow Queen's' Decades-Long Story Problems." Accessed November 25, 2020. http://

jimhillmedia.com/editor_in_chief1/b/jim_hill/archive/2013/10/18/countdown-to-disney
-quot-frozen-quot-how-one-simple-suggestion-broke-the-ice-on-the-quot-snow-queen
-quot-s-decades-long-story-problems.aspx.

Hillard, Molly Clark. *Spellbound: The Fairy Tale and the Victorians*. Ohio State University Press, 2014.

Hone, William. "The Political House That Jack Built." *Romantic Circles*, March 1, 1998. https://romantic-circles.org/editions/hone/jacktext.htm.

Houghton, Walter E. *The Victorian Frame of Mind, 1830–1870*. Yale University Press, 1985.

Huffman, Joan B. *Lady Frances: Frances Balfour, Aristocrat Suffragist*. Troubador Publishing Ltd., 2018.

Hughes, John. "'Hang There like Fruit, My Soul': Tennyson's Feminine Imaginings." *Victorian Poetry* 45, no. 2 (July 23, 2007): 95–115. https://doi.org/10.1353/vp.2007.0024.

Hughes, Linda K. "Transatlanticism." *Victorian Literature and Culture* 46, no. 3–4 (2018): 917–24. https://doi.org/10.1017/S1060150318001183.

Hurd, Earl. "Peter Pan Notes," October 3, 1939. Walt Disney Archives.

Hurley, Dorothy L. "Seeing White: Children of Color and the Disney Fairy Tale Princess." *Journal of Negro Education* 74, no. 3 (2005): 221–32.

Huston, John. *The Man Who Would Be King*. Columbia Pictures, Devon/Persky-Bright, Allied Artists Pictures, 1975.

Hutcheon, Linda. *A Theory of Adaptation*. Routledge, 2012.

Huxley, Aldous. "Letter to Anita Loos," October 13, 1945. *The Significant Letter Collection of Victor Niederhoffer*. https://issuu.com/rrauction/docs/rr_auction_historical_letter _june_2.

Huxley, Aldous. "Synopsis for *Alice in Wonderland*." Edited by David Leon Higdon and Phill Lehrman. *Review of English Studies* 43, no. 169 (1992): 67–74.

Huxley, Thomas Henry. "Science and Culture." In *The Norton Anthology of English Literature*, edited by Catherine Robson and Carol T. Christ, 1451–57. 9th ed., vol. E: The Victorian Age. W. W. Norton & Company, 2012.

Iger, Robert. *The Ride of a Lifetime: Lessons Learned from 15 Years as CEO of the Walt Disney Company*. Random House, 2019.

"I Want Your Job: McDonald's Corporate Archivist." *College Today*, College of Charleston Office of University Communications. Accessed November 17, 2021. https://today.cofc .edu/2014/10/01/want-job-mcdonalds-corporate-archivist/

Jackson, Kathy Merlock. *Walt Disney, a Bio-Bibliography*. Greenwood Press, 1993.

Jackson, Kathy Merlock. "Walt Disney as Reader and Storyteller: The Books in His Library and What They Mean." In *Walt Disney, from Reader to Storyteller: Essays on the Literary Inspirations*, edited by Mark I. West and Kathy Merlock Jackson, 9–19. McFarland, 2014.

Jackson, Kathy Merlock, and Mark I. West. *Disneyland and Culture: Essays on the Parks and Their Influence*. McFarland, 2010.

Jackson, Kathy Merlock, and Mark I. West. *Walt Disney, from Reader to Storyteller: Essays on the Literary Inspirations*. McFarland, 2014.

Jackson, Lee. *Palaces of Pleasure: From Music Halls to the Seaside to Football, How the Victorians Invented Mass Entertainment*. Yale University Press, 2019.

Jackson, Mary V. *Engines of Instruction, Mischief, and Magic: Children's Literature in England from Its Beginnings to 1839*. University of Nebraska Press, 1989.

Jackson, Wilfred. *Mickey's Mellerdrammer*. Walt Disney Pictures, 1933. http://www.imdb.com/title/tt0024331/.

James, Henry. "The Limitations of Dickens." In *The Dickens Critics*, edited by George Harry Ford and Lauriat Lane, 48–54. Cornell University Press, 1961.

James, Henry. *William Wetmore Story and His Friends: From Letters, Diaries, and Recollections*. Houghton, Mifflin & Company, 1903.

James, Louis. *The Victorian Novel*. Wiley, 2008.

Jaques, Zoe, and Eugene Giddens. *Lewis Carroll's "Alice's Adventures in Wonderland" and "Through the Looking-Glass": A Publishing History*. New ed. Ashgate Pub Co, 2013.

"Jean Hersholt Humanitarian Award." Academy of Motion Picture Arts and Sciences, July 17, 2014. https://www.oscars.org/governors/hersholt.

Jeffords, Susan. "The Curse of Masculinity: Disney's *Beauty and the Beast*." In *From Mouse to Mermaid: The Politics of Film, Gender, and Culture*, 175–92. Indiana University Press, 1995.

Jenkins, Henry, and Kristine Brunovska Karnick. *Classical Hollywood Comedy*. Psychology Press, 1995.

Jobson, Christopher. "Welcome to Dismaland: A First Look at Banksy's New Art Exhibition Housed Inside a Dystopian Theme Park." *Colossal* (blog), August 20, 2015. https://www.thisiscolossal.com/2015/08/dismaland/.

John, Juliet. *Dickens and Mass Culture*. Oxford; New York: Oxford University Press, 2011.

Johnson, Ted. "Disney, Marvel to Boycott Georgia if Religious Liberty Bill Is Passed." Reuters, March 23, 2016. https://de.reuters.com/article/variety-idUSL3N16V4UN.

Johnston, Eileen Tess. "'This Were a Medley': Tennyson's *The Princess*." *ELH* 51, no. 3 (1984): 549–74. https://doi.org/10.2307/2872937.

Johnston, Phil, and Rich Moore. *Ralph Breaks the Internet*. Walt Disney Animation Studios, Walt Disney Pictures, 2018.

Jones, Katie. "The World's 25 Most Successful Media Franchises, and How They Stay Relevant." *markets.businessinsider.com*, November 22, 2019. https://www.visualcapitalist.com/successful-media-franchises/.

Jordan, Lawrence. *Eddie Izzard: Dress to Kill*. Ella Communications Ltd., 1999.

Joseph, Gerhard. "Tennyson's Three Women: The Thought within the Image." *Victorian Poetry* 19, no. 1 (1981): 1–18.

Kapurch, Katie. "Something Else Besides a Daughter?: Maternal Melodrama Meets Postfeminist Girlhood in Tangled and Brave." *Lion and the Unicorn* 40, no. 1 (2016): 39–61.

Kaiser, Matthew. *The World in Play: Portraits of a Victorian Concept*. Stanford University Press, 2011.

Kelly, Chris. "Banksy Dismaland Show Revealed at Weston's Tropicana." BBC News, August 20, 2015, sec. Bristol. https://www.bbc.com/news/uk-england-bristol-33999495.

Kern, Kevin M., Tim O'Day, and Steven Vagnini. *A Portrait of Walt Disney World: 50 Years of The Most Magical Place on Earth*. Disney Editions, 2021.

Kincaid, James Russell. *Child-Loving: The Erotic Child and Victorian Culture*. Routledge, 1992.

King, Margaret J., and J. G. O'Boyle. "The Theme Park: The Art of Time and Space." In *Disneyland and Culture: Essays on the Parks and Their Influence*, edited by Kathy Merlock Jackson and Mark I. West, 5–18. McFarland, 2010.

Kipling, Rudyard. "The Man Who Would Be King." In *The Norton Anthology of English Literature*, edited by Catherine Robson and Carol T. Christ, 1853–77. 9th ed., vol. E: The Victorian Age. W. W. Norton & Company, 2012.

Knoepflmacher, U. C. "*Little Lord Fauntleroy*: The Afterlife of a Best-Seller." *Princeton University Library Chronicle*, vol. 73, no. 2 (2012): 185–213.

Knoepflmacher, U. C. *Ventures Into Childland: Victorians, Fairy Tales, and Femininity*. University of Chicago Press, 2000.

Konnikova, Maria. "How 'Frozen' Took Over the World." *New Yorker*, June 25, 2014. https://www.newyorker.com/science/maria-konnikova/how-frozen-took-over-the-world

Kooistra, Lorraine Janzen. "The Moxon Tennyson as Textual Event: 1857, Wood Engraving, and Visual Culture." In *BRANCH: Britain, Representation and Nineteenth-Century History*, edited by Dino Felluga. Accessed November 27, 2020. http://www.branchcollective.org/?ps_articles=lorraine-janzen-kooistra-the-moxon-tennyson-as-textual-event-1857-wood-engraving-and-visual-culture.

Kooistra, Lorraine Janzen. "Poetry in the Victorian Marketplace: The Illustrated 'Princess' as a Christmas Gift Book." *Victorian Poetry* 45, no. 1 (2007): 49–76.

Korkis, Jim. "The Origin of the Disneyland Wienie." Accessed November 23, 2020. https://www.mouseplanet.com/11371/The_Origin_of_the_Disneyland_Wienie.

Korkis, Jim. *The Vault of Walt*. United States: Ayefour Publishing, 2010.

Kosnik, Abigail de. "2021 Will Launch the Platinum Age of Piracy." *Wired*, December 12, 2020. https://www.wired.com/story/2021-platinum-age-piracy-streaming.

Krämer, Peter. "The Walt Disney Company, Family Entertainment, and Global Movie Hits." In *The Oxford Handbook of Children's Film*, edited by Noel Brown, 569–90. Oxford University Press, 2022.

Kramnick, Jonathan. "What We Hire in Now: English by the Grim Numbers." *Chronicle of Higher Education*, December 10, 2018, sec. Advice. https://www.chronicle.com/article/what-we-hire-in-now-english-by-the-grim-numbers/.

Krutnik, Frank. "A Spanner in the Works? Genre, Narrative, and the Hollywood Comedian." In *Classical Hollywood Comedy*, edited by Kristine Brunovska Karnick and Henry Jenkins, 17–38. Psychology Press, 1995.

Kuhn, William M. "Queen Victoria's Jubilees and the Invention of Tradition." *Victorian Poetry* 25, no. 3–4 (1987): 107–14.

Kunze, Peter C. "Don Bluth and the Disney Renaissance." In *The Oxford Handbook of Children's Film*, edited by Noel Brown, 630–48. Oxford University Press, 2022.

Kunze, Peter C. *Staging a Comeback: Broadway, Hollywood, and the Disney Renaissance*. Rutgers University Press, 2023.

Kutzer, M. Daphne. *Empire's Children: Empire and Imperialism in Classic British Children's Literature*. Routledge, 2000.

Laird, Karen. *The Art of Adapting Victorian Literature, 1848–1920: Dramatizing "Jane Eyre", "David Copperfield", and "The Woman in White."* Ashgate Publishing, 2015.

Latour, Bruno. "Why Has Critique Run out of Steam? From Matters of Fact to Matters of Concern." *Critical Inquiry* 30, no. 2 (January 1, 2004): 225–48. https://doi.org/10.1086/421123.

Leavis, Frank Raymond. *The Great Tradition: George Eliot, Henry James, Joseph Conrad.* New York University Press, 1963.

Ledbetter, Kathryn. *Tennyson and Victorian Periodicals: Commodities in Context.* Ashgate Publishing, 2007.

Lee, Julia Sun-Joo. "The Return of the 'Unnative': The Transnational Politics of Elizabeth Gaskell's *North and South.*" *Nineteenth-Century Literature* 61, no. 4 (2007): 449–78. https://doi.org/10.1525/ncl.2007.61.4.449.

Lee, Sir Sidney. *Queen Victoria: A Biography.* J. Murray, 1904.

"Legacies of British Slave-Ownership." University College of London Department of History. Accessed November 28, 2020. https://www.ucl.ac.uk/lbs/.

Leitch, Thomas. *Film Adaptation and Its Discontents: From Gone with the Wind to The Passion of the Christ.* Johns Hopkins University Press, 2007.

Leitch, Thomas. "Twelve Fallacies in Contemporary Adaptation Theory." *Criticism* 45, no. 2 (2003): 149–71.

Leitch, Thomas, ed. *The Oxford Handbook of Adaptation Studies.* Oxford University Press, 2017.

Lepore, Jill. "The Lion and the Mouse: The Battle That Reshaped Children's Literature." *New Yorker,* July 14, 2008. https://www.newyorker.com/magazine/2008/07/21/the-lion-and-the-mouse.

Lethem, Jonathan. "The Ecstasy of Influence." *Harper's,* February 2007. https://harpers.org/archive/2007/02/the-ecstasy-of-influence/.

Levine, Caroline. *Forms: Whole, Rhythm, Hierarchy, Network.* Princeton University Press, 2015.

Levine, Caroline. "From Nation to Network." *Victorian Studies* 55, no. 4 (2013): 647–66. https://doi.org/10.2979/victorianstudies.55.4.647.

Levy, Rom. "Upcoming: Banksy 'Dismaland' Pop-Up Exhibition @ Weston-Super-Mare." *StreetArtNews,* August 19, 2015. https://streetartnews.net/2015/08/upcoming-banksy-dismaland-pop-up.html.

LIFE Walt Disney: From Mickey to the Magic Kingdom. Time Inc. Books, 2016.

Linde, Andrew. "My Ice Gown Is in the Closet: Disney's Frozen Will Surprise You." Accessed November 25, 2020. http://www.agentsofguard.com/frozen-will-surprise-you-by-andrew-linde/.

Linetsky, Barry. *The Business of Walt Disney and the Nine Principles of His Success.* Bob McLain Media, 2017.

Longford, Elizabeth. *Queen Victoria.* History Press, 2011.

Loos, Anita. "Aldous Huxley in California." *Harper's,* May 1, 1964. https://harpers.org/archive/1964/05/aldous-huxley-in-california/.

Lovett, Charles C. *Alice on Stage: A History of the Early Theatrical Productions of Alice in Wonderland.* ABC-CLIO, 1989.

WORKS CITED

Lowe, Lisa. *The Intimacies of Four Continents.* Duke University Press, 2015.

Lutz, E. *Animated Cartoons.* Applewood Books, 2014.

Lydall, Ross. "Forget Disneyland, Try Dickens World." *Evening Standard,* April 6, 2005.

Lynch, Deidre Shauna, and Jack Stillinger, eds. *The Norton Anthology of English Literature.* 9th ed., vol. D: The Romantic Period. W. W. Norton & Company, 2012.

Macaulay, Thomas Babington. "A Minute on Indian Education." In *The Norton Anthology of English Literature,* edited by Catherine Robson and Carol T. Christ, 1640–42. 9th ed., vol. E: The Victorian Age. W. W. Norton & Company, 2012.

Mackrell. "Hans Christian Andersen's Failed Career as a Dancer." *The Guardian,* November 1, 2004, sec. Stage. http://www.theguardian.com/stage/2004/nov/01/dance.

"Mad Tea Party | Rides & Attractions | Disneyland Park." Accessed December 3, 2020. https://disneyland.disney.go.com/attractions/disneyland/mad-tea-party/.

Malcolm, Derek. "Busby Berkeley, Patron Saint of Movie Camp." *The Guardian,* March 16, 1976, sec. Film. https://www.theguardian.com/film/2016/mar/16/busby-berkeley-obituary-hollywood-archive-1976.

"Manifesto of the V21 Collective," March 2015. http://v21collective.org/manifesto-of-the-v21-collective-ten-theses/.

Marcus, Sharon. "Victorian Theatrics: Response." *Victorian Studies* 54, no. 3 (April 1, 2012): 438–50.

Marcus, Steven. *The Other Victorians: A Study of Sexuality and Pornography in Mid-Nineteenth-century England.* Routledge, 2009.

Marks, Laura Helen. *Alice in Pornoland: Hardcore Encounters with the Victorian Gothic.* University of Illinois Press, 2018.

Marsh, Joss. "Dickens and Film." In *The Cambridge Companion to Charles Dickens,* edited by John O. Jordan, 204–22. Cambridge University Press, 2001.

"Mary Pickford Back from Europe; Proposes to Appear in 'Alice in Wonderland,' Animated by Walt Disney. Would Offer 'Peter Pan'; Star Says Public Is Tired of Sex and Gangster Films and Is Ready for Change." *New York Times,* March 31, 1933, sec. Archives. https://www.nytimes.com/1933/03/31/archives/mary-pickford-back-from-europe-proposes-to-appear-in-alice-in.html.

Matos, Angel Daniel. "Conceal, Don't Feel: A Queer Reading of Disney's Frozen," January 19, 2014. https://angelmatos.net/2014/01/19/disneys-frozen-queer/.

Mattacks, Kate. "Acts of Piracy: Black Ey'd Susan, Theatrical Publishing and the Victorian Stage." In *Pirates and Mutineers of the Nineteenth Century: Swashbucklers and Swindlers,* edited by Grace Moore, 117–32. Ashgate Publishing, 2011.

Mauro, Jason Isaac. "Disney's Splash Mountain: Death Anxiety, the Tar Baby, and Rituals of Violence." *Children's Literature Association Quarterly* 22, no. 3 (1997): 113–17. https://doi.org/10.1353/chq.0.1208.

McGann, Jerome J. "The Crisis in the Humanities." *Journal of Philosophy: A Cross Disciplinary Inquiry* 5, no. 12 (March 22, 2010): 53.

McGann, Jerome J. *The Romantic Ideology: A Critical Investigation.* University of Chicago Press, 1985.

McGurl, Mark. *The Program Era: Postwar Fiction and the Rise of Creative Writing.* Harvard University Press, 2009.

McKernan, Luke. "The Familiarity of the New: The Emergence of a Motion Picture Industry in Late Nineteenth-Century London." *Nineteenth Century Theatre and Film* 33, no. 2 (November 1, 2006): 30–44. https://doi.org/10.7227/NCTF.33.2.4.

McNary, Dave. "Disney World Updates Controversial 'Pirates of the Caribbean' Ride Bride Auction Scene." *Variety*, March 21, 2018. https://variety.com/2018/film/news/disney-world-pirates-of-the-caribbean-bride-auction-scene-1202733112/.

Mee, Jon. "Recent Studies in the Nineteenth Century." *SEL Studies in English Literature, 1500–1900* 53, no. 4 (November 13, 2013): 913–40. https://doi.org/10.1353/sel.2013.0040.

Meikle, Kyle. *Adaptations in the Franchise Era: 2001–16*. Bloomsbury Publishing USA, 2019.

Mcisel, Martin. *Realizations: Narrative, Pictorial, and Theatrical Arts in Nineteenth-Century England*. Princeton University Press, 1984.

Mendelson, Scott. "Review: 'Frozen' Is Disney's Triumphant Reaffirmation of Its Cultural Legacy." *Forbes*. Accessed November 25, 2020. https://www.forbes.com/sites/scottmendelson/2013/11/19/review-frozen-is-disneys-best-toon-in-years/.

Merritt, Russell, and J. B. Kaufman. *Walt in Wonderland: The Silent Films of Walt Disney*. Johns Hopkins University Press, 2000.

"Mickey Mouse's New Affiliation." *New York Times*, June 26, 1932, sec. Archives. https://www.nytimes.com/1932/06/26/archives/mickey-mouses-new-affiliation.html.

Miller, Carl F. "'Worth Melting For': The Legacy of Difference and Desire in Hans Christian Andersen's 'The Snowman.'" *International Research in Children's Literature* 10, no. 2 (November 23, 2017): 162–77. https://doi.org/10.3366/ircl.2017.0235.

Miller, Diane Disney. "A Conversation with Diane Disney Miller." *Oh My Disney*, February 14, 2012. https://ohmy.disney.com/insider/2012/02/13/a-conversation-with-diane-disney-miller/.

Miller, Diane Disney, and Pete Martin. "My Dad, Walt Disney." *Saturday Evening Post*, 1956–57.

Miller, Susan, and Greg Rode. "The Movie You See, The Movie You Don't: How Disney Do's That Old Time Derision." In *From Mouse to Mermaid: The Politics of Film, Gender, and Culture*, 86–104. Indiana University Press, 1995.

Moody, Jane. *Illegitimate Theatre in London, 1770–1840*. Cambridge University Press, 2007.

Moore, Grace. "Pirates for Boys: Masculinity and Degeneracy in R. M. Ballantyne's Adventure Novels." In *Pirates and Mutineers of the Nineteenth Century: Swashbucklers and Swindlers*, edited by Grace Moore, 165–80. Ashgate Publishing, 2011.

Moses, Belle. *Lewis Carroll in Wonderland and at Home: The Story of His Life*. D. Appleton, 1910.

"The Most Popular High School Plays and Musicals." *Morning Edition*, July 30, 2020. https://www.npr.org/sections/ed/2019/07/31/427138970/the-most-popular-high-school-plays-and-musicals.

Muir, Robin. *The Disney Princess Phenomenon: A Feminist Analysis*. Bristol University Press, 2023.

Murray, Simone. *The Adaptation Industry: The Cultural Economy of Contemporary Literary Adaptation*. Routledge, 2012.

Murray, Simone. "Phantom Adaptations: Eucalyptus, the Adaptation Industry and the Film That Never Was." *Adaptation* 1, no. 1 (March 1, 2008): 5–23. https://doi.org/10.1093/adaptation/apm002.

Nadel, Ira B. "Portraits of the Queen." *Victorian Poetry* 25, no. 3–4 (1987): 169–91.

Nagra, Daljit. *Look We Have Coming to Dover!* Faber & Faber, 2010.

Napolitano, Marc. "Of Mice and Men: Eve Titus's Basil of Baker Street and Disney's The Great Mouse Detective as Holmesian Adaptations." *Victorian Studies* (2016): 35.

Napolitano, Marc. *Oliver!: A Dickensian Musical.* New York: Oxford University Press, 2014.

Nelson, Claudia. *Precocious Children and Childish Adults: Age Inversion in Victorian Literature.* JHU Press, 2012.

Nelson, Claudia. "Writing for Children." In *The Cambridge History of Victorian Literature*, edited by Kate Flint, 311–28. 1st ed. Cambridge University Press, 2012.

Nesbit, E. *The Railway Children.* Project Gutenberg, 1906. https://www.gutenberg.org/files/1874/1874-h/1874-h.htm.

Nikolas, Akash. "The Pro-Gay Message Hidden in Every Disney Film." *The Atlantic*, April 23, 2014. https://www.theatlantic.com/entertainment/archive/2014/04/its-not-just-frozen -disney-has-always-been-subtly-pro-gay/361060/.

Novak, Daniel A. *Realism, Photography and Nineteenth-Century Fiction.* Cambridge University Press, 2008.

O'Flynn, Siobhan. "Data Science, Disney, and the Future of Children's Entertainment." In *The Palgrave Handbook of Children's Film and Television*, edited by Cassie Hermansson and Janet Zepernick, 507–31. Palgrave Macmillan, 2019.

"'Oliver.' Prod. #0421 Rough Working Copy," August 8, 1986. Walt Disney Archives.

"'Oliver Twist' Musical Feature. Character Descriptions," October 24, 1985. Walt Disney Archives.

"'Oliver Twist' Musical Feature. Story Outline, Rough," October 21, 1985. Walt Disney Archives.

"'Oliver Twist' Musical. One Additional Story Concept for You to Consider.," October 1, 1985. Walt Disney Archives.

"'Oliver Twist' Musical (Untitled Memo)," September 24, 1985. Walt Disney Archives.

"'Oliver Twist' Musical (Untitled Memo)," September 26, 1985. Walt Disney Archives.

O'Malley, Andrew. *The Making of the Modern Child: Children's Literature in the Late Eighteenth Century.* Taylor & Francis, 2003.

O'Neill, Brendan. "Bemusement Park: Where Dickens Meets Disney." *Christian Science Monitor*, May 25, 2007. http://www.csmonitor.com/2007/0525/p20s01-woeu.html.

Orenstein, Peggy. *Cinderella Ate My Daughter: Dispatches from the Front Lines of the New Girlie-Girl Culture.* HarperCollins, 2011.

Orwell, George. "Charles Dickens." In *The Collected Essays, Journalism, and Letters of George Orwell.* Harcourt, Brace & World, 1968.

Otto, Peter. "Artificial Environments, Virtual Realities, and the Cultivation of Propensity in the London Colosseum." In *Virtual Victorians: Networks, Connections, Technologies*, edited by Veronica Alfano and Andrew Stauffer, 167–87. New York: Palgrave Macmillan US, 2015. https://doi.org/10.1057/9781137393296_9.

"Our History." *Madame Tussaud's.* Accessed December 16, 2020. https://www .madametussauds.com/london/information/our-history/.

Packard, Jerrold M. *Victoria's Daughters.* St. Martin's Publishing Group, 1999.

Pallant, Chris. *Demystifying Disney: A History of Disney Feature Animation.* Bloomsbury Publishing USA, 2011.

Parody, Clare. "Franchising/Adaptation." *Adaptation* 4, no. 2 (September 1, 2011): 210–18. https://doi.org/10.1093/adaptation/apr008.

Patterson, Ada. *Maude Adams: A Biography.* Creative Media Partners, 2018.

Pearce, Charles E. *Madame Vestris and Her Times.* Paul, 1900. http://archive.org/details/madamevestrisher00pear.

Perkins, Al. "Research Report for Alice in Wonderland (May)," May 27, 1938. Walt Disney Archives.

Perkins, Al. "Research Report for Alice in Wonderland (Sept)," September 6, 1938. Walt Disney Archives.

"Peter Pan Meeting Notes," October 21, 1939. Walt Disney Archives.

"Peter Pan Meeting Notes," December 27, 1943. Walt Disney Archives.

Petersen, Kierran. "Disney's Frozen and the 'Gay Agenda.'" BBC News, March 27, 2014, sec. Echo Chambers. https://www.bbc.com/news/blogs-echochambers-26759342.

Peterson, Linda H. "Tennyson and the Ladies." *Victorian Poetry* 47, no. 1 (May 2, 2009): 25–43. https://doi.org/10.1353/vp.0.0040.

Petzold, Jochen. "Victorian Gendered Photography in the *Boy's Own Paper* and the *Girl's Own Paper.*" *Victorian Periodicals Review* 52, no. 1 (Spring 2019): 57–79.

Pickering, Samuel F. *John Locke and Children's Books in Eighteenth-Century England.* University of Tennessee Press, 1981.

Pinch, Adela. "Recent Studies in the Nineteenth Century." *SEL Studies in English Literature, 1500–1900* 54, no. 4 (December 1, 2014): 943–1002. https://doi.org/10.1353/sel.2014.0039.

"The Pirates League. | Rides & Attractions | Disneyland Park." *Disneyland Resort.* Accessed December 3, 2021. https://disneyparks.disney.go.com/au/disneyworld/events-tours/pirates-league/.

"Pirates of the Caribbean | Rides & Attractions | Disneyland Park." *Disneyland Resort.* Accessed December 3, 2021. https://disneyland.disney.go.com/attractions/disneyland/pirates-of-the-caribbean/.

Plotz, Judith. *Romanticism and the Vocation of Childhood.* New York: Palgrave, 2001.

Plunkett, John. *Queen Victoria: First Media Monarch.* Oxford University Press, 2003.

Pollack-Pelzner, Daniel. "Shakespeare Burlesque and the Performing Self." *Victorian Studies* 54, no. 3 (2012): 401–9. https://doi.org/10.2979/victorianstudies.54.3.401.

Pond, Doug, and Cory Doctorow. "Interview with Cory Doctorow." *Massachusetts Review* 45, no. 4 (2004): 742–54.

Porsdam, Helle. *Copyright and Other Fairy Tales: Hans Christian Andersen and the Commodification of Creativity.* Edward Elgar, 2006.

Powell, Manushag N. *British Pirates in Print and Performance.* Springer, 2015.

"Prefatory Note." *Victorian Studies* 1, no. 1 (1957): 3.

Prince, Alison. *Hans Christian Andersen: The Fan Dancer.* Allison & Busby, 1998.

"Princess Louise to Josephine Butler," March 27, 1869. Josephine Butler Letters Collection, Women's Library Archives. https://archiveshub.jisc.ac.uk/search/archives/60c86e80–940c-3a71-b138-2a0b3ea347b3?component=5b84db52-8864-37c4-a1fc-034d50244349&terms=Louise.

Pulver, Andrew. "Frozen Lambasted as Pro-Gay Propaganda by Christian Pastor." *The Guardian*, March 12, 2014, sec. Film. https://www.theguardian.com/film/2014/mar/12/frozen-gay-propaganda-christian-pastor-colorado.

Pykett, L. "The Changing Faces and Spaces of Victorian Studies." *Critical Quarterly* 55, no. 1 (2013): 9–23. https://doi.org/10.1111/CRIQ.12037.

Pyle, Howard, and Merle Johnson. *Howard Pyle's Book of Pirates: Fiction, Fact & Fancy Concerning the Buccaneers & Marooners of the Spanish Main.* Harper & Brothers, 1921.

"Queen Victoria's Journals," October 3, 1896. Accessed December 1, 2020. www .queenvictoriasjournals.org.

Rahn, Suzanne. "The Dark Ride of Snow White: Narrative Strategies at Disneyland." In *Disneyland and Culture: Essays on the Parks and Their Influence,* edited by Kathy Merlock Jackson and Mark I. West, 87–100. McFarland, 2010.

Railton, Stephen. "The Howard Family & Uncle Tom's Cabin." *Uncle Tom's Cabin & American Culture.* Accessed December 1, 2020. http://utc.iath.virginia.edu/onstage/ performin/howarditinerary.html.

Ramirez, Michael. "New Adventures with Princess Tiana Coming to Disneyland Park and Magic Kingdom Park." *Disney Parks Blog* (blog), June 25, 2020. https://disneyparks .disney.go.com/blog/2020/06/new-adventures-with-princess-tiana-coming-to -disneyland-park-and-magic-kingdom-park/.

Rather, Dan. "The AIDS Metaphor in 'Beauty and the Beast.'" *Los Angeles Times,* March 22, 1992. https://www.latimes.com/archives/la-xpm-1992-03-22-ca-7396-story.html.

Renfro, Kim. "Why Elsa Doesn't Have a Love Story, Gay or Otherwise, in 'Frozen 2.'" *Insider,* November 22, 2019. https://www.insider.com/why-elsa-has-no-love-interest-frozen-2 -2019-9.

Rezek, Joseph. *London and the Making of Provincial Literature: Aesthetics and the Transatlantic Book Trade, 1800–1850.* University of Pennsylvania Press, 2015.

Rhys, Jean. *Wide Sargasso Sea.* W. W. Norton & Company, 1992.

Richards, Thomas. *The Commodity Culture of Victorian England: Advertising and Spectacle, 1851–1914.* Stanford University Press, 1990.

Richards, Thomas. "The Image of Victoria in the Year of Jubilee." *Victorian Studies* 31, no. 1 (1987): 7–32.

Richardson, Alan. *Literature, Education, and Romanticism: Reading as Social Practice, 1780–1832.* Cambridge University Press, 2004.

Ricks, Christopher. "*The Princess* and the Queen." *Victorian Poetry* 25, no. 3–4 (1987): 133–39.

Roberts, Diane. "Harriet Beecher Stowe and Florida Tourism." In *Literary Tourism and Nineteenth- Century Culture,* edited by Nicola J. Watson, 196–209. Palgrave Macmillan UK, 2009. https://doi.org/10.1057/9780230234109_18.

Robson, Catherine. *Heart Beats: Everyday Life and the Memorized Poem.* Princeton University Press, 2012.

Robson, Catherine, and Carol T. Christ, eds. *The Norton Anthology of English Literature.* 9th ed., vol. E: The Victorian Age. W. W. Norton & Company, 2012.

Rodosthenous, George, ed. *The Disney Musical on Stage and Screen: Critical Approaches from "Snow White" to "Frozen."* Methuen Drama, 2017.

Rodriguez, Ashley. "Disney, Built on Franchises, Says Not Everything Needs to Be a Franchise." *Quartz,* February 28, 2018. https://qz.com/1217178/disney-built-on -franchises-says-not-everything-needs-to-be-a-franchise/.

Romano, Aja. "The Racist Backlash to *The Little Mermaid* and *Lord of The Rings* is Exhausting and Extremely Predictable." *Vox*, September 17, 2022. https://www.vox.com/culture/23357114/the-little-mermaid-racist-backlash-lotr-rings-of-power-diversity-controversy.

Rose, Jacqueline. *The Case of Peter Pan: Or The Impossibility of Children's Fiction*. Springer, 1994.

Rosenstein, Elliot. "Disney Animation Reveals the Tech behind Rendering Realistic Snow in Frozen." *geek.com*, November 26, 2013. https://www.geek.com/news/disney-animation-reveals-the-tech-behind-rendering-realistic-snow-in-frozen-1578165/.

Ross, Deborah. "Escape from Wonderland: Disney and the Female Imagination." *Marvels & Tales* 18, no. 1 (April 15, 2004): 53–66. https://doi.org/10.1353/mat.2004.0016.

Rowell, George. *The Old Vic Theatre: A History*. Cambridge University Press, 1993.

Rowland, Herbert. *More Than Meets the Eye: Hans Christian Andersen and Nineteenth-Century American Criticism*. Fairleigh Dickinson University Press, 2006.

Rushdie, Salman. "Imaginary Homelands." In *The Norton Anthology of English Literature*, edited by Jahan Ramazani and Jon Stallworthy, 2749–51. 9th ed., vol. F: The Twentieth Century and After. W. W. Norton & Company, 2012.

Ruskin, John. "Of Queen's Gardens." In *The Norton Anthology of English Literature*, edited by Catherine Robson and Carol T. Christ, 1614–16. 9th ed., vol. E: The Victorian Age. W. W. Norton & Company, 2012.

Ruskin, John. "Pre-Raphaelitism." In *The Norton Anthology of English Literature*, edited by Catherine Robson and Carol T. Christ, 1468–70. 9th ed., vol. E: The Victorian Age. W. W. Norton & Company, 2012.

Ruskin, John. *Stones of Venice*. Bryan, Taylor, 1894.

Sadoff, Dianne F. *Victorian Vogue: British Novels on Screen*. Minneapolis: University of Minnesota Press, 2009.

Said, Edward W. *Culture and Imperialism*. Knopf Doubleday, 2012.

Said, Edward W. *Orientalism*. Knopf Doubleday, 2014.

Salmon, Edward. *Juvenile Literature as It Is*. London: Henry J. Deane, 1888.

Salvatore, Steven. "Disney's Frozen." *Steven Salvatore* (blog), June 24, 2014. https://stevensalvatore.com/2014/06/24/disneys-frozen/.

Sammond, Nicholas. *Birth of an Industry: Blackface Minstrelsy and the Rise of American Animation*. Duke University Press, 2015.

Sanders, Chris, and Dean DeBlois. *Lilo & Stitch*. Walt Disney Pictures, 2002.

Sanders, Julie. *Adaptation and Appropriation*. Routledge, 2005.

Sandlin, Jennifer A., and Julie C. Garlen. *Disney, Culture, and Curriculum*. Routledge, 2016.

Sayers, Frances Clarke. "Walt Disney Accused." *The Horn Book*, December 1965. http://archive.hbook.com/magazine/articles/1960s/dec65_sayers.asp.

Schaffer, Scott. "Disney and the Imagineering of Histories." *Postmodern Culture* 6, no. 3 (January 5, 1996). https://doi.org/10.1353/pmc.1996.0028.

Schickel, Richard. *The Disney Version: The Life, Times, Art and Commerce of Walt Disney*. Simon & Schuster, 1968.

Schwartzel, Erich. Beauty and the Backlash: Disney's Modern Princess Problem." *Wall Street Journal*, Nov. 17, 2018. https://www.wsj.com/articles/beauty-and-the-backlash-disneys-modern-princess-problem-1542430801?

WORKS CITED

Scribner, George. *Oliver and Company*. Walt Disney Studios Home Entertainment, 2009.

Sedgwick, Eve Kosofsky. *Between Men: English Literature and Male Homosocial Desire*. Columbia University Press, 2015.

Sedgwick, Eve Kosofsky. *Epistemology of the Closet*. University of California Press, 1990.

Sedgwick, Eve Kosofsky. "Jane Austen and the Masturbating Girl." *Critical Inquiry* 17, no. 4 (1991): 818–37.

Sedgwick, Eve Kosofsky. *Tendencies*. Duke University Press, 1993.

Seldes, Gilbert. "Mickey-Mouse Maker: Walt Disney at Thirty." *New Yorker*, December 19, 1931. https://www.newyorker.com/magazine/1931/12/19/walt-disney-profile-mickey-mouse-maker

Sells, Laura. "'Where Do the Mermaids Stand?': Voice and Body in The Little Mermaid." In *From Mouse to Mermaid: The Politics of Film, Gender, and Culture*, 175–92. Indiana University Press, 1995.

Shannon, Dr Mary L. *Dickens, Reynolds, and Mayhew on Wellington Street: The Print Culture of a Victorian Street*. Ashgate Publishing, 2015.

Shelley, Percy. "England in 1819." In *The Norton Anthology of English Literature*, edited by Deidre Shauna Lynch and Jack Stillinger, 790. 9th ed., vol. D: The Romantic Period. W. W. Norton & Company, 2012.

Shesgreen, Sean. "Canonizing the Canonizer: A Short History of *The Norton Anthology of English Literature*." *Critical Inquiry* 35, no. 2 (2009): 293–318. https://doi.org/10.1086/596644.

Shortsleeve, Kevin. "The Wonderful World of the Depression: Disney, Despotism, and the 1930s. Or, Why Disney Scares Us." *Lion and The Unicorn* 28, no. 1 (2004): 1–30.

Shuttleworth, Sally. *The Mind of the Child: Child Development in Literature, Science, and Medicine, 1840–1900*. Oxford University Press, 2010.

Sichol, Lowey Bundy. *From an Idea to Disney: How Imagination Built a World of Magic*. Houghton Mifflin Harcourt, 2019.

Siemann, Catherine. "'But I'm Grown up Now': Alice in the Twenty-First Century | Semantic Scholar." *Neo-Victorian Studies* 5, no. 1 (2012). /paper/%22But-I%27m-grown-up-now%22%3A-Alice-in-the-Twenty-First-Siemann/6b0f9d8ec4f00b844e877929e1a60a085b4a2480.

Slater, Michael. *Charles Dickens*. New Haven: Yale University Press, 2009.

Smiles, Samuel. *Self-Help*. Edited by Peter W. Sinnema. Oxford University Press, 2002.

Smith, Dave, and Steven Vagnini. *Disney A to Z: The Official Encyclopedia*. 6th ed. Disney Editions, 2023.

Smith, David R. "Comics and Cels: The Walt Disney Archives." *California Historical Quarterly* 56, no. 3 (1977): 270–74.

Smith, Michelle J., and Rebecca-Anne C. Do Rozario. "Race, Species, and the Other: 'Beauty and the Beast' in Victorian Pantomime and Children's Literature." *Nineteenth-Century Contexts*, vol. 38, no. 1 (January 2016): 37–53.

Smith, Robert. "OMG TPP." *Planet Money*. Accessed November 30, 2020. https://www.npr.org/sections/money/2015/11/06/455055023/episode-662-omg-tpp.

Smith, Victoria Ford. *Between Generations: Collaborative Authorship in the Golden Age of Children's Literature*. University Press of Mississippi, 2017.

Snow, Richard. *Disney's Land: Walt Disney and the Invention of the Amusement Park That Changed the World*. Simon and Schuster, 2019.

Solomon, Charles. *The Disney That Never Was: The Stories and Art from Five Decades of Unproduced Animation*. Disney Editions, 1995.

Spivak, Gayatri Chakravorty. "Three Women's Texts and a Critique of Imperialism." *Critical Inquiry* 12, no. 1 (1985): 243–61.

St Clair, William. *The Reading Nation in the Romantic Period*. Cambridge University Press, 2004.

Stam, Robert. "Beyond Fidelity: The Dialogics of Adaptation." In *Film Adaptation*, edited by James Naremore, 54–76. Rutgers University Press, 2000.

"Statistics—Broadway in NYC." *The Broadway League*. Accessed December 1, 2020. https://www.broadwayleague.com/research/statistics-broadway-nyc/.

Stevens, Dana. "That Weird Sexy-Makeover Moment at the Heart of Frozen's 'Let It Go' Leaves Me Cold." *Slate Magazine*, February 15, 2014. https://slate.com/culture/2014/02/let-it-go-idina-menzels-frozen-ballad-it-sends-the-wrong-message.html.

Stevenson, Deborah. "Sentiment and Significance: The Impossibility of Recovery in the Children's Literature Canon, or The Drowning of the Water Babies." *Lion and the Unicorn* 21, no. 1 (June 1, 1997): 112–30. https://doi.org/10.1353/uni.1997.0010.

Stevenson, Robert Louis. *A Child's Garden of Verses*. In *The Norton Anthology of Children's Literature*, edited by Jack Zipes et al., 1181–201. Norton, 2005.

Stevenson, Robert Louis. "The Strange Case of Dr. Jekyll and Mr. Hyde." In *The Norton Anthology of English Literature*, edited by Catherine Robson and Carol T. Christ, 1677–1720. 9th ed., vol. E: The Victorian Age. W. W. Norton & Company, 2012.

Stevenson, Robert Louis. *Treasure Island*. Edited by R. H. W. Dillard, reprint edition. New York: Signet Classics, 1998.

Stewart, Garrett. "Curtain Up on Victorian Popular Cinema." In *BRANCH: Britain, Representation and Nineteenth-Century History*, edited by Dino Felluga, 2011. http://www.branchcollective.org/?ps_articles=garrett-stewart-curtain-up-on-victorian-popular-cinema-or-the-critical-theater-of-the-animatograph.

Stewart, James B. *DisneyWar*. New York: Simon & Schuster, 2006.

Stone, Marjorie. "Genre Subversion and Gender Inversion: *The Princess* and *Aurora Leigh*." *Victorian Poetry* 25, no. 2 (1987): 101–27.

Storey, John. "Introduction: Making Popular Culture." In *The Making of Popular Culture*, edited by John Storey. Routledge, 2016.

Strachey, Lytton. *Queen Victoria*, 1921.

"Summary of the Most Recent Discussions of Peter Pan Musical Feature," January 22, 1947. Walt Disney Archives.

Summerfield, Geoffrey. *Fantasy and Reason: Children's Literature in the Eighteenth Century*. Methuen, 1984.

Sumpter, Caroline. *The Victorian Press and the Fairy Tale*. Palgrave, 2008.

Susanin, Timothy S. *Walt before Mickey: Disney's Early Years, 1919–1928*. University Press of Mississippi, 2011.

Susina, Jan. *The Place of Lewis Carroll in Children's Literature*. Routledge, 2010.

Sutton, Angela. *Pirates of the Slave Trade: The Battle of Cape Lopez and the Birth of an American Institution*. Prometheus Books, 2023.

WORKS CITED

Sweeney, Meaghan M. "'Where Happily Ever After Happens Every Day': Disney's Official Princess Website and the Commodification of Play." *Jeunesse* vol. 3, issue 2 (Winter 2011): 66–87.

Swift, Simon. "What the Dickens?" *The Guardian*, April 18, 2007. http://www.theguardian.com/books/2007/apr/18/classics.travelnews.

Szumsky, Brian E. "'All That Is Solid Melts into the Air': The Winds of Change and Other Analogues of Colonialism in Disney's Mary Poppins." *Lion and the Unicorn* 24, no. 1 (January 1, 2000): 97–109. https://doi.org/10.1353/uni.2000.0012.

Szwydky, Lissette Lopez. *Transmedia Adaptation in the Nineteenth Century*. Ohio State University Press, 2020.

Taylor, Jesse Oak. *The Sky of Our Manufacture: The London Fog in British Fiction from Dickens to Woolf*. University of Virginia Press, 2016.

Taylor, Jesse Oak. "Where Is Victorian Ecocriticism?" *Victorian Literature and Culture* 43, no. 4 (December 2015): 877–94. https://doi.org/10.1017/S1060150315000315.

Tennyson, Alfred. "*In Memoriam A. H. H.*" In *The Norton Anthology of English Literature*, edited by Catherine Robson and Carol T. Christ, 1186–235. 9th ed., vol. E: The Victorian Age. W. W. Norton & Company, 2012.

Tennyson, Alfred. "*The Princess.*" In *Tennyson's Poetry*, 129–203. 2nd ed. W. W. Norton & Company, 1999.

Teukolsky, Rachel. *Picture World: Image, Aesthetics, and Victorian New Media*. Oxford University Press, 2020.

Thackeray, William Makepeace. *Vanity Fair*. Edited by Helen Small. Oxford University Press, 2015.

Thiong'O, Ngugi Wa. "Decolonising the Mind." In *The Norton Anthology of English Literature*, edited by Jahan Ramazani and Jon Stallworthy, 2737–41. 9th ed., vol. F: The Twentieth Century and After. W. W. Norton & Company, 2012.

"Top Comments: A Queer Perspective on Disney's Frozen," February 21, 2014. https://www.dailykos.com/story/2014/2/21/1279401/-Top-Comments-A-Queer-Perspective-on-Disney-s-Frozen.

Tremblay, Christopher. "Disney in the Academy (and Other Disney Educational Experiences on College Campuses)." *College and University* 92, no. 4 (October 1, 2017): 49.

Tucker, Phillip Thomas. *Anne Bonny the Infamous Female Pirate*. Feral House, 2017.

Turley, Hans. *Rum, Sodomy, and the Lash: Piracy, Sexuality, and Masculine Identity*. New York University Press, 1999.

The Ugly Duckling. Walt Disney Pictures, 1931. https://www.youtube.com/watch?v=wolYx1937-E.

The Ugly Duckling. Walt Disney Pictures, 1939. https://www.youtube.com/watch?v=RCX-mPstrPU.

Underwood, Ted. *Why Literary Periods Mattered: Historical Contrast and the Prestige of English Studies*. Stanford, California: Stanford University Press, 2013.

Vagnini, Steven. "Disney Archives." Personnel correspondence, July 28, 2014.

Vallone, Lynne. *Becoming Victoria*. Yale University Press, 2001.

VanDerWerff, Emily. "Why Elsa from Frozen Is a Queer Icon—and Why Disney Won't Embrace That Idea." *Vox*, November 22, 2019. https://www.vox.com/culture/2019/11/22/20975178/frozen-2-elsa-girlfriend-lesbian-queer-review.

Varty, Anne. *Children and Theatre in Victorian Britain: "All Work, No Play."* Palgrave Macmillan, 2008.

Vidor, Charles. *Hans Christian Andersen.* MGM, 2001.

Viswanathan, Gauri. *Masks of Conquest: Literary Study and British Rule in India.* Columbia University Press, 2014.

Walkowitz, Judith R. *Prostitution and Victorian Society: Women, Class, and the State.* Cambridge University Press, 1982.

Walt Disney World Resort. "Walt Disney's Carousel of Progress." Accessed December 21, 2020. https://disneyworld.disney.go.com/attractions/magic-kingdom/walt-disney-carousel-of -progress/.

Wasko, Janet. *Understanding Disney: The Manufacture of Fantasy.* John Wiley & Sons, 2020.

Watson, Jeanie. "Tennyson's *The Princess*: The Ideal of 'Like in Difference.'" *South Central Review* 4, no. 1 (1987): 63–81. https://doi.org/10.2307/3189602.

Watts, Steven. *The Magic Kingdom: Walt Disney and the American Way of Life.* University of Missouri Press, 2001.

Watts, Steven. "Walt Disney: Art and Politics in the American Century." *Journal of American History* 82, no. 1 (June 1, 1995): 84–110. https://doi.org/10.2307/2081916.

Wells, Paul. *Animation and America.* Rutgers University Press, 2002.

Weltman, Sharon Aronofsky. "'Can a Fellow Be a Villain All His Life?': Oliver!, Fagin, and Performing Jewishness." *Nineteenth-Century Contexts* 33, no. 4 (September 1, 2011): 371–88. https://doi.org/10.1080/08905495.2011.598673.

Weltman, Sharon Aronofsky. *Victorians on Broadway: Literature, Adaptation, and the Modern American Musical.* University of Virginia Press, 2020.

Weltman, Sharon Aronofsky. "Victorians on the Contemporary Stage." *Journal of Victorian Culture* 13, no. 2 (January 1, 2008): 303–9. https://doi.org/10.3366/E1355550208000386.

Westover, Paul. "How America 'Inherited' Literary Tourism." In *Literary Tourism and Nineteenth- Century Culture*, edited by Nicola J. Watson, 184–95. London: Palgrave Macmillan UK, 2009. https://doi.org/10.1057/9780230234109_17.

Whipple, E. P. "Dickens's American Notes." *The Atlantic*, April 1877. https://www.theatlantic .com/magazine/archive/1877/04/dickenss-american-notes/306680/.

Whitten, Sarah. "The 13 Highest-Grossing Film Franchises at the Box Office." *CNBC*, January 31, 2021. https://www.cnbc.com/2021/01/31/the-13-highest-grossing-film-franchises-at-the -box-office.html

Williams, Carolyn. *Gilbert and Sullivan: Gender, Genre, Parody.* Columbia University Press, 2012.

Williams, Carolyn. "Melodrama." In *The Cambridge History of Victorian Literature*, edited by Kate Flint, 193–219. 1st ed. Cambridge University Press, 2012.

Williams, Kate. *Becoming Queen Victoria: The Tragic Death of Princess Charlotte and the Unexpected Rise of Britain's Greatest Monarch.* Random House, 2010.

Williams, Kate. "Ethel Lang, the Last Victorian, Has Died but Victorianism Lives On." *The Guardian*, January 18, 2015, sec. Opinion. https://www.theguardian.com/ commentisfree/2015/jan/18/ethel-lang-last-victorian-dies-victorian-values-live-on.

Wills, John. *Disney Culture.* Rutgers University Press, 2017.

WORKS CITED

wmfrank. "Creative Fiction, or CC SF." *Creative Commons* (blog), July 27, 2005. https://creativecommons.org/2005/07/27/creativefictionorccsf/.

Wojcik-Andrews, Ian, and Jerry Phillips. "Telling Tales to Children: The Pedagogy of Empire in MGM's Kim and Disney's Aladdin." *Lion and the Unicorn* 20, no. 1 (June 1, 1996): 66–89. https://doi.org/10.1353/uni.1996.0002.

Wolstenholme, Elizabeth C. "The Education of Girls, Its Present and Its Future." In *Woman's Work and Woman's Culture: A Series of Essays*, edited by Josephine Butler, 290–330. Cambridge University Press, 2010.

Woolf, Virginia. "Mrs. Dalloway." In *The Norton Anthology of English Literature*, edited by Jahan Ramazani and Jon Stallworthy, 2155–264. 9th ed., vol. F: The Twentieth Century and After. W. W. Norton & Company, 2012.

Woolf, Virginia. "Professions for Women." In *The Norton Anthology of English Literature*, edited by Jahan Ramazani and Jon Stallworthy, 2272–75. 9th ed., vol. F: The Twentieth Century and After. W. W. Norton & Company, 2012.

Wordsworth, William. "Lines Composed a Few Miles above Tintern Abbey." In *The Norton Anthology of English Literature*, edited by Deidre Shauna Lynch and Jack Stillinger, 288–92. 9th ed., vol. D: The Romantic Period. W. W. Norton & Company, 2012.

Wordsworth, William. "Steamboats, Viaducts, and Railways." In *The Norton Anthology of English Literature*, edited by Deidre Shauna Lynch and Jack Stillinger, 348. 9th ed. vol. D: The Romantic Period. W. W. Norton & Company, 2012.

Wordsworth, William. "The Prelude." In *The Norton Anthology of English Literature*, edited by Deidre Shauna Lynch and Jack Stillinger, 349–402. 9th ed., vol. D: The Romantic Period. W. W. Norton & Company, 2012.

Wullschlager, Jackie. *Hans Christian Andersen: The Life of a Storyteller*. University of Chicago Press, 2002.

Wunderlich, Richard, and Thomas J. Morrissey. *Pinocchio Goes Postmodern: Perils of a Puppet in the United States*. Routledge, 2014.

Wyland, Russell. "Public Funding and the 'Untamed Wilderness' of Victorian Studies." *Romanticism and Victorianism on the Net*, no. 55 (2009). https://doi.org/10.7202/039554ar.

Yolen, Jane. *Sea Queens: Woman Pirates Around the World*. Christine Joy Pratt, illustrator. Charlesbridge, 2010.

Yonge, Charlotte Mary. "Children's Literature of the Last Century, Part III: Class Literature of the Last Thirty Years." *Macmillan's Magazine* XX (October 1869): 448–54.

Young, Alan R. "Henry Irving's Hamlet: Some Visual Sources." *Nineteenth Century Theatre and Film* 32, no. 2 (December 1, 2005): 3.

Zemka, Sue. *Time and the Moment in Victorian Literature and Society*. Cambridge University Press, 2011.

Zipes, Jack. "Breaking the Disney Spell." In *From Mouse to Mermaid: The Politics of Film, Gender, and Culture*, edited by Elizabeth Bell, Lynda Haas, and Laura Sells, 21–42. Bloomington: Indiana University Press, 1995.

Zipes, Jack. *Hans Christian Andersen: The Misunderstood Storyteller*. Routledge, 2014.

Zipes, Jack. *Victorian Fairy Tales: The Revolt of the Fairies and Elves*. Routledge, 2016.

Index

Page numbers in *italics* indicate an illustration.

Academy Awards, 8, 18–19, 22, 95, 97–99, 101, 105, 107, 112
Achebe, Chinua, 151, 153
Adams, Maude, 18, 147–48, *148*
adaptation studies, viii, 57, 157, 165–67; fidelity, 36, 57–58, 102, 109, 147; importance of intervening adaptations, 17, 19, 68
Adventures of Ichabod and Mr. Toad, The, 17, 169, 186n61
Adventures of Tom Sawyer, The, 11, 164
Aladdin (1992), 37, 104, 159
Albert (prince). *See* Prince Albert
Alcott, Louisa May, 7
Alexander, Carl, Duke of Weimar, 84
Alice comedies, 41, 50–53, 65, 188n131
Alice Hunting in Africa, 50
Alice in Cartoonland. See Alice's Wonderland
Alice in Wonderland (1924), 17–18, 45, 51, 53–54, 56, 59, 67, 179n20
Alice in Wonderland (1951), xv, 3, 25, 28, 42, 45, 58–60, 65, 70–71, 145, 186n61
Alice in Wonderland (2010), 70–71, 107
Alice in Wonderland (dark ride), 69
Alice in Wonderland: A Dream Play for Children, 43, 44, 82
Alice the Jail Bird, 50
Alice the Peacemaker, 50
Alice the Piper, 50
Alice's Adventures in Wonderland, 42, 45, 49, 51, 61–69
Alice's Day at Sea, 50
Alice's Spooky Adventure, 50
Alice's Wild West Show, 50

Alice's Wonderland, 41, 47–50, 58
Almar, George, 35
American Weekly, 41–42, 45, 51, 57–58, 60, 64–65
Andersen, Hans Christian: autobiographies, 73–74, 84–85, 94–95; and Charles Dickens, 26, 79–80, 87; Disney biopic, 65, 73–74, 98–99, 188n144; "The Emperor's New Clothes," 83, 87, 98–99; and the fairy tale tradition, 73, 78, 82, 87–88, 108, 186n53; links to Victorian culture, 78–83, 164; "The Little Match Girl," 88, 102, 188n131; "The Little Mermaid," 33, 87–88, 98–101, 103–7, 166; "The Nightingale," 83, 86, 93–94, 97–98, 207n229; "The Red Shoes," 88, 99, 108; sexuality, 74, 87–94, 100, 102–12, 184n3; "The Snow Man," 109–10; "The Snow Queen," 74, 107–9, 111–12, 186n61; "The Steadfast Tin Soldier," 80, 85, 101–3, 185n39, 188n147; translations, 78, 83, 87, 97; "The Ugly Duckling," 73, 81, 83, 94–97, 98, 100–101. *See also* Collin, Edvard; Lind, Jenny; Scharff, Harald
Anderson, Ken, 53
"Angel in the House, The," 115–16, 125–26
Animatronics. *See* Audio-Animatronics
Arnold, Matthew, xii, 4, 12–13, 61, 151, 153, 173n58
Arnold, Thomas, 60–61, 183n140
Artist's Dream, The, 48
Ashman, Howard, 37, 40, 103, 105–6
Atencio, X, 149
Audio-Animatronics, 26, 139, 154, 171n6

229

230 INDEX

Aurora Leigh, 116
Austen, Jane, xi, 141, 151
Ayers, Harry Morgan, 57

Bailey, Halle, 107
Balanchine, George, 101
Banksy, 153–55
Barnett, C. Z., 35
Barnum, P. T., 86, 93, 162, 173n85
Barrett Browning, Elizabeth, 80–81, 116, 140
Barrie, J. M., 18, 22–23, 56, 83, 145–46, 169n8;
    Peter Pan, 22, 144–47
Barrymore, John, 147
Bart, Lionel, 25, 36–38, 178n231
Baskett, James, 18–19, 98
Bassano, Alexander, 124–25
Beauty and the Beast (1991), 37, 70, 73,
    104–5, 113, 138
"Beauty and the Beast" (fairy tale), 5
Bennett, Louise, 153
Bentley, Richard, 78–79, 87
Bentley's Miscellany, 33, 79
Berkeley, Busby, 104
Berne convention, 4. *See also* copyright
Bertie (Victoria's son). *See* Edward VII
Black Beauty, 160–61, 199n21
Black Ey'd Susan, 142
blackface, 19–20, 174n109
Blank, Dorothy, 18, 56–57, 147–48
Borodin, Alexander, 102
Boucicault, Dion, 21
Bowman, Isa, 82
Boy Called Twist, 153
Boy Castaways of Black Lake Island, The, 145
boyhood, 149. *See also* masculinity
Boy's Own Paper, 7, 15
Brandstrup, Kim, 100
Brave, 114, 117, 138
Brave New World, 60
Bray, John Randolph, 48
Braybrooke, Patrick, 56, 147
Broadway, 27, 37, 51, 147, 165, 175n131,
    178n237
Bronson, Betty, 18, 23
Brontë, Charlotte, 116, 151, 153; *Jane Eyre*, 61,
    151, 153, 155, 165
Browne, Roscoe Lee, 37

Browning, Elizabeth. *See* Barrett Browning,
    Elizabeth
Browning, Robert, 56, 80
Buchanan, Stuart, 60
Bulwer-Lytton, Edward, 81
Burnett, Frances Hodgson, 22–23, 131
Burney, Frances, 23
Burton, Tim, 70–71
business (cartoon comic element). *See* gags
Butler, Josephine, 116, 128–30, 133
Butler, Judith, 117
Byron, George Gordon, Lord, 81, 120, 142

Campbell, Frances, 193n83
Carlyle, Thomas, 12, 27, 81
Carroll, Lewis, 7, 22, 41–45, 51, 57–60,
    61–71, 82, 83, 126, 161; *Alice's Adventures
    in Wonderland*, 42, 45, 49, 51, 61–69;
    Through the Looking-Glass, 25, 42–43,
    45–46, 54–55, 67, 71
Carter, Helena Bonham, 70–71
Chapek, Bob, 106, 170n15
Chaplin, Charlie, 36, 53
childhood, 5–7, 15, 32, 66, 77, 80, 82, 86, 99,
    114, 142–43
children's media: film, 23, 47, 139; literature,
    xv, 4, 5–7, 30–31, 43, 56–57, 79, 82–83, 139,
    146, 158, 162, 165; poetry, 64, 143; theater,
    22–23
Child's Garden of Verses, A, 143
Christmas, 10, 18, 43, 87, 102, 133, 135
Christmas Carol, A, 10, 35, 87, 150, 197n2
Cinderella (1950), 73, 105, 138
Cinderella (2015), 70
"Cinderella" (fairy tale), 5, 119–20, 155
Cinderella's Castle, 75
Clarke, Henry Savile, 22, 43–44, 56–57, 82
Clements, Ron, 33, 103, 149
Clemmons, Larry, 166
Coleridge, Samuel Taylor, 12
Collin, Edvard, 74, 89–92, 95, 103
Collin, Jonas, 74, 84, 87, 92
Collingwood, Stuard Dodgson, 57, 63
Collins, Wilkie, 28, 80
Collodi, Carlo, 150, 169n8, 181n96
colonialism. *See* imperialism
Conrad, Joseph, xi, 151

INDEX   231

Coogan, Jackie, 36
Cooper, Gary, 45
Cooper, James Fenimore, 142
copyright, 4, 8–11, 19, 22, 35, 45, 53, 87, 98, 154, 164; of *Alice* books, 45, 47; of *Peter Pan*, 145
Creedon, Dick, 98
Cruikshank, George, 26, 34, 36, 78, 120
Crystal Palace, 4, 28–29

Darton, F. J. Harvey, 56, 147
Davis, Marc, 109
Davis, Virginia, 47–50
de la Mare, Walter, 57
de Maris, Merrill, 98
Deja, Andrea, 104, 106
Del Vecho, Peter, 109
Depp, Johnny, 71, 139, 141, 149
DeSantis, Ron, 106–7
Diamond jubilee, 125
Dickens, Catherine, 80
Dickens, Charles, xv, 4, 13–14, 16–17, 26–27, 31–35, 80, 127, 142, 166–67, 177n213, 185n21; *A Christmas Carol*, 10, 35, 87, 150, 197n2; and copyright, 9–11, 22, 35, 87; *Dombey and Son*, 14; *Great Expectations*, 14–15, 70, 153; *Hard Times*, 13, 23, 32; *Nicholas Nickleby*, 9, 136; *Oliver Twist*, 19, 33–36, 40, 78–79; *The Pickwick Papers*, 33–34; visit from Hans Christian Andersen, 26, 79–80, 87
Dickens, Kate, 79
Dickens World, 31–32
Dismaland, 153–55
Disney, Roy, 33, 53, 56, 58, 76
Disney, Roy E., 103
Disney, Walt, xi–xiii, 3–4, 6, 8–9, 13, 16, 18, 22, 28, 32, 48, 53, 64, 73, 75–77, 85, 97, 139, 144, 147, 155; the Alice comedies, 41, 50–53, 65, 188n131; comments on *Alice in Wonderland*, 41–42, 45, 47, 51–52, 60, 66, 69, 71; competing biographies of, 75–77; early films in Kansas City, 41, 47–49; feature films, 6; television and "uncle Walt," 34; visit to Europe, 28, 112
Disney archives. *See* Walt Disney Company Archives, The

Disney Miller, Diane. *See* Miller, Diane Disney
Disney Princess (brand), xvi, 67, 107, 109, 111, 113–14, 116–19, 138, 145, 159, 170n12, 191n6, 191n21
Disney renaissance, 13, 37, 75, 100–106, 158, 170n12
Disneyland (television special), 4, 13, 16, 42, 68, 75–76
Disneyland (theme park), xii–xiv, 4, 16–17, 26, 31, 42, 68–69, 85, 99, 112, 114, 139, 142, 145, 154–55
Divine (performer), 104, 106
Doctorow, Cory, 153–54
Dodgson, Charles. *See* Carroll, Lewis
Dombey and Son, 14
Douglass, Frederick, 164
Down and Out in the Magic Kingdom, 153–54
Dracula, 27
Driscoll, Bobby, 18
D23 fan club, xiii
du Maurier, Gerald, 146

Ebert, Robert, 103
Edison, Thomas, 15, 173n85
education, 7, 11, 12–13, 29; women's, 116, 128, 131–34, 136
Education Act of 1870, 7
Edward VII, 126
Eisenstein, Sergei, 17, 166, 200n60
Eisner, Michael, xii–xiii, 8, 11–12, 16, 33, 36, 40, 75, 100–104, 149, 154, 175n131
Eliot, George, xi, 12, 27, 81, 97, 116; *Middlemarch*, 12, 27, 81, 97
Eliot, T. S., 3, 4
"Emperor's New Clothes, The," 83, 87, 98–99
Europe, 7, 73, 78, 81, 84–85, 90, 94–95, 112, 118, 126–27, 144, 162, 169n8
Evelina, 23, 25–26

Fairbanks, Douglas, 53
Fairy Tale of My Life, The, 73, 85–86
fairy tales, 5, 22; Disney and, 47, 52, 97, 165, 181n96; Hans Christian Andersen and tradition of, 73, 78, 82, 87–88, 108, 186n53; princesses and, 119, 121, 131

fallen woman, 115
Fantasia, 98
Fantasia 2000, 74, 101–3
Felix the Cat, 49–50
fidelity (adaptation concept), 36, 57–58, 102, 109, 147
Fields, W. C., 45
Fierstein, Harvey, 109
fireworks, 23, 26–27, 29, 91
Fleischer, Max and Dave, 48–49, 58
Forster, John, 35, 185n21
Four Musicians of Bremen, The (1922), 48
franchises, 4, 16, 22, 25, 39–40, 139, 161, 165; Disney Princess, 109, 113–14, 116–19, 138, 145, 159, 170n12, 191n6, 191n21; Disney's *Alice in Wonderland* as, 42, 66–72
Freedman, Claire, 139
Frozen, 74, 107–12, 116–17, 138
Frozen 2, 112
Frozen Deep, The, 80
Fuller, Margaret, 132

gags, 13, 20, 46–55, 59, 64–67, 95, 111, 116, 182
Gaiman, Neil, 139
Gaskell, Elizabeth, 151
General History of Pyrates, A, 140–41
George III, 118–21
German Popular Stories. See Grimm, Jacob and Wilhelm
Ghosh, Amitav, 153
Gilbert, W. S., 26–27, 136
Gilbert and Sullivan, 10–11, 22, 26–27, 133, 136, 143–44; *H. M. S. Pinafore*, 10, 143; *The Pirates of Penzance*, 10–11, 143, 146; *Princess Ida*, 133, 136
golden age of children's literature, xv, 7, 162
golden age of illustration, 133, 136, 140
golden age of piracy, 141, 144
Golden Jubilee, 125
Goldwyn, Samuel, 73–74, 98–99, 109, 188n47
Gosse, Edmund, 86
Grahame, Kenneth, 17, 56, 83, 169n8, 186n61
Grant, Cary, 45, 145, 158
Great Exhibition, 4, 16, 28–30
Great Expectations, 14–15, 70, 153
Great Mouse Detective, The, 100, 103
Greenaway, Kate, 56

Greene, Timothy, 153
Griffith, D. W., 53, 158
Grimm, Jacob and Wilhelm, 5, 78–79, 166
Guinness, Alec, 36
Gupta, Tanika, 153

H. M. S. Pinafore, 10, 143
Hall, David, 60
Hallam, Arthur Henry, 132
Hamid, Mohsin, 153
Hanks, Tom, 105
Hans Christian Andersen (1954), 74, 99–100
Hard Times, 13, 23, 32
Hargreaves, Alice. *See* Liddell, Alice
Harman, Fred, 48
Harman, Hugh, 179n20
Harris, Joel Chandler, 19, 169n8
Hays Code. *See* Motion Picture Production Code of 1930
Hayter, George, 121, *122*
Heart of Darkness, 151
Hercules (1997), 104
Hersholt, Jean, 97–98, 188n135
Hogarth, Georgina, 80
Hone, William, 118–19
Household Words, 26, 80
Howitt, Mary, 78–79, 85
Huemer, Dick, 64
Hurd, Earl, 147
Huxley, Aldous, 60–65, 171n28, 173n57
Huxley, Thomas Henry, 12–13, 60, 183n140

Iger, Robert, xiii, 16, 106, 155
illustration, 5, 21, 26, 45, 78, 120, 133, 135–36, 144–45, 149, 166–67; of the *Alice* books, 42–43, 45, 47, 53–56, 58, 70–71; of Dickens novels, 16–17, 33–34, 36; influence on film adaptations, 36, 45, 56, 58, 166–67; of pirates, 144, 165; of Tennyson, 133, 135–36
imperialism, 29, 106, 140, 150–54
"In the Duckyard," 97
intellectual property. *See* copyright
Irving, Henry, 26–27, 63, 147
Irving, Washington, 169n8
Ising, Rudolph, 50, 179n20
It's a Small World, 139, 171n6

INDEX

Jake and the Neverland Pirates, 139
James, Henry, xi, 32, 80–81, 164
Jane Eyre (1944 film), 61
Jane Eyre (2011 film), 165
Jane Eyre (novel), 151, 153, 155
Jazz Singer, The, 15, 19
Jekyll and Hyde. See *Strange Case of Dr. Jeckyll and Mr. Hyde, The*
Jerdan, William, 78
Jerrold, Douglas, 80, 142, 195n161
Joel, Billy, 37, 39
Johnson, Charles, 140–41
Jubilee celebrations, 125
Jungle Book, The (1968), 150, 152–53, 166, 186n61
Juvenile Literature as It Is, 7
juvenile periodicals, 7, 83, 142–43

Katzenberg, Jeffrey, 33, 36, 39–40, 103
Kaye, Danny, 74, 99–100
Kean, Charles, 30
Keane, Glen, 109
Kierkegaard, Søren, 89
Kim, 151
Kimball, Ward, 68
Kingsley, Charles, 70, 160
Kipling, Rudyard, 83, 150–53, 166, 186n61
Kurtz, Bob, 98

La Gallienne, Eva, 17–18, 45, 51, 56, 58–59
Lady Frances. See Campbell, Frances
Lang, Andrew, 52–53, 181n78
Laugh-O-Gram, 48–50, 179n21
Lean, David, 36
Leavis, F. R., xi–xiv, 13, 31–32
Leicester Square, 15, 28–29
libraries, 6, 47, 158
Liddell, Alice, 42, 51, 126, 179n7
Life magazine, 41, 45, 75
Lilo & Stitch, 101, 103
Lind, Jenny, 86, 93–94, 97, 99
Lion King, The, 27, 37, 63, 104
literacy, 7–8, 121
Little Artist, The, 48
"Little Ida's Flowers," 108
Little Lord Fauntleroy, 22–23
"Little Match Girl, The," 88, 102, 188n131
Little Match Girl, The (2006), 102

Little Mermaid, The (1989), 37, 74, 100, 103–6, 111, 138, 154, 159, 166
Little Mermaid, The (2023), 107
"Little Mermaid, The" (story), 33, 87–88, 98–101, 103–7, 166
Little Red Riding Hood (1922), 47, 52
Little White Bird, The, 145, 169
Lloyd, Frank, 36
Longfellow, Henry Wadsworth, 86
Loos, Anita, 61
Ludwig II, 3–4, 85
Lumiére brothers, 23
Lutz, Edwin G., 47
Lyceum theater, 26–27, 63

MacDonald, George, 131, 186n61
Maclise, Daniel, 135–36
Macmillan, 43, 56, 62–63
Madame Tussaud, 25–26
magazines. *See* periodicals and magazines
magic lanterns, 25, 43
Major, Charles, 169n8
Mansfield Park, 151
Many Adventures of Winnie the Pooh, The. See *Winnie the Pooh*
Martin, Mary, 145
Martin, Pete, 76
Marvel, xiii, 16, 67, 113
masculinity, 12, 87–89, 114, 132, 136–37, 159, 195n156; pirate, 117–18, 139–49
Maurice, F. D., 132–33, 163
Mayhew, Henry, 25
melodrama, 20–21, 30, 34–35, 115, 141–43, 149
Menken, Alan, 37, 103, 105, 109
merchandising, 4, 9, 16, 43–43, 67, 69–70, 76
MGM (Metro Goldwyn Mayer), 61, 101, 188n147
Mickey Mouse, 8, 15, 19–20, 22, 41, 51, 54–55, 67, 75–76, 98, 113, 174n109, 188n147
Mickey Mouse Club, The, 76
Mickey Thru the Mirror. See *Thru the Mirror*
Mickey's Christmas Carol, 150
"Mickey's Mellerdrammer," 19–20, 190n111
Middlemarch, 12, 27, 81, 97
Midler, Bette, 37–38, 104
Millais, John Everett, 127, 142

Miller, Diane Disney, 3, 5, 8, 65
Milne, A. A., 17, 83, 186n61
minstrelsy. *See* blackface
Mintz, Charles, 8, 50, 179n20, 188n131
Moana, 114, 117, 138
Mooney, Andy, 113, 118
Moses, Belle, 57, 63
Motion Picture Production Code of 1930, 6
Moxon, Edward, 133, 135
Mrs. Dalloway, 14
Mudie's library, 6–7, 171n17
Müller, Edward, 91
music halls, 15, 23–25, 29–30
Musker, John, 149
Mysteries of Udolpho, The, 25

Nagra, Daljit, 153, 155
National Academy of Art, 127
nautical melodrama, 141–43, 149
Nesbit, Edith, 25
Neuschwanstein, 3–4
Newbery, John, 5
Nicholas Nickleby, 9, 136
Nichols, Grace, 153
Nicholson, William, 146
Nielson, Kay, 98–99, 166
Nightingale, Florence, 130
"Nightingale, The," 83, 86, 93–94, 97–98, 207n229
North and South, 151
Norton, Edgar, 53–54
Norton Anthology of English Literature, The, 170n9

O'Brien, Margaret, 61
Oliver! (film), 36
Oliver! (stage musical), 25, 36–37, 175n131
Oliver, Edna May, 45
Oliver & Company, 33, 36–40, 100, 103–4; early drafts in Walt Disney Archives, 37–39
Oliver Twist (1948), 36
Oliver Twist (novel), 19, 33–36, 40, 78–79; film adaptations of, 35–36, 153; theatrical adaptations of, 33–35
Only a Fiddler, 78, 89
Orenstein, Peggy, 113–14
Orwell, George, 32
Oscars (award). *See* Academy Awards

Oswald the Lucky Rabbit, 8, 50–52, 179n20, 188n131
Out of the Inkwell, 48–50, 58
Oxford University, 42, 61–64, 133

panoramas, 16, 27–28, 30
pantomime, 5, 25, 82, 179n14, 179n16
Paramount Pictures, 17–18, 45, 51, 53–54, 56, 59, 67, 179n20
Patmore, Coventry, 115–16
Paul, Robert W., 15
Penner, Ed, 149
Penny Dreadful, 165
penny dreadfuls, 7
periodicals and magazines, 7, 26, 43, 78, 80, 132, 142–43; juvenile, 7, 42, 83, 142–43; *Life*, 41, 45, 75
periodization, xii–xiii, 163–65; of The Walt Disney Company, xiii, 170n12
Perkins, Al, 17, 56–61, 63–65, 67, 98, 144, 147
Perrault, Charles, 78
Peter and Wendy, 145, 147, 169n8
Peter Pan (1953 animated musical), 144–49, 152, 186n61; early drafts, 17–18, 56–57, 147–49, 171n28
Peter Pan (play), 17–18, 22–23, 145–49, 169n8
Peter Pan in Kensington Gardens, 145
Peter Pan's Flight, 69, 145
photography, xv, 4, 14–15, 21, 30, 62–63, 145; of Queen Victoria, 30, 124–25
Pickford, Mary, 23, 51–56, 71
Pickwick Papers, The, 33–34
Pinocchio (1940), 56, 60, 150, 181n96
Pinocchio (novel), 150, 169n8
piracy. *See* copyright; pirates
Pirate Stew, 139
pirates, 42, 114, 117–18, 139–49; in history, 139–41; sexuality, 117–18, 141, 149; in Victorian culture, 142–44, 146, 149
Pirates Love Underpants, 139
Pirates of Penzance, The, 10–11, 143, 146
Pirates of the Caribbean (franchise), 26, 42, 67–68, 71, 139–45, 149
plagiarism. *See* copyright
Poet's Bazaar, A, 89
postcolonial theory, xiii, 151–54, 163
Pre-Raphaelite Brotherhood (PRB), 127–28, 133, 135

Pride and Prejudice, 61
Prince Albert, 28, 80, 123–26, 132–33
Princess, The, 131–39
Princess Alice, 125, 128
Princess and the Frog, The, 18
"Princess and the Pea, The," 83
Princess Beatrice, 62, 126–27
Princess Caroline of Denmark, 84
Princess Charlotte, 119–23
Princess Helena, 126–27
Princess Ida, 133, 136
Princess Louise, 125–31, 193n83
princesses, 113–14, 118–23, 126–31, 136, 155, 159, 191n21; Disney, 18, 107, 109–11, 113–14, 116–18, 138, 149, 159, 170n12, 191n6, 191n21; fairy tale, 5, 115, 119–20
publishing industry, 5–7, 10–11, 14–15, 21, 34, 43, 78, 83, 87, 121
Pyle, Howard, 149, 196n209

Queen Victoria, xii, 30, 61–64, 80, 118–19, 121–25, 127–28, 130–31, 133, 151, 162–63; comments on gender equality, 128, 131–32, 135

Radcliffe, Anne, 25
railroads, 13–14, 21, 29, 121
Railway Children, The, 125
Ralph, Sheryl Lee, 37
Rathbone, Basil, 147
Red Rover, 142
"Red Shoes, The," 88, 99, 108
Red Shoes, The (1948), 99
Reid, Elizabeth Jesser, 133
"Reluctant Dragon, The," 56, 169n8
Reluctant Dragon, The (1941), 56, 186n61
Rhys, Jean, 153, 155
Rob Roy, 145, 169n8
Robin Hood, 145
Robinson, Edwin Arlington, 70
Rossetti, Christina, 116
Royal Academy of Art, 127
Ruggels, Mary Jane, 109
Rushdie, Salman, 152–53
Ruskin, John, 81, 115, 127, 131, 160

Saabye, Augustus Vilhelm, 82–83
Salmon, Edward, 7, 79
Sayers, Frances Clarke, 158

Scharff, Harald, 90, 92, 99–100, 110, 191n229
Scott, Walter, 142, 145, 160, 169n8
Scudder, Horace E., 83
Sears, Ted, 98
Self Help, 12
separate spheres, 115–16, 128, 131–32, 135, 137–38
Sewell, Anna, 160
sexuality, xvi, 6, 33, 39, 42, 87–89, 93–94, 104, 117–18, 138, 141, 143, 155, 179n7, 195n156; of Hans Christian Andersen, 74, 87–94, 100, 102–12, 184n3; pirates and, 117–18, 141, 149
Seymour, Robert, 33–34
"Shadow, The," 90
Shakespeare, William, 9, 12, 21, 26–27, 31, 37, 161
Shelley, Percy, 119, 124
Sherlock Holmes, 33, 100, 165
Shostakovich, Dmitri, 101
Silly Symponies, 56, 74, 76, 94, 98, 188n131
slavery, 19–20, 140–41, 163, 164
"Sleeping Beauty," 5, 119–20, 135
Sleeping Beauty (1959), 73, 115
Sleeping Beauty's Castle at Disneyland, 4, 31, 85
Smiles, Samuel, 12–13, 173n58
"Snow Man, The," 109–10
"Snow Queen, The," 74, 107–9, 111–12, 186n61
"Snow White," 5, 119–20
Snow White and the Seven Dwarfs, xii–xiv, 8, 16, 32, 46, 56, 58, 60, 67, 76, 97, 105, 115, 138, 145, 160, 166–67, 181n96
Snow White's Scary Adventure, 69
Song of the South, 18–19, 65, 98–99, 152, 169n8
Sontag, Susan, 105
stage adaptations. *See* theater
Stampe, Henrik, 91, 93
Star Wars, xiii, 16, 67, 113
"Steadfast Tin Soldier, The," 80, 85, 101–3, 185n39, 188n147
Steamboat Willie, 8, 13–15, 19, 67, 75, 95
Stevenson, Robert Louis, 7, 15, 142–46, 149; *A Child's Garden of Verses,* 143; *The Strange Case of Dr. Jeckyll and Mr. Hyde,* 15; *Treasure Island,* 7, 142, 144–45, 149, 169n8

Stoker, Bram, 27
Story, William Wetmore, 80
*Story of Robin Hood and His Merrie Men,
The*, 145
Stowe, Harriet Beecher, 11, 19, 174n112
Strachey, Lytton, 61
*Strange Case of Dr. Jeckyll and Mr. Hyde,
The*, 15
suffrage, 128–29, 131, 193n83
Sullivan, Arthur, 26. *See also* Gilbert and
Sullivan
Sullivan, Pat, 49
Sword and the Rose, The, 145, 169n8

Taylor, Edgar, 5, 78
Tenniel, John, 17, 43, 45, 47, 53–54, 56, 58, 61,
70–71, 167
Tennyson, Alfred, 15, 131–33, 160; *The
Princess*, 131–39
Ternan, Ellen, 80
Terry, Ellen, 26, 62, 63–64, 142
Terry, Paul, 48
Thackeray, William, 24, 160
theater, 5, 10–12, 16–23, 25–27, 30, 35–36, 43–
45, 51, 56, 63–64, 84, 120, 142–43, 166–67;
Broadway, 27, 37, 51, 147, 165, 175n131,
178n237; children's, 22–23; melodrama,
20–21, 30, 34–35, 115, 141–43, 149; panto-
mime, 5, 25, 82, 179n14, 179n16
theme parks, 4, 8, 16, 23, 27, 30, 31–34,
67–69, 75–76, 114, 139–41, 153–55, 167.
See also Dickens World; Disneyland;
Dismaland
Thiong'o, Ngũgĩ wa, 152
Thornycroft, Mary, 127
Three Little Pigs, The, xi, 52–53, 56
*Through the Looking-Glass and What Alice
Found There*, 25, 42–43, 45–46, 54–55,
67, 71
Thru the Mirror, 54–55, 65
Thurber, James, 53
Tin Toy, 101
Tivoli Gardens, 3–4, 112, 191n229
Toad of Toad Hall, 17
Toy Story, 101
trains. *See* railroads
Treasure Island (1950), 18, 144–45
Treasure Island (novel), 7, 142, 144–45, 149,
169n8

Treasure Planet, 33, 149
Tree, Beerbohm, 147
Trolley Trouble, 51
True Story of My Life, The, 94
Twain, Mark, 11, 162, 164
20,000 Leagues Under the Sea (1954), 99,
150
20,000 Leagues Under the Sea (novel), 150,
169n8

"Ugly Duckling, The," 73, 81, 83, 94–97, 98,
100–101
Ugly Duckling, The (1931), 94–95
Ugly Duckling, The (1939), 95
Uncle Remus stories, 19, 98, 169n8
Uncle Tom's Cabin, 11, 19, 174n11
United Artists, 53
Universal Pictures, 50–51

Vanity Fair, 24
vaudeville, 48, 59
Verne, Jules, 7, 150, 169n8
Victoria. *See* Queen Victoria
Voight, Christian, 91–92
von Angeli, Heinrich, 125
voting. *See* suffrage

Walbrook, H. M., 147
Walt Disney Archives, The, xii, 17, 33, 37,
40, 127, 147, 150, 160. *See also* Blank,
Dorothy; Perkins, Al
Walt Disney Family Museum, The, 75
Walt Disney World, 13, 29, 31, 106–7, 154
Warner Bros. Studios, 49, 101, 188n131
Watts, Isaac, 64
waxworks, 16, 25–26, 120, 139
Wells, H. G., 14
When Knighthood Was in Flower, 169n8
Wide Sargasso Sea, 153, 155
Wilde, Oscar, 82, 88
Wind in the Willows, The, 17, 158, 169n8
Winkler, Margaret, 49–50
Winnie the Pooh, 186n61
Wolstenholme, Elizabeth C., 133
Woman in the Nineteenth Century, 132
Woman in White, The, 28
Woman's Work and Woman's Culture, 128,
130, 133
women's suffrage. *See* suffrage

Woolf, Virginia, 14, 115
Woolverton, Linda, 138
Wordsworth, William, 6, 13
World War I, xii, 76, 186n61
World War II, 32, 36, 41, 71, 144, 147, 161, 169
World's Fairs, 4, 28, 30; in 1964, 4, 13, 26, 139.
    See also Great Exhibition
Wreck It Ralph 2, 116, 159
Wulff, Henriette, 86

Yonge, Charlotte, 81, 83
Young, Pete, 33
Young Folks Magazine, 7

About the Author

Photo courtesy of the author.

Patrick "PC" Fleming is the author of *The Legacy of the Moral Tale: Children's Literature and the English Novel* (2016) and *Nineteenth-Century Children's Literature: A Companion* (forthcoming). He received his PhD from the University of Virginia and is former director of the honors program at Fisk University. He currently lives in northern Virginia and is a program officer at the National Endowment for the Humanities (NEH). This book represents his own views and not those of the NEH or the United States government.